THE MAN
WHO WARNED
AMERICA

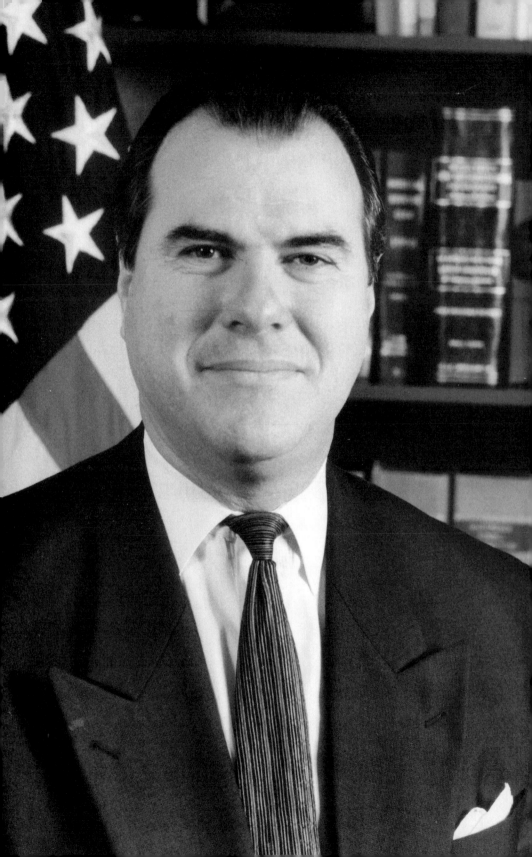

THE MAN WHO WARNED AMERICA

★ THE LIFE AND DEATH OF ★

FEB. 6, 1952 **JOHN O'NEILL,** SEPT. 11, 2001

THE FBI'S EMBATTLED
COUNTERTERROR WARRIOR

MURRAY WEISS

ReganBooks

An Imprint of HarperCollins*Publishers*

HarperCollins books may be purchased for educational, business, or sales promotional use. For information please write: Special Markets Department, HarperCollins Publishers Inc., 10 East 53rd Street, New York, NY 10022.

FIRST EDITION

Designed by Rymn Massand

Printed on acid-free paper

Library of Congress Cataloging-in-Publication Data

Weiss, Murray.
     The man who warned America : the life and death of John O'Neill, the FBI's embattled counterterror warrior / Murray Weiss.—1st ed.
        p. cm.
     Includes bibliographical references.
     ISBN 0-06-050822-1 (acid-free paper)
        1. O'Neill, John P., 1952–2001. 2. United States, Federal Bureau of Investigation—Officials and employees—Biography. 3. United States. Federal Bureau of Investigation. National Security Division—Officials and employees—Biography. 4. Terrorism—United States—Prevention. I. Title.

HV7911.O45W45 2003
363.3'2'092—dc21
[B]
                                                                                        2003047206

03 04 05 06 07 WBC/RRD 10 9 8 7 6 5 4 3 2 1

For John O'Neill,
and all the victims of September 11

CONTENTS

Foreword: Mary Jo White   *viii*

Acknowledgments   *xi*

I The Real Inspector Erskine   *1*

Prologue   *3*

1. On the Boardwalk   *7*
2. Thinking out of the Box   *21*
3. "My Kind of Town"   *36*

II Fundamentalism and Fanaticism   *55*

4. In the Name of God   *57*
5. "You Can't Make This Shit Up"   *76*
6. The Birth of Al Qaeda   *91*
7. The Obstructionists   *110*

III Domestic Troubles and Foreign Affairs   *137*

8. Silencing the Critics   *139*
9. O'Neill Takes Manhattan   *152*
10. The Man Who Knew   *177*
11. "They Can Strike Anytime"   *206*

IV   **New York, New York**   *229*

12.   So Nice They Named It Twice   *231*

13.   The Voice of God   *247*

14.   The Briefcase Incident   *270*

V   **"We're Due for Something Big"**   *285*

15.   The Tip of the Spear   *287*

16.   Face-to-Face with the Enemy   *313*

17.   Forced Out   *336*

18.   September 11, 2001   *355*

     Epilogue   *389*

     Notes   *401*

     List of Interviewees   *421*

     Timeline   *425*

     Photograph Credits   *435*

     Index   *437*

FOREWORD

Our nation and our world are in the midst of the war against global terrorism. Right now, it seems that we will be in this state forever—and perhaps we will. Although no attack has occurred on American soil since September 11, many innocent lives have been taken by the terrorists in Tunisia, Bali, the Philippines, and Riyadh, Saudi Arabia, and more are sure to follow. Osama bin Laden, the evil but charismatic leader of al Qaeda, and his second in command, the even more dangerous Ayman al-Zawahiri, remain at large, as they remind us periodically with audiotapes calling for further bloodshed directed at America and Americans worldwide.

We heard that threat and warning before, in early 1998, when Osama bin Laden issued his *fatwah* against Americans. But few took it seriously then. One who did was John O'Neill, the former head of the FBI's counterterrorism efforts, in both Washington, D.C., and New York. His first assignment in 1995 in his counterterrorism role at FBI headquarters was to monitor the Bureau's efforts to capture Ramzi Yousef in Pakistan, and return him to New York to be tried for bombing the World Trade Center in 1993. John O'Neill accomplished that mission, but soon came to recognize the grave risk that al Qaeda and, specifically, Osama bin Laden, posed to the United States and all Americans, both abroad and within our own borders. In this book, Murray Weiss, with a wealth of important sources and insights, chronicles the complex life of John O'Neill and takes the reader through his education and ours about international terrorism prior to the deadly attacks of September 11.

John O'Neill went to East Africa when our embassies were bombed in August 1998; he went to Yemen in the fall of 2000 and led the difficult investigation of the bombing of the USS *Cole*. He literally traveled the world and brought his counterparts from around the world to the United States as he forged the global relationships essential to detecting and defeating international terrorism. John O'Neill spoke up about the terrorism risk he perceived and worked tirelessly to try to combat it and to make people who were in a position to try to do something about it listen. He did this and much more to identify and defeat the enemy. But he failed, as did we all.

September 11 happened—an attack stunning both in its massiveness and in its simplicity. By midmorning, three thousand innocent civilians and those who tried to rescue them were gone, including John O'Neill. Then a civilian in charge of security at the World Trade Center, which had survived Ramzi Yousef's terrorist bomb in 1993, John O'Neill was at his new post doing what he could to save lives and manage the crisis he had predicted would occur someday. John O'Neill survived the impact of both planes only to succumb in the act of attempted rescue when he went back into the south tower before it collapsed. He died as he lived, fighting international terrorists bent on world destruction.

In the end, we will win this war. It will take a very long time and more deaths before we do. But at least we are finally fighting it on the scale that is required, as John O'Neill believed was necessary before September 11. We will vindicate John O'Neill's death and honor his life, by finishing this war and by never again failing to recognize and imagine the depth and reach of the terrorist dangers that confront us. We will never forget John O'Neill and all that he tried to do. And, as he refused to do while he lived, we will not say good-bye to a friend; "Friends don't say good-bye." We will instead remember John O'Neill for all that he was—a brilliant and driven investigator, a very complex person who had flaws and could ruffle feathers, but also a man who lived and worked to the fullest. We will remember what he told us in

1997: "When bin Laden speaks, we have to listen. They have the capability to strike American soil any time they choose."

—Mary Jo White,
    former U.S. Attorney,
    Southern District of
    New York

New York, New York
May 28, 2003

ACKNOWLEDGMENTS

When Judith Regan asked me in late November 2001 whether I would be interested in writing a book about John O'Neill, a friend, I knew immediately just how difficult a task it would be. Re-creating anyone's life, much less someone involved in such a complex and secretive universe as John O'Neill's, would be an extraordinary chore, and one made even more challenging because of his tragic death. I did not, however, begin to imagine the full extent of this incredible assignment, with its unusual obstacles, until I started the journey.

I completed this book with the help of many people, and I want to extend heartfelt gratitude to those who have graciously assisted me, especially to those who loved O'Neill, or worked alongside him, or both, and who have provided personal recollections and insights that made the project a reality. While this book is the result of untold hours of research, *The Man Who Warned America* is the story of a heroic life that I pieced together largely from the more than six hundred interviews I conducted over the last year and a half. I have listed most of these people at the end of the book, but there are others who wished to remain anonymous. For all of them, my only hope is that I have proven worthy of their trust.

While everyone has my sincere appreciation, there are several people I must single out for special thanks.

Foremost, let me express my warmest regards to Valerie James, Anna DiBattista, and Mary Lynn Stevens, who shared some of their most personal moments, thoughts, and observations with me. I cannot say how much respect I have for them, and how much I appreciate their assistance. In addition, when I set out on the path of uncovering O'Neill's life, I held only modest expectations of cooperation from those still working in government, especially at the FBI. In the end, however, the cooperation I received was unprecedented, for which I must express particular gratitude to Joseph Valiquette, Jay Manning, Kevin Donovan, Thomas Donlan, Michael Rolince, and James Margolin, all of the FBI, and Tom Houston and Paul O'Donnell of the Naval Criminal Investigative Service.

I would also like to express my thanks to Lisa Hamilton and Aliza Fogelson, my gifted editors at ReganBooks, and to Conor Risch and the rest of the ReganBooks staff. Steve Kettmann assisted with a skilled eye and deft hand at the finish line. Thanks also to Philip Messing, my *New York Post* colleague and wordsmith, who was a valued sounding board, and to Ed Hayes, Jay Berg, and Alice McGillion, for their counsel. Also, this project could not have been accomplished without the *New York Post* library staff—Laura Harris, Susan Vanella, Kenneth Moy, Bruce Furman, Andre Freeman, Eric Seadale, and Judy Ausuebel—who always fielded queries with tolerance and precision; and Joseph Amari, Pierre Mena, and Linda Arellano in the photo department. A special thanks goes to Col Allen, the *New York Post* editor in chief, and Jesse Angelo, the metropolitan editor, for their personal cooperation and support. And finally, the words have not been penned to express my gratitude to the wondrous and patient Anne Weldon, who supported me throughout this amazing project.

Lastly, for John O'Neill's family, friends, and colleagues, I extend my personal condolences for the very deep loss of a truly unique and loving person.

THE MAN
WHO WARNED
AMERICA

THE REAL
INSPECTOR
ERSKINE

O'Neill in his 1970 graduation photograph, Holy Spirit High School, Atlantic City, New Jersey. As far back as junior high school, O'Neill was telling friends and teachers he planned to become an agent with the Federal Bureau of Investigation.

PROLOGUE

The writer A. E. Hotchner summed up the pecking order at Elaine's restaurant in New York in a July 2002 *Vanity Fair* article describing the four levels of greetings from the legendary restaurateur Elaine Kaufman: she gave a nod of the head to newcomers, a handshake to semiregulars, a peck on the cheek to her regulars, and, finally, for her favored few, there was a stand-up kiss and hug. John P. O'Neill, the self-styled bon vivant and secret agent, and the new head of the FBI's national security division in New York, had been a fixture in the best spots in town from Chicago and Washington to Rome, Paris, and Cairo. But his first few times at Elaine's in 1999, he was just another face at the bar. He didn't rate even the obligatory nod when he first walked through the double wooden doors, took a spot in the crowd, and ordered his customary Chivas with a twist from Elaine's famous bartender, Thomas Carney.

O'Neill's anonymity at Elaine's did not last long. He soon made an impression at the celebrity-studded saloon, entertaining tables of terrorist hunters and spies from Scotland Yard and MI-6, the real James Bonds of the United Kingdom. Carney recalled looking out from behind the bar one evening and seeing O'Neill with his pals from Scotland Yard, and then, a few days later, turning on the TV and seeing the same investigators back in England searching for clues inside the crime-scene tape after a bombing. Other foreign terror hunters followed. Some were from the Spanish national police, others from the Bundes Kriminal Ambt in Hamburg, and eventually even the Saudi and Yemeni secret police.

One wintry night in February, O'Neill breezed into Elaine's with a group of African officials who were in New York as part of the investigation into the African embassy bombings. Because they were not acclimated to the frigid Northeastern cold, O'Neill went out that day and purchased overcoats for them using his credit cards, so they would not freeze. "They were sitting around wearing coats that did not quite match their clothes, eating steaks and pasta," Elaine recalled with a chuckle.

O'Neill's flair for stylish entertaining may have reached its high point during an official visit from the Saudi crown prince's security detail and Saudi intelligence in 1997, the year after the Khobar Towers bombing that left seventeen American servicemen dead and another four hundred people wounded. Word reached O'Neill that when the Saudis had visited Washington, they were treated with little fanfare. He was appalled. That was no way to treat people who considered themselves royalty. Many were in fact from the royal family, and had to be treated accordingly if the FBI was going to make headway in winning their friendship and cooperation. O'Neill insisted the Saudis come to New York, where he put them up at the Plaza Hotel and wined and dined them, wowing them with the O'Neill tour of the attractions of the Big Apple. He submitted an eye-popping twenty-five thousand dollars in expenses for the short visit, which sent shock waves through the bureau and infuriated the bean counters.

But O'Neill was not one to deny himself the pleasure of entertaining visiting agents and VIPs in the way he felt was appropriate and recharging his batteries at fancy establishments. He was a regular at Cité, Bruno, and Kennedy's as well as Elaine's. FBI agent Vincent Sullivan, a fellow counterterrorism agent, recalled joining O'Neill on several sojourns to Bruno restaurant. Once, O'Neill sat upstairs in the piano lounge with a Scotch in one hand, a cigar in the other, singing Sinatra songs with a group of Mafia wise guys and their *goumadas*, or girlfriends. On another occasion, O'Neill and Sullivan were joined by several visiting terrorist investigators from

Madrid. O'Neill gave them the full treatment—dinner, wine, and song—and then gestured for a cigar box to be brought to the table.

"It was the size of a small child's casket," Sullivan said, assuming the humidor belonged to the restaurant's stylish owner, Bruno Selimaj.

"No, Vinny, the humidor's mine," O'Neill corrected him.

Sullivan still laughs, thinking about the impression O'Neill made on the Spaniards that night.

"They loved him," he said. "They were 'JPO'd.'"

O'Neill's unique style of doing business was what distinguished him from other, more conservative, by-the-book FBI agents. He ran up huge debts, entertaining foreign visitors at his own expense. But his ability to "JPO" foreign officials and agents, whether they were visiting New York, or O'Neill was in Amman, Tel Aviv, or Ankara, created an important network of personal relationships that spanned the globe, and assisted him and the FBI in carrying out its missions all over the world.

Because of this extensive network of intelligence contacts and his own exhaustive knowledge of the subject, John O'Neill was, notably, one of the first people in counterterrorism to understand the threat posed to the United States and its interests abroad by Islamic fundamentalists, particularly Al Qaeda. He established a desk in the FBI's New York office dedicated to monitoring Osama bin Laden and his Al Qaeda network, and remained convinced throughout the last six years of his career that the terrorist leader, who had masterminded the 1998 bombings of two American embassies in Africa, the 1993 "Black Hawk Down" incident in Somalia, and the USS *Cole* bombing in Yemen in 2000, would eventually strike on U.S. soil.

His warnings often fell on deaf ears. Higher-ups and presidents had their own agendas, or perhaps assumed that the terrorism that had struck so tragically in far-flung parts of the world would not materialize at home. Yet despite being "the man who knew," as he came to be known after his death, O'Neill found that bin Laden remained an elusive quarry, so much so that when O'Neill left the FBI in August 2001 for a post as head of security at the World Trade Center, he was forced to downsize his mission from protecting the world from Al Qaeda to protecting the Twin Towers from Al Qaeda. It was a task that, spectacularly and ironically, he was unable to complete.

O'Neill's departure from the FBI after a notable thirty-one-year career came sooner than he had expected, and was dogged by several infractions of FBI procedure that had brought embarrassment to the perfectionist who had dreamed of being an agent all his life, and who had lived for the bureau. But what no one who knew O'Neill would deny was the passion, commitment, and dogged determination he brought to the job, and the fervent and visionary methods he used to complete what he called his "mission." O'Neill had some understanding of the trait that was both his greatest asset and his greatest limitation: "My passion holds all of my wealth and all my liabilities," he once wrote. "It is the best of me and it is the worst of me. But it is me."

1

ON THE BOARDWALK

Thirteen-year-old John P. O'Neill took his usual spot on the living-room couch a few minutes before his favorite television program would begin. He didn't want to risk missing even one minute of the show. It was a Sunday evening in 1965, more than a decade before casinos and hotels would sprout up behind the O'Neills' modest walk-up on Atlantic Avenue, and transform Atlantic City. Finally, at 9 P.M., the screen on the family's small black-and-white showed the opening sequence of the hit ABC-TV series *The FBI*, and O'Neill was transported to a world of polish, dedication, and skill, where dashing federal agents protected people like him from harm.

O'Neill was enthralled. He loved watching the way the calm agent Lewis Erskine, played by Efrem Zimbalist Jr., methodically tracked down his quarry of murderers, racketeers, and saboteurs. O'Neill decided he wanted more than anything to become an agent. Millions of American kids dreamed of becoming a famous buttoned-down agent like the television character, but for John O'Neill this was a mission, not a fantasy. He began to count the days until he could leave Atlantic City and join J. Edgar Hoover's bureau.

"It was not 'This is what I'm thinking of doing.' It was 'This is what I'm *going* to do! I'm going to join the FBI!'" remembers Jack Caravelli, one of O'Neill's closest boyhood friends.

O'Neill's working-class Irish background helped instill in him both an outsized determination and a clear sense of purpose. He always knew he wanted out of Atlantic City, which was not the kind of place that could accommodate his dreams. For more than a century, well-heeled Northeasterners had carried on a love affair with Atlantic City's world-famous herringbone boardwalk with its hotels, its quaint Steel Pier, and the kitschy Miss America pageant. In its heyday, Atlantic City was known as the "Queen of Resorts," bordered by gleaming fine white sand and dotted with nightclubs that attracted entertainers from W. C. Fields and Frank Sinatra to the Beatles.

But there was always an "us versus them" friction between the thirty-seven thousand locals and the outsiders—the "Shoe-bees," as they were derisively called—who descended on the beach for the day carrying shoe boxes packed with sandwiches. Atlantic City was like a small Middle American city where young people either coveted the cocoon of family and friends or hungered for broader horizons. "There were those in Atlantic City who could not get the sand out of their shoes, and others who could not help but leave," said Caravelli.

By 1952, when O'Neill was born, the city was already losing its allure. Elegant neighborhoods were giving way to vacant lots, and racial strife and crime were increasing. Resorts sprang up nearby, siphoning off tourists from Atlantic City and forcing its grand hotels into disrepair. The boardwalk became deserted much of the year, except for a season-ending rush for the Miss America pageant. The Democratic National Convention in 1964 may have represented Atlantic City's last hoorah.

Life was a struggle for O'Neill's parents. The family of three lived in a working-class neighborhood on a section of Atlantic Avenue where shops today sell "All Items 69 Cents," if they are open at all. The Atlantic City Expressway emptied onto the boardwalk only a few blocks away, the Atlantic City Hospital was down the street, and Green's Army/Navy Store and the city newspaper's offices were nearby. The family's small fourth-floor walk-up had a modest kitchen, a living room, and two bedrooms that shared a bathroom.

Starting in the late 1950s, the O'Neills owned a taxi medallion and operated the Dial-a-Cab company out of their apartment. Most of the time, it dispatched one car—theirs—but at its height in the early 1960s, the operation dispatched a fleet of fifteen taxis, according to Murray Rosenberg, owner of the rival Yellow Cab Company in Atlantic City. "It was the high point of their life," he said. "They were unique in that they purchased new cabs, which helped attract business." O'Neill's mother would drive the cab during the day—and still does—and his father drove at night.

"Like most drivers, when he finished his shift and the workday ended, he had a couple and played the ponies," Rosenberg said. "He liked to drink a bit, but he was a helluva guy and that did not make him a bad guy. John was a nice guy, the kind of guy to shoot the breeze with. I have nothing to say except they are solid, honorable people."

More than a dozen taxi companies went out of business in those years, he said. "It was a tough business. There was no gold in the streets." O'Neill's father's taxi gamble, and the decline in the economy, eventually cost the O'Neills their fleet of taxis, but they stayed in business, driving their one cab eighteen hours a day and barely making ends meet even at the height of tourism season. O'Neill's mother would do what she could to pinch pennies, even darning socks for the family, and also worked shifts as a waitress when times were tough.

"It was a wonderful time moral-wise, but a difficult time financial-wise," she has said.

Even after the passage of the 1976 Casino Gambling Referendum, which brought in big-money developers who erected highrise casino hotels along the famed but fading boardwalk, there was little change in their circumstances. The boom that local politicians had preached never materialized for area merchants and residents.

Unlike Las Vegas, which attracted guests who arrived by jet, Atlantic City gamblers were mostly day-trippers who came by car or bus from New York City, Philadelphia, and Washington, D.C.;

these low-rollers were given free lunches and bonus dollars to insert in slot machines as incentives. Even after the glittering lights of Bally's and the Sands framed the sky behind the O'Neill's walk-up, driving a cab was still a grind.

"I was always fascinated how he got out of a place like that and became John O'Neill," said Valerie James, who lived with O'Neill in New York starting in 1997.

O'Neill grew up to be much more like his father than he ever expected. The elder O'Neill, a painter by trade, was gregarious, charismatic, well dressed, and quick with a joke, just like his brother, Bob, a popular piano player and singer at the Hialeah Club and other local clubs. "That's where John got his personality," said James. "He was smooth," recalled Rosenberg. His father also enjoyed drinking and gambling, had a feisty personality, and was, by all accounts, very much his own man. He largely left his wife to care for their young son. That son later told FBI colleagues he was the only official to have a father who was once investigated by the bureau.

"I think John admired and respected his dad, but he wanted to be different," an FBI colleague said.

Dorothy O'Neill—"Dotty," to her friends—was the real breadwinner. Even now, in her midseventies, she still drives a cab out of the same Atlantic Avenue apartment where she raised her son. She was a gritty woman determined that her "Johnnie," the light of her life, would have all that he would need to take advantage of life's possibilities.

"John's mother and father were the nicest people in the world," said John Heanon, one of O'Neill's boyhood friends, now an Atlantic City detective. Heanon often saw Dotty O'Neill behind the wheel of her cab. "It was a tough, tough way to make a buck—dealing with people who think they are kings and queens," he said. "I would be on the street and, whenever John's name appeared in a newspaper, his mother would pull up in her taxi and she would pull out a Xerox of a story about him."

She did not smoke or drink and—though she was not a Catholic like her son and his father—she encouraged him to serve as an altar boy at the ornate St. Nicholas of Tolentine Church on nearby South Tennessee and Pacific Avenues. O'Neill's parents sent him to the new Catholic school, the Holy Spirit High School, which cost them $450 a year. The sprawling complex, built on thirty-one acres on the outskirts of town, offered an alternative to the city's decaying public schools.

"We were the second class to go through Holy Spirit," said Fred Dalzell, now a local orthopedic surgeon. "Atlantic City was having racial tensions. It was getting run-down. John's parents, like so many others, made sacrifices for their children to go to Holy Spirit. There weren't many other choices."

The school dress code called for boys to wear slacks, dress shirts, ties, and suit jackets. Girls wore plaid skirts and patent-leather lace-ups. But this was the late sixties, and some of the students defied tradition. Some girls wore shorter skirts. Some boys wore longer hair. Not O'Neill. He kept his hair short, almost like a fresh recruit in his first weeks at boot camp, and wore a conservative blue blazer and gray slacks.

O'Neill was tall, nearly six-one, fresh-faced and polite. Friends remember his dry, understated sense of humor. He was an average student but excelled in subjects he enjoyed. His best grades were in religion, the Old and New Testament, and morality, and he had more trouble with algebra and chemistry. He was not a star student by any stretch, but he had a focus and seriousness of purpose that set him apart. "Motivation is much more important than innate intelligence," said Joseph Adams, who is still the school's guidance counselor. "Students who are motivated tend to go farther than the ones to whom it comes easy. My strongest image of John was his gentleness, his manner, the way he talked, his politeness. There was nothing fake or phony about him."

O'Neill and his friends, like Caravelli, gained an invaluable education growing up in Atlantic City at that time. It was a motley collection of losers and dreamers who rolled into town, providing useful early training for a later career in law enforcement. "When you spend summers in Atlantic City, the world comes past you," Caravelli recalled. "Rich and poor, socialites and beggars. You really learn a lot, not like living in the suburbs."

Caravelli and O'Neill—who double-dated on Easter Sunday the year they were in eighth grade—would both rise to top positions in law enforcement. Caravelli first went to work at the CIA as an expert on Russian affairs, later as a director of the National Security Council in the White House, and then as a director of international nuclear material protection and cooperation at the Department of Energy. The two remained friends during college and throughout their careers, frequently meeting to compare notes on the serious problems facing the world. O'Neill was drawn to law enforcement not only "to get bad guys," his old friend remembers.

"It was something more than that," Caravelli said. "I think for John it was that mixture of service and clarity of absolutely being on the side of good and having the cachet of glamour attached to it."

O'Neill was always a complicated personality. He was a confident teenager who liked being with people, just as he did throughout his life. But he also had a darker side. He could be fragile and insecure, and could never quite shake his incessant hunger for approval and acknowledgment. This side of his personality, too, would be with him throughout his life. Even when he was at the top of his profession, providing masterful briefings on global terrorist threats to top White House officials, he would always be asking how he did and what he could have done better. "Nothing," he would be told.

"He very much cared about what people thought of him," Caravelli said. "He was never indifferent to how people saw him. And I think he got a lot of emotional support outside his family."

O'Neill was popular, and used that to his friend's advantage when Caravelli ran for student-council president in spring 1969 during their junior year. As campaign manager, O'Neill organized rallies in the cafeteria and put up flyers around the school. Caravelli's father rented a small plane that flew along the beach and over the school, trailing a "Caravelli for President" banner, which may have been the most important factor in the contest. But Caravelli was also helped by O'Neill's warm and winning personality, which helped bring out the voters, especially the underclassmen. "John was just such a great ambassador to the younger kids," Caravelli said, remembering how warm his friend could be in reaching out to others, even though at other times, he could be difficult.

"In class, whether he was right or wrong, he always thought he was right. And that 'Irish thing' would surface, but there was always humor in it, with a wink and nod and a bit of Irish blarney. When I was in the White House, his colleagues in the FBI saw that same trait in John, but they saw it in a positive light, a quiet confidence which they clearly respected."

O'Neill was not a gifted athlete, but clearly wished he was. He ran middle-distance events on the track team, and had high expectations for himself. "When he lost he would get mad," said Frank Formica, a track teammate whose family owns the renowned Atlantic City bakery. "But John was pretty much your average all-American guy. He was not too serious, but he did have a little bit of an edge to him as far as he wanted to seem tough. But the worst thing we ever did was to go out and find a six-pack."

O'Neill was fit enough to pull off a small coup and win a job as a beach lifeguard, which took some effort. "Being a lifeguard is the most prestigious position you can have during the summer—and not a bad way to meet chicks," said Formica. "Probably three or four mayors were former lifeguards. You cannot believe how politically savvy it is to become one. And the way you basically got the job was to have someone with contacts help you. But John got it through sheer determination and training. If you cannot swim or row that boat, it is like the Marines, you're not getting the job.

That was just hard work and determination, given his family was not connected. You have to be that good."

O'Neill hawked newspapers on the boardwalk to earn some change, and sometimes embellished the news. "Extra, Extra, Liz Taylor Is Dead!" he would yell, and people would rush up and buy all his papers, and he would run off before the unsuspecting buyers learned the truth. "You have to give people what they want," he once told Kevin Duffy, a manager at Elaine's.

He helped his mother by taking shifts in her taxi and waiting tables at a local restaurant, experiences that helped him keep a sense of perspective later in life. Even though at times he would be too easily impressed by wealth and its trappings, he was widely known in the FBI as someone who respected people regardless of their station. He related to people whether they were on the wait staff in the fancy restaurants he came to love or the vendors selling trinkets for small change outside the J. Edgar Hoover Building in Washington, D.C.

"You would walk into Elaine's or Bruno with him and everyone from the owner to the waiters to the guy who cleaned the floor would look up, and the amazing thing is they would all have a private discussion with him at some point," R. P. Eddy, an NSC director, told *The New Yorker*. "The waitress wanted tickets to a Michael Jackson concert. One of the wait staff was applying for a job with the bureau, and John would be helping him with that. After a night of this, I remember saying, 'John, you've got this town wired,' and he said, 'What's the point of being sheriff if you can't act like one?'"

His senior year, O'Neill started dating Christine Shutz, an attractive blonde on the girls' track team. "She was a sweetheart, just a jovial person," Heanon said. "You meet her once and you fall in love with her." O'Neill soon started to discuss marriage, even though he was a long way from being ready for the responsibilities of having a family. O'Neill knew his first few years in the FBI would be difficult, and he needed someone to provide him with support and approval after he left Atlantic City. That need, a lifelong characteristic, led him to make some unusual choices in his personal life over the years.

O'Neill and Caravelli graduated from Holy Spirit High in June 1970 and departed for the nation's capital. Caravelli studied at Georgetown and worked in the school's law library. O'Neill headed for the FBI and American University. To become an agent in the FBI, you either started as a clerk or you needed a bachelor's degree. O'Neill decided to pursue both options. He figured that would give him the best chance of realizing his dream. "He put everything into his goal," said Adams, his guidance counselor.

O'Neill applied to become a humble fingerprint clerk and FBI tour guide to get his foot in the door, and to support himself as he attended American University. Not many of his fellow students saw the world the way he did. The nation was deeply split over the Vietnam War, and campuses were gripped by massive antiwar demonstrations and a growing distrust of all government institutions.

"By any measure, we ran counter to the grain," Caravelli said. "I remember when we were eighteen in 1970 and they did the birthday draft. We would ask each other what we would do if you had a low number and were called to serve. We had a lot of questions about where we were heading. My father served in World War II. My brother served in 'Nam. He came back with stories. I would have gone to Vietnam with great trepidation. Although those were radical days swirling around us, John had an internal compass of what the country meant to him. There were longer-term beliefs and fundamentals. Our families were the great unwashed middle class trying to give their children a better life. Maybe joining the bureau was his answer."

The Vietnam protests tested O'Neill's beliefs. On the one hand, he was deeply troubled by the direction of the war and how it was being waged, and he could not help but be moved by the passion of the demonstrators. On the other hand, he loved his country and was committed to becoming part of the very U.S.

government so reviled by the demonstrators. "He wondered, 'If we were so good and righteous, how could we be doing these things and getting these results?'" Caravelli said. "It was not 'right versus wrong' for John. Things were more subtle and complicated for him than that. Mostly we were all trying to figure things out."

That meant taking a few tentative steps toward taking part in the youth culture of the time, but mostly trying to remain as unaffected as possible. O'Neill and Christine were married in Linwood, New Jersey, on January 23, 1971, while she was still of high school age, and between family and the FBI, O'Neill had a much different set of priorities than those around him. "I actually had a beard in college and John's hair was longer," Caravelli said. "Neither of us qualified as an Abby Hoffman radical. We were just two pretty straitlaced guys."

Caravelli remembers one large protest in May 1971 that brought 150,000 antiwar demonstrators to the area around the Washington Mall. It seemed as though they stretched as far as Caravelli and O'Neill could see. Protesters closed the Key Bridge linking Roslyn with downtown, and the police had to drive the young marchers back onto the Georgetown campus, sometimes clubbing them in the head.

"I remember when we went down to the Washington monument, the grounds were surrounded with a hundred and fifty thousand kids from all over the country with a commitment and you could not help but take notice of it, intellectually," Caravelli said. "We were really seeing something extraordinarily unusual, a landmark moment that could not be dismissed."

O'Neill was moved by the convictions of the antiwar protesters, but he would have fought in Vietnam if called, he always said, even though he had responsibilities at home. O'Neill was only twenty when his son, John P. O'Neill Jr., was born on September 8, 1972. The O'Neills lived in an apartment in suburban Alexandria and drove around in a Volkswagen beetle. Christine was working as a waitress, and John was working as a clerk in the FBI's Fingerprint Identification Unit. He quickly became a full-time tour guide, and carried a full course load at night at American University's school of justice. He studied government and law enforcement and the impact of politics, economics, and the environment on public policy in Washington and around the world.

"I could never have married as early as he did," said Caravelli. "There always seemed to be a larger internal compass driving John, first his career and then the antiterrorism, which was like a Holy Grail."

Most clerks took one tour around the building each day, but not O'Neill. He always took two, and sometimes three. Other tour guides teased O'Neill because he was so serious, always rushing around seeking information. "John was an interesting character," John Blaha, another former clerk, remembers. "He was always striving to be better than he was, always trying to get to the next tier, struggling for an identity, an education, and a job as an agent, and later as a supervisor."

All that hurrying left O'Neill rumpled. The shirts and ties he wore as a tour guide were often creased and unkempt. When he raced around, working up a sweat, his colleagues began to call him "Stinky," a name he never forgot. Years later, Blaha visited O'Neill in New York soon after he became national security division head. "John was sitting behind this desk with a magnificent view of Manhattan and he said, 'So are you still going to call me Stinky?' and flashing that trademark O'Neill smile," Blaha said.

O'Neill made the most of his time shepherding visitors through the Department of Justice. He made a good first impression, with his mellifluous baritone and crisp, detailed accounts, and met heads of states and other top government officials who would later prove useful to him. He boned up and was awash in information about the different points of interest along the FBI tour, including displays on everything from Mafia bosses to the Rosenberg case to the 1950s Brinks Depository Robbery in

Boston, as well as the famed laboratory on the seventh floor and the firearms range in the basement. "He always felt he was the best tour giver," recalled Warren Flagg, another former clerk. "Anything short of being the best was not in John's vocabulary."

"This place really meant something to him, you could really tell," said Rex Tomb, also a former clerk. "John was really bright, extremely focused. He really stood out from the rest of us, very, very ambitious in school and getting classes out of the way."

O'Neill's tours, which he would later credit with giving him confidence as a public speaker, took on a special quality because he was especially alert. He was always studying the FBI more closely than other tour guides, paying attention to current events that involved the FBI and its internal planning and administrative changes. He would go out of his way to watch anything on television—there were only three major networks at the time—that had to do with the FBI.

"If there was a special news program, he would catch it," said Tomb, who now is the chief of the fugitive publicity special services unit. "John really wanted to be an agent. He just thought it would be a really good, honorable, and rewarding profession that would earn him respect wherever he went. And I knew that no matter how high John O'Neill got, he would always call you back and he did not forget you."

Tomb also recalled how O'Neill would stick up for the powerless. He defended the vendors who worked outside the FBI headquarters. Most agents dismissed these lowly salespeople as an annoyance when their pushcarts and ice-cream trolleys distracted people on the tours, or their garbage soiled the clean steps of the building. But O'Neill came to know them personally. "He never looked down his nose, even on the vendors, some of them foreigners, who would sell pop or ice cream to tourists," Tomb said. "He would go out and talk to them, know their names and their kids'. He'd say, 'These people are here trying to make a living.'"

O'Neill would overpay the vendors, showing his generosity,

but he would also borrow money from friends for the candy machine and never pay it back. "It was understandable, though, he had a wife and child," Tomb said. He could often be blunt and competitive to a fault. Warren Flagg recalled how intense O'Neill was when the clerks played basketball in the basement gym. Just as in high school, O'Neill was not the most gifted player, but he was determined to win. "Anything short of winning was unacceptable," Flagg said.

O'Neill enrolled in the challenging masters-of-science program in forensic sciences at George Washington University, after graduating from American University in 1974, but continued to give tours at the FBI and clerk in the fingerprint unit. The masters program was essentially created to teach federal agents how to gather and document evidence properly. Subjects included serology, legal medicine, forensic pathology, toxicology, firearms ballistics, and forensic chemistry. Professor Walter Roe, a distinguished forensic-science educator at GWU, said O'Neill was one of the few students who could handle the tough curriculum while working or training full-time at the bureau. "I don't think we had many students who could do that," he said.

In July 1976, after more than five years of clerking for the FBI, O'Neill was finally selected to join a class of about thirty students who would train to become agents. During the four months of training, prospective agents moved into the FBI's Quantico training facility in Virginia. For the first month, they remained under virtual lockdown. The grueling regimen was designed to weed out the weak. Tests were only given once, and a passing grade was eighty-five. When an agent flunked out, expulsion was swift and brutal: supervisors would call the disappointed agent out of a morning class, and by lunchtime, his bed would be neatly made and he would be gone. "It was all done to put as much pressure on you to see where your breaking point was," said Flagg, who later became a highly regarded agent.

Although O'Neill and the others had to sleep at Quantico,

they could leave the grounds in the evening. O'Neill would hitch-hike to D.C. to attend his graduate classes, and then thumb a ride back to Virginia, slipping inside the building after curfew by shimmying through an open window. "It was during those early years that I knew John would go as high in the bureau as they would take him," Flagg said.

Some agents who joined the FBI directly from college or law school poked fun at the ones who started as clerks, referring to them sarcastically as "clerk-agents." O'Neill was sensitive about the mocking wisecrack, but he did not waste time explaining himself to others. He was on a mission to become an agent, and eventually a supervisor, and he was a person whose work ethic and expertise would silence any critic. After nearly six long years of tours, clerking, and attending college, the mission O'Neill embarked upon as a ninth-grade boy growing up in gritty Atlantic City and watching television's Inspector Erskine became reality. In October 1976, John P. O'Neill graduated Quantico and became one of the FBI's nine thousand "special agents."

2

THINKING OUT OF THE BOX

O'Neill did not waste any time making a name for himself as an inventive and skilled investigator in the Baltimore field office, his first assignment. But he wasn't only smart and resourceful. He was also a natural at reaching out to people and forging alliances. He was back at Quantico for a scheduled retraining session when he learned that his office would finally be getting its first female agent. Pleased by the news and strongly in favor of the FBI including women as equal partners, O'Neill immediately went looking for the new agent, Kathy Hartnett Kiser, the daughter of a respected New York City cop and the seventy-eighth female FBI agent to make it through Quantico. He wanted to welcome her and offer his support.

"He said, 'Hi, I'm John O'Neill and if there is anything I can do or answer any questions, please free to ask me,'" Kiser recalled. "I said, 'Great.' From the moment I met him he was cordial, personable, and that was the way he always was with me. When he is a friend, he is a friend for life."

O'Neill gained a reputation in Baltimore for being brilliant, insightful, dogged, creative, and fiercely protective of his staff and colleagues. He also recognized early on the importance of reducing interagency squabbles in law enforcement. He socialized with local cops and prosecutors, building bridges that helped out later on, whatever mission he had undertaken. And when Kiser was hospitalized after a car crash, he visited her nearly every day. "He had a heart of gold," she said.

Even as a young agent, O'Neill had a knack for digesting huge amounts of complicated information and distilling it down to its essence as easily as if it were a child's math question. He tried not to come across as arrogant. He would argue ferociously over a strategic turn he wanted to take, and would typically throw an arm around the shoulder of a disbeliever, making him a friend and ally. And his philosophy was clear: the FBI investigates to get to the truth—without prejudice and until every question has been answered.

"One day John asked me, 'What is it we do?' and I said, 'We put people in jail,'" said Gary Stevens, who worked with O'Neill in the Baltimore office. "John disagreed. He said, 'No, we don't. We investigate. Maybe we put them in jail. Maybe we don't.'"

This philosophy served O'Neill well. It helped him keep a sense of perspective whether he was pursuing drug dealers, killers of abortion doctors, domestic terrorist Timothy McVeigh, or Islamic fundamentalist radicals. He was less inclined to be judgmental of his targets, and more focused on investigating a case until he was satisfied that every avenue had been checked and every question answered. The outcome rested solely on where the evidence took him.

"It was hard to close out cases with John," said Stevens. "John did not want to give up on a case, even when it became apparent you had to close it out. He would still have you tying up loose ends and we would say, 'Why the hell are we doing this?' He just would not let you close a case while there was a second thought or unless it was as dead as a doornail."

Wes Wong was a young agent working on Chinese gangs in 1978 when he was dispatched from New York to Baltimore. His assignment was to help O'Neill guard key witnesses in a case against Chinese gang members who were extorting money from the owners of a Chinese nightclub. One of the witnesses was a singer in the nightclub who was prepared to testify against the gang members, and needed protection. The FBI suspected that the gang, Ghost Shadows, would send a team of hit men from

New York's Chinatown to silence her. Wong and another senior Chinese gang expert from New York worked with O'Neill at the Holiday Inn where the witness was kept under wraps.

Wong remembered not knowing what to expect from the agents in the smaller Baltimore office, and immediately being impressed by O'Neill's cool professionalism and big-city manner. A major shoot-out seemed imminent one afternoon during the assignment when a car with New York plates pulled up outside the Holiday Inn, and four young Chinese men stepped out. "They started walking around the hotel as though they were casing it," Wong recalled. "It was too much of a coincidence." O'Neill, Wong, and the others moved into position to defend the room where the witness was stashed, and shoot it out with the would-be assassins, if necessary. But the four young men gave up without finding the woman, and headed back to New York empty-handed. Wong and the other New York agent told one another that this John O'Neill was someone to watch.

"There was just something about him," said Wong. "You knew he was going to move up. I remember saying John was going to be an SIC someday. I used to kid with him, all the way until the end, that 'The first day I met you I knew you were going places.' I can't put my finger on it. He was a leader. He had the demeanor. It was just something I sensed."

When Kiser arrived in Baltimore in April 1978, the twenty-six-year-old O'Neill was in the midst of an important pornography case. Kurt Schmoke, later the mayor of Baltimore, was a young United States attorney handling the pornography investigation when John O'Neill took it over. The case was fraught with obstacles and had been languishing, with a revolving door of agents and prosecutors passing it along as they were transferred to other assignments.

The target owned a variety of strip clubs and other X-rated businesses in Baltimore and Washington. A federal assault on such clubs might seem inconsequential today, when adult videos are readily available at shopping malls and cybersex is just a mouse click away. But in 1978, the investigation carried a high priority, especially when it became clear that this was not some small-time smut peddler. O'Neill and his fellow agents soon determined that he was part of a larger network, connected to the Mafia, that dealt in pornography and the white slave trade. But the case was complicated by the vague definition—then and now—of what constitutes pornography.

"No one could tell you what was or was not pornography," Agent James Duffy said. "It was up to the 'community standards.'"

O'Neill realized he had to find a novel way of claiming federal jurisdiction in the case. He ordered his men to canvass every lightbulb manufacturer in neighboring states to determine if the pornographer was purchasing lightbulbs from outside Maryland. He told his agents to collect invoices going back several years. They thought O'Neill was insane. 'What the hell do you have us doing?'" they wondered, according to Schmoke.

But O'Neill was working to exploit a recently enacted weapon in the FBI's arsenal against crime known as "RICO," the Racketeering Influence and Corrupt Organizations Act, which later would be used to topple the godfathers of New York's five Mafia families. O'Neill was "way ahead" of other FBI agents in how he used RICO, Schmoke said. "Everyone thought the big case was going nowhere," he said. "John was just out of school, a beginning agent. In order to try to show that indeed there was interstate activity, John had his agents do an inventory of the number of lightbulbs this guy bought for his X-rated theater houses."

Schmoke used the evidence involving thousands of lightbulbs as a "predicate act," a specific criminal offense, in a draft indictment of charges involving transporting goods across state lines to further a pornographic enterprise. With the foundation laid for a RICO case, O'Neill took to the streets. It was unusual at that time for FBI agents to embark on late-night, undercover operations. This was long before undercover agent Joe Pistone infiltrated

New York's Bonnano crime family pretending to be "Donny Brasco," a mob fence. But O'Neill and his agents spent countless late nights trying to find an employee at the strip clubs and movie houses who might be willing to cooperate.

O'Neill finally found a peep-show doorman who was ready to flip. He was ideal for a federal case because he worked in Baltimore, Maryland, and in Washington, D.C. "John was always looking for an interstate aspect," Schmoke said. But winning his confidence was not easy. Agents all wore suits and ties back then, and O'Neill was so clean-cut, Schmoke remembers him looking like a real "Boy Scout," trying to win over the doorman, who was black.

"He looked like a character out of the *Mod Squad* television show, with big squared-off Afro, bell-bottom pants, and big platform shoes," said Schmoke. "Remember he worked in a peep show and striptease joints. He was one slick, 1970s dude."

The suspicious informant wanted a guarantee from a prosecutor that O'Neill would deliver on promises he made in exchange for his cooperation against the pornographer. This presented one last hurdle—prosecutors and peep-show doormen do not work the same hours. O'Neill set up a meeting for well past midnight, and drove the informant to the federal courthouse to demonstrate he was who he said he was.

Other agents were waiting inside the building. They were there to baby-sit Schmoke's kids because the prosecutor's wife was out of town attending a medical conference. "John called me to meet the guy at like two A.M., and I had to bring my children and had to bring them down and find a couch and a rocker for them. It was one of the most unusual moments I ever had in the U.S. attorney's office," said Schmoke, who described himself as a "buttoned-down, African-American Ivy Leaguer."

The *Mod Squad* doorman did not immediately agree to cooperate. That took some time. "We played a cat-and-mouse game," said Schmoke. "He wanted to hear the offer and know that John was in fact dealing with a prosecutor. Obviously that worked out.

It seems pretty standard stuff now, but it was pretty unusual then."

O'Neill's cooperation with Schmoke was typical. He always saw his work as an FBI agent as part of a larger mosaic that also included local cops and prosecutors. He was one of the few agents who attended the huge annual law enforcement barbecue, "The Steak Out," at the Pikesville, Maryland national-guard armory. He would shake hands and smile, then collect and hand out business cards—and, just as important, take the time to listen to people from different law enforcement disciplines. It all came naturally to him, but beyond that, he was always very aware of the importance of expanding his universe of contacts.

O'Neill had to show toughness, too, to make a mark in the bureau. Shortly after the pornography case, he was transferred to the white collar crime division, which had become a bureau priority following several historic FBI corruption investigations, including one of Vice-President Spiro Agnew, the former governor of Maryland, who was imprisoned for taking bribes in the White House bathroom. O'Neill's transfer to white collar was personally ordered by Dana Caro, then the legendary head of the Baltimore office. Caro could be flinty and difficult, and agents who worked for him either loved him or hated him. There was no in-between. Caro told O'Neill to devise a program to investigate two local politicians, a senator and a congressman, and when it came time for O'Neill to present his ideas for getting an undercover operative close to the targets, Caro played devil's advocate.

"Dana began slowly and then he built up steam as he started his barrage of questions: 'Do you know this?' 'Have you explored that?' 'Do you know undercover operations could come back and bite us in the ass?'" remembered George Andrew, then a young supervisor. "Once Dana smelled blood, he pounded away, and in front of your peers. He was unmerciful with John. By the time Dana had finished, I saw tears in John's eyes."

O'Neill went straight back to his office to start drafting another attack plan, which was later approved. If he ever complained about Dana's treatment, Andrew never heard it. "John did not sulk or pout," he said. "John went out and changed the operation and became a pet agent just by working hard. Some agents thought he was a 'blue-flamer,' someone who would make a mark and then burn out. The others thought he was just a hard-charging, young, energetic kid."

Caro saw more than energy in O'Neill. He saw real talent. In fact, he was about to make O'Neill one of the youngest FBI supervisors in the country, giving him a squad to fight labor and political corruption, even though O'Neill barely had the required seven years in the bureau to earn such a promotion. One of Caro's top lieutenants asked why he was elevating an agent so light on experience to such an important post.

"He is the smartest agent I ever met," Caro replied.

Far from letting Caro's challenge hurt him, O'Neill had turned it to his advantage, impressing the boss and getting a great new opportunity. Andrew was amazed when he heard about Caro's lavish praise of O'Neill.

"It kind of put me back a step," he said. "I said, 'Wow,' Dana did not give out accolades like that. But John was an amazing person to study, brilliant guy, just great capacity for investigations, for names, for prior events, and he was very energetic. I was thinking how far John recovered from Caro's initial belittling."

O'Neill's promotion in 1983 was a vindication of his belief in using every tool he could to sharpen his focus on a given challenge. "I swear John had a beeper before anyone else I knew," Kiser said. "He had all the gadgets." He also worked long hours, and expected his people to do the same. He was not a stickler about a spit-and-polish dress code or arriving to work with military precision, but his agents needed to be available. "When he called you on a Sunday to get something done, he wanted you without excuses, whether it was surveillance or supporting someone for a wiretap," said Stevens.

"And you could not keep up with him. He was way ahead. If you wanted to lay out a scenario for a case, he would jump in and say, 'If you do this or that, you would be way ahead.' And he was always right. I am not sure you ever knew a case better than John O'Neill, even if the case was yours."

O'Neill's energy level amazed people. Stevens remembers a time when his squad was working a public corruption case that suddenly spun out into a complicated drug probe with political overtones. A stack of intelligence data took the investigation into O'Neill's home state, New Jersey, where the DeCavalcante crime family held sway. Several DeCavalcante associates were running the drugs, apparently into Baltimore. O'Neill and a team of agents, including Stevens, went to Newark to review wiretaps recorded by the local cops.

The agents spent all day Saturday listening to boring conversations about food and TV, and soon found that O'Neill was not above such tedious grunt work. He sat with his men as they searched for a revealing snippet of conversation. At night, they broke for dinner and then everyone went to sleep—except O'Neill. He and a Newark cop sped off to Atlantic City, where they gambled all night and returned in time to meet Stevens the following morning, as he finished attending mass, to listen to another round of recordings. O'Neill was not a big gambler; that was not the point of the trip. Rather it was part of his credo: work hard, play hard. "Listening to tapes is boring even if you are wide-awake," said Stevens. "But John was there ready to go. He had that kind of energy."

Back in Baltimore, O'Neill organized an early morning meeting with local federal prosecutors to lay out the case, and breezed into the office only minutes before the briefing the next day. "Let's go," he barked at Stevens, then walked into the meeting without having looked at a single scrap of paper, and rattled off every piece of evidence as though he had spent days writing down each word he was going to say. "His capacity to absorb was just phenomenal," Stevens said. "Everyone conceded that, even people who did not like him."

There were always more than a few who did not like O'Neill. He could seem to be a little too full of himself for some tastes. But he welcomed legitimate challenges to his ideas. He never wanted subordinates to express problems without stepping up with possible solutions. In fact, he encouraged give-and-take that might lead to new ways of addressing an investigation. He would sometimes concede a point. More often, he would prevail, either because people came to see he was right or because of what he liked to think of as the O'Neill Irish charm.

"Just about everyone at one time or another would have knock-down-drag-out shouting matches with John about how to do the case," Stevens said. "John would start out on his side of the desk and you on the other, and you knew it was going to be a bad one. You'd go at each other tooth and nail. Somewhere along the way . . . he would come around and sit next to you to cajole you and win you over to his side. And when it came time for him to rate your performance, you would never know that you had argued. It just did not come up. He rated you just on how you did the job. Not on whether he liked you or not."

O'Neill's long hours took a toll on his family life. He tried to provide a traditional home life with Christine and their son, J.P., but that desire clashed with his ambition to throw everything he had into being a top agent. Christine had left her job as a waitress and tried hard to make things work. Even when O'Neill worked past midnight, she would go out of her way to take care of him.

"John would come in the next day saying, 'You know, Chris got up and made me dinner,'" Kiser recalled. "And I said, 'My God, she is a great woman, making dinner after midnight.' She was home with J.P., who was an adorable, cute little boy. I remember John was very proud of his son, attending his sporting events. He was very, very close to his son. He was his heart."

Agent Duffy recalled attending cross-country track meets with John where their sons competed on a field in Westchester, where the Baltimore Colts football team used to conduct spring training. A decade later, O'Neill would dispatch Duffy to Afghanistan to hunt killers of an American and three European tourists. But at those Baltimore track meets, they were just two dads sitting in the stands proudly watching their kids.

Christine, John, and J.P. would sometimes join other agents and their families at McDonald's, but such family outings were the exception to the ominous reality. If it came down to a choice between giving his all to the bureau and saving his marriage, O'Neill would always pick the FBI. Other agents would hear him on the phone with his wife, reassuring her that he loved her.

"John's work was something he lived for," Kiser said. "He would say, 'Kathy, I have always wanted to do this.' And he earned it. He had a thirst for adventure. But Chris was just lower key. She was quieter and content with being at home. You could tell their roads were parting." Caravelli, who was at the CIA at the time, said there was no way to reconcile such a grueling work schedule with a normal family life. "John was making his choice," he said. "He was married to the FBI."

But O'Neill made other choices that hurt his marriage—and had nothing to do with the FBI. He and a colleague went for a drink at the nearby Hilton Hotel, which had a popular dance club, and an attractive young woman named Janet Murray, who worked for ATT, approached. She asked O'Neill's colleague to dance, and then O'Neill, who used to boast that he was such a good dancer he had appeared on *American Bandstand* as a teen back in Atlantic City. A four-minute dance at the Hilton turned into a two-year affair.

"John told me he was separated and getting a divorce from his wife," Murray recalled. "He said they were staying together until his son had finished school, and his wife would be moving back to Atlantic City."

Murray believed him, though by then O'Neill had begun to develop a pattern of deception about his personal life even to those who loved him. Murray said she and O'Neill spoke every day, saw each other often, and played golf on Saturdays. O'Neill even took her several times to meet his parents, who apparently knew his marriage was rocky.

"I was in love," she said. But her patience ran out. O'Neill kept putting her off with false promises, and she finally confronted him and learned that O'Neill and his wife were still together. "I would never date a married man," she said. "I was led to believe that they were divorcing."

When Christine O'Neill learned that her husband was dating another woman, the revelation rocked their marriage. Murray broke up with O'Neill, telling him to call her when he really got a divorce. O'Neill apologized to his wife, asked for forgiveness, and assured her such infidelity would never happen again, and the couple had their second child, Carol, on June 1, 1984.

But even the arrival of a lovely new baby could not save the marriage, and the O'Neills soon separated. Christine returned to Atlantic City, a single mother with two children, one of them an infant girl with an eye ailment. Christine's plight was more than many young women could accept, but she managed to successfully raise her children, attend nursing school, and become an integral part of her community working in the local medical examiner's office.

O'Neill once pointed to an office building downtown and told Stevens, "That is where my divorce attorney is," but in fact, the O'Neills never did divorce. "It's a Catholic thing," O'Neill would say if forced to explain. Perhaps he was driven by pragmatism. Staying married guaranteed government health insurance for his family, which was especially important for his daughter, who might require special medical attention. If he died, Christine and the children would receive his pension and life-insurance payout.

However O'Neill explained the choice to himself, his decision not to divorce Christine skewed any future relationships he would have. He always seemed to be lying about some aspect of his life. Although he was a charismatic man with a spellbinding career and an infectious lust for life, he could not easily tell a woman he was married because it would stop a relationship before it could start. And that may have preselected the type of women he could date— all were independent, had careers of their own, and enjoyed life without yearning for marriage or children.

Most of O'Neill's colleagues knew almost nothing about his personal life. Even with prospective girlfriends, O'Neill was guarded. He initially acknowledged he had a son. But it was generally only after the relationships were cemented that he confessed he also had a daughter—telling himself that his new companion might be reluctant to become involved with a "divorcé" with two children. O'Neill became so accustomed to shading the truth, he often was at a loss to understand his own insatiable need always to line up another woman who loved him and admired him. For a man who spent his life digging for the truth, he was remarkably willing to leave major parts of his own psyche unexplored and mysterious.

"I don't know what was wrong with me," he would confess years later to an intimate. "I would date two people, and on my night off, I would look for another. I don't know why."

O'Neill began to seriously date a married woman who had returned from maternity leave and was assigned to work for him in the Baltimore office. They fell in love, and she eventually left her husband. She was not demanding, and understood the rigors of his long hours on his job. But after an extended relationship, this union also fizzled when she began to talk about marriage and children. Any woman who wanted to send O'Neill back to the cover of round-the-clock work for the bureau only had to discuss marriage, and he might leave.

As always, O'Neill's work was demanding and important. In 1985, he was named head of labor and public corruption in Baltimore at a time when the nation's most important public corruption investigation involved the Wedtech Company of New York, which was suspected of winning military contracts by bribing a host of government officials. The investigation had links to two major political figures in Maryland, Clarence M. Mitchell III, a former state senator, and his brother, State Senator Michael B. Mitchell. The brothers were suspected of accepting $110,000 in payoffs in 1984 and 1985 to block an investigation of Wedtech by the House Small Business Committee, which was headed by their uncle, Congressman Parren Mitchell, who was not implicated in the scheme.

"Public corruption cases are like elephant hunting," O'Neill would say. "You have one shot. It must be right. You can't wound the elephant. It is not right to the elephant or the system."

Stevens was one of the investigators O'Neill put on the complicated case. They built the case from scratch using surveillance and wiretaps and culling thousands of documents and records. "John was like no one I ever worked for," Stevens said. "He was a stickler for paperwork."

O'Neill was headed for big things, and everyone knew it. "Any boss who did not see it and take advantage of it was foolish," said Kiser. "He was classic for management. He was not afraid to state his opinion. He was very bright. He could put his finger on things and not waste time on nonsense." She and Agent James McAllister stood outside of O'Neill's glass-enclosed office one time, discussing his future. "See that man in there?" said McAllister. "John is going to be a special agent in charge of an office one day, and we will sit back and say, 'We knew him when.'"

O'Neill was transferred from the Baltimore office to the new J. Edgar Hoover Building and named supervisory special agent in the white collar crime section, a position rarely given to an agent with less than eleven years in the bureau. It was quite a feat for a man who was still only thirty-seven. One evening he stopped in at Anton's Loyal Opposition, a restaurant near Capitol Hill, and took a seat at the bar and ordered a Chivas with a twist and a splash, and sat watching C-SPAN, which had uninterrupted video of Chinese students demonstrating in Tiananmen Square.

Mary Lynn Stevens, an attractive blond executive at one of the nation's largest military credit unions, walked in. "Is there a spot at the bar?" she asked the owner. "Yeah, just one over there next to that lucky guy," he replied, motioning to an empty stool next to O'Neill. Stevens asked if the bartender knew the man. "No, I've never seen him before. He must be new."

She sat down next to O'Neill, and for the next three hours they talked about politics, world affairs, life, art, and Irish history. "He said I was the smartest women he ever met," Stevens said. O'Neill also said he was divorced and had dated another woman, but that the relationship had ended. "I had a sense that he was a man of principle, not a runaround," she said, noting that she had been "a play-the-field kinda" woman. "He conveyed a sense of stability that you could hook into. He was giving you something solid, a strong set of values."

Stevens was slightly older than O'Neill and extremely independent. They eventually became intimate and carried on a relationship, often long distance and over the telephone, until the day O'Neill died. Only then did she learn how much she had been sharing him with other women. "I loved him," she said. "And love is unconditional, relationships are not. He was a great sounding board. He was a very good friend. Sometimes I wanted to see him more than once a week, but he was working most of the time and had the perfect excuse. I understood that his personal life was squeezed into the margins by his work."

In 1991, while still working at FBI headquarters, O'Neill was assigned to the bureau's inspections division, where he impressed Neil Gallagher, then the section chief of counterterrorism. The two men traveled to Alaska to conduct an analysis and critique of the FBI's field office in Anchorage. O'Neill's work ethic and his ability to brilliantly assess the work of the office and write a detailed report impressed Gallagher. That favorable impression changed the direction of O'Neill's life. When an opening developed to head the Chicago field office later that year, to be the assistant special agent in charge, the "ASAC," for violent crime, white collar crime, and organized crime, Gallagher told the higher-ups he knew just the agent for the job. In July 1991, O'Neill was promoted to one of the bureau's most important field offices.

"Me and another agent who worked with John still talk about him," said agent Stevens. "We still do all those little last things to tie up the loose ends of a case. Sometimes, we say it is a waste of time and we ask ourselves, 'Why are we doing this?' And the answer is, 'We do it because we are John O'Neill–trained.'"

3

"MY KIND OF TOWN"

Chicago was O'Neill's kind of town, right from his first days there. Arriving in the Windy City in July 1991 was like a coming-out party for the kid from Atlantic City. He loved being in a world-class city that was cosmopolitan and self-confident, and went out and splurged on a silver Buick Regal with blue seats to make the drive from Washington to Chicago in style. He was one of the FBI's up-and-coming officials now, and for his playground he had a city with a rich history of great blues and jazz clubs, and sophisticated restaurants and taverns where sports stars, entertainment celebrities, and millionaires mingled.

Washington, for all its status as the nation's capital, remains a provincial, stuffy town compared to Chicago or New York. Bars and restaurant shut down by 1 A.M., with last call often half an hour earlier. Worse still from O'Neill's perspective, FBI agents do not rank very high in the pecking order of a town jammed with bureaucrats. U.S. senators and representatives rate special tables alongside diplomats and foreign dignitaries. Even lowly White House and congressional aides hold sway over agents. But in grittier, working-class cities like Chicago, gun-toting lawmen are often treasured, and a fancy G-man with panache and a federal badge had cachet that translated into a hefty measure of respect. Sometimes it seemed as if everyone in Chicago knew John O'Neill.

"You would walk into a restaurant with him and he was like Elvis," Jay Manning said. "I would say, 'John, you got this town wired,' and O'Neill would smile that John O'Neill smile and say, 'There's no sense living in a town unless you can own it.' "

O'Neill rented a $1,200-a-month apartment on the fortieth floor of the sixty-story Onterie Center apartments at 441 East Erie Street, across from the Playboy Building. The high-rise had a breathtaking view of Lake Michigan and offered tenants such amenities as a private gym, saunas, and whirlpool on the roof, and a high-end shopping mall on the ground level. O'Neill had no furniture. He had given it all to an ex-girlfriend in Baltimore when they split, an obvious gesture to ease the separation and guilt. He rented simple, comfortable furniture for the place. It may not have been flashy, but it was perfect for an FBI official who did not plan on spending many hours at home.

O'Neill, always a quick study, read dozens of nightlife and entertainment magazines and guidebooks about Chicago before he arrived, and quickly hit all the best nightspots, taverns, and restaurants. He would earn his well-deserved reputation for working extraordinary hours and then staying out even later, seemingly without the need for sleep. The front-row seats at Wrigley Field ball games, a dignitary's perch for St. Patrick's Day festivities and well-positioned tables at crowded boîtes satisfied O'Neill's fun-loving side, but the lure of Chicago never distracted him from his work at the FBI's offices inside the Dirksen Federal Building. It was as though the glad-handing and late-night action was a release that enabled O'Neill to reenergize.

Chicago was the fourth-most-violent city in America, averaging 32.5 murders, rapes, assaults, and robberies for every thousand Chicagoans. The city was awash in serious crime, and its poorest residents were stuck in sprawling housing projects, all but held hostage by violent drug and street gangs. National news programs seemed to carry a report at least once a week on the slaughter of children caught in the cross fire of warring Chicago gangs. The Chicago Police Department had twelve thousand cops and one thousand detectives, but was hard-pressed to break the vise-like grip of the youth gangs carving up territory and to end the tidal wave of violent crime.

O'Neill had not only been boning up on nightlife guides before he arrived, he had also immersed himself in a study of Chicago's cycle of crime. As always, he was brimming with confidence that law enforcement could make a breakthrough and he had fresh ideas to try to create that reality. The first step would be to take advantage of his skill in knocking down barriers and selling others on cooperation. O'Neill started by reaching out to Jack Townsend, the Chicago Police Department's chief of detectives. Townsend also oversaw the task forces that worked closely with the FBI, so O'Neill knew he needed to have Townsend as an ally for whatever plans he might want to unleash. But the quality that always set O'Neill apart was that he looked at cooperation as a two-way street.

"We hit it off right then and there," Townsend said. "I just liked him, his forthrightness and his honesty. John said, 'We're here to help you,' and he meant it. He was not that type of federal official who promises you cooperation and you wind up giving everything and getting nothing in return. If he told you he was going to do something, he did it. If he said he would call back with information, he did it. He was a different breed. He was down-to-earth. You could sit and talk to John O'Neill, and the minute you sat down, you knew where he was coming from. There was no bullshit. That is how we started off. I told John, 'If there's a problem, I will bring it up and we will deal with it.' And that's the way he wanted it and that's the way we built our friendship."

O'Neill was pleased to find that he had inherited two supervisors in the Chicago office who were experienced and aggressive. But Kenneth Pierneck and Grant Ashley both had strong-willed styles that were sure to lead to clashes with O'Neill, given his sometimes oppressively hands-on approach. Pierneck, who also lived in O'Neill's swank apartment building, had a law degree and a master's. A former field agent, he had been a supervisory agent working Eastern European counterintelligence out of FBI headquarters when he was transferred to Chicago in 1989 to supervise the office's counterintelligence unit. Ashley, a strapping amateur baseball player, ran the elite violent crime squad, which comprised both the gang and fugitive units. Ashley's wife was a flight attendant and traveled often, giving him the luxury of spending long hours working violent crime cases without sacrificing his personal life.

Ashley's squad had been working overtime handling a spate of kidnappings by drug gangs, and within a week of O'Neill's arrival, he received a blunt introduction into just how hands-on O'Neill could be. A dope dealer in the projects had been snatched off the street at gunpoint by a rival gang. Ransom was set at 1.6 kilos of cocaine (worth about seventy five thousand dollars). Ashley's task force of agents and cops had already handled countless similar cases. In fact, they had an unblemished 20–0 record in recovering "victims" without incident or injuries.

"We did kidnappings all the time," said Ashley, now the head of the FBI's criminal investigative division. "We used to say, 'We were so good, we made it safe to be a drug dealer.' But John began asking a million questions. 'What about this?' 'What about that?' His questions were pounding us. I was on the Los Angeles violent crime squad for nine months before this. He wanted to see if I knew what I was doing."

Ashley told O'Neill a family member of the victim would serve as go-between. "I'm not going to get an agent killed in one of these," he said. Ashley assured his boss he would get the victim back unharmed, but O'Neill bristled. He told Ashley he was risking his career with that attitude. The two nearly came to blows.

"We had a fight," said Ashley. "I finally said, 'If you're asking all these questions because you're concerned about your career, if it goes wrong, it's my squad.' And then I cursed."

O'Neill insisted no action be taken without his personal

authorization. He wanted to establish that he was in charge, and he was also being cautious, eager to avoid a mishap during his first days on the new job. "I don't think he didn't trust me, I think he didn't trust anyone, including himself," Ashley observed.

But Ashley was not about to give in without resisting.

"We don't work that way," he told O'Neill.

Ashley had a point. Agents in the field need to be able to make snap decisions. It made no sense to impose an unwieldy chain of command on a unit that had proven its skill so often. So Ashley made his point, and then smoothed over the dispute with his new boss: Ashley gave in to O'Neill's request, and made an announcement over the FBI's radios that there should be no action taken without O'Neill's authorization. But by then, the agents had already made their move. They had saved another drug dealer. Their record was now 21–0.

"Even though everything was all right, John was pissed he did not give the command," Ashley recalled.

And another confrontation developed.

"That's the wrong message to give out," Ashley told O'Neill. "I don't think agents should wait when they're already playing for years in the Super Bowl."

O'Neill just glared at Ashley. The silence dragged on, and Ashley figured he was due for another tongue-lashing.

"Yeah," O'Neill said finally. "You're right."

O'Neill had conceded the point, but he was still worried about establishing his authority. A few days later, O'Neill called Ashley into his office for another face-to-face power struggle, but Ashley continued to insist, "I'm running this squad!"

O'Neill reached into his desk and pulled out his pay stub.

"You're writing checks that you can't cash," he fired back.

It was Ashley's turn to back down.

"You're right," he said finally.

Two strong personalities had found a way past an impasse. Ashley knew that within the rigid universe of the FBI, any blame to be doled out if anything went wrong would reach O'Neill, too, not just Ashley. For his part, O'Neill felt he had made his point. His authority had to be respected. Soon he lightened up and allowed the violent crime expert to run his squad with little interference. "I saw maturation," Ashley said. "He let me do the job."

That didn't mean O'Neill was going to stop yelling. "You could go toe-to-toe with John with convictions," said Pierneck. "He liked warlords who would go toe-to-toe, put our stuff through the crucible and melt it down, and see if something better came out."

O'Neill and Ashley still fought like brothers, which in a way they were. Both started out at the FBI as clerks—"C-WAGs," O'Neill said, as in "clerk with a gun." Both worked hard, and both could be hotheads. One time, they were driving down the highway in O'Neill's bureau Thunderbird when Ashley challenged O'Neill's judgment and it looked like the two were going to start trading punches.

"If you want my opinion, I'll give it, but if you want your ass kissed, go to someone else," Ashley said.

"I'll kick your ass all over the road," O'Neill shouted.

He offered to pull the car over to the shoulder, so they could go at it, but instead they drove along in silence.

"We glared like a married couple, afraid what we might say next," Ashley said. "I was younger and in better shape, but I would not want to fight John. He was one tough guy."

Late that afternoon, Ashley got a call in his office. A voice that sounded like Porky Pig asked, "Is da wittle supervisor still mad at me?"

Ashley cursed and slammed down the phone.

"Get your coat," O'Neill said about an hour and a half later, showing up at Ashley's door. "We're getting drunk."

The move was revealing. O'Neill liked strong personalities who challenged him, but he also liked to feel in control. He could not intimidate Ashley, but maybe he could win him over through other sides of his personality. O'Neill liked to play tough, but in many ways he was motivated by that most basic of all impulses, the desire to love and be loved, by his people, and by the various women who filled his life.

A few mornings later, a disturbed woman snatched a newborn baby from Cook County Hospital and took the South Shore subway to Indiana. Ashley did not hesitate to charge into the jurisdiction of the smaller Gary, Indiana, office to pursue the investigation. A turf battle developed. When the child was recovered safely a few days later in South Bend, Indiana, officials in Gary did not want to release him to the Chicago FBI or surrender the case. Ashley asked his agents in Indiana only about the child's condition. The baby was fine, he was told.

"Good, bring the kid back to his mother," he said. "Get a doctor's exam saying he's okay and be sure to bring a child safety seat. This is not evidence we're talking about."

O'Neill let Ashley handle the delicate matter, standing in the door listening with his patented half smile, nodding approvingly.

"Just get the kid in the car and bring him back to his parents," Ashley barked.

"It's the right thing to do, for the right reason," O'Neill told Ashley. "And don't worry about the heat. I'll take it when they complain to headquarters that we encroached on their territory."

Later that night, O'Neill and Ashley were at a pub when the evening news showed a press conference O'Neill had given on the rescue. The bartender looked at O'Neill, then up at the screen, then back at O'Neill.

"Was that you?" he asked. "The guy with the FBI who saved the kid?"

"No," O'Neill said, pointing to Ashley. "This guy and his squad did. I'm just his boss."

Applause broke out all along the bar and throughout the pub, and the barkeep tore up O'Neill's bill.

"There were so many days like that, rescuing people and children," Ashley recalled. "There is nothing like it. Who but God and doctors get to bring people back?"

It took several months before O'Neill really felt accepted by Ashley and his agents. A *Chicago Tribune* columnist named John O'Brien interviewed O'Neill about a bank robber who had struck eighty times that year. The columnist quoted O'Neill on the importance of giving seminars to bank tellers urging them to keep focused during a robbery on descriptive information like "how tall the guy was." O'Brien, obviously impressed by O'Neill, compared him in the column to the late actor Kent Taylor, who played Boston Blackie in a 1950s television show by the same name about a resourceful private detective.

A few nights later, O'Neill joined Ashley and his squad for beers. It wasn't enough just to meet at the popular Chicago bar Boston Blackies, near the *Tribune*, which had a mural of the real John "Boston" Blackie with his slicked-back black hair. The agents also blew up a picture of O'Neill that ran with the column, and attached twenty copies of the shot to rulers, which they held up in front of their faces when O'Neill arrived.

"Does that mean they like me?" O'Neill asked Ashley, who reassured him they did. "The guys really came to love him, and he loved them."

One evening, O'Neill was alone in his apartment reading Chicago PD crime and intelligence reports about the gang violence that was largely responsible for the city's murders. He had an idea that these gangs based in the projects could be viewed federally as ongoing organized criminal enterprises, like the Mafia, and could be prosecuted under the new RICO law, which he had effectively used in Baltimore against the pornography kingpin. O'Neill picked up the phone and called Pierneck, who was surprised to hear his boss's voice.

"Hey, Ken," O'Neill said. "If you're not busy, why don't you come down here?"

Pierneck did not know it at the time, but that call marked the beginning of the end for violent gangs in Chicago. He took the elevator down to O'Neill's floor of their apartment building and found him waiting with a bottle of Captain Morgan's rum. O'Neill poured two glasses with ice. "He was impressed that I didn't need dilutions with my ablutions," Pierneck said.

O'Neill got right to the point. "What's the number one problem here that's not being addressed?" he asked. "Gangs," Pierneck said. O'Neill agreed. They had a couple more drinks and O'Neill asked Pierneck to devise an attack plan. Two weeks later, they had polished the plan to reflect an awareness of how the FBI could use its resources most wisely. "John had great instincts," Pierneck said. "Rather than do what the cops did best, which was small corner arrests, we wanted to go after the hierarchy, the leaders, who called themselves Governors."

The "Governors" collectively formed the most dangerous organization, the Black Gangsta Disciple Nation, which was a confederation of gangs with upward of thirty thousand members. The plan called for a task force of FBI, Chicago police, Illinois State Police, and county sheriffs, a coalition like none that had ever been put together. O'Neill's team would ultimately serve as a template for the rest of the nation, just as he would later create the template for investigating international terrorism after two U.S. embassies were bombed in Africa. O'Neill also changed the tone of the relationship between the FBI and the CPD by taking the unusual step of ordering some of his agents to report to a police precinct on East 111th Street in a rough section of the South Side. That simple move impressed Jack Townsend, the chief of detectives.

"When you work with the FBI, you always go to the federal building, but John asked me if it was all right to have it the other way," he said. "And I said it was just fine. He clearly demonstrated that he thought out of the box. The two words that really show the relationship: *communication* and *cooperation*. I think that's what made him unique. The other FBI people like to keep everything to themselves. Not him. John was a 'man's man, and a policeman's policeman.'

"No matter what we talked about on the phone, even if we talked three times a day, at the end he'd ask, 'Are we all right?' And I'd say, 'Of course we are.' I asked him why he could not just say good-bye. And he answered, "Friends don't say good-bye.'"

Cooperation would be the only way to have a chance against gangs that had grown so confident and blatant that Larry Hoover and his Supreme Leaders gang invested drug proceeds in a political action campaign, 21st Century Vote, to try to influence African-American voters. The Drug Enforcement Administration was going after Hoover, and O'Neill agreed to stay away from the Supreme Leaders and attack their prime competitor, the Vice Lords, who were composed of a dozen gangs, and the Latin Kings, an organization formed among convicts in prisons.

"John wanted me to whack them, and whack them hard," said Pierneck. "He wanted them to know there was a new kid on the block."

But the task force got off to a shaky start. One of O'Neill's agents wrote a letter to Townsend accusing a Chicago police supervisor of taking bribes from the Governors, noting that the supervisor refused to allow certain patrols in his precinct. The timing of this serious allegation could not have been worse. O'Neill's task force had only recently been put in place, and he was scheduled to sit down with Townsend's deputy chief for gang operations to discuss working closely. When they met, the Chicago gang chief pulled out the crudely written, rambling missive from the FBI agent and slid it across the table. O'Neill read it and rolled his eyes at the wild, unsubstantiated charge.

"John did a masterful job sewing up the tear, personally talking and talking to assure that it was not condoned," Pierneck said. "He charmed the pants off the Chicago police."

O'Neill even persuaded Department of Justice officials to leave their cushy Washington offices and come to Chicago. He wanted them to see for themselves what the projects were like at night. "We would roll down the windows and say 'Listen, just listen,' and they would hear the rattle of the machine guns and Uzis in the darkness," Pierneck said. "They were amazed. They would talk about that, and John, for years."

Justice granted permission for O'Neill to monitor cell phones and conduct wiretaps. The task force was soon conducting undercover drug buys and selling weapons to the unsuspecting gangs. The work was getting dangerous. Agents were getting so close to the action, they were nearly hit on several occasions.

"Gangsters on one side of the street were shooting literally in front of our car, putting rounds into a joint," Pierneck said. "I told John we might get clipped. They might even shoot up the van just for the fun of it."

O'Neill had a temporary solution. He obtained large Kevlar blankets that the agents could put up inside the van while he ordered a special surveillance van that came with Kevlar already in the skin.

"John was always big on protecting his people," Pierneck said. "If you were one of John's and loyal to him, he took care of you, even if he beat the shit out of you. He was a hard guy. He was tough. He could actually be brutal. But he was the best, most loyal person you could have in your corner. He never held grudges. But if you were a snake, and tried to cut his throat, he was remorseless. John and I had it out a few times. I think he was pissed some of my people were not sufficiently respectful. He came in and said something to me. We were toe-to-toe, finger-pointing and cursing, and then we went out drinking that night."

The task force spent several months on its pursuit of the Governors, and then O'Neill decided it was time to step up the attack and launch a series of massive sweeps. Helicopters would hover overheard, and sharpshooters would be in position on nearby rooftops, as five hundred cops and agents went from apartment to apartment, taking out hundreds of suspects. It took six months before the first Governor fell, but he was one of the most fearsome and revered in the projects.

His name was "Boo-G." He had seventeen illegitimate children and he swaggered and dressed like his role model, Al Capone, the famous Chicago mobster of the 1920s. The feds arrested Boo-G with forty kilos of cocaine and $1.7 million. He was in shock, which was precisely the effect O'Neill wanted to have on him and the rest of the Governors. Boo-G never made bail that night. He was ultimately sentenced to life in jail, and never seen again.

Dealers who were now rounded up in Chicago quickly decided to cooperate rather than face a lifetime in jail under the new RICO laws. Every few months, another Governor was toppled. Soon the gang's reign of terror began to recede in the projects, where law-abiding citizens had felt like prisoners in their own homes. And the city's intractable homicide rate began to decline.

The cooperation needed to achieve this impressive victory against gang violence was a testament to O'Neill's ideas and his drive and leadership. Pierneck remembers watching O'Neill gain more confidence, and transform himself from a young supervisory agent with his Atlantic City background into a big-city bon vivant with sharp clothes, fancy cigars, and a slight swagger in his step. O'Neill often favored his "nightclub wardrobe," dark shirts under dark jackets paired with the see-through socks worn by the Chicago wise guys his agents chased.

"I went to all the police retirement parties," O'Neill once told ABC-TV's John Miller. "But the part I was proudest of in Chicago was every time we put a wise guy away, I was invited to his 'going away to prison party' because they knew we'd got them fair and square and they respected that."

O'Neill, inevitably, decided he had to have a pinkie ring. Standing at the counter trying on one diamond after another, and checking it out in the mirror, O'Neill reminded Pierneck of the actor Joe Pesci checking out rings in a riotous skit on television's *Saturday Night Live.* O'Neill eventually selected a plain Irish Claddah, with a heart. "He was big Irish," Pierneck said. "But before he did he kept wagging his hands, asking, 'Well, what do you think about this one or that one?' He was worried it might make him look effeminate."

If O'Neill gained more polish and style in Chicago, it had a lot to do with the influence of Valerie James, whom he met only a few weeks after he arrived in town. O'Neill was at Centro's, one of the hot restaurants he had read about in the Chicago nightlife magazines, when James walked in the front door. She saw him standing near the coatrack at the entrance, glass of Chivas in his hand, and thought he "looked kind of sad and vulnerable."

She asked the bartender who he was. "He's new in town," he told her. So James, the daughter and niece of fundamentalist ministers, playfully did something she had never done before—and insists she will never do again. She bought him a drink, and had the bartender take it over.

She was drawn to O'Neill by his eyes. "He was slightly pudgy, but he had the most compelling eyes I had ever seen," she said. "He had jet-black hair combed back, and a great smile. But those eyes . . ."

James was director of sales for a women's clothing company, and a single parent with two children, Jay, then twelve, and Stacy, then eighteen. She is a striking woman, with dark hair and deep blue eyes, and a soft gravelly edge to her voice that reminds listeners of the actress Lauren Bacall. James had just emerged from a broken relationship when she and a friend dropped by Centro's that night. O'Neill asked the bartender who sent him the drink, and he pointed at James. He walked right over and introduced himself.

"We both thought we hit the jackpot at that point," James recalls.

O'Neill told her he was with the FBI.

"I know, I'm with the CIA," she shot back, thinking he was joking.

James asked O'Neill if he was single. "I told him I would never date a married man or a man who had children . . . I already had two of my own," she said.

O'Neill told her he was divorced without children, then pulled out a business card and scrawled his home number on the back.

"We stayed out all night," James said. Everywhere they went, people knew O'Neill. There was Harry Carey's, a salsa club, and even a jazz joint where the waiter knew O'Neill. "That is what made John O'Neill, John O'Neill," she said. "He immersed himself in everything he did. I thought John was a ton of fun. He was the best dancer I ever danced with in my life. A fabulous dancer. He said he once danced on *American Bandstand.*

"John was a take-charge guy. The next weekend, he had a lot of plans, living this frenetic life that he usually lived. 'Okay, Saturday we have plans for dinner,' he said. 'Sunday we have a party.' Does a man like John come home to eat chicken and potatoes?"

O'Neill dated James for five whirlwind months, squiring her around the Windy City in his 1991 blue Buick Regal, before they became intimate. The first morning she woke up in his apartment, she said, "You can never wake up in a bad mood here." She loved the seemingly endless blue water stretching off into the distance. "You felt God was right there," she said. "The sun would rise, and there was all of Lake Michigan in front of you. One time, I remember sitting in the tub on the roof and snowflakes were falling."

The interior of O'Neill's apartment seemed odd, though.

"There were no pictures," she said. "I have pictures of my kids everywhere. John did not have a single photo, not one. The apartment looked nice. It worked. But it told me he was not a man of material stuff."

It took another month of dating before O'Neill told James that he had a son. It wasn't until March 1995 that he felt comfortable enough to tell her he had still another secret—a daughter. By then, James was willing to forgive him.

Ashley and his wife, Linda, knew O'Neill was married. O'Neill reminded Linda Ashley of the actor Jack Nicholson with the handsome face and slicked-back hair—he's "lovable but a character," she would say. The Ashleys warned O'Neill, however. "If you want to parade women through your life, we won't give you cover." O'Neill understood and adjusted to suit them, keeping them out of his personal affairs.

He began to see more and more of James. On weekends, she stayed in his apartment in Chicago. During the week, he practically moved into her house in nearby Oak Park, where he kept up his regime of scouring four morning newspapers while drinking coffee and watching CNN news. On Halloween, he filled the hallways with hay lined with corn, candles, and pumpkins. And his special treat was a ten-dollar haircut and a hot shave on Saturdays at the local barbershop.

Cozy as he became with James, O'Neill would still see Mary Lynn Stevens sometimes. When he left her behind in Washington and moved to Chicago, O'Neill asked Stevens to remain faithful. He told her he wanted their relationship to be exclusive. She agreed, and they kept their relationship going, primarily with what she felt were sincere telephone conversations. "He was a great sounding board," she said. "The things we shared. We tried to talk fairly regularly, twice a week."

Occasionally, when James was out of town on business, Stevens would visit from Washington and stay in O'Neill's apartment. During one visit, however, James called and left a message on O'Neill's machine. Stevens heard her voice, and sensed the truth. She threatened to leave O'Neill, but he pleaded and begged and swore he and James were not an item.

"He literally got on his knees," she said. "I was trusting and I loved him."

Pierneck soon realized O'Neill was a very private man who

"had a lot of sides that he did not easily share." O'Neill opened up rarely, but did confide that he was still married and that divorce was something he would not do as a Catholic. O'Neill, he learned, also had more than one girlfriend. But he did not know how he had the time or the energy to see them, considering how hard he worked and how hard he played.

"John was generally in before everyone and he generally left work after everyone else, and he was a voracious reader," he said. "John would run twenty-four hours a day. He could bounce all night. He knew every bar in downtown. There was one that had some people with steel in their face and funny-colored hair. Bars that opened at two or three in the morning. I had no clue. After a while, I said, 'I can't do this. I'm with my guys at night and I need my rest.' I just backed out. But he worked until ten or eleven at night and then would go out. He would run hard with little sleep and then would crash and sleep a whole weekend and be down. I told him the pace was going to kill him."

O'Neill just smiled at that.

"It's okay," he said. "I just run like this and crash for a day."

Pierneck remembered one morning when O'Neill was summoned to see his boss, Bill Brannon, who was in charge of the entire Chicago FBI office. O'Neill walked in and took his seat next to Brannon. He looked immaculate. His hair was slicked back, Boston Blackie–style. His suit was military pressed. Everything was in place and he looked perfect. O'Neill turned his head slowly toward Pierneck and through clenched teeth said, "Ken, how do I look?"

"You look fine," he replied, knowing that O'Neill rarely got drunk or even tipsy because he was such a control freak.

"That's good," O'Neill said, still smiling through the pain of a rare morning hangover, "because every strand of hair on my head hurts."

Besides the Gold Sardine piano bar across the street from his apartment in the Playboy Building, O'Neill loved Pasta Tutti, one of Chicago's best Italian restaurants, with its high-rollers, corporate executives, investment bankers, and stock-market traders. "They all knew him," Pierneck said. "He knew how to speak to people. He was larger than life. He was a New York kind of guy."

But even as O'Neill was establishing the "Prince of Darkness" persona that would define him in later years, gaining in sophistication, he was becoming more of an enigma to some people who knew him. He could recommend the best orthopedic surgeon in town, and knew all the important people, but was he ever comfortable enough with himself just to be who he was without having to hold back part of the truth? Good friends of O'Neill's earlier in life were struck mostly by his sense of purpose. But by the time O'Neill was making his mark in Chicago, he was impressing some people as a man on the run from himself in certain essential ways.

"He was a complicated human being, and no one really ever knew the real Johnny," former FBI official George Andrew said.

Ashley agreed.

"Nobody ever knew the real John P. O'Neill," he said. "He only let you see what he wanted you to see."

Ashley remembers getting a rare glimpse deeper into O'Neill's soul one day. There had been a spate of cab shootings and a task force was hunting the killers in Chicago. Ashley was driving O'Neill to headquarters when a cabbie cut him off. "I'm not sure it's not okay to kill a cabbie," Ashley joked, prompting O'Neill to reach across the front seat and grab his knee. "Hey, my dad and mom drive a cab," O'Neill told him. "You have no idea how dangerous it is to be at someone's mercy."

O'Neill always wanted to be liked, and admired, even if it meant living beyond his means. His fast-paced lifestyle was slowly putting a sizable dent in his bank account, especially with the money he still gave his estranged wife. If the brakes on his car needed repair, he would ignore the problem until it cost him three times as much when they completely wore out. He was "pissing away money," living paycheck to paycheck, a former colleague said. He managed money by borrowing on credit cards, skillfully finding those with the lowest interest rates.

Despite all that, he was generous to a fault. When a young boy walked up to O'Neill and Ashley near the Chicago Loop one afternoon, collecting for an African American charity, O'Neill whipped out a twenty-dollar bill that he could barely afford to part with. "Get a receipt," Ashley said. O'Neill just smiled and walked on. He simply enjoyed life too much to squirrel away his pay. Money wasn't something to be saved. Money was a tool to be used to savor life.

Like many agents, Ashley was also a certified public accountant, and O'Neill turned to him for advice. Although Ashley rarely ventured into O'Neill's personal life, he once asked if he would consider divorce because it might save him a lot of money and grief. "But John made it clear about his obligations to Christine and the kids," he said. "He would never abrogate them. The love for his children was unbounded."

Nonetheless, Ashley felt compelled to warn O'Neill that he could end up "an old man waiting for a check to come in," if he didn't get his fiscal house in order. "I'd say, 'You have to save for the future, John.' "

But O'Neill brushed aside that kind of talk.

"Oh, I probably won't live long enough to enjoy it," he replied.

FUNDAMEN-
TALISM AND
FANATICISM

*On June 26, 1996, a truck bomb destroyed the Khobar Towers, a
U.S. military facility in Dhahran, Saudi Arabia, killing nineteen
Americans and injuring hundreds more. The bomb was the work of
a Hezbollah terrorist cell linked to Iranian officials and Osama bin
Laden. Saudi officials blocked O'Neill and U.S. investigators trying
to find the suspects.*

4

IN THE NAME OF GOD

O'Neill was sitting in his office in the Dirksen Federal Building when Robert "Bear" Bryant, the assistant director for the FBI's national security division, called in early August 1994 and asked if he was available for a special project. Bryant warned that the project was a tremendous challenge, "fraught with a lot of internal, external, and political minefields."

He wasn't exaggerating. An antiabortion extremist who had previously appeared on *The Phil Donohue Show* showed up outside a Florida clinic where a doctor had been assassinated the year before, and opened fire. His point-blank shotgun blasts claimed the lives of a sixty-eight-year-old physician and his seventy-four-year-old colleague. President Clinton called for "a quick and thorough investigation into this tragic incident," which he said was a form of domestic terrorism. The Department of Justice and the FBI soon realized that the Violence Against Abortion Providers Conspiracy, or VAAPCON, would require an investigation of unprecedented sensitivity and complexity.

Bryant told O'Neill that Attorney General Reno wanted the investigation run nationally out of headquarters, with all available bureau resources involved in probing for conspiracies. She also wanted constant progress reports, and she would be assigning a special prosecutor from the civil rights division to work with the FBI. "Frankly, I did not particularly want the case," Bryant said. "But they said, 'Congratulations, you have it.'"

Bryant decided the case needed a top-level manager who could oversee the probe from FBI headquarters and serve as a liaison between the Washington field office, Reno and FBI Director Louis Freeh. "I feared it could spiral out of control," he recalled. Given the sensitive political and First Amendment issues involved, Bryant thought his choice would need to balance the rights of the right-to-life activists against those of the pro-choice proponents without allowing personal politics to get in the way. He needed someone a lot like John O'Neill, in other words, someone whose motto was "We investigate, that's all we do, until all the *T*s and *I*s are dotted," as O'Neill had once told agent Gary Stevens.

Bryant remembered O'Neill from the early 1990s when Bryant was deputy assistant director for drug and organized crime and O'Neill worked at headquarters in the white collar crime division. Bryant asked O'Neill to analyze and make recommendations about "how resources should be utilized" by the Washington field office. Three weeks later, O'Neill handed Bryant a complex program report that called on field agents to honestly project the kind of resources they needed for criminal and counterintelligence issues. Bryant and the bureau's other top bosses grilled O'Neill about this report, and he had all the answers ready, without ever looking at notes.

"I could tell when someone does his or her homework," Bryant said. "It was very well put together."

O'Neill's report was quickly signed off on by then FBI director William Sessions and implemented. "What that gave us was the ability to go to Congress and ask for what we needed," Bryant said. "I dislike people who bring problems without answers. He brought ideas, and they were very well expressed. I found him a breath of fresh air."

Bryant wanted O'Neill for the abortion-clinic case. It wasn't just his skills as an investigator, and his reputation for hard work. Bryant knew that O'Neill was well versed in the nuances of FBI guidelines and was smart enough to make sure he followed them. "I had absolute confidence in his judgment," he said. O'Neill did not hesitate at the opportunity to take over such an important case, even after Bryant explained to him in detail all the potential difficulties and pitfalls he would have to expect. In fact, Bryant thought O'Neill seemed ready for a change.

The investigation gave O'Neill his first brush with a theme that would preoccupy him in the years ahead: religious fanaticism. "At first he knew nothing about that, but he read everything there was about fundamentalism," said Valerie James, the daughter of a fundamentalist preacher. "He used to say, 'Fundamentalist anything, in the extreme, is wrong and dangerous.'" O'Neill was Catholic, and proud of that fact, but he had never looked at these issues in so much detail before. "As a Catholic boy from Atlantic City, I never knew what a third-trimester abortion was," he told agent Kevin Giblin.

The issue erupted into a full-fledged national controversy on March 10, 1993, when a physician working at an abortion clinic became the first murder victim in the war over a woman's right to choose. Peter Jennings, the ABC-TV anchor, opened his broadcast that evening with the following report. "We're going to begin in Pensacola, Florida. There have been hundreds and thousands of anti-abortion demonstrations outside abortion clinics all across the country in the last several years. Today, in Pensacola, one of them ended in murder. While demonstrators tried to disrupt business at an abortion clinic there, one demonstrator shot and killed the clinic's doctor."

The physician was David Gunn, a slight forty-seven-old from Kentucky who walked with a limp because of polio. An obstetrician who devoted his practice to abortion, he was in high demand throughout the South because of a combination of low pay for most doctors and the aggressiveness of antiabortion protests, which had driven many less committed souls away. Gunn was "a circuit rider," making the rounds from one clinic to another in lesser cities in Georgia, Alabama, and Florida.

To zealots in the antiabortion movement, Gunn had become a

visible symbol. As far as they were concerned, he personified the legions of misguided physicians slaughtering unborn fetuses in the wake of *Roe* v. *Wade*. A fiery crowd led by John Burt, who ran Our Father's House, a home for troubled and pregnant girls, had burned Gunn in effigy a few months earlier on the twentieth anniversary of the Supreme Court ruling that women have a constitutionally protected right to choose abortion. Burt and his followers depicted Gunn wearing bloody gloves, near an inscription from Genesis 9:6.

The spectacle made an impression on Michael Griffin, who had served as an ensign on a U.S. Navy nuclear submarine. Griffin, the son of a Pensacola dentist, had been raised as a mainline Methodist, but joined Burt's zealous flock of fundamentalists after his stint in the military. He sat down with his wife and two children one afternoon and watched *The Hard Truth*, a graphic abortion video. Twelve days later, he took five hours of weapons training conducted by the local police.

Griffin could not believe his eyes when he pulled into an Exxon Station in Pensacola on March 5, 1993, and saw Gunn sitting there in his car, drinking coffee before heading into the Ladies Center Clinic to perform abortions. "I thought it was Providence," Griffin said later. "I knew he was getting ready to go kill children that day." Griffin walked over to his car, tapped on the window, and told him: "David Gunn, the Lord told me to tell you that you have one more chance."

Griffin waited outside the clinic that afternoon for five hours until Gunn departed, and again confronted him. "I felt like I had another word from the Lord for him: that he was accused and convicted of murder and that his sentence was Genesis 9:6, 'Whosoever sheds man's blood, by man his blood shall be shed.'" He demanded of the doctor: "David Gunn, are you going to kill children next week?" and claimed that Gunn replied, "Yeah, probably." Five days later, as picketers protested the Pensacola Women's

Medical Services Center, Griffin waited for Gunn to step out of his car, then shot him in the back three times with a .38.

Gunn's murder was the first of what quickly became a wave of bombings and other violence against clinics. A "born-again" Oregon woman named Rachelle Ranae (Shelley) Shannon joined the most radical fringe of the antiabortion movement's Operation Rescue. She communicated in prison with Griffin and received her inspiration from a manual titled *Army of God:* "We, the remnant of God-fearing men and women of the United States of Amerika, do officially declare war on the entire child killing industry . . . Our most Dread Sovereign Lord God requires that whosoever sheds man's blood, by man shall his blood be shed."

Documents later found on Shannon's computer described a string of firebombings she mounted in several states. She drove to the Catalina Medical Center in Ashland, Oregon, tossed gasoline inside, and then lit a birthday candle and tossed it through a window. As she waited for a fire to erupt, she prayed, "Lord, if you want that fire going, you're going to have to light it." The candle ignited an explosive blaze. At the end of July, she flew to Kentucky for a round of visits with imprisoned clinic attackers. After one visit, she had a vision to kill George Tiller, a pro-choice leader.

"This morning in bed it seemed God asked, 'Is there any doubt?' " she wrote. "No Lord. Please help me do it."

On August 18, 1993, she arrived at the Oklahoma City bus station with a .25-caliber handgun she'd practiced with at target ranges. She rented a car and drove north to Tiller's clinic in Wichita, Kansas, walked up to him as he got into his car, and fired six times at point-blank range, striking him three times in his arms.

Until then, the Justice Department and the FBI had been keeping a close watch on the growing violence but not taking action. They lacked clear legal justification to step in, and tended to view the incidents as unrelated, sporadic, and best left to local authorities. But that fall Congress responded to mounting pressure from free-choice advocates and the Clinton White House, and passed the Freedom of Access to Clinic Entrances Act, which made it a federal crime to block access to clinics or to commit acts aimed at denying a woman access to an abortion. The act directed federal law enforcement to use RICO against conspirators and provide protected "buffer zones" around clinics for doctors and other employees.

"There was a sense there was a national conspiracy to violently attack clinics," said Robert Blitzer, then assistant section chief for FBI counterterrorism. "The attorney general and the FBI director were under tremendous pressure from the Hill to do something about it."

Attorney General Janet Reno established a task force led by the FBI to crack down on the violence and focus on the strident religious fanatics taking their direction from *The Army of God* manual. "Bear" Bryant, then the special agent in charge of the Washington field office (WFO), recognized the importance of the issue to Reno and the White House. Newly elected president Bill Clinton and his wife, Hillary, were both strong supporters of the pro-choice movement. Bryant selected John Lipka, an aggressive young agent, to establish the VAAPCON probe. His goal was to assemble evidence from field offices around the country to try to determine if there was a link between the antiabortion adherents that could lead to federal indictments.

Debby Stafford, a former elementary-school math teacher turned FBI antiterrorism supervisor, was placed above Lipka and put in charge of the investigation to serve as liaison with headquarters. Over the next several months, FBI and ATF agents from Boston to California were executing search warrants and interviewing prospective witnesses for grand jury appearances across the country. In Wichita, prosecutors were bringing attempted murder charges against Shannon, the born-again Oregon woman who shot and injured Tiller at his clinic. In Portland, her daughter was being questioned about other conspirators. In Florida, Gunn's killer was being tried.

By May 1994, the federal investigation was going full blast and involved more than fifty agents. President Clinton had just signed into law the FACE bill passed by Congress months earlier. A confidential FBI Teletype confirmed the enormous priority the abortion-clinic violence warranted, asking all field offices to free up agents to track antiabortion activists. Then, on July 12, 1994, the investigation assumed new purpose. Paul Hill, a vocal antiabortion leader who had appeared on *The Phil Donahue Show*, mailed a letter using the biblical concept of "blood guilt" to rev up his supporters.

"Our tiny planet is saturated with the blood of the innocent," he wrote. "The blood guilt that hangs over our head is unspeakably staggering. Yet few seem to notice and fewer still take a stand."

Hill headed off to Kansas City later that week to attend a three-day seminar conducted by Gregg Cunningham, a former member of the Pennsylvania House of Representatives who served in the Justice Department during both the Reagan and Bush administrations. Attending the sessions on how to become a full-time antiabortion activist, and staying with a longtime advocate of justifiable homicide, Hill wondered if it was time to show his resolve. "I was thinking who might take the next action," Hill later told investigators. "And then I began to think, 'Well, what would happen if I did it?'"

Soon he was stalking Dr. John Britton, the sixty-eight-year-old physician who replaced Gunn at the Ladies Center Clinic in Pensacola after his murder. Hill soon found out that whenever Britton arrived in Pensacola, he was met at the airport by Jim Barrett, a seventy-four-year old retired air-force lieutenant colonel, and his wife, June, sixty-eight and a retired nurse and U.S. Public Health Service captain. On Friday, July 29, 1994, Hill arrived at the clinic with a shotgun stashed inside a cardboard tube. He had extra ammunition strapped to his leg, he said, "like a good boy scout." He hid the weapon in the grass and planted twenty white wooden crosses in the ground. A cop came by and made him remove the crosses. Then, at 7:27 A.M., Britton arrived in a Nissan pickup driven by Barrett with his wife in the jump seat behind him.

"I picked up the weapon and stepped out from behind the fence and fired three times directly at the truck," said Hill. "I aimed directly at the abortionist, but the driver was directly between me and him, so their heads were almost blocking one another."

The shotgun blasts slammed Barrett out of the car and onto the ground. Hill reloaded, turned to Barrett's terrified widow, June, and asked if Britton had his gun with him. "No," she replied, taking cover on the floor and closing her eyes. "I fired directly into [Britton], five rounds, and then laid the shotgun down and walked away, slowly with my hands down to my side."

The grisly double murder led to a new level of national condemnation, and set in motion the sequence of events that brought O'Neill to Washington to lend his singular talents to the case. "We needed to find out if there was conspiracy and we wanted to prevent any more attacks," Bryant said. "There was definitely smoke and a lot of noise, and I wanted O'Neill to do the investigation."

Bryant's decision to bring in someone from outside of headquarters met with a predictable amount of resistance. Many agents, including the hard-charging Lipka, had already spent months on the investigation and were not exactly eager to have a new face telling them what to do. "All of a sudden the bureau anointed someone as an inspector over the case to provide management and supervision, even though he was already an ASAC in Chicago," Lipka recalled. "As you can imagine, we had been working that case for a long time and thought we had a handle on it. All of a sudden, he appears and shows up in the Washington field office."

O'Neill came straight from the airport, a few days after Bryant's call, and made an immediate impression on the VAAP-CON team. Here he was, a top man at the Chicago office, the assistant special agent in charge, and he was decked out in his finest wiseguy garb. "He was wearing a very expensive pair of pants, no tie, a noncollared shirt and a very nice sport coat and very expensive shoes, and he had just flown in," Lipka said. "I introduced him to the squad and gave him a status briefing and, in a quick study, he immediately started asking, 'What have we done?' and 'What we can do?'" Lipka recalled. "I remember saying to myself, 'Quick study, good criminal background, but who the hell is this guy?'"

Lipka leaned over to a couple of agents and cops on one side, including Elaine Xydis, the case agent who later became his wife, and one of his closest friends, Mike Brooks, a metro cop. He asked them what their first impression was of the flashy new supervisor. "Be careful," Xydis warned him, "One day you may be working for him." Lipka just laughed.

"The rumor mill had preceded John, with his double-breasted suits and his hair slicked back," said Stafford, who would become one of the bureau's top terrorism experts. "People always laughed and joked that John always looked like an organized crime figure, and he had a sense of humor about it. He was a schmoozer who knew that to get the job done you needed to develop high-level contacts."

Lipka and Stafford quickly recognized that O'Neill would be a demanding, dynamic overseer. He shuttled back to Chicago, and later that week, Lipka and several members of the task force were undercover at a motel all weekend on a surveillance mission. Lipka was eating pizza with a couple of cops around sunrise on Sunday morning when the door suddenly opened and the burst of bright morning light blinded the FBI team, who had been awake all night in the dark. Blinking and adjusting to the sunlight, they finally made out the image of John O'Neill standing in the doorway, dressed impeccably with a silk shirt under a sport coat in what Lipka described as his "*Miami Vice* look."

"How are you guys doing?" he asked cheerfully. It turned out O'Neill had come straight from the airport to the stakeout, which was not exactly standard operating procedure. "It caught me off guard, someone of John's rank coming out to talk to the coppers and me on a Sunday morning," Lipka confessed. But O'Neill wanted to work, not just make a point by showing up. He took a seat on a bed and received a briefing from Lipka. He then provided some of his own investigative guidance. "It was very helpful," Lipka recalled.

But as impeccably as he was dressed, O'Neill could be touchy. He did not like jokes at his expense, as Lipka soon learned. "Nice socks," the agent quipped. But O'Neill was not wearing any socks. He looked down and chuckled, then asked Lipka if he could step outside for a private word. "Look," O'Neill said. "You work hard. You are forward leaning. You remind me of myself. But don't embarrass me in front of the cops."

Lipka apologized. He said he was from Philadelphia and the quip was only meant as a bit of East Coast humor. After all, Lipka knew O'Neill was from New Jersey, and he thought he would understand. "Just don't do it in front of other people," O'Neill insisted.

Despite the warning, Lipka was impressed with O'Neill. Although he had received a dressing-down, O'Neill did it in a way that was not embarrassing for Lipka and, at the same time, O'Neill paid him a compliment about his work. O'Neill left the motel knowing the surveillance was in competent hands.

When he had spare time in Washington, O'Neill had dinner or a drink with Mary Lynn Stevens, whom he had been dating before he was transferred to Chicago. Valerie James, who was busy with her job and children, would sometimes visit. On September 20, 1994, O'Neill met yet another vivacious, independent woman when he and a colleague stopped for a drink at the Old Ebbitt Grill, an inside-the-Beltway establishment popular with congressmen and senators and Secret Service agents working the president's detail.

O'Neill was sipping Chivas at the bar when a striking woman with golden-brown hair and dark eyes walked in with a friend. Anna DiBattista was the daughter of an Italian mason who laid marble at the White House and other monuments before he returned to Italy, leaving Anna and her mother in America. She was lively and bright, a national account executive for a major travel agency. But she had just broken up with the dashing playboy son of a congressman and was a reluctant patron at the Old Ebbitt that night. Anna and her friend took seats next to O'Neill and his buddy, but as much as O'Neill stared at her, DiBattista made it clear that she didn't want to have anything to do with him. "I had the attitude," she said. "But John liked a challenge."

"Do you get to Chicago?" O'Neill asked her.

"No," Anna replied. "I don't frequent that city."

For O'Neill, the conversation was like pulling teeth. DiBattista told her friend she wanted to leave and she slid off her chair. O'Neill reached into his briefcase and pulled out a business card. "I get to Washington once a week," he said. "If you would ever want to have lunch or a drink, call me sometime," he said.

"I don't call," Anna said, handing him her card. "You call me."

As the women left the Ebbitt, Anna's friend examined O'Neill's card, and said, "Special agent. What does that mean?" Neither woman was certain what to make of it. But O'Neill called the next time he was in town DiBattista thought O'Neill might be interesting, and the couple began dating when he had free time. He explained what a special agent was and what he did. But he was less than candid about other aspects of his life. Of course, the names Valerie James and Mary Lynn Stevens never came up. He claimed he was estranged from his wife and that he had a son, which was fine with DiBattista. It would be months before O'Neill acknowledged he had a daughter.

O'Neill would take DiBattista with him on vacations periodically over the years, and he became friends with her mother and family, spending weekends or an occasional holiday with them. "We were inseparable when he was in Washington," she said. O'Neill took Anna to meet his mother, which was assuredly a sign of her importance to him, but he also introduced his mother to virtually all his other female friends and lovers until the day he died.

Over the next several months, O'Neill spent most of his time in Washington, overseeing the abortion-clinic probe. He was consumed by the work. He gained valuable face time with Reno and Freeh, and demonstrated his gift for masterful presentations about complex aspects of the case seemingly without peering at a note. His single-minded focus on the investigation rubbed off on others. "It was John's style, whatever he was doing at the moment, he invested himself 110 percent," Fran Townsend, then a top deputy to Attorney General Reno, told PBS's *Frontline*. "Once John was there, we worried far less about the pace and focus of the investigation."

O'Neill put pressure on the agents to dig up every morsel of information they could find on protesters and fringe activists and their movements across state lines. He also directed agents to examine how the activists used the federal mail system. O'Neill wanted a clear template placed over the entire investigation to coordinate information into a central intelligence bank in order to pinpoint people's movements and contacts.

In his gut, he believed there could be a national conspiracy case to make because the leaders of the movement—although insulated from the actual crimes—were aware that their fiery orations were directly influencing the people who planted the bombs or pulled the triggers. O'Neill wanted to keep the focus on the prospects of a nationwide conspiracy, insisting every angle be checked out, and every question asked. Just as Agent Stevens had realized in Baltimore nearly fifteen years earlier, when it came to investigations, O'Neill was a like a dog rooting up a bone in the backyard. He would not close out a case until every inch of ground was dug up.

But Reno's prosecutors at the Department of Justice, along with a number of VAAPCON supervisors, including the FBI's Lipka, Stafford, and Raymond Mislock, saw the investigation differently. They were coming to the collective opinion that the attacks—at least according to law—were each an isolated crime, subject to state rather than federal jurisdiction. Griffin, Shannon, and Hill were each charged and convicted by state prosecutors. Other assailants also faced local justice. The FBI compiled a tremendous investigative database, but they felt it established no conspiracy, and no set leadership of the antiabortion groups. But O'Neill thought they just weren't paying enough attention.

"John did not think they had done enough to peel back the layers of the onion," said Robert Blitzer, then deputy FBI director for counterterrorism. "He was pissed. He felt there were just too many holes. He would get this shit in his head and you would just want to kill him because he just felt there was more to do. He would always call me—'Bobby, this is fucked up'—and he would go on and on that there could be a conspiracy. I think he still felt that way even after the attorney general made the decision we could not conclude a conspiracy, and cut the investigation off."

Right up to the moment Reno pulled the plug on VAAPCON, O'Neill was lobbying for more time. "Everyone agreed to end the case except John O'Neill," Lipka said. "He thought we should have gone a little longer. He got mad, but he was no screamer." Ray Mislock, a Vietnam veteran and another FBI supervisory agent on the case, believed O'Neill took Reno's decision personally, as though it reflected on his leadership rather than on the merits of the case. "We looked up the same facts but had a different opinion," said Mislock, who later worked with O'Neill after the Africa embassy bombings. "That case was the only situation where John and I were a hundred and eighty degrees apart."

In November, just four months after O'Neill was brought into the abortion-clinic probe, a coveted position opened as the section chief for counterterrorism in FBI headquarters, a job that included oversight over international terrorism, domestic terrorism, and weapons of mass destruction. Domestically, there were dangerous "fascist-skinheads," right-wing hate groups such as the World Church of the Creator and the Aryan Nations, and extreme patriotic militias espousing antigovernment hysteria or racial supremacy. And there were anarchists and extremist socialist groups decrying the World Trade Organization, and separatist terrorists such as the Armed Forces of the Puerto Rican National Liberation (FALN), who had carried out deadly bombings to win Puerto Rican independence. Even more sinister were virulent anti-Western Muslim fundamentalists, who made up a small fraction of the religion's 1.2 billion followers across the Middle East and the rest of the world. These fundamentalists were committing acts of terrorism against secular governments and political leaders with links to the United States, and their influence was increasing.

By all accounts, O'Neill was no terrorism expert. But he wanted the promotion. He needed the promotion. The prospect of more action, and the high-profile nature of the new position, promised to fulfill his secret dreams of honor, duty, and serving one's country while expanding his horizons far from the carnival boardwalk of Atlantic City. And although his own belief in a conspiracy in the abortion cases was a vision that his superiors did not share, his tenacity in defending himself and his unpopular position made him an excellent candidate for such a daunting job.

"It was the kind of position that would give him visibility," said Blitzer, the deputy counterterrorism chief. "No one had a crystal ball and I don't think anyone could have foreseen what was coming. But there was so much action. It was a hot spot. He was attracted to it. He jumped after it. And he got it."

In December 1994, O'Neill was inside the J. Edgar Hoover Building when he received word that FBI Director Louis Freeh had formally printed his initials, *J.P.O.*, next to O'Neill's name on the short list of candidates to become the next chief of the counterterrorism section. To say he was ecstatic would be an understatement. After stopping to thank "Bear" Bryant for his support, O'Neill walked down a flight of steps and directly to the cubicle where John Lipka was seated.

Lipka had also been promoted. He was named a supervisor in international terrorism, where his expertise and aggressive style would be needed in the newly emerging undeclared war. O'Neill strode up without being noticed and stuck his smiling Irish face over the side of Lipka's cubicle. "I looked up, and there he was, O'Neill smiling down on me," Lipka said.

"How are you doing?" O'Neill asked.

"Fine, sir," Lipka replied.

"I'm your new boss," O'Neill announced, prompting Lipka to remember how Agent Elaine Xydis warned him to watch the wisecracks about O'Neill because he might be working directly for him one day.

"Congratulations," Lipka politely said.

O'Neill's smile broadened, and he winked.

"Are you ready to rock and roll?" O'Neill asked.

"Yes, sir," Lipka said.

O'Neill recognized that he and Lipka were very similar. They were both devoted to the FBI and both had a slavish work ethic. Lipka's dedication to his job had also cost him a marriage. During the next two years, the two driven FBI men worked almost nonstop investigating bombings around the world. But O'Neill would always insist that their day not end without a meal and a libation, usually at the Old Ebbitt or Les Halles. But while Lipka headed home after a long day's work and evening out, O'Neill went back to the Hoover Building, where he would work even more.

"The next morning, I would see anywhere from five to forty-five e-mails from O'Neill to agents around the section," Lipka said. "And he would be back in the office before seven o'clock when most people had not arrived for work. He would be there all day and then leave for no more than three or four hours. He would go to his apartment. Shower. Catnap. And come back in a clean suit.

"The long hours were a detriment to his family. I had a daughter in Annapolis and got divorced. I knew he had a son and daughter and a wife who lived in New Jersey. I knew they were estranged. And that he cared a lot for his children. As for his relationships, my read was that he got something from each of them. I don't know what he promised. I told him, 'I am not the moral police.' But I know he cared for each of them in a unique and genuine way, with all of them. He was not a user. And I think they got something from him. They enjoyed being with him."

O'Neill returned to Chicago about a week before Christmas 1994. He had yet to tell Valerie James about his promotion, which also meant moving back to Washington. There was every reason for him to be reluctant. He had recently discussed the possibility of moving into her home and giving up his apartment in the Onterie Center. Marriage had also come up. O'Neill did not know how to break the news to James, so he decided to at least wait until after Christmas Day to avoid ruining everyone's holiday season.

But he had a hard time keeping the secret, particularly since everyone at the bureau knew that he was leaving for headquarters sometime in the next ninety days. He had to follow James around at the office Christmas party, trying to keep her from talking to any agent. "When we went to his company dinner dance, there was something odd about it," she said. "It was fun. We danced.

We had dinner. But he kept me secluded. When I went to the rest room, he escorted me and waited outside the door."

Shortly after Christmas, O'Neill finally told her the truth—he was becoming one of fewer than two dozen section chiefs in the FBI. But he should have gone further, and not just by revealing that he was still married to Christine. He should have told her what all his colleagues and friends understood about John P. O'Neill—he was married to the FBI, and everyone else was a mistress, including her.

"Val," he began. "I am really sorry, but I have to do this to get to the next level."

As a working woman managing a career and two children, James actually admired O'Neill's ambition and independence. "It was his job before all else," she said. "I understood it. I kind of liked that about him."

O'Neill told her his goal was to become the head of the FBI's flagship office in New York City. A tour of duty in FBI headquarters was a prerequisite for any ambitious agent to obtain a higher position in the bureau, such as special agent in charge, or "SAC," of one of the FBI's fifty-six field offices. The head of the New York office, however, has a slightly higher designation, considering the office's unique responsibilities: Wall Street, the United Nations, the Mafia, spies, terrorists, and corrupt politicians. The special agent in charge of New York supervises 1,100 agents and carries an assistant director in charge, or "ADIC," rank.

The requirement that agents spend time in headquarters to earn a promotion proves to be a double-edged sword. Agents who work in headquarters quickly learn that the only thing that can derail their potential promotion is a mistake, and that realization instills in far too many would-be supervisors the hope that nothing serious happens on their watch. In short, their motto becomes: Big cases, big problems; small cases, small problems; no cases, no problem. But that was never the O'Neill way.

He told James he would spend no more than a year in Washington before getting a new assignment, preferably in New York, where she could join him. She worked for Bob Mackie, a New York–based fashion company, and once her son, Jay, graduated high school in a couple of years, she could move to New York, join him, and expand her own career. Which is just what she did. "That was always our plan," she said.

O'Neill was preparing for the move to Washington when he received word of another bloodbath at an abortion clinic on December 30, 1994. John C. Salvi III, a twenty-two-year-old New Hampshire hairdresser and former altar boy who quoted Scripture and displayed colored photographs of aborted fetuses in his pickup, burst into the waiting room of a Planned Parenthood clinic in the Boston suburb of Brookline, Massachusetts. Salvi opened fire with a .22 caliber rifle, killing a receptionist and wounding three others. He then drove to another clinic two miles away and continued firing, killing another receptionist and injuring two more. He escaped in his pickup.

O'Neill immediately flew to Boston to see if the killing spree could prove to be the linchpin of a pattern that would persuade Reno to keep the VAAPCON probe open to investigate new conspiracy connections. He registered at the Cambridge Hyatt, and then raced over to the FBI command post. Michael Rolince was running the case. O'Neill introduced himself and then stood aside in a doorway, allowing Rolince and his agents to run the investigation without interruption from the boss—just as he done with Grant Ashley months before, in the child abduction caper in Gary, Indiana.

After two anxious days, Salvi turned up in Norfolk, Virginia, and fired nearly two dozen shots at an abortion clinic. A cop who was nearby heard the gunfire and raced to the clinic. Salvi tossed down his weapon. "I'm not mad at you," he said. O'Neill realized the mentally impaired Salvi was apparently another lone assailant whose actions would not serve as a catalyst to change Reno's mind about a conspiracy. The Justice Department's VAAPCON investigations would continue as the number of clinic arsons and bomb threats doubled over the next year. But each new case failed to reveal a broader conspiracy, Reno said, and the prosecutions were ultimately handled by local authorities.

On December 31, 1994, O'Neill flew from Boston back to Chicago to spend the evening with James, who preferred ringing in the New Year with a quiet home-cooked dinner. A few days later, Rolince received a note from O'Neill, saying how much he appreciated his work, particularly the sacrifice he and the other lawmen made over the Christmas holidays. "John became my mentor," Rolince said. "He never took the attitude that 'I know your job because I did it.' He was always understanding and would say, 'I understand the pressure cooker you're in, and you might want to do this or that.'"

In February 1995, O'Neill began to pack up his office and personal belongings for the twelve-hour drive to Washington. But on the day he was to leave, he and James had a serious fight over another secret O'Neill had been keeping from her. The wife of an agent in the Chicago office told her that O'Neill was married, and she confronted him. O'Neill could have used the confrontation as an opportunity to tell the truth, but instead he insisted he was divorced.

"We had a fight, and then I felt badly because I was supposed to be driving with him," James said. "At the very last minute, I said, 'Do you want me to go with you?'"

"I rode into this town myself," O'Neill shot back. "And I will ride out of it by myself."

He drove all night, eight hundred miles from Chicago to Washington, and went straight to his office without dropping off his belongings. He was hanging French Impressionist pictures on the wall, completely unaware of fast-moving developments halfway around the world that would catapult him into the global theater—and change his life forever.

5

"YOU CAN'T MAKE THIS SHIT UP"

Unlike the people of Europe, Americans were used to thinking of terrorism as something that always took place somewhere else, far away in an unpronounceable city you could never find on a map. Terrorism claimed hundreds of lives, including those of many Americans, but since the attacks occurred thousands of miles from America's shores, there was no clamor from the U.S. public for strong, sustained action against terrorism. Even the devastating truck bombing that killed 241 U.S. Marines in Beirut in October 1983 failed to prompt a full-scale U.S. response, partly because the killings did not take place on American soil and partly because the Reagan administration invaded the small Caribbean island of Grenada just days after the Beirut disaster.

International terrorism, left largely unchecked, evolved into ever more dangerous strains. Libya, Iran, Iraq, and the Sudan all delved into state-sponsored terrorism, using outlaw organizations as surrogates to promote their dark agendas. They provided funding, intelligence, and munitions in exchange for "plausible deniability" for any attack, including bombings of commercial jets carrying hundreds of innocent passengers. The most infamous of these state-sponsored terror acts was the December 1988 bombing of Pan Am flight 103 over Lockerbie, Scotland, which killed 270 people. President Ronald Reagan ordered multiple air strikes on the Libyan capital of Tripoli in retaliation for Pam Am 103 and the West Berlin disco bombing, which killed two U.S servicemen. Several of Libyan strongman Muammar Qaddafi's family members were hurt in the attacks, and a chastened Qaddafi moved away from sponsoring terrorism.

Other U.S. actions also helped curtail international terrorism. U.S. economic and diplomatic sanctions against countries linked to terrorism played a role, but more important was the massive display of high-tech weaponry during the 1991 Gulf War to remove Iraqi forces from Kuwait, which alerted the world to a new generation of U.S. weapons. Intelligence services noted a reduction in overt operational activities among state sponsors of formal terrorist networks. But the U.S. and its allies failed to eliminate the terrorist threat, and extremist terrorist groups found a way to alter their operations and make them less dependent on the tacit and direct support of governments.

Just how much harm terrorist groups could inflict was painfully demonstrated on February 26, 1993, when a truck packed with explosives was driven into a parking garage beneath the World Trade Center in New York. The bomb killed six people and injured more than a thousand others. Several conspirators were quickly arrested after one suspect returned to a Ryder Truck company in New Jersey to collect a deposit on the rented van. But Ramzi Yousef, the operational mastermind, escaped on a flight to Pakistan, and later Malaysia, only minutes after the bomb sent plumes of smoke rising through the shaken towers, forcing tens of thousands of people to rush into the street, coughing from the smoke and desperate for air.

That June, the FBI interrupted another group of Islamic fanatics preparing a "witches' brew" of explosives in a Queens warehouse. The terrorists, followers of Blind Sheikh Abdul Rahman, an Egyptian, planned to blow up landmarks throughout the city, and wanted to bomb both the Lincoln and Holland Tunnels to cause maximum chaos. The interrupted plot was only tangentially related to the World Trace Center bombing, but many of the participants in both shared similar backgrounds. They were "mujahedeen," or holy warriors, who had fought in Afghanistan in the successful U.S.-backed struggle to expel the Red Army.

Instead of seeing the two cases as linked together in international terrorism, the United States treated them as law enforcement issues, with suspects to be hunted down, arrested, tried, and imprisoned, if possible, as though they were a gang of bank robbers with no connection among them. Yousef was quickly listed as the United States' most wanted fugitive, a two-million-dollar reward was posted for his capture, and a global manhunt was launched to find him. Osama bin Laden, the son of a politically connected Saudi Arabian billionaire businessman, turned up on a list of donors to an Islamic charity in New York that helped finance Ramzi's bombing of the World Trade Center. By 1994, shortly before O'Neill was named the head of counterterrorism, conspirators were heard referring in taped conversations to "Sheikh Osama," and the CIA began to refer to "financier Osama bin Laden."

Bin Laden was not high on the lists of most U.S. intelligence and counterterrorism experts. They believed Hezbollah and Hamas posed far graver threats to the United States and U.S. interests than the lanky, bearded Saudi "financier." O'Neill disagreed. He would soon argue that bin Laden was emerging as the most strident terror leader in the world. O'Neill always trusted his instincts, and his instincts told him that the extremism that drove bin Laden to leave his affluent life in Saudi Arabia to help fight the Russians in Afghanistan would push him in dangerous directions. Inflicting a humiliating defeat on the Russians was only the beginning. Bin Laden's religious quest demanded nothing less than driving all "infidels" from Muslim soil.

"No, this man is not a financier," O'Neill would soon warn President Clinton's top counterterrorism advisers. "Yes, he's got some of his own money, and he's very good at raising money. But that's not all he's about. The money is for a purpose. He's building a worldwide terrorist network, the point of which is going after the United States. We've got to get this guy. Everything leads back to him."

Richard Clarke, President Clinton's national coordinator for counterterrorism, was reading intelligence reports in his office on the morning of February 5, 1995, when he came upon a report indicating that Ramzi Yousef had been spotted in Pakistan. Clarke knew it was critical to move as quickly as possible to capture the WTC mastermind. He dialed the FBI, and heard an unfamiliar voice on the other end of the line.

"Who's this?" Clarke demanded.

"Well, who the hell are you? I'm John O'Neill," the new FBI section chief fired back.

"I'm from the White House," Clarke said. "I do terrorism. I need some help."

Over his classified phone line, Clarke explained the situation to O'Neill, who had driven through the night from Chicago and had come straight to his new office that morning. Everyone tried to keep optimism in check. There had been numerous false reports on Yousef since the WTC attack, most by con artists trying to scam the FBI out of the two-million-dollar reward advertised on thousands of matchbook covers airdropped in Muslim lands. The FBI was accustomed to running down clues that went nowhere.

The call that came in that morning to Robert Blitzer, O'Neill's new deputy, was different. Alan Digler of the Diplomatic Security Service had called and told Blitzer, "Hey, I think we have a hot lead on Yousef. We think he's in Islamabad."

"How do you know?" Blitzer asked.

"A guy came into the home of an embassy employee and asked to speak to someone in the embassy. A regional officer went out to talk to this guy and he described Yousef to a T."

The report was intriguing, but Yousef look-alikes had been

taken into custody in several countries over the last two years. Blitzer needed to be sure. He gave Digler specific questions for the agents in Islamabad to ask the informant, including one that dealt with Yousef's escape from the Philippines. "The informant had all the right answers," said Blitzer, who immediately ordered the FBI's Special Investigations and Operations Center to be opened, and notified his supervisors, "Bear" Bryant and O'Neill.

"John instantly realized this was really big-time stuff," said Bryant. "This was no bank embezzlement. This was high profile and you're dealing in the highest echelon of our government and other governments."

Clarke, too, remembers O'Neill hitting the ground running.

"He had never worked on the case before, but he obviously knew the importance of it and he went into action," he told PBS's *Frontline*. "He was first of all incredibly bright. He may not have had a Ph.D. from MIT or something like that, but his IQ was clearly off the charts. And he had stamina, an energy that was just unending."

For the next three days, O'Neill went without sleep, fielding calls and faxes and orchestrating the complexities of a capture nine thousand miles away. He so completely disappeared that DiBattista feared he had a secret life and was married. "He never left the office," Clarke said. "He worked the phones out to Pakistan, he worked the phones to the Pentagon, and he worked the phones at the State Department"—all to coordinate the possible capture of a diabolical religious fanatic whose picture had just appeared on the cover of *Newsweek* magazine.

By 1995, Ramzi Yousef had carried out two other bombings besides the 1993 Twin Towers attack. One in Iran killed twenty-six pilgrims in the shrine of Reza. Another, in the Philippines, was without casualties. Yousef also devised a scheme to assassinate Pope John Paul II, President Clinton, and Pakistani Prime Minister Benazir Bhutto, and conceived a plan to simultaneously blow up twelve American commercial airliners in flight with tiny undetectable explosive devices he invented that could be assembled on a plane. Each deadly concept would have had a high chance of succeeding, investigators believe, had it not been for an accidental fire in his Philippine apartment.

Ramzi Yousef was born on April 27, 1968, to a Pakistani mother and a Palestinian father, investigators believe. He grew up in Fahaheel, a working-class Kuwait City suburb. Like many displaced Palestinians, he and his family had difficulty adjusting to life as second-class citizens, exiles in a diaspora. They despised Israel for "taking their land," and hated the U.S. for supporting the Jewish state. From 1986 to 1989, Yousef, who speaks Urdu, the main Pakistani language, as well as Arabic and perfect English, studied electronic engineering at Swansea University in Wales. In 1989, he traveled to Afghanistan just after the mujahedeen rebels, backed by the U.S., drove the Soviets troops out of that country after ten years of fighting.

"[The Islamic fighters] in Afghanistan were told that if you have your faith you don't need anything else to demolish all the superpowers," former Pakistani Prime Minister Bhutto told journalist Simon Reeve. "They were brought up to believe you can demolish both the Soviet Union and the United States and the entire world. And having driven the Soviet Union out of Afghanistan, they feel they have the power to drive America out as well."

Yousef trained as a guerrilla fighter in the Afghanistan camps set up by bin Laden, and studied munitions in Peshawar, near the lawless Khyber Pass frontier. "I'm an explosives expert," he later boasted. His twisted passion was not directed at ridding Afghanistan of the Russian invaders. Instead, he wanted to create a new form of terrorism that inflicted mass destruction and casualties on the United States and other Western targets that he perceived as enemies of the Palestinians and of Islam. He claimed his views were reinforced in Peshawar when he befriended Sheikh Abdul Rahman, the fiery Egyptian cleric, who was waging jihad of his own against Western influences.

Yousef returned to Kuwait in August 1990, just as Saddam Hussein ordered his troops into the small gulf sheikhdom. A year later, as U.S. soldiers streamed into the area during Desert Storm, he left Kuwait City and headed for Pakistan as part of a mass exodus of hundreds of thousands of non-Kuwaiti nationals. Later he moved on to the Philippines, where he joined a little-known Muslim extremist group, Abu Sayyaf, which stood for "Bearer of the Swords." The group was waging a guerrilla war with support from bin Laden, and hoped to gain independence for the southern island of Mindanao, where the minority Muslim population was concentrated.

Using a false Iraqi passport, Yousef flew to JFK International Airport in New York on a flight from Pakistan on September 1, 1992. His traveling companion was Ahmad Mohammed Ajaj, a Palestinian expelled from Israel. Yousef immediately asked for political asylum as a dissident and was released, despite his phony passport, pending a hearing. Ajaj was not as fortunate. He was arrested with a fake Swedish passport and a suitcase filled with bomb-making manuals. The connection between the two men was not made, or Yousef would doubtlessly have been detained.

Once in the United States, Yousef raised $8,500 from friends and relatives to make bombs. At a mosque in Jersey City, he was working with Blind Sheikh Abdul Rahman and his followers, who had developed a plot to bomb the United Nations and other New York landmarks. Utilizing his Afghanistan munitions training, Yousef developed a new, more powerful bomb that he believed would shear a support column beneath the World Trade Center and topple one of the 110-story towers, sending it crashing into the other tower and killing 250,000 people.

He used 1,200 to 1,500 pounds of the chemical fertilizer urea nitrate mixed with ammonium nitrate to make his bomb, and would have made it larger if he had not run out of funds. On February 26, 1993, the second anniversary of the retreat of Iraqi forces from Kuwait City, the bomb was driven into the parking garage beneath the World Trade Center. It killed six people, including a pregnant woman, injured another thousand and sent smoke and panic rising through the snow descending on New York City that winter day.

But Yousef watched in disappointment from the Jersey City waterfront as smoke poured from the still-upright towers in Lower Manhattan. He quickly boarded a jet for a flight to Pakistan that he had booked two weeks earlier. Back in Pakistan, he stepped up his militant activities and joined a small, violent Islamic political party called Sapha-i-Sahaba, a six-thousand-member group that adheres firmly to the tenets of Islam's Sunni sect. In July 1993, he was disfigured when a bomb he was mixing blew up in his face, nearly blinding him. He had hoped to use the bomb to kill Prime Minister Bhutto, who, as a woman, Yousef believed, could not under Islamic law be a government leader. Yousef recuperated and returned to the Afghanistan camps.

In early 1995, bin Laden's senior officers asked Yousef to travel to an Abu Sayyaf secret base on the small island of Basilan in the Sulu seas, 550 miles south of Manila, an encampment reachable only via a ninety-minute ferry ride. Basilan and Zamboanga are part of the southern Philippine region of Mindanao and the Sulu archipelago, which comprises one-third of the country's seven thousand islands. Although the country is largely Catholic, this region has been inhabited by Muslims for five centuries, since before the Spanish conquest of the islands and the arrival of Christian Jesuit missionaries. Bin Laden believed Yousef could instruct Abu Sayyaf in bomb-making and foment an insurrection that could lead to the creation of a separate Islamic state.

Yousef was happy to return to the modern city of Manila after weeks of serving as a terrorist instructor. For all his religious zeal, Yousef fancied himself a playboy who enjoyed women, wine, and song and who was not too sophisticated or religious to avoid the city's red-light district. But his weakness for these joys of the flesh somehow did not temper his hatred for the American "infidels."

In Manila, Yousef devised the plan to blow up eleven American jetliners, a scheme he called "The Bojinka Plot," which is Serbo-Croatian for "the explosion."

For weeks, Yousef taught himself to make a stable, liquid form of nitroglycerin, the explosive component of dynamite. He tested his device in a movie theater. Then he decided he could smuggle it and other tiny components for a bomb onto the airplane, assemble the device in the toilet, and leave it under a seat before he disembarked. The flight would continue and explode, and he would be miles away. He made several test runs, smuggling the materials onto planes. Then on December 11, 1994, he boarded a Philippines Airlines flight that was due to stop in Cebu, 350 miles to the south, before continuing on to Tokyo.

In a tiny space beneath the calculator on a Casio digital watch, Yousef installed electronic wiring attached to the watch alarm. Two cords that formed a fuse were then welded in place. Attached to a contact-lens case, he had lightbulb filament. Two nine-volt batteries needed to charge the explosive were hidden in the hollowed-out heels of his shoes and went undetected in the airport X-ray machines. Yousef initially took seat 35F on the Boeing 747-200, but asked a stewardess to move him so he could have a better view and ended up in 26K. Halfway through the flight he disappeared into the bathroom and fashioned his bomb. He returned to his seat and placed the device under his new seat.

Yousef left the plane in Cebu, as planned. Two hours into the final leg of the flight, a flight attendant noticed smoke coming out from under seat 26K, which was now occupied by Haruki Ikegami, a twenty-four-year-old engineer heading home to Japan. Moments later, an explosion ripped Ikegami's body in half, severely wounding five others. The blast also blew a small hole in the floorboards and severed cables that controlled the plane's flaps. Captain Ed Reyes quickly dumped fuel and managed to make a safe emergency landing at Naha Airport in nearby Okinawa.

Yousef was pleased with his handiwork. He realized he had

only to increase the explosive power to bring down a jet. He anonymously telephoned the Associated Press office in Manila to claim responsibility for the near disaster for Abu Sayyaf. He returned to his apartment in the Dona Jesefa apartment building and began to meticulously study 747 blueprints for seat locations above central fuel tanks. He also pored over flight schedules and times of connecting flights, and worked on false identifications and disguises to carry out his Bojinka plot, saving all his plans on his computer.

The Dona Jesefa apartment was chosen because it was on the route Pope John Paul II was scheduled to take during a papal visit to Manila planned for January 12, 1995. Yousef was planning to assassinate the pontiff, and was just as meticulous in formulating this plot as he was with the Bojinka scheme. The terror mastermind sent recruits to buy Bibles, crucifixes, priest vestments, a large photograph of the pontiff, and a tobacco pipe that could be used to hide a small quantity of plastic explosives. He even obtained confessional manuals and tunic buttons similar to ones worn by Filipino cardinals.

Six days before the pope's visit, Yousef was heating chemicals in a cooking pot when a small fire erupted, and smoke seeped out into the hallway. A startled guest called security guard Roman Mariano, who raced up to the apartment, where he found Yousef and Abdul Hakim Murad trying to blow the smoke away. "Don't worry, we were just celebrating a late New Year's Eve," Yousef said. But Mariano went inside and saw chemicals and wires and knew the smoke did not come from firecrackers. By the time he turned around, however, both men had vanished. Yousef was last seen calmly walking out of the building, talking into a cellular phone.

The two terror suspects reunited at a nearby karaoke bar. Yousef convinced Murad to return to the apartment to retrieve his laptop with the secrets of the terror plans, which Murad did. But as he was nearly escaping with the computer, a squad of senior officers arrived with a search warrant. Murad was arrested and the computer seized. David Swartzendruber, a former San Diego drug-enforcement-narcotics-task-force forensic computer specialist working for Microsoft, finally recovered deleted files stored on backup disks waiting to be overwritten. The information revealed Yousef's nightmarish terror plan, including flight schedules and projected detonation times. The files also contained a business card advertising Yousef's name and occupation: International Terrorist.

In the early hours of January 7, 1995, Yousef paid $848 in cash for a first-class flight from Manila to Hong Kong and on to Singapore, where he caught a jet to Pakistan. On January 23, 1995, Yousef contacted a friend, Ishtiaque Parker, a Muslim student at Islamabad's militant Islamic University. Parker's South African passport made him a good recruit. With it he could travel freely anywhere in the world. Yousef had befriended Parker months earlier and now asked him to come to the Pearl Guest House in Islamabad. Parker was told his mission was to plant a bomb on an American jet. But Parker, who was married with children, had second thoughts. He did not board the plane, and told Yousef that airport security was inspecting luggage and demanding fingerprints from passengers.

Parker returned to Pakistan, where Yousef was already planning more kidnappings and devising new attacks against the Israeli consulate in Bombay and the Israeli embassy in New Delhi. The possibility of such wanton destruction was too much for Parker, who called the U.S. embassy in Pakistan on February 3, 1995, and nervously said he had information about the terrorist fugitive who blew up the World Trade Center.

"He knew what Yousef wanted him to do could hurt innocent people and that it would not conform to the teachings of the prophet Muhammad and the tenets of Islam," said Lipka, who would become a friend of Parker's.

Parker didn't even know there was a reward when he came forward, although he eventually did receive it. Two diplomatic security agents met the slightly built, nervous Parker, disguised him, and brought him to the embassy for questioning. Soon he had answered Blitzer's queries and Blitzer—who would earn an attorney general's award for his work—telephoned Ralph Horton, legal attaché in Bangkok, and told him they had a lead on Yousef that he needed to follow up on immediately.

So in Washington, O'Neill found himself in an initiation by fire. There were countless rapidly changing issues to deal with around the clock: calling the military to arrange a plane, notifying the State Department to determine which countries the U.S. could fly over, finding the ambassador involved in Pakistan, preparing a hostage team, getting a physician and a fingerprint expert to ensure the suspect was Yousef, and notifying Pakistani authorities. O'Neill dealt with the State Department to obtain country clearance for the FBI personnel to enter Pakistan, and spent days and nights with the military establishing midflight rendezvous points for the plane to refuel along the way.

"This was going on for days, and at all hours of the day and night," said Thomas Pickard, assistant special agent in charge of national security in the New York office. "We even discussed how [Parker] would get his money. Is it cash or goats or what?"

A decision was made to send Pickard to collect Yousef and bring him back to New York to face justice. "Finally John says he's got military and crew lined up," Pickard recalled, "and I say we need people from a hostage rescue team, a photographer to get Ramzi's picture and show he is okay, a doctor, and most importantly a fingerprints expert."

But in Pakistan, there was suddenly no time to wait for a military transport. Parker called diplomatic security agent Bill Miller early on February 6 to say Yousef was back in the city preparing to board a bus to Peshawar, a bandit region where tribal fighters commonly walk around with AK-47 assault rifles. Peshawar was popular with terrorists because it provided easy access to Afghanistan through the Khyber Pass.

A small team of agents was cobbled together, composed of Horton, agents from the DEA, and the DDS agents. O'Neill and the other FBI officials in SIOC communicated with the State Department to ensure that the Pakistani government, which had no formal extradition agreement with the United States, would cooperate with them if they captured Yousef. Bhutto said she would. "Ramzi Yousef was an important terrorist, but he was a soldier in a larger group. We could not allow fringe groups to dictate the agenda," she told writer Simon Reeve. The local military provided soldiers to join the American team.

The team raced over to the tidy white Su-Casa guest house, where Yousef was believed to have been staying under a false name since early February 7. Parker went into the guest house and upstairs to Yousef's room, where he had a brief conversation with him before returning to the street. He took off his hat and ran his fingers through his hair, giving the prearranged signal for the agents who had the building under surveillance.

The team of federal agents rushed up to the second floor, Room 16, tapped on the door, and awakened Yousef. Soon they had him pushed up against the wall, and an agent pulled out a photo of the most wanted man in the world. They placed a black hood over his head, bound his feet, and carried him downstairs as he demanded to see an arrest warrant. O'Neill, Pickard, and the rest of the FBI team held off on celebrating. "We didn't want to say anything until he was here," Pickard said.

Bill Galvin, the head of the New York office, took over for Pickard when he became too ill to make the eighteen-hour trip in a U.S. government jet. The plane landed the following morning, and in a quiet section of the airport, Galvin's team greeted Yousef's captors. The fugitive's fingerprints were taken and faxed to New York, where they were matched against the ones the U.S. had from a British immigration application.

"We were still holding our breath as the fax came in," Pickard said. Word of the successful match then reached New York and SIOC. Soon Galvin's plane was "wheels up" with Yousef aboard. Everyone stood and applauded. O'Neill stood in the front of the room, looking calm and beaming with satisfaction. It was February 7, around 10 A.M. There was one more step before a glass of Chivas Regal would be hoisted to celebrate the capture: getting Yousef safely on American soil.

On the flight back to New York, Yousef boasted how he had hoped to topple one tower into the other and kill a quarter of a million people. He claimed he would have attacked Israeli targets, but they were too well defended. At one point, he sketched the parking garage beneath the tower and the route he took with the bomb, and then ripped out the page, crumpled it up, popped it into his mouth, and ate it. He didn't want it used as evidence against him.

The plane landed at Stewart Air Force Base, north of New York City, and was met by an FBI team including Lewis Schiliro. Galvin, Schiliro, and Yousef flew to Manhattan on a Port Authority Sikorksy S-76A helicopter, and as they neared the towers, Galvin removed Yousef's blindfold so he could see the towers "are still standing."

"They would not be, if I had enough money," Yousef replied ominously.

Schiliro had been one of the first agents to respond to the blast beneath the towers, and would never forget looking down six stories into what was then New York's first "Ground Zero."

"They'll never take the towers down," he said.

Schiliro repeated those words to John O'Neill years later, when he was the head of the New York office and O'Neill was in charge of the national security division. "John knew differently,"

Schiliro said. "John said, 'You're wrong, Louie. They will never stop.' John, more than anyone, instinctively knew the level of hate and violence."

Yousef's arrival on American soil finally touched off celebration in SIOC command, a scene that would play out again nine months later with the capture of Yousef's accomplice, Wali Khan Anim Shah, a suspect in both the WTC bombing and the Bojinka–Manila Air bombing. But on February 7, 1995, O'Neill was still a novice at fighting terrorism. He stood at the front of the command center, amazed at the vast universe he had navigated during his first seventy-two hours as the section chief for counterterrorism.

"I think John was absolutely astounded," Bryant said. "There was an immediate recognition of the tremendous complexity and the politics of the situation. And I mean the international politics, just how difficult they could really be. You are always dealing with interagency rivalries here, but you are on the world stage and these cases are just all-consuming. I think he immediately grew into it."

O'Neill finally telephoned James in Chicago to tell her about his three-day experience. "Val, you are not going to believe this," he said, before providing her with a quick overview of his whirlwind series of days. Then he uttered a phrase he would frequently repeat over the coming years. "You know," he said, "you can't make this shit up." John O'Neill had truly found his calling.

6

THE BIRTH OF AL QAEDA

*There's Miller Time. And there's O'Neill Time. He was like Las Vegas.
There were no clocks on his walls. Whenever he was around, it was a
major event.*

—KEVIN GIBLIN, CHIEF OF TERRORIST WARNINGS, FBI

O'Neill assumed his new position as FBI section chief for counterterrorism at a unique moment in American history. The FBI
was first catapulted into national prominence when it began chas-
ing Depression-era hoodlums like John Dillinger, Pretty Boy
Floyd, and Baby Face Nelson. It briefly delved into a broader
international arena in the 1950s when the bureau actively pursued
suspected communists like Ethel and Julius Rosenberg, but
remained overwhelmingly concerned with domestic crime. The
FBI had maybe its finest hour in the 1990s when it arrested and
convicted the godfathers of the nation's top Mafia families. In
New York alone, all five crime families witnessed the conviction
of their bosses and many of their underbosses, consiglieres, and
capos.

However, as counterterrorism chief, O'Neill recognized
immediately that he was involved in the most important new game
in town, and through sheer force of personality and intensity, he
soon had his agents working feverishly. "We went from zero to a
hundred miles per hour, without stopping at twenty, thirty, or
forty," said Giblin, now the chief of FBI terrorist warnings.

"Look," O'Neill told several of his new charges. "I am a section chief at the age of forty-four. You better grab my coattails,

because there's no telling what I will be by the time I leave the bureau."

George Andrew, who had once seen O'Neill near tears in Baltimore, said some agents in Washington were put off by his brash confidence and what they perceived as his arrogance. "The smart ones, though, they took his coattails," Andrew said. Once these agents signed on to the O'Neill way of working, they found their lives transformed. "It was like someone suddenly moved in with your family," Giblin said. "There would be these ubiquitous e-mails at two A.M. and calls on the weekends. It was nonstop!"

Wherever he went and whatever challenge he took on, O'Neill always impressed people with his complete immersion in whatever he was doing. If he was planning a vacation to Italy, he read ten books about various Italian restaurants and tourist destinations. When he arrived in Washington in 1994 to take over the abortion-clinic investigation, he read books on Catholic fundamentalism and the history of the right-to-life movement. The same was true of his introduction to the fanatical world of international terrorism after he became involved in the capture of Yousef. He demanded complete files on every case his section was investigating, and spent his first weeks in Washington absorbing as much information as he could on whether the country was fully prepared to head off any terrorist threat.

"John made himself the terrorism expert, and then he started educating Louis Freeh and his other immediate bosses," said Andrew.

O'Neill's first order of business was to hold a battery of briefings with unit supervisors, particularly those involved in the radical fundamentalist division established a few years earlier by O'Neill's deputy, Robert Blitzer. O'Neill was bluff and direct, but encouraged dissent as long as it was productive. "I don't want yes people," O'Neill said. "I want people who can identify problems and think of viable solutions."

He typically spent an hour listening and then would spend the next hour asking questions. If agents did not have answers to his questions, O'Neill insisted they get the information and report back to him. "I've briefed a lot of people," said Thomas Corrigan, a NYPD detective who was one of the founding members of the Al Qaeda squad that O'Neill formally created in New York in 1997. "With John, there was never 'Here's the information and I'm out of here.' He would ask questions and then give his response, and then you couldn't leave work until you had all the answers for him by the morning. He could be brutal, but it was always for the right reasons."

O'Neill's fresh perspective on counterterrorism helped him recognize that terrorism constituted a looming danger to the U.S. national security. There had been hundreds of attacks on Americans overseas, some nine hundred around the world, but only one so far involving foreign terrorists on American soil—the 1993 World Trade Center bombing. Historically, U.S. officials believed international terror groups would never attack on American soil because so much of their funding came from U.S. sympathizers whose donations would surely diminish in the backlash of a direct attack.

O'Neill disagreed. He believed the 1993 attack was the first, rather than the last, attack and that a sea change was taking place in the methods and targets of terrorist groups. That opinion put him at odds with the prevailing view. The White House, National Security Council, State Department, and federal law enforcement groups perceived Yousef's bombing as an isolated crime, albeit on a grand scale.

U.S. policy for all previous attacks was to investigate the assault, identify suspects, use diplomacy as a means to track them down, and then, if possible, bring them to the U.S. to face American justice. It was a tidy formula that the majority of Americans could understand and it produced little political fallout. The notion of exploring broader conspiracies, which might uncover other dangerous threats to the United States, just was not in the nation's diplomatic, intelligence, and law enforcement playbook, numerous administration and law enforcement officials said. In fact, evidence that could have connected attacks on American soil to Muslim extremists was ignored.

One glaring example of that failure was the November 1990 shooting of Rabbi Meir Kahane, the founder of the Jewish Defense League. Kahane, a member of the Israeli parliament, was assassinated in a Manhattan hotel conference room by an Egyptian fanatic, El Sayyid Nosair. Investigators followed a trail that led within twenty-four hours to his rented apartment in New Jersey, where they found U.S. military documents and training materials, maps of several New York landmarks, including the World Trade Center, and two Middle Eastern men, Mahmoud Abouhalima and Mohammed Salameh. But the inquiry was shut down with the airtight arrest of Nosair. Twenty-eight months later, Abouhalima and Salameh assisted Yousef in bombing the World Trade Center. Similarly, intelligence on Yousef's connections to Al Qaeda in Afghanistan, Pakistan, and the Philippines was allowed to wither on the vine, along with the mountain of information uncovered during the arrest of Blind Sheikh Rahman that pointed to overseas connections to the plot to destroy New York landmarks in 1993.

Tensions within the U.S. government also got in the way of an effective response to international terrorism. President Clinton's top advisers, including national security adviser Sandy Berger, did not trust the CIA's intelligence. The CIA, fearful of being second-guessed, was reluctant to provide intelligence to the White House unless it came from an unassailable source. The limited intelligence the agency offered made it harder for the White House to develop policy. "Berger was frustrated by the CIA," said Jack Caravelli, a former top CIA official and NSC member. "The CIA under Clinton never wanted to look bad or wrong. If their intelligence did not come off a satellite, they would not give it any credence. But that kind of intelligence, at best, is fragmentary."

It was understandable that the Clinton White House would be leery about taking actions that could backfire, or "blow back," on the United States. An infamous instance of "blowback" occurred in Afghanistan in the early 1990s, when the U.S. supported bin Laden and the mujahadeen against the Russians. After they routed the Soviets, the U.S. found that bin Laden and the mujahadeen had aligned themselves with the Taliban before turning their hostility toward the U.S.

Under O'Neill's leadership, different law enforcement agencies would make strides toward better coordination and cooperation, which was essential to make sense of all that was unfolding. In New York in early 1995, U.S. Attorney Mary Jo White was building a case against Yousef and two other suspects in the 1993 World Trade Center bombing. Her prosecutors were also preparing for the trial of Sheikh Rahman, whom they charged as the mastermind of the plot to blow up New York's landmarks, bridges, and tunnels. There was also the international manhunt for Mir-Aimal Kansi, who shot and killed two CIA employees and wounded three others with an assault rifle outside the CIA on July 25, 1993; it was thought Kansi was possibly connected to the Afghan mujahedeen. The VAAPCON abortion-clinics investigation had yet to be completed. O'Neill's office was also monitoring skinhead, neo-Nazi, and Aryan Nation groups operating in the United States.

Added to all these domestic terrorism issues was the growing threat of radical Islamic fundamentalism spreading throughout the Middle and Far East, and the spectral figure of Osama bin Laden. Referring to conversations with other agents shortly after Yousef's capture, Schiliro said, "I remember all of us discussing Yousef's return and Yousef's comment that 'Next time, we'll take the towers down.' I never thought they would. But John understood that it was not a onetime deal. He said that the mujahedeen claimed there were two devils in the world. They eliminated the Russians. And there was one standing, the United States."

Five days after starting his new job, O'Neill was introduced to another frightening aspect of international terrorism, one with no ties to the Islamic world. Late at night on March 3, 1995, he received a communiqué about a nightmarish gas attack in the Tokyo subway system using sarin gas, the deadly gas developed by Nazi scientists during World War II. It had been unleashed at the height of the crowded morning rush hour, at least 6 people had been killed, and several thousand more were vomiting, fainting, and convulsing, with more than 550 requiring hospitalization.

The attack paralyzed the city's transportation network and strained medical units and required a call for military troops to assist the injured and help control the chaos. Two subway lines were completely shut down and twenty-six stations were closed. Yet the toll could have been far worse if the terrorist who mixed the three quarts of sarin used in the attack had mixed it properly. Hundreds of people would have died within minutes.

O'Neill did not wait for approval from higher-ups to dispatch agents from Washington to Tokyo. He always believed in the urgent need to get people on the ground providing timely, unfiltered information as quickly as possible after a terrorist attack. O'Neill's first question in Tokyo was whether the gas attack represented a broader, global terror threat. Japanese authorities quickly determined that the attack was the work of a wayward Buddhist doomsday cult, the Aum Shinrikyo Cult, led by blind, forty-year-old Shoko Asahara. O'Neill was advised the cult had been trying to buy Russian nuclear warheads and had set up an advanced laboratory on a 500,000-acre ranch in Australia to figure out a way to deliver it. Prompted by the potential for more violence, investigators around the world raced to learn more about the shadowy group, whose name meant "Supreme Truth."

The cult had accumulated more than a billion dollars and was said to have more than fifty thousand converts in at least six countries. In the United States, O'Neill dispatched agents to cities where the cult had members in order to ensure no terror attacks were planned for American targets. There were none, but the sarin gas attack in Tokyo allowed the FBI and other U.S. agencies to study Tokyo's emergency response to the world's first large-scale chemical terrorist strike in order to determine an appropriate U.S. reaction to a similar domestic incident.

"When John was around, there wasn't a week that went by when there was not a major incident," Giblin said. "In fact, there was not a day."

On March 8, five days after the sarin attack, a report about bin Laden crossed O'Neill's desk. At the time, the U.S. and Saudi Arabia were pressuring the Sudanese to exile bin Laden from his palatial home in the Sudan. Bin Laden responded with a diatribe against the Saudi royal family, which he blasted for living in lavish palaces while it bankrupted the country, for following "manmade laws" rather than Islamic law, or *sharia*, and for allowing the U.S. military to establish bases in the Muslim holy land. He said the Saudi government was corrupt and co-opted by its alliance with the U.S.

The Saudi royal family had good reason to fear that bin Laden's words could incite unrest. Before he fled to the Sudan from Afghanistan in 1991, the Saudis had issued a warrant for his capture and were mounting an assassination attempt with Pakistan intelligence officials when the plot was leaked to bin Laden. As a result, he donned a disguise, fled to the Sudan on a private jet, and holed up on a $250,000 farm that a close aide, Mohammed Rashed Daoud al-'Owhali, had purchased for him months earlier in preparation for exile near Khartoum.

Bin Laden told the Sudanese officials he wanted to help develop their country and improve their crumbling infrastructure, just as his father had done in Saudi Arabia years before. But the wily bin Laden also had a secret plan: he wanted to develop a terrorist training ground in the Sudan as well. With his tens of millions of dollars, bin Laden was treated as a special guest and given hundreds of passports for his recruits. He returned the favor handsomely, opening a huge construction company that employed hundreds of Sudanese. Bin Laden built the country's highway infrastructure, and just as his father had done, he diversified his holdings to gain virtual monopolies of Sudanese exports. Soon he had cornered the market on corn, sunflower, sesame products, and gum, which is derived from Sudanese acacia tree sap.

Bin Laden in this period appeared to be a gentleman and a country squire, enjoying his horse farms and soccer fields, but he was a shrewd handler of his money. He wisely moved portions of his wealth abroad, notably to Cyprus, Malaysia, Dubai, and London, all the while continuing to funnel millions of dollars to build Al Qaeda. As his influence in his adopted country grew, he used his considerable sway to influence local Somali tribal leaders to step up their threats against the Saudi royal family. Decrying the presence of "American infidels" near Islam's holiest shrines, he urged a direct attack. The Saudi government responded by ordering his assets frozen, and officially denouncing him as an enemy of the state.

The influence of bin Laden was not always so easy to detect. When the U.S. landed twenty-eight thousand American troops in Somalia in 1993 as part of Operation Restore Hope, a UN mission to feed starving Somalis, many Muslims saw it as a cover for the U.S. to expand its military presence in the region. In Yemen, the U.S. arrival prompted Al Qaeda supporters to bomb a hotel that was a pit stop for troops heading to Somalia. The blast killed an Australian tourist. Another small group of Al Qaeda–trained terrorists were caught at Aden Airport in Yemen, preparing to launch rockets at U.S. planes.

The Somalia mission soon became embroiled in the infighting between clans that was consuming the capital of Mogadishu. U.S. authorities identified Mohammed Adid, the most powerful clan leader, as the prime obstacle to peace in the country and decided to try to capture him. But in the attempt to take Adid, the U.S.

soldiers came under intense fire. Rocket-propelled grenades downed three American Black Hawk helicopters by striking their vulnerable tail rudders—grenade launchers that could only have been fired by men trained during the U.S.-supported war against the Soviets in Afghanistan.

Grisly television images of the mutilated body of a U.S. serviceman being dragged through the streets of Mogadishu were aired across America and the world. Eighteen Americans had been killed in the fighting. Within a week, the United States forces pulled out of Somalia. Few American intelligence officials knew that bin Laden was secretly involved in the attack. His role would only become clear years later when he proudly declared his support for the attack.

The U.S. departure from Somalia struck bin Laden as another intoxicating "victory" for Al Qaeda, one that demonstrated the "weakness, frailty and cowardice" of U.S. soldiers and filled him with notions of vanquishing the American superpower as he had helped vanquish the Soviets in Afghanistan. "One day our men shot down an American helicopter," he told Al Jazeera in 1999. "The pilot got out. We caught him, tied his legs and dragged him through the streets. After that 28,000 U.S soldiers fled Somalia. The Americans are cowards."

The United States soon joined other countries in stepping up pressure on the Sudanese to stop their covert support of Islamic radicals. The Saudi government gave every sign of backing the United States in this fight, and formally withdrew bin Laden's citizenship in 1994. Bin Laden replied by denouncing King al-Saud and the Western hold on the Saudi regime and established his own "Advice and Reform Committee," which served as a platform to harshly criticize the Saudi government and unwanted Western influence in the Arab peninsula.

But the Saudis were playing a double game. They also tried to distance themselves from the United States, and sent word to bin Laden through intermediaries that his fight was with America, not Saudi Arabia. The Saudis reportedly even offered bin Laden up to four hundred million dollars to back down and declare that Saudi Arabia was a solidly Muslim nation, a pronouncement that would have held wide sway with the Muslim population. But bin Laden refused. So the Saudis tried a different approach: assassination. Bin Laden's home in the Sudan became a war zone when four mercenaries opened fire on his security guards with AK-47 assault rifles. Three attackers and two guards died in the ensuing firefight, but bin Laden was unhurt.

Years later, O'Neill came to believe that the Saudi government developed a handshake relationship with bin Laden, appeasing him and dampening hostilities by providing funds and cover for his associates. "All the answers, everything needed to dismantle Osama bin Laden's organization, can be found in Saudi Arabia," he said.

But back in March 1995, he was still scrambling to get more information. He spent most of the night of March 8 poring over bin Laden's words in his new communiqué and studying the FBI's file on the Al Qaeda leader. In the morning, O'Neill spoke with the CIA to learn their assessment of bin Laden's latest diatribe, and also reached out to the NSC and other government agencies for their source information on the Al Qaeda leader. A few days later, Bear Bryant held what he described as one of his morning "A-meetings," which began promptly at 7:30 A.M.

"You better be there on time and you better be prepared," Bryant told O'Neill.

Bryant was aware that O'Neill "worked both ends of the candle pretty hard," as he put it. He told his new charge that he did not care where he was the night before, or how tired he was, or if he showed up in his slippers and pajamas. "Just be there," he told him. And O'Neill always was.

O'Neill arrived at the A-meeting armed with his developing belief that Osama bin Laden was in fact the world's most pressing threat. His frantic study had indicated to him a pattern among fundamentalist Islamic radicals, and bin Laden and his Al Qaeda organization were right at the center of the web. Bryant never forgot the insight O'Neill showed that day in alerting him to a problem that would plague every U.S. law enforcement official for years to come.

"The first time I ever heard of bin Laden was from John O'Neill," Bryant said. "John basically started explaining that bin Laden was a relative of a wealthy Saudi family and they had a construction company and he had left for the Sudan, which was basically identified as a state sponsor of terrorism."

O'Neill told Bryant and the other FBI officials about bin Laden's history of fighting with the mujahedeen against the Soviets and that bin Laden had turned his hatred toward America because he viewed U.S. policy as undermining the Islamic world. O'Neill explained that a terrorist with bin Laden's kind of wealth, money, and connections could cause America enormous harm. He wrapped up his presentation by saying he was already speaking with the CIA to glean more information, and to prompt them to gather more information on bin Laden.

Less than a month into his new job, O'Neill began discussing bin Laden with Richard Clarke, the national coordinator for counterterrorism and an NSC director. O'Neill compared bin Laden to a young Adolf Hitler, making ominous threats that no one took seriously until it was too late. "It's like *Mein Kampf*," O'Neill said. "Bin Laden's just like this. When you read what this guy says he's going to do, he's serious. There are a lot of people who support him." O'Neill pointed out that bin Laden was raking in donations from sympathizers around the world and that he had to be taken seriously because "what he says he's going to do is go to war with the United States."

"If you asked most terrorism experts in the mid-1990s to name the major terrorist organizations that might be a threat to the

United States, they would have said Hezbollah, Hamas," Clarke said. "Most people wouldn't have known that there was Al Qaeda. But not John. He knew what Al Qaeda was."

He also understood how it worked, and delivered a chilling warning to Clarke: bin Laden's network extended inside the United States. "It is inconceivable that they are not here," he said.

Despite its obvious importance, counterterrorism was never a clearly defined or specially funded discipline within the government. There wasn't enough funding for translators to deal with the mountain of foreign-language newspapers and communications gathered from around the world. Intelligence was stored at the CIA, and often hoarded. The State Department had its own information, which diplomats and Foreign Service personnel had gleaned, and the FBI collected its own information as well. There was no central clearinghouse.

O'Neill wanted to get his arms around it all—but couldn't. The lines of authority within the law enforcement, diplomatic, and intelligence communities were at best blurred. The groups were often at loggerheads with one another, fighting for turf and clinging to their own idiosyncratic institutional identities. The intelligence community wanted to string the terrorists along to get more intelligence. Law enforcement wanted to catch terrorists and string them up. The diplomatic community tended to broker agreements that maintained the status quo.

O'Neill was unique at the FBI in that he went outside traditional boundaries and met with scholars for their insights, rather than relying solely on the perspectives of insiders and lawmen. Frank Ciluffo, now a member of the White House Home Security Office, met O'Neill in the early 1990s when Ciluffo was with a Washington-based think tank, the Center for Strategic and International Studies. "If you look at counterterrorism in the early 1990s, it always fell between bureaucratic gaps," he said. "John understood you could not look at counterterrorism solely through law enforcement, or State Department diplomacy, or a military prism alone. He was very good at breaking down those walls, and he wore his views on his sleeves, and that was refreshing in many ways. Because there was no single entity that owned the mission, it was personality driven as much as process driven. He was an FBI person driven not by politics, but by results, and he would break a lot of glass to get there."

To O'Neill, the way to get results was for the FBI to be the lead agency in the event of a terrorist attack in the United States, or overseas if an American citizen had been hurt. He began lobbying NSC members to establish clearer lines—primarily *his* lines—of authority. In a matter of weeks, an event of such staggering proportions occurred that Clinton quickly settled the debate by signing a nationwide presidential directive giving the FBI what O'Neill wanted: the lead in investigating an act of terrorism. Tragically, the directive came with a heavy price tag.

On April 19, 1995, a truck bomb exploded outside the Alfred P. Murrah Federal Building in Oklahoma City. At the time, the country was more interested in Clinton's sexcapades and the O. J. Simpson murder trial than in terrorists like Blind Sheikh Rahman, who was on trial in New York City and barely attracting media coverage. But the images of destruction in the heartland of the United States jarred the nation. The explosion was massive, shearing off the front of the eight-story building like a knife cutting through a giant layer cake. The scene evoked a horror not often seen outside the Middle East. Bodies were strewn on the street, including those of children from an obliterated day-care center inside the Murrah Building. Scores of bloodied survivors were carried away. In all, 267 men, women, and children were killed, and more than 1,000 were injured.

Within minutes of the blast, speculation was rampant that Middle Eastern fanatics were behind the carnage. The television airways were filled with so-called experts on terrorism, particularly those with self-described expertise on Muslim extremists. But O'Neill did not share their opinion. Amid the chaos of those early hours in the command center, he told his colleagues not to rush to the judgment that Hamas, Hezbollah, or other Islamic fundamentalist fanatics were behind the attack. He had another theory to explore before troops and other resources were needlessly dispatched abroad.

O'Neill thought the attackers were probably homegrown. "John said it right away: April nineteenth was the anniversary of Waco," Bryant said, recalling with admiration how O'Neill immediately linked the date to the infamous siege in Texas that ended in the fiery death of an estimated eighty followers of Branch Davidian cult leader David Koresh. "John came up with the idea right away that it was a domestic incident. It was incredible, and incredibly smart."

Timothy McVeigh, an Operation Desert Storm veteran from Buffalo, New York, was taken into custody on a traffic violation after a trooper spotted his battered Mercury with a hanging license plate and found a weapon in the car. McVeigh resembled an FBI sketch of a possible suspect. No one knew it at the time, but McVeigh harbored extreme right-wing antigovernment views. The FBI quickly established links between McVeigh and a Michigan man, Terry Nichols. Agents were dispatched to their homes and to hotels where their credit cards had recently been used.

For the next month, O'Neill, Bryant, and Blitzer supervised what became a nationwide investigation, coordinating the efforts of more than a thousand agents and prosecutors as leads were followed to anyone who had had contact with either McVeigh or Nichols. "John was great making sure the details were covered," Bryant said. "There were fifteen offices involved, including Chicago, Detroit, Buffalo, Phoenix, Oklahoma City, Los Angeles, Knoxville. Anytime there was a portion of something in one place, John had a conference call to make sure everything was coordinated."

O'Neill was also the point man giving briefings to FBI Director Freeh, Attorney General Janet Reno, and the White House. By mid-May, with the focus of the investigation squarely on McVeigh and homegrown fanatics, O'Neill and Bryant handed off the investigation to a task force of lawmen pulled together by O'Neill. He and the other supervisors realized that the devastating Oklahoma City bombing raised the bar on terror attacks.

"It was the supersizing," Giblin said. "It was the 'force multiplier.'"

As usual, it took a disaster to wake up the politicians. The Senate and Congress started asking what resources the FBI needed to fight terrorism at home and abroad. As a result of the tragedy, O'Neill's units would double in size within a few years. Just weeks after McVeigh's arrest, President Clinton gave the FBI what O'Neill wanted: lead authority to investigate terrorism when an American or an American interest was threatened, in the United States or abroad. The signing of Presidential Decision Directive 39 on June 21, 1995, was a defining moment, because it brought representatives from several other federal agencies, including the Federal Emergency Management Administration, the Department of Environmental Protection, and the Department of Health, into the antiterrorism program.

International cooperation was also essential, and in June 1995, O'Neill embarked on a grueling, three-week trip that took him to London, Paris, Rome, Japan, the Philippines, and Australia. Blitzer had recommended the trip because of O'Neill's previous success in gleaning information from French and Italian law enforcement officials while investigating Middle Eastern terrorist cells. "We had good relations with the British, but he really wanted to reach out to the British because they were farther ahead of us," Blitzer said. "The French had worked on Islamic radicalism; the Italians had uncovered an Egyptian terrorist cell."

The trip was a heady experience for O'Neill, who as a boy in Atlantic City had dreamed of expanding his horizons far beyond the boardwalk and beach. Blitzer joined O'Neill for the first leg of the trip, and remembers one night in Paris when they had a round of meetings with their French counterparts, then dined in a restaurant on the Champs Élysées near the Arc de Triomphe, and afterward walked along the Seine. "This is great," O'Neill told Blitzer, lighting up a cigar under a clear sky. The rest of the trip might not have lived up to that standard for glamour, but it was productive. O'Neill continued on to a string of countries, ending in Australia, where he met with antiterrorist officials from Sweden, Canada, Egypt, and India. By the end of the long trip, "he had been through every time zone around the world, but he was energized," Blitzer said.

Back in Washington that July, O'Neill moved into the Saratoga Building on Connecticut Avenue, near Chevy Chase. His schedule had prevented him from spending much time with Mary Lynn Stevens, whom he had started to date in 1989 during his first assignment to headquarters. But his unavailability did not seem to worry her or make her suspicious. "John was the type of man that when you were with him, he gave you his undivided attention," she said. "He always made me feel that I was the most important person in the world. He was tender and kind and he listened." And he did one more thing that made her feel special. "He said 'I love you' all the time," Stevens said.

O'Neill and Stevens occasionally attended Sunday mass at her church, St. Peter's, near the James Madison Library of Congress. O'Neill had encouraged her to become a reader, and she did, later becoming the parishioner in charge of all the church's readers. He also accompanied her to numerous black-tie affairs, which she was invited to because of her position as vice president of a huge credit union that handled military personnel. "My friends were all charmed by him," Stevens said. "I never met a man who enjoyed wearing a tuxedo more than John O'Neill."

A gourmet cook, Stevens often made O'Neill dinner at her house, but she was never invited over to his place. He told her he didn't have an apartment, but lived in an FBI "safe house" that was strictly off limits for social visits. The charade provided O'Neill with the freedom he desired to pursue other women. He was even able to smooth things over when she found out through her hairdresser, Jim Rennie—whose sister lived in Atlantic City and was a friend of Christine O'Neill—that O'Neill was married. He said he told everyone he met that he was divorced. And when he started to date Stevens, he feared telling her the truth because she might end their relationship.

Stevens described herself as "the perfect girlfriend" for O'Neill because she was both independent and trusting. "If you want to lie to me, that's your problem," she said. "I'm not going to turn into a suspicious person. In hindsight, I worked very well for him. But in a sense, he fit in with what I wanted. I have my career and I actually enjoy going places on my own. What he gave worked well for me."

Valerie James, who was busy in Chicago with her own job and two children, only visited O'Neill occasionally in Washington, usually bringing her son, Jay. When they visited, they stayed with O'Neill and went with him on tours of the White House and other landmarks and museums. "We shuttled back and forth, with John coming back to Chicago a number of times," James said. He often assured her they would marry, apparently to ease the strain his move to Washington had placed on their relationship.

Anna DiBattista, meanwhile, lived just four miles away from O'Neill in Kensington, Maryland. The two frequently saw each other at night for dinner or drinks. When he was stuck at work, the five-foot-eight, brown-eyed DiBattista would bring food to his fifth-floor counterterrorism office. On Monday evenings, they went for dinner at DiBattista's mother's home in Kensington, and occasionally he would take her to his black-tie socials or a diplomatic party. DiBattista soon began keeping some of her belongings at his place. On those many mornings she didn't see him, he would call around 7 A.M. "This is your morning wake-up call," he would say.

Some Sundays he did double duty, attending church in the morning with Stevens and later attending 5:30 P.M. mass with DiBattista at her church, St. Matthew's. DiBattista had no reason to doubt O'Neill's story that he was divorced and had two children who lived with their mother. "I knew he had dated a Valerie James in Chicago for a few years, but he told me he had broken up with her," she said. In fact, when O'Neill returned from his whirlwind three-week trip around the world in July, it was DiBattista who picked him up at the airport. He arrived in time for Fourth of July celebrations at the Capitol, which featured a fireworks display and a rousing rendition of the *1812* Overture, which was one of O'Neill's favorites. He and DiBattista sat in the front row with tickets O'Neill had obtained.

But O'Neill could never escape the horror of terrorism for even one day. On July 5, he awakened to news that an American neuropsychologist, Donald Hutchings, had been kidnapped along with five other tourists in the foothills of the Himalayas, in Kashmir, India. He would not know the full truth about the reason for the action until years later: the kidnapping incident would ultimately put him in pursuit of Ahmed Omar Saeed Sheikh, a Muslim terrorist who would transfer funds for bin Laden that were used in carrying out the September 11 attacks. Sheikh would also emerge as the instigator of the 2002 kidnapping and murder of *Wall Street Journal* reporter Daniel Pearl.

Like so many youths who espoused terrorism, Sheikh had enjoyed a privileged background before becoming an Islamic fanatic. At the time, he was a fresh-faced twenty-one-year-old British-born citizen, the son of Pakistani nationals who owned a booming garment business, Perfect Fashions. Sheikh graduated from public school and studied applied mathematics at the London School of Economics. While at university, he became a world-class arm wrestler who competed at international championships in Spain and Switzerland. He was also an active member of the university's Islamic Society.

After watching a gripping film called *The Destruction of a Nation* about the Serbian slaughter of Muslims in Bosnia, he dropped out of school and went to Bosnia to assist in bringing aid to the injured. In Bosnia, he met mujahedeen veterans of the Afghanistan war who had arrived to fight alongside fellow Muslims. Sheikh eventually met Al Qaeda members who steered him to bin Laden's training camps in Afghanistan, where he was tutored in everything from surveillance and countersurveillance, to cryptology, disguise, and interrogation, to weapons and explosives.

His first Al Qaeda assignment was to travel to India to use kidnapped tourists as bargaining chips to free Islamic activists. But he himself was shot and captured, leading Muslim terrorists to embark on a more ambitious kidnapping to try to secure his release and that of other jailed Muslims. That was how Donald Hutchings and the others found their camp taken over by gun-toting militants on the Fourth of July. O'Neill dispatched several agents to India, including James Duffy, his former colleague in Baltimore who had become an expert hostage negotiator. The action marked the first time O'Neill exercised the power afforded him under provisions of the new presidential directive giving the FBI authority over terror investigations.

7

THE OBSTRUCTIONISTS

The visits to Paris and other foreign cities left O'Neill eager for more travel, and in July 1995, he and Anna DiBattista took off for eight days in Barbados, where they stayed in the beautiful home of the FBI's legal attaché. They rode mopeds, jogged along mile after mile of beautiful beach, and rented a car to explore the island. Once again, O'Neill was well armed with guidebooks, and he and DiBattista dutifully explored the historical sights and restaurants they recommended. O'Neill snuck in a round of golf one day at a private club, but mostly he and DiBattista hit the beaches and made the most of the chance to enjoy the blue-green Caribbean. O'Neill was watching DiBattista wade into the water one day in her revealing fishnet swimsuit when an eighteen-year-old boy swam up to her and tried to talk her up. O'Neill didn't sit still for that. He marched into the water, carrying a towel to wrap around DiBattista, and jealously escorted her back to their spot on the beach.

"Did you see how he was looking at you?" O'Neill demanded.

But the visit to Barbados, like O'Neill's escapes to Elaine's and other top nightspots, only offered a transitory suspension of reality. O'Neill could sometimes lull himself into the illusion that his life was as carefree and full of laughter as anyone's. He might momentarily be unencumbered of the horrific pressure of worrying about where in the world a terrorist was planning an attack that he was not sure he could prevent. But he knew the pressure and responsibility were inescapable. As he liked to put it, comparing himself to Babe Ruth and other baseball Hall of Famers who made outs far more often in their careers than they got hits, "I can never strike out."

The situation in Kashmir had not improved while O'Neill was getting in his beach time. Al Faran, the Muslim extremist group that had taken the hostages in the Pahalgam Woods in south Kashmir, had not released any of its prisoners. Norwegian hostage Hans Christian Ostro was found beheaded, with the initials *A.F.*—for Al Faran—carved into his chest. But an American businessman named John Childs was later able to escape. That left Hutchings, German Dirk Hasert, and Keith Mangan and Paul Wells of Britain in the hands of the Kashmiri separatists, who demanded the release of Sheikh and thirty-eight other Muslims being held in Indian jails before they would turn over their prisoners. Ostro's severed head was found in August with a note calling for the immediate release of Sheikh and others.

Duffy telephoned O'Neill from India with a grim status report on his investigation into the disappearance of Hutchings and the others. "We had established a negotiating policy with India that allowed us to try to deal with the terrorists because there was an American victim and a violation of American law," Duffy recalled. But direct communication with the hostage takers had proven impossible. Duffy said it might take a long time to get results, but that was all right with O'Neill.

"John understood that the foreign culture often won't allow you to move so quickly," Duffy said. "Every day I was there, two or three police officers were killed. Every fifty feet, there was an armed soldier standing in the street."

The kidnappers were mostly a ragtag group of young kids, sixteen to twenty years old. But eventually it was determined that the leader of the group was a veteran of the fight against the Russians in Afghanistan, Abdul Hamid Turki, who was now part of a Pakistan-based group, Harkat-ul Ansar, that was fighting for an end to Indian rule in Kashmir so the region could be under Muslim control. Seven years after the kidnapping, the fate of the hostages was still uncertain, since their bodies were never recovered, but it appears likely they were murdered. Indian intelligence sources would later tell reporters they believed the four were killed in December 1995. Jane Schelly, Hutchings's wife, held a memorial service for him on September 15, 2001, finally concluding that there was no longer any hope.

Sheikh would serve nearly five years in jail, but he was freed in December 1999 as part of a ransom deal with the Indian government in which prisoners were exchanged for 154 passengers aboard a hijacked Indian Airlines flight. The mere fact that Sheikh was part of the deal showed he held a prominent place in bin Laden's terror organization, which should have alerted the Indian authorities to his importance. In January 2002, Sheikh kidnapped Daniel Pearl of the *Wall Street Journal,* luring him to a meeting with an e-mailed promise of introducing him to Muslim extremists linked to bin Laden. In exchange for Pearl, Sheikh and his accomplices demanded two million dollars and the release of Al Qaeda suspects held by the U.S. at Guantánamo Bay in Cuba. But they murdered Pearl, cutting his throat. Sheikh was captured, convicted, and sentenced to death later that year.

Pearl's widow found some closure with the discovery of her husband's body. Hutchings's family was not that fortunate, but it wasn't for a lack of effort on the part of O'Neill. He met several times with Hutchings's widow to assure her that the FBI would not give up. "We spent millions trying to recover the remains of the American and the other people," Duffy said. "He clearly knew it was not going to be solved overnight, and he invested in it. Their bodies literally disappeared off the face of the earth." No one has been brought to justice, but there are still FBI agents checking leads, "hoping something will pop up."

Movement did come on another front in the last months of 1995, however. Evidence turned up that November that Ramzi Yousef's accomplice in both the 1993 World Trade Center attack and the 1994 Bojinka plot, Wali Khan Anim Shah, had been spotted working as a cook in a shabby restaurant in Qatar. Shah was easily identifiable: he was stocky, and he was missing two fingers on his left hand. O'Neill pushed the State Department to see if Qatar would make a deal and help arrest Shah, just as Pakistan had done with Yousef.

"Sometimes the State Department can be difficult," said Andrew, then the head of FBI counterintelligence at the Washington field office. "They can keep you at arm's length. They don't want anyone to mess up their diplomacy and sometimes they look at the FBI as though we are thugs."

O'Neill used an NSC meeting chaired by Richard Clarke, the president's national coordinator for counterterrorism, to push for an operation to return Shah to U.S. soil to face justice. "I asked John what he was going to do," recalled George Andrew, who had known O'Neill since Baltimore. "And he said, 'Why don't you come over with me?' I sat like a bird on a tree limb and watched the interaction in this meeting. It was not two minutes into the meeting that I felt that all the power and all the attention shifted to John. John controlled the meeting, and that is what impressed me. He had all the answers, but he didn't take power away from anyone. Everyone turned to him and listened to him."

Some of O'Neill's mastery of meetings had to do with preparation. He had done his homework, typically, and he often reached out to others attending a meeting beforehand to sound them out—or more than that. Fran Townsend insists that he would sometimes do so much advance work, "the meeting was over before everybody ever got in the room," as she put it to PBS. "He would make phone calls. He would see what people's positions were. He would cajole them, persuade them to a consensus. So by the time he walked in the room, everybody in the room knew they had spoken to John. Everybody in the room knew that John knew where this was going, and it was basically cooked by the time you got into the meeting."

Townsend may have exaggerated O'Neill's sorcery, but she is

hardly alone in having been impressed by the way O'Neill handled a meeting. Andrew, too, was forced to give O'Neill credit for the NSC meeting that day at the White House. "I was friends with John and was not a big believer—I was jealous," he said. "But this meeting went so very smoothly and made the bureau look smart. And it took no longer than an hour, which for D.C. is a pretty short meeting."

O'Neill won White House approval. Qatar officials agreed to assist the U.S., but did not want any public disclosure of their role—no "fingerprint" to indicate they had been helpful. "They just wanted to get rid of a terrorist and get a marker from us," one official said. In making the arrangements, O'Neill used the same template that brought Yousef to New York, but this time Tom Pickard was healthy enough to travel.

Khan was badly dehydrated, and looked weary by the time Pickard arrived to collect him. A Qatar police officer guarding Khan introduced him to the tall American. "I said I was the FBI, and you are going to stand trial," Pickard recalled. "He knew he was in trouble when they picked him up. He had no idea he was heading to the United States."

Pickard radioed back home, "We have the package." As his colleagues rejoiced, O'Neill was busy asking more questions. He wanted to know what Qatar police had recovered at Khan's apartment. "Did they find laptops?" O'Neill asked. They had, but the CIA had gotten to them first. The agency said it would not share its information with the FBI, but O'Neill was not about to accept that without a fight. "John could use heavy-handed methods to get what he wanted," said Bryant. "He just put a lot of pressure to bear, everywhere." Eventually, David Cohen, the CIA station chief in New York, intervened. O'Neill got his data.

Khan was flown to New York and safely jailed in the Metropolitan Corrections Center in Lower Manhattan, but there was barely time for O'Neill to savor the capture before another problem arose. On November 13, 1995, word came of a bombing in

Saudi Arabia, bin Laden's homeland. The attack occurred just nine months after bin Laden issued his "ARC Communiqué #17" that severely criticized the Saudi royal family's alliance with the United States. A small battered pickup truck containing about two hundred pounds of explosives exploded in Riyadh, the capital, ripping an outside wall off a three-story building occupied by U.S. personnel sent to Saudi Arabia to train security forces. The facility, formerly called the Office of the Program Managers for Saudi Arabian National Guard, or "OPM-Sang," was actually the second target selected by the terrorists. Their first, the U.S. embassy, was passed over because it had scores of Saudi nationals working inside.

The powerful OPM-Sang explosion killed five Americans and two Indian servicemen, and wounded more than sixty others. Two shadowy and previously unknown organizations, the Tigers of the Gulf and the Islamic Movement for Change, claimed responsibility. The two groups had issued a statement in April that set a June deadline for the withdrawal of U.S. troops from Saudi Arabia, which had been Washington's closest and most powerful ally during the Gulf War. Saudi Arabia was by far the largest purchaser of U.S. arms and fighter jets, and had allowed the U.S. to station troops there since the Gulf War. The OPM-Sang blast was the first attack on U.S. military in Saudi Arabia since the Gulf War, when Iraq had fired Scud missiles into the kingdom and one hit a U.S. barrack, killing more than twenty soldiers.

Speculation immediately centered on bin Laden as the culprit behind the attack, but O'Neill was among those at the FBI who cautioned that several neighboring countries, including Iran and Iraq, could easily have been responsible. O'Neill dispatched twenty FBI forensic and explosives experts to Riyadh to help with the investigation. The agents recovered valuable crime-scene evidence that enabled the Saudis to focus their investigation on tracing where the explosives and the truck were purchased. For possible suspects, Saudi police turned their attention to a list of nearly fifteen-thousand Saudi nationals who had fought as mujahedeen in Afghanistan. But the Saudi government was afraid of more threats from outside its borders and worried about saboteurs from within its own ranks, and was not about to share anything it learned with American investigators. That would only have risked inflaming their fundamentalist Muslim critics even more.

"There were possible connections to Saudi Shiites and Iran and the Iranian National Guard or the Iranian MOIS [intelligence service]," said John Lewis, who was the deputy assistant director for operations in the national security division. "When we go overseas, we are totally dependent on the cooperation of the host service in a foreign country. We may have all kinds of power in the U.S., but in Saudi Arabia, they would not allow us to interview Saudi nationals even with their police present."

On November 29, 1995, the Egyptian embassy in Islamabad was hit by a powerful truck bomb that killed fifteen and injured eighty. The attack was attributed to Al Qaeda and resulted in the arrests of more than 150 Arabs, including the director of bin Laden's ARC Services Office. O'Neill hoped the attack on another country with a secular government and ties to the United States would jar the Saudis into cooperating with the U.S. investigation. But it only hardened their position and reinforced their fear. "I think it was just Saudi independence," Lewis said. "They did not want to be viewed as submitting to United States law enforcement."

Frustrated, and unable to pursue a proper investigation into the attacks, O'Neill brought his contingent back to the United States in a matter of weeks. A few days after their return, he was sitting in his fifth-floor office when the phone rang.

"O'Neill," he announced.

"Hey, schmuck!" a voice said. "What're you doing? Are you still a hack?"

"Fuck you, asshole," he shot back, recognizing the voice right away.

It was Jack Caravelli, the boyhood buddy O'Neill helped get elected student-council president. Caravelli was by now not only an expert in Russian affairs and a major official in the CIA, he was also serving in the White House as an NSC expert on weapons of mass destruction.

"My job dealt with international affairs, particularly with Russia and other nations or terrorist groups that were trying to take nuclear weapons across the borders or transfer missile technology for mass destruction weapons from one place we care about to another," Caravelli explained. "A lot had happened in those years. The Berlin Wall had come down. As the Soviet Union was breaking down, we saw a rise in terrorist groups seeking to acquire weapons of mass destruction, trying to take advantage of the situation. There was a lot of good intelligence about which states were in play, countries like Iran and more radical entities such as Iraq."

U.S intelligence uncovered hard evidence that Saddam Hussein was trying to acquire weapons of mass destruction after the Gulf War. That came as no surprise, given the Iraqi dictator's record of thuggery and past use of chemical weapons. But evidence had also been accumulating that bin Laden was trying to acquire weapons of mass destruction. Caravelli believes bin Laden's several attempts over the years to acquire weapons-grade plutonium have been unsuccessful, but that he has acquired other radioactive material which could be used in a so-called dirty bomb that could kill thousands.

As far back as 1993, bin Laden allegedly approved a plan for several Al Qaeda members to buy enriched uranium from the former Soviet Union. But the black marketers soon recognized that the Al Qaeda bargainers were unsophisticated when it came to nuclear weapons, and took advantage. Bin Laden spent several hundred thousand dollars, thinking he was getting one hundred kilograms of enriched uranium. But instead, it was mercury and low-grade reactor fuel that could never have been used to make weapons.

"That is one of the great ironies, bad guys getting fleeced by other bad guys," Caravelli said.

Caravelli had walked up to an FBI expert on mass destruction after a White House interagency meeting in November 1995 and made small talk with him.

"Hey, I had a longtime friend named John O'Neill," he told the FBI agent.

"O'Neill? You've got to be kidding," the agent replied. "He's a big-time guy just back in D.C."

Caravelli and O'Neill were both pleased by the way their lives were overlapping again. The FBI is only five blocks from the White House, and the two old friends were soon meeting regularly for lunch to share off-the-record insights and information. Caravelli had been aware of bin Laden, but O'Neill told him in their private talks that the United States had only scratched the surface of recognizing how dangerous Al Qaeda was. He was trying to make the administration understand that the attacks would not be isolated to single events and would not stop at the U.S. border.

"John was convinced we were extremely vulnerable," he said. "He saw the threads and elements and was trying to put together a response to go after it, earlier than almost anyone. John felt that the administration was not aggressive enough in donating resources to stamp out the danger at its source. He knew that terrorists would only be constrained by opportunity and resources. They have made a pact with the devil and are committed to fostering as much destruction as they can."

O'Neill discussed ways to overcome his frustration with the State Department and the CIA for slowing down investigations of terrorism against Americans overseas. "John was hard-charging, but with the State Department it was always 'go slow.' Although the White House was beginning to recognize that this problem had nasty tentacles, the policy response was probably lacking, not as aggressive, and certainly there was a question of the willingness to commit military resources."

In January 1996, O'Neill mapped out a landmark change for his counterterrorism division. He recognized that the scope of terrorism was growing exponentially, and concluded that the only way to devote proper attention to the various threats was to create separate divisions for domestic terrorism and international terrorism. The decision would remove domestic terrorism from his direct control, and few bureaucrats willingly surrender a piece of turf, but O'Neill was unique. He designated Robert Blitzer, his deputy, to be section chief for the domestic side. "John saw that the future major threat was international terrorism," said Bryant. "I tended to agree with him."

Once Freeh signed off on the change, O'Neill turned his attention to helping create a new CIA-based station, code-named "Alex," where FBI agents would partner with the CIA to go after bin Laden. The mission of the Alex station was not just to track down bin Laden, but to focus on his infrastructure, his capabilities, his funding sources, his bases of operation, his training centers, and the movement of his people.

To counter the lack of cooperation from foreign law enforcement and police agencies, O'Neill also made it a requisite part of his job to entertain every foreign cop, intelligence officer, and government official he encountered. His reasoning was pragmatic, because such hospitality meant that a well-timed phone call might provide access to invaluable assistance that would help to catch a terrorist, save a life, or foil a threatened attack. "Most successes in life are built on relationships, and not legal documents," he liked to say.

Late-night bonding sessions over drinks and meals were not the norm at the stuffy FBI. In fact, they were frowned upon. But

O'Neill did not care. He paid his expenses out of his own pocket, to avoid confrontations with bureau bean counters, and never hesitated to take advantage of a chance to make a new acquaintance who might one day be useful. He described his nights on the town as his "night job," and O'Neill clearly loved the work. "Life is meant to be gulped, not sipped," he told agent Anne Beagan.

O'Neill was constantly on the phone, doing favors, massaging contacts, and building such a huge Rolodex of friends and acquaintances that he categorized his Palm Pilot by world geography, types of law enforcement agencies, employment, and businesses. "John's approach to law enforcement was like that of the old Irish ward boss in regards to governance: you collect friendships, debts and obligations, because you never know when you're going to need them," Clarke told the *New Yorker* magazine.

Then, in April 1996, O'Neill and Bryant came up with such an innovative idea to bridge the gap between the FBI and the CIA that the mere mention of it was an act of heresy in an agency founded by the almighty J. Edgar Hoover: they discussed bringing over a CIA counterterrorism specialist and making him O'Neill's deputy for international terrorism. "John would say, 'If you put the resources and talents of the CIA counterterrorism center and the FBI's counterterrorism section together on any issue, there isn't anything we cannot solve, but we need both,'" Lipka explained.

O'Neill's friendship with Caravelli might have given him the nerve to act on this radical idea. His proposal ran counter to the way different branches of law enforcement usually behave. They talk about cooperation, but insist on autonomy. But O'Neill saw the threat of terrorism as a challenge that could only be met by creative thinking and planning, and he was looking at the big picture. He called Lipka into his office and told him of his plans to bring an outsider from the CIA into the FBI family. He selected Lipka because he knew he would resist the idea.

"John called me into his office and says, 'There is an individual at the CIA counterterrorism center who works hard and puts in long hours and he likes the FBI as much as you like the CIA.'"

"So what does that mean?" Lipka asked.

"I want you to work closely with him," O'Neill said. "There are very few counterterrorism issues that the CIA and the FBI can't solve together."

Bryant and O'Neill suggested Jeff O'Connell, the CIA's deputy for counterterrorism, later the Tel Aviv station chief, and CIA Director George Tenet approved the temporary transfer.

"John was FBI from his underwear out," Bryant said. "He was resistant to the agency being in our knickers, but he knew for the success of the mission, it was the right thing. I told him, 'Let's just do it and let everyone know this is an order.'"

Like Nixon going to China, O'Neill was in a way just the sort of figure required to make a major breakthrough in relations between the bureau and the agency. O'Neill was not only an FBI man to the core, someone who literally knew he was going to be an FBI agent before he even knew who he was, he was also a diffi-cult personality whose style could put people off. If O'Neill of all people could get along with O'Connell, the CIA man, and even become friends with him, it sent a signal throughout the ranks of the bureau that times had changed. O'Neill let it be known that O'Connell needed to be treated with every respect and courtesy.

"He went so far as to instruct the agents that when he was not around, the CIA official was in charge," said Giblin. "He wanted to merge our information and get the best bang for U.S. dollars. Frictions were absolutely gone. Whenever a dinosaur showed up, John made sure they knew the CIA was involved. We made a major breakthrough."

The time was right to cooperate against bin Laden. The three-million-dollar reward for information about the OPM-Sang bombing led to the arrests of four Saudi men whom Saudi authorities said had confessed to crossing over from Yemen and setting off the truck bomb. Once again, the Saudis refused to let

U.S. investigators interrogate the men. They would not even release videotaped confessions, which meant there was no way for the U.S. to know if the men were mere scapegoats set up to take the fall. Eventually, the United States was given an opportunity to view the confessions—along with the rest of the world. The Saudis broadcast the confessions over national television. Several of the suspects admitted to training in bin Laden's camps. Although none said the Muslim terror leader had directly ordered the bombing, they acknowledged that they were inspired by bin Laden and his *fatwas* against America.

The public release of the confessions represented a calculated decision by the Saudis, who had to maintain a delicate balancing act in trying to satisfy both their Western allies and their extremely vocal and dangerous Muslim critics. But the public airing of the confessions lent urgency to the behind-the-scenes pressure both the Saudis and U.S. State Department were exerting on the Sudan to expel bin Laden, a move the United States hoped would place him in a less protected environment. By April 1996, the Sudan politely asked bin Laden to leave.

His travel options were limited for a number of reasons. He would only live in a Muslim nation, but several of them would not take him. The Saudis did not want him to return because they feared he would incite unrest and violence and because he hated the Saudi royal family even more than the United States for allowing the "crusaders" to set foot on their holy soil. Other countries were not inclined to have such a powerful revolutionary catalyst living in their midst. Wherever he went, his departure from Sudan would offer the United States an opportunity to grab him, but prosecutors had yet to formally indict bin Laden and had no legal authority to snatch him. This turned out to be their last chance to get bin Laden before September 11, 2001.

The Al Qaeda leader chose to return to Afghanistan, the country where he rose to mythic status fighting the Soviets and where a Muslim fundamentalist group, the Taliban, was taking control that year. Mullah Mohammed Omar, the Taliban leader, sent word that he considered it an honor to provide protection for bin Laden, whose sacrifices for the jihad were well known. On May 18, 1996, bin Laden and his three wives, along with many of his children and 150 supporters who had trained on his Sudan bases, boarded a chartered C-130 plane, and landed several hours later in Jalalabad, near the Khyber Pass in eastern Afghanistan.

Bin Laden would settle into a virtually impenetrable stronghold, a cave tunneled into the side of a mountain to protect against air attacks. From there he could direct terror attacks with near impunity, protected by rugged mountains, hundreds of miles of desert, and an oppressive regime that welcomed him like a brother. Located above the city of Jalalabad, the cave could only be approached from a narrow ravine, and was guarded by several hundred heavily armed men. His cave was sparsely furnished, but equipped with modern laptops and a satellite phone. However, he rarely spent more than a few nights in one place, moving around with a caravan of vehicles, guarded by men with automatic, high-powered weapons—including a Stinger missile, in case of air attack. Bin Laden also renewed his relations with the powerful Pakistani Inter-Services Intelligence Agency (ISI), which had backed the Taliban following the successful war with the Soviets.

Two weeks after bin Laden flew to Afghanistan, the U.S. embassy in Saudi Arabia received word from the Saudis that the four suspects apprehended in the OPM-Sang bombing had been sentenced to death. The executions would step up the risk of reprisals from Islamic fundamentalists who had been making threats of new terrorist attacks on U.S. installations in Saudi Arabia. The Pentagon had already ordered the Defense Department to carry out detailed security reviews of its installations after the OPM attack. Now stepped-up patrols were ordered around U.S. facilities. Air-force employees living in the Khobar Towers installation in Dhahran, Saudi Arabia, pressed the Saudi civilian police to patrol the perimeters more aggressively. After all, the Khobar installation was headquarters for the air force's 4404th Air Wing. Since the Gulf War, it had enforced a no-fly zone in southern Iraq with F-15 and F-16 jet fighters, and had a battery of Patriot surface-to-air missiles.

Incredibly, the Saudis dismissed the threat of retaliation against American interests, and carried out the executions shortly after announcing them. The four newly sentenced terrorists were beheaded without the U.S. investigators ever having a chance to ask them questions. The executions only increased the already high number of threats against Americans in Saudi Arabia. But the U.S. Air Force commander in Dhahran, Brigadier General Terry Schwalier, said Saudi officials were so unconcerned about the potential for an attack that they refused to place safety barriers around the Khobar Towers, which was home to nearly half the five-thousand-member American military force in Saudi Arabia, and maintained only a paltry thirty-five-yard perimeter around the base.

The rising tensions in Saudi Arabia came as O'Neill was organizing a barbecue at the FBI's Quantico training center. Borrowing a page from his days in Baltimore, breaking bread at the annual law enforcement "Steak Out," O'Neill planned an informal session to foster good relations between the CIA and the FBI. "I referred to it as 'O'Neill's Love Fest,'" Lipka said. "But John would tell me, 'Stop it, I just want to bring the good men and women together from the CIA and FBI counterterrorism and have a little picnic and discuss working together and how much we can do.'" The picnic took place June 26, and by late morning, scores of agents from both agencies were on the fields of Quantico grilling burgers and hot dogs.

It was nearly 10 P.M. in Saudi Arabia. Staff Sergeant Alfredo Guerrero and two other air-force security policemen were on heightened alert, patrolling the roof of the eight-story Khobar Towers barracks. They had reached the northernmost corner of the roof when what appeared to be a large gasoline truck and a passenger car pulled up to the perimeter fence. The vehicle was a truck normally used to clean latrines, and for that reason, it could be driven close to the barracks without inspection, since Muslims saw it as "unclean." But this truck was filled with several thousand pounds of explosives, and its driver soon sprinted out of the truck to the waiting passenger car and sped off.

Sergeant Guerrero immediately knew it was a bomb. He and the other MPs ran into the building yelling for everyone to get out. But Guerrero only made it down two flights of stairs before an explosion four times more powerful than McVeigh's Oklahoma City bomb tore the front off the Khobar Towers and sent a scorching fireball through the crippled structure, killing nineteen American servicemen and wounding 400 other people, including 250 Americans. The bomb was the largest ever used against a U.S. target in the Middle East. Prince Bandar bin Sultan, the Saudi ambassador to the United States, visited the wounded soldiers and promised injured airman Sergeant Harold Jautakis, "We'll catch the guys who did this. And I promise you it won't be an O. J. Simpson trial."

O'Neill's love fest at Quantico turned into a sea of pinging beepers, but even when he learned of the magnitude of the Dhahran bombing, O'Neill decided to stay at the picnic. "Everyone's cooking and drinking soda and John instructs me, 'Go back to Washington. You've done this before. Get the ball rolling!'" Lipka said. O'Neill was taking the longer view, staying calm and thinking one step ahead of most people around him. He was not about to pass up the rare opportunity to make inroads with CIA agents. He finally made it back to headquarters late that afternoon.

"When he got up there, he was like a whirling dervish," Lipka said. "It was like a Steven Spielberg production."

A cadre of employees remained at headquarters two or three

days straight, deploying significant numbers of people, equipment, and communication devices to Saudi Arabia, obtaining visas, and sending waves of people and assets to the airport and off to the Arabian peninsula. Meanwhile, at the White House, President Clinton decried the attack as the work of terrorists. "I am outraged by it," he said. "The cowards who committed this murderous act must not go unpunished. Let me say this again. We will pursue this. America takes care of our own."

But despite the strong rhetoric, Clinton was not inclined to take firm action. U.S. intelligence indicated the attack might have been sponsored by Hezbollah, the Lebanon-based terror group supported by the Iranians. And since Iran had been moderating its position in recent months, the U.S. was unlikely to strike back at them. The Saudis remained inclined to resist cooperation because of their fears of being viewed as tools of the United States. "You weren't going to get the Saudis to do any work," Bryant said. "We would do the work and have to give it to them and then have to wonder if they were ever going to even share any information with us even if they cut off heads again."

The FBI deployment to the Khobar Towers site was the largest ever mounted overseas. More than a hundred agents, a handful of whom spoke Arabic, arrived in Saudi Arabia within forty-eight hours. Ray Mislock and Debby Stafford were among the first FBI supervisors dispatched from the Washington field office to the Saudi desert, where temperatures exceeded a parching 120 degrees during the day. Mislock's first reaction at seeing the blasted apartment complex was shock. There was a crater four hundred feet wide and forty feet deep in front of the building, which resembled the Murrah Building in Oklahoma City after that bomb blast. "It was the worst devastation I have ever seen, and I served in Vietnam," recalled Mislock, who went on to work for the CIA and at the White House.

The eight-story, precast-concrete building had entirely lost its outer wall. A mattress hung crazily from an upper floor, and pipes and wires were sheared and twisted. There were rows of exposed bathtubs from the top floor to the ground floor, which made the building resemble an open dollhouse. The bomb wounded people up to three-quarters of a mile away and left other buildings in the complex structurally unsound.

The conditions could not have been more difficult or oppressive for the investigators. Under doctor's orders, agents were required to drink a pint of water every fifteen minutes to avoid dehydration and heat exhaustion. Scores of agents ultimately succumbed to the conditions, given the difficulty of acclimating so quickly to the harsh change in time zone and temperature. Daytime investigations were halted after a few days, and conducted only at night, when the sun had set and the temperature dropped to a mere one hundred degrees. "In other locations, we could work twenty-hour hours a day," Mislock said. "We made a decision to stay in the barracks until nightfall."

Agents slept ten and fifteen to a room in bunk beds, and had to use bottled water for everything, including showers. The command post was set up next to a men's bathroom in a mess hall. But there were few complaints. The agents were joined by the military personnel, some bandaged from injuries, all with their fingers on the triggers of their M-16s, volunteering to sift through the sand and rubble for clues to the bombing.

"It was inspiring, seeing them," Stafford said. "They lost their buddies and best friends. The military are the walking targets. They suffer the greatest risk and in many ways it is a thankless task. But to be part of it, there is no bigger cause or motivation."

Once again, the thorny issue was the lack of Saudi cooperation. Mislock told O'Neill and Freeh that the Saudis were keeping him and his agents on an extraordinarily tight leash. Agents could not examine cars or phone records. They were barred from leaving the site. They could not interview residents in the local neighborhoods, where agents believed the attackers had taken an apartment and conducted surveillance of the Khobar Towers.

Instead they were told to interview people inside the fence at the time of the explosion, which meant only Americans. Even meetings with the powerful local regional director of the Saudi intelligence service never seemed to go anywhere.

"They were an absolute waste of time," Mislock said. "They were nice enough and promised to help and then absolutely nothing occurred. We wanted to go door-to-door in neighborhood housing to see if anyone witnessed anything. The Saudis' reasoning was that it would do no good and would be a waste of time."

The Saudis took a number of people into custody the first week after the attack, but U.S. investigators were not allowed to speak with them. Agents were forced to submit questions in writing and then patiently wait—often for days—for answers that provided little, if any, information. Mislock soon concentrated on meetings with local law enforcement and diplomatic personnel. Freeh had arranged with Saudi Crown Prince Abdullah for Mislock to meet Prince Nayef, the Saudi minister of the interior, but the session consisted of a brief U.S. request for more security at the local American school, just down the street from the embassy, and a forty-five minute monologue from Nayef.

"I had a meeting with the Prince of Darkness," Mislock recalled. "He had a circular conversation in Arabic, which essentially translated into, 'It was a dangerous world, even for kids,' and 'Don't let the door hit you in the ass on the way out.' . . . We did get some cooperation in some areas, but not the things we really wanted, such as access to suspects in ways we would expect. We all had the view that with their cooperation, we could have solved the case."

Many CIA experts believed the bombing was tied to bin Laden, primarily because he hated his native Saudi Arabia even more than he hated the United States. Bin Laden had developed his distaste for the Saudi ruling family in the early 1990s when they failed to support his efforts in Afghanistan. After the Russians were defeated and bin Laden returned home, he expected a hero's welcome. Instead he was treated as a pariah because of his harsh criticism of the royal family. Even the vast wealth and influence of bin Laden's family, which operated a behemoth global corporation, could not temper the royals' hostility toward him.

Finally, when Saddam Hussein was poised to invade Kuwait, bin Laden told the royal family and their defense minister, Prince Sultan, that "there was no need for American troops" to assist their efforts to stave off Saddam. In a letter to King Al Saud, bin Laden laid out a military strategy that involved marshaling all the Arab mujahedeen to defend the tiny Kuwait kingdom. Having beaten the Soviets, bin Laden argued that with the support of other Muslims, his hardened religious warriors could easily defeat the Iraqis, a weaker opponent.

But to bin Laden's dismay, the Saudi and Kuwaiti leaders allowed the Americans to place warships in the Gulf and troops on the ground to launch counterstrikes to liberate Kuwait. Despite the rebuff from the king and Prince Sultan, bin Laden asked Muslim religious leaders to call for a *fatwa*, a call to arms that brought thousands of soldiers to his land in Jeddah. But bin Laden was placed under virtual house arrest, to avoid such a show of force, and could not take action. The presence of U.S. personnel and warships on holy Muslim soil was another sign for bin Laden that the Saudis had made their deals with the devil.

O'Neill was not so certain that bin Laden was behind the Khobar Towers attack. He thought there were ties to Iran. The Saudis' lack of cooperation supported that belief. The Saudis feared that if the U.S. became convinced the Iranians were behind the bombing, U.S. air strikes would be launched against Iran. Such retaliation would create more unrest for the region, and particularly Saudi Arabia, which was already at risk.

Freeh decided that he, O'Neill, and other top bureau officials would visit Saudi Arabia to encourage more Saudi cooperation and support the agents toiling in the oppressive desert. Such a trip would normally be made aboard a C-130 transport, a heavy, uncomfortable military aircraft. But O'Neill, who was making his first trip outside the United States on a major terrorism investigation, used his considerable persuasiveness to convince an air-force adjutant general to lend the FBI one of its more comfortable Gulf Stream jets. Then he walked into Lipka's office to tell him he was coming along on the trip and ordered him to compile a detailed briefing book for the director on the Khobar Towers case, all within a few hours.

"I don't have time," Lipka said.

"I want it," O'Neill told him.

If O'Neill wanted it, Lipka had no choice but to stay up all night and do the work. He thought the entire exercise was a waste of time. He figured the director probably would not have time even to thumb through his briefing book. But he was wrong. The Gulf Stream flew Freeh, O'Neill, Bryant, and Lipka to Gander, Newfoundland, and then Ramstein, Germany, where the crew had to rest overnight. O'Neill insisted that another crew take over for them. "John told them the FBI had to keep going," Lipka said. The FBI contingent showered, boarded the jet with a fresh crew, and flew off to Cairo, with Freeh and Bryant in the front discussing Lipka's briefing book with its highlighted sections and notes in the margin.

"I had a similar feeling when we briefed O'Neill in the VAAP-CON case," Lipka said. "It was visionary of O'Neill that he wanted the briefing book, and he had no qualms about asking someone to stay up all night because it was exactly what we needed."

The Gulf Stream arrived at night in Dhahran. Mislock and Stafford were on the tarmac waiting to greet the director and the FBI hierarchy. The plan called for Freeh, O'Neill, and the others to visit the troops and then survey the charred crime scene with its mountains of rubble. After that, Freeh and the others would seek a meeting with the King Abdullah and his top aides on the issue of cooperation.

Mislock had warned O'Neill and the others to dress appropriately for the desert. Yet the five FBI officials came off the plane in suits, which were in stark contrast to the fatigues the agents at the scene wore. Lipka remembers being hit with a furnacelike blast of heat as they left the jet. "When I walked down the steps I was instantly soaked in sweat," he said.

O'Neill and Freeh traveled to the dusty, parched crime scene, which took on an eerie glow under klieg lights that resembled those of a movie set. Freeh's agents were wearing borrowed clothes, while the two bureau officials were still in suits and ties. Freeh, followed by O'Neill, walked down the line of agents, shaking hands along the way. The director recognized some agents from the Washington field office and headquarters. So did O'Neill. He spotted his friend Michael Brooks, the six-foot-six D.C. metro cop assigned to the joint terrorist task force. There was no handshake when O'Neill reached Brooks. Instead, O'Neill threw his arms around the tall cop and gave him a trademark bear hug and slap on the back and said, "How you doing, Brooksie?"

"John and the director paid a visit under horrific conditions at a horrific terrorist act and it meant a lot to the agents and to the people who had lost friends," Stafford said. "Their reaction to the devastation was similar to everyone else's. You're looking at a building with the face torn off and you're wondering why this could not have been prevented. They wanted to make sure we had what we needed, about intelligence, and they wanted to see what else they needed to do."

Freeh addressed his troops, extolling the value of their work and his appreciation of their dangerous assignment, and then went off for a status briefing at the command post next to the men's room. He and O'Neill soon got their first taste of the sloth-like Saudis' response to the investigation. The Saudis conduct business at night, which meant the FBI brass had to cool their heels at their hotel waiting for word that the Saudis were finally available. The call never came before 11 P.M., and the Saudi participants were rarely officials of high rank. "If we were lucky, we saw the hierarchy," said Bryant. "We called the meetings 'death marches.'"

The Khobar Towers were located in an eastern province near Kuwait. During the summer, the king remains in the north at his summer palace in Jeddah. Freeh flew to Jeddah seeking a meeting with the king, but never got to see him. "I don't think anyone gets to see the king," Mislock said. "It was a typical Saudi deal. You show up at ten P.M. or midnight and wait and wait and wait and then they tell you he is not available. This was not 'dissing Louie.' This is the way they do business."

"We tried very hard to get through to them," Bryant said. "There was O'Neill, liaison-building with the Saudi intelligence and military. He was not sweating. He looked good. No question about it. A class act. But we did not make much headway. The Saudis were concerned about the politics with Syria and Iran. They were afraid of how the population would react and the negative publicity."

John Lewis said the bureau felt handcuffed by the Saudis. "When you look at it, what are our options? Sanctions, covert action, diplomacy, law enforcement, and military. All too often the administration would take a law enforcement response because they could simply say they would bring criminals and terrorists to justice. But you have to have a big stick on the diplomatic side to get things done."

Despite the Saudi obstructionism, Freeh's visit to the devastated Khobar Towers left an indelible mark on him. Perhaps his instincts told him the case could be solved. Until the day he retired from the FBI, Freeh was consumed with trying to find justice in the rubble of Dhahran. He flew back from Saudi Arabia five days after leaving Washington without seeing the king and without obtaining a promise of tangible cooperation, but said on the flight home that he was hopeful they had made headway with the Saudis. O'Neill was less optimistic, and told Freeh what he thought. But despite claims that he told the director, "They were blowing smoke up our ass," a lifetime FBI man like O'Neill would never be that disrespectful to Freeh or any FBI director.

O'Neill's experience with the Saudis taught him a number of immediate lessons. First, he and Freeh decided to expand the FBI's legal attaché program in the Middle East beyond Saudi Arabia, where they had a Muslim agent permanently stationed, and beyond France, Britain, and Israel to a host of new nations, including Jordan, Pakistan, Turkey, and the Philippines. A legal attaché was in a unique position to develop close ties with counterparts in their host country and was available to fly elsewhere in a region in an emergency to establish an immediate FBI presence. Beyond that, he reached out to anyone with ideas who might be able to help formulate new strategies, the way he had done when he turned the *Mod Squad* doorman in Baltimore into an informant and when he developed strategies in Chicago that took down the murderous drug gangs. He began to discuss the establishment of a global database for storing and sharing information about bombings anywhere in the world.

"John realized we needed to offer our resources to non-U.S. agencies to develop and share critical forensic information to enhance our intelligence base," Lipka said. "He suggested the FBI and other foreign services store evidence collected at various bombings in a vast data bank for all law enforcement to share to find commonalities among events."

Freeh decided the FBI brass should return to Saudi Arabia for another face-to-face attempt to win the kind of assistance they really required. Freeh had met with the families of some of the victims of the Khobar Towers blast, and he refused to let the investigation drop. He ordered O'Neill back to Dhahran, but the trip was not as comfortable as when Freeh accompanied them. They flew on a C-130, with web-type seats and loud roaring motors that nearly shattered their eardrums. The food was precooked lasagna for which the FBI had to reimburse the military.

Once in Saudi Arabia, O'Neill found it a heady experience being the highest-ranking FBI official there. He stayed three days, conducting a whirl of meetings and dinners, but only achieved modest concessions from his Saudi counterparts, who finally agreed to accept questions in writing from the U.S. investigators and then respond with answers. "We would never get detailed answers, just summaries," Lewis said. "They had a tendency to give conclusions about interviews in writing, without telling us how they got from point A to point B, which was helpful for our understanding, but useless in the event of a prosecution." It would be months before the Saudis allowed FBI agents to inspect the car they believed was used by the bombers to make their escape.

From his fortress in Afghanistan, bin Laden praised the attack and exulted in the killings. "Only Americans were killed in the explosions," he said. "No Saudi citizen suffered any injury. When I got the news about these blasts, I was very happy. This was a noble act. This was a great honor, but unfortunately, I did not conduct these explosions personally. But I would like to say to the Saudi people that they should adopt every tactic to throw the Americans out of Saudi territory."

The frustrating trips to Saudi Arabia left O'Neill with a sinking feeling, which he finally identified years later. "Do you know what's wrong with this whole terrorism thing with the Saudis?" he asked his friend John Blaha. "It's one word: *oil*. The diplomacy is controlled by oil." To another colleague, Mark Rossini, he added that U.S. policy should not be held hostage by the gyrations of the oil markets. "If we just had a policy of saying, 'How much do you want for a barrel of oil?' and not get involved in the politics of every country, we would be much better off," he said.

For the next five years, O'Neill and Freeh would both be obsessed with trying to convince the Saudis to help bring the Khobar Towers bombers to justice. Freeh was even more consumed with the case than O'Neill. Then, Hani Al-Sayegh, an alleged participant in the attack and a prominent member of

Saudi Hezbollah, was arrested in Canada in September 1997. He quickly agreed to cooperate with American authorities. But the deal fell through and he was ultimately deported to Saudi Arabia, leaving Freeh angry with the office of the U.S. attorney in Washington, who was overseeing the case. In 1998, Freeh reluctantly gave the order to pull out all of his agents with the exception of his lone legal attaché and liaison to the Saudis. Frustrated with Clinton and the White House's inability to focus on convincing the Saudis to cooperate with the FBI, Freeh contacted former President George H. W. Bush, who enjoyed a strong relationship with Crown Prince Abdullah because of the U.S. role in the Gulf War in 1991. Then in November 1998, Freeh arranged a meeting with Crown Prince Abdullah when the Saudi leader visited the United States. Finally there was a breakthrough to get access to information the Saudis had obtained in the Khobar Towers case.

Freeh's détente with the Saudis, and O'Neill's own growing relations, finally paid off. FBI agents were permitted to directly witness interviews with a handful of bombing suspects held in Saudi prisons, and on June 21, 2001, a day before Freeh stepped down as FBI director, a federal grand jury in Virginia indicted fourteen militants, thirteen of them Saudi and one Lebanese, and charged them with the June 1996 murders of the nineteen American airmen at the Khobar Towers. The complete list of suspects, eleven of whom are in Saudi jails, and evidence of their possible links to foreign governments, had been kept under seal, although the opening page of the indictment states the groups behind the bombing "were inspired, supported, and directed by elements of the Iranian government."

Factions of the royal Saudi family attacked the indictments. Saudi defense minister Prince Sultan, a brother of Saudi leader King Fahd, sharply rebuked the U.S., saying "only Saudi Arabia has the right" to prosecute the case. Iranian officials denied any involvement in the bombing. It remains unclear despite Freeh, O'Neill, and the FBI's efforts, if any of the eleven suspects being held in Saudi jails will ever be tried in an American court.

DOMESTIC TROUBLES AND FOREIGN AFFAIRS

O'Neill, then the head of the FBI Counterterrorism Division at headquarters in Washington, D.C., with Director Freeh and Special Agent Kenneth Maxwell amid the collected remains of TWA Flight 800, which exploded shortly after takeoff from JFK International Airport in New York City on July 17, 1995.

8

SILENCING THE CRITICS

The summer of 1996 was an uneasy time. In New York City, concerns about a terrorist attack were extremely high. The FBI and the U.S. Marshals Service established security zones with concrete barricades around the federal courthouse, where a jury was in the process of being selected for the trial of Ramzi Yousef in the 1993 World Trade Center bombing and charges stemming from the Bojinka plot to blow up a dozen American commercial airliners. Arabic newspapers abroad and in the United States were filled with unusually vitriolic anti-American sentiment.

"They were basically saying, 'We're going to get you, you scum. You will be shocked. It will bring you to your knees. It will be horrendous,'" recalled James Kallstrom, then the head of the FBI's flagship office in New York.

O'Neill was engaged in efforts to map out security strategies for the upcoming Olympics in Atlanta, in addition to his hefty responsibilities in the Khobar Towers investigation. On July 17, at 8:45 P.M., O'Neill was dining with Lipka in one of his favorite Italian restaurants in Georgetown when both of their pagers went off. A jet had exploded shortly after takeoff from JFK Airport and, in a ball of flames seen for miles, plunged into the sea off the southern coast of Long Island. All 230 passengers and crew aboard doomed fight TWA 800 were missing and presumed dead.

FBI agent Lewis Schiliro, then the head of New York's criminal division, was in a hospital emergency room attending to his son, who had been injured playing baseball. Schiliro lived on Long Island and was less than fifteen miles from the crash site, and he was the first FBI agent to reach the scene. The sight of the burning wreckage spread across hundreds of square miles of ocean would haunt him forever. "It was one of the most incredible nights of my life," said Schiliro.

Sal Emilio, an ATF agent on the joint terrorist task force, was leaving a cousin's funeral on Long Island when he heard about the crash from the head of his office, Jack Ballast. Emilio raced from the cemetery to the crash scene, where he joined agents collecting debris from the private boats that were combing the water, looking for survivors. "CNN had hired an old landing craft from World War Two, where the front opens and troops come out," he said. "A car pulled out and they started collecting pictures. They lied about being a search boat. We immediately commandeered a coast-guard boat to inspect any boats to prevent any media boats from coming close."

Thomas Pickard, the special agent in charge of the New York office's national security division, was at home when he received a call from the command post that a plane had disappeared. "This just doesn't happen," the FBI duty officer quoted his counterparts at the FAA as saying. Pickard's next call was to O'Neill, who had already left the restaurant and returned to his office, where he was pushing for answers and lining up scuba teams, heavy salvage equipment, and manpower to be sent to New York. Schiliro said he was barely on board a helicopter to view the disaster and O'Neill was already dispatching computer technicians, metallurgists, and rescue teams to Long Island. "I was amazed to see his ability to get it organized," Schiliro said.

Initial speculation focused on the possibility that a bomb smuggled onto the plane had caused the explosion. But nothing was ruled out, and rumors were rampant that a Stinger missile had brought down the plane. "We needed more information on missiles," Pickard said. "Were there any subs in the area? Some people thought the military was doing exercises. We wanted to lock down all manifests, toll telephone records, all flights within twenty-four hours, boats, military, what people saw on the beaches, was anything suspicious or anything in the wreckage, what kind of missile could do this, if any."

The FAA initially reported spotting a radar blip on their tapes that indicated there was another plane or projectile near TWA Flight 800 when it exploded. "Our initial feelings were, 'Aha, something ran into the plane or a missile ran up from the ground,'" recalled George Andrew, who was working for Pickard as the ASAC for counterterrorism in New York. But the FAA needed a couple of days to study the tapes to ensure it was not a false-positive reading.

The following day, O'Neill sat silently in his office in Washington, listening as the FAA dropped a bombshell during its conference call with the FBI. There was no blip. There were no missiles picked up on the JFK scanners. "All of sudden they came back and said there was nothing, that it was an anomaly," Andrew recalled.

"How can that be?" Kallstrom demanded during the conference call. He was a former Marine commander with as bluff a manner as O'Neill's. "One day you say there is something and now there is nothing there?"

But none of the FBI men on the call knew enough about radar to dispute the FAA's account. As they sat in near disbelief, wondering what their next step would be, O'Neill's baritone voice weighed in with a solution that might allay some of the bureau's concerns. "I'll tell you what," he said. "I'll put together all the federal agencies that have any intelligence radar in that area that night. Let's see what their technicians come up with and what's on their various monitoring systems."

O'Neill told the others on the call that he would get back to them shortly after calling various agencies. The others were impressed but skeptical. "O'Neill's idea was brilliant," Andrew said. "But what an undertaking, assembling every agency and their electronic information!"

O'Neill was back in touch with the others within a few hours, announcing that he had contacted every agency linked to the investigation, and set up a meeting forty-eight hours later in Washington. "I'll have them assembled and, George, you brief them and we'll see what they can bring to the table," O'Neill said.

Andrew caught the shuttle to Washington two days later. "Sure enough, I met John at headquarters and we went over to the FAA and there were tech people from every agency I can name," he said. Andrew told the experts what the FBI knew, and what they needed to explain, including the fact that witnesses reported seeing a streak of light heading up in the sky rather than down. Those puzzling accounts would lead to even more outlandish speculation that O'Neill and the FBI would later have to quell.

The FAA began by trying to explain that anomalies are routine and inevitable. They said that "somewhere between raw data and light on a screen there can be what they call 'noise,' and that is where you get the anomaly," Andrew recalled.

In addition to having federal agencies attend the summit, O'Neill also convinced private-sector companies like Sikorsky Aviation Corporation, the helicopter manufacturer that is now a subsidiary of the United Technology Company, to contribute its radar reports from the time period when Flight 800 went down. It also showed nothing unusual. "I was so impressed with John," Andrew said. More important, so was Kallstrom.

The hard-charging head of the New York office had barely heard O'Neill's name before the initial TWA 800 conference call, but he knew he liked O'Neill's action-oriented, problem-solving style. "Once he saw that John could do something like that, he and John became inseparable," Andrew recalled. "He went to John directly after that, a lot."

Thomas Corrigan, a New York City Police Department detective who served on the joint terrorist task force and was an original member of the Al Qaeda squad, became the lead investigator on the TWA Flight 800 investigation. As the months of arduous recovery and investigative work continued, the FBI and the other agencies involved in investigating the disaster had accomplished two major feats.

Using scuba divers and military dredging ships to comb the murky ocean water, the FBI recovered more than 90 percent of the huge 747, and reassembled every piece—all 100,250 pounds of metal and wire—on a giant steel skeleton frame they had built inside a hangar at the Calverton Airport in Suffolk County on Long Island. Forensic experts trained in ballistics and explosives pored over every inch of the sprawling metal carcass looking for clues to the cause of the crash. They swabbed for residue of explosive materials and checked for shrapnel strafing marks on the fuselage, luggage compartments, overhead racks, toilet seats, and even the clothing dragged form the murky, often turbulent waters.

All the evidence pointed away from a bomb or a criminal act and toward a mechanical disaster as the cause of the explosion—specifically toward a spark from the hundreds of miles of wires running through the giant plane that might have ignited a combustible pocket of fumes collected in the fuel tank. There was even an explanation for the troubling witness accounts of seeing flames ascending in the sky. O'Neill and Pickard believed the blast caused the jet to split into two pieces. The smaller piece—the cockpit—descended, but the rest of the plane continued to thrust higher into the sky, trailed by flaming fuel as it climbed, creating the illusion of an ascending fiery missile.

The challenge was finding a way to demonstrate the point conclusively for skeptics, and O'Neill again had a solution: he persuaded the CIA to do a video simulation of his scenario. The CIA's intricate simulation clearly explained what the civilians along the beach had really seen when they thought they were seeing a missile hitting a plane. Yet despite the vast investigative effort, the thousands of manpower hours, and the reconstruction of the doomed jet that eliminated any conceivable possibilities of foul play, there remained a small but vocal chorus of disbelievers.

Pierre Salinger, President John F. Kennedy's former press secretary, was now a rogue television commentator for ABC-TV from his home in Paris. His time working with Kennedy gave him stature and credibility, and when he became a vocal conspiracy theorist and insisted terrorists had brought down TWA Flight 800, his charges resonated with the public. Worse, rumors soon circulated on the Internet that a former American Airlines pilot claimed that he had seen a missile fired from the USS *Normandy* at the TWA plane. Salinger's insistent fear mongering would prove to be a complication that O'Neill would have to address before the FBI and the Justice Department could convince an anxious American public that the jet had in fact suffered a catastrophic accident.

The TWA 800 investigation was the largest since the Oklahoma City bombing case, and developments were prominently featured on the nightly news and in daily newspapers from the time the jet went down on July 17. But O'Neill's attention was not focused solely on that case. Agents continued to sift through the desert in Dhahran looking for clues in the Khobar Towers case. And there were even more disturbing developments taking place in Afghanistan that went largely ignored by the American government and the public at large, but not by O'Neill.

Bin Laden had stepped up his operations soon after arriving in Afghanistan, and spread the word that he was offering money for room and board for recruits and their families who traveled to Afghanistan for training in jihad. Hundreds upon hundreds of Islamic fundamentalists flocked to his training camps from around the Middle East, and bin Laden soon issued his first "declaration of war" against the United States, calling for a "holy war" to expel American forces from the Arabian peninsula. He condemned U.S. policy from the time of President Franklin D. Roosevelt onward in his twelve-page document, "The Declaration of Places," issued on August 23, 1996, "from the peaks of the Hindu Kush, Afghanistan."

"Expel the heretics from the Arabian Peninsula," he urged. "The Muslims have realized they are the main target of the aggression of the coalition of the Jews and the Crusaders. The latest of these assaults is the greatest disaster since the death of Prophet Muhammad, the occupation of the country of the two sacred mosques—the home ground of Islam. Our Muslim brothers throughout the world, your brothers in the country of the two sacred places and in Palestine request your support. They are asking you to participate with them against their enemies, who are also your enemies—the Israelis and the Americans—by causing them as much harm as can be possibly achieved."

Bin Laden's rhetoric would quickly grow even more threatening. He would broaden this threat to include all Americans, not only those in the military and those who worked at U.S. foreign offices or embassies in the Middle East. In November, bin Laden told an Arab newspaper reporter that Arabs affiliated with his Al Qaeda network were involved in the killing of American troops in Somalia in 1993. It was the first time that a clear connection had been made between bin Laden and the "Black Hawk Down" incident, as it came to be known.

The boasts dovetailed with information the FBI and prosecutors in New York had gleaned from Jamal al-Fadl, a top Al Qaeda insider who had recently defected. Al-Fadl, a native of the Sudan, had immigrated to New York, studied in the Al-Khifah Refugee Service office in Brooklyn, and raised money for bin Laden before heading off to Afghanistan to fight against the Soviets. He eventually became a founding member of Al Qaeda and a confidant of bin Laden's inner circle, which included Dr. Ayman al-Zawahiri, the head of the Egyptian Islamic Group, and Blind Sheikh Rahman's son. Eventually, al-Fadl became close to bin Laden himself. He was entrusted with the important job of preparing for bin

Laden's move to the Sudan in 1991, and was sent ahead to find living quarters for bin Laden and his followers and farmland on which they could train.

Al-Fadl later was in charge of administration and payroll for Al Qaeda, and worked under bin Laden's private secretary in a Khartoum town house. He also screened the veteran mujahedeen who streamed into Sudan seeking bin Laden. In June 1996, al-Fadl entered the U.S. embassy in Asmara, the capital of Eritrea, and whispered to a clerk that he had vital information about threats against American interests. His motivation was unclear. Although he had stolen hundreds of thousands of dollars from bin Laden, he claimed his break with Al Qaeda was made on ideological grounds.

Al-Fadl outlined bin Laden's vast holdings. He described Al Qaeda's dizzying array of members and its sophisticated relationships with other terrorist organizations throughout the Middle East. He talked about bin Laden's desire to attack America, and to obtain uranium to produce nuclear weapons. He also confirmed bin Laden's purported role in the Black Hawk Down incident in Somalia. Al-Fadl was debriefed for months by the CIA and then the FBI and placed in the Witness Protection Program. A secret grand jury sitting in the Manhattan Federal Court would soon indict bin Laden and a host of other terrorists, largely on the strength of al-Fadl's testimony about the killing of U.S soldiers in Somalia.

O'Neill always had an eye on moving up the FBI ladder, and always viewed it as his destiny to take over one of top jobs in the bureau. He started talking about taking a job as a special agent in charge heading up a field office somewhere around the country. Six such jobs were opening up, and the position was considered a prerequisite for higher promotion. O'Neill liked the idea of living in sunny Tampa, near golf courses where the lefty-swinging duffer could play the only sport he still enjoyed.

But by coincidence, the top job at the Washington field office became available—and Freeh selected Pickard, which created an opening in New York for a special agent in charge of the national security division. O'Neill, the head of counterterrorism at headquarters, was the natural replacement. Freeh was already a fan of O'Neill's, and Pickard recommended him to Kallstrom to succeed him. Kallstrom had been impressed with O'Neill's work, especially in the TWA case, and jumped at the chance to add O'Neill and his problem-solving energy to the team.

"What I liked about John was . . . he was emotionally engaged in the work he was doing," Kallstrom said. "He read, he absorbed, and he knew his stuff and did not have to delegate to get the answers. If you called him in the morning and asked him about something, he would get back with an answer by the end of the day. That was John O'Neill. He was a cut above everyone. He wanted to satisfy, sometimes to a fault."

Despite the glamour of New York, many federal agents actually do not want to work there. Apartments are expensive, and the cost of living is high. Federal agents on modest government salaries often live far out in the suburbs and face a long, difficult commute. Generally they cannot take full advantage of a city where theater tickets can run a hundred dollars a seat and a hot dog and beer at a Yankee or Mets game costs fifteen dollars. Most agents come from small cities and towns, and assignment to other field offices seems more comfortable. "There weren't many people who wanted to come to New York," said Neil Herman, then the joint terrorist task force supervisor.

O'Neill was different. He frequently told colleagues he would never have considered his career complete had he not worked in the Big Apple. If joining the FBI had been his boyhood dream in Atlantic City, this assignment to New York was the fulfillment of the adult dream he had harbored since becoming an agent:

becoming the head of the FBI's flagship office. He loved the idea of working for Kallstrom, but he also knew that Kallstrom was nearing retirement age. O'Neill privately hoped to replace him. "He had a fire for what he was doing," Kallstrom said. "I knew he would instantly take control and there would be a smooth transition [with Pickard]." O'Neill was also pleased to return to what he did best, which was working in the field on investigations, away from the office politics at headquarters, where his bluff style had bruised egos and made him enemies.

An excited O'Neill telephoned James in Chicago to give her the great news.

"Hey, babe," he said. "New York came through. I'm going to New York."

Since their Chicago days, their plan had always been for her to join him in New York. "Babe," O'Neill said, "I promise you the Chicago days," meaning they would again be together as a couple. James was just as pleased. "I'm coming, too," she said.

O'Neill ran out and starting getting copies of all the New York newspapers and magazines such as *Time Out* listing restaurants and goings-on. He pored over them for weeks in anticipation of his move, just as he had when he was promoted to Chicago.

"He was so excited to get out of D.C. and to be his own person again in the field," James said. "Headquarters had aged him."

Mary Lynn Stevens was pleased for O'Neill, but she saw the transfer as just another career move. "It didn't matter to me," she said. "The long-term plan was still in effect, that nothing was going to happen until he retired. He knew I would never follow him unless we were married. And I had a very full life. I was always out, going on vacations, trips, and I had a lot of friends. I have a season subscription to the opera, season tickets to the Washington Redskin football games, and do a magnificent tailgate. I golf, garden, and cook. I did not miss out at all."

Anna DiBattista was less easily placated. He had talked about marriage with her, and had told their friends he was "going to bring Anna with me," even though DiBattista was never as enamored of New York life as O'Neill was. "We used to fight about that all the time," she said. "I just was not impressed with all that, and he hated that."

The week before Christmas, DiBattista helped him pack up his old apartment and office. He insisted on taking his plants with him to New York. "One was six feet tall," she said. "He was a kook about his plants. He always had fresh flowers. He loved tulips." That weekend, they drove a rented van filled with his office belongings to New York, stopping along the way at a Baltimore sandwich shop O'Neill loved, then returning later to Baltimore that night after she helped unpack O'Neill's effects in his new office at 26 Federal Plaza in Manhattan.

O'Neill, as an only child, generally spent Christmas Day with his parents, which had helped him avoid conflicts about where and with whom he would spend the holiday. He would drive to Atlantic City to visit his parents and drive back that evening. James recalled that "he would take them out for dinner and they would sometimes bicker back and forth. But he would go to make a nice day of it."

On Christmas Day in 1996, O'Neill stayed with DiBattista at her brother's home in Washington. He left Washington for good the following day. DiBattista, who was in the travel business, had arranged a room for O'Neill in the Suites Hotel in Gramercy Park. "John was saying he could not stand to leave me," DiBattista said. "He was insisting, 'You have to come up for the weekend.' He was emphatic."

To those who knew him at FBI headquarters, the prospect of O'Neill "going operational" and working and playing harder in New York than he had in Washington seemed unfathomable, if not outright life-threatening. "The question was not whether John was ready for New York, the question was whether New York was ready for John," said Joe Billy, who would be O'Neill's deputy in New York.

Giblin said O'Neill would go out for the evening and then come back to work, make a peanut-butter-and-jelly sandwich, and fire off e-mails until 2:30 A.M. "When we were in the command center, he would literally be there all day, leave for no more than three or four hours, shower, and come back in a clean suit," Lipka said. "He was always focused on solving the case. He would walk by and he would ask people, 'Have you solved the case?' and I would say, 'Sir, I'm working on it,' and he would repeat, 'Solve the case, solve the case.' I think his work ethic, and aggressive, forward-leaning style, rubbed some people the wrong way. It may have made some people jealous."

Most agents were drawn to O'Neill because of the passion and energy he devoted to his job while still finding the time to meet with families of victims and network socially with dignitaries and foreign law enforcement officials in the United States and overseas. "I once said to him, 'You are a manager and a leader, and you might be dressed in Gucci shoes, but I would go through a door with you,'" Lipka recalled.

Lipka believed that trying to keep up with O'Neill could be dangerous to his health. "John once came back from having an upper and lower GI, and the doctors said he had to return the next day. Instead, there was some counterterrorism threat and he went to work. I told him he should not have come in. 'Don't worry about it, I will be okay,' O'Neill said." O'Neill's laserlike focus on his work prevented him from allowing any health issue to come first if it was anything short of life-threatening.

Mike Rolince, then assistant special agent in charge of the counter intelligence and counterterrorism programs in Washington, could not imagine O'Neill surviving the even more accelerated pace of New York. "There was one day during a crisis he just got so sick he literally crawled to an elevator, got to his car, and checked himself into George Washington Hospital with exhaustion," he said. "He stayed two days and was pumped with fluids and then he was back at work."

Everyone wondered when O'Neill slept. Lipka thought O'Neill was something of a vampire. "I don't know when you sleep," he told O'Neill.

"What do you mean?" the perplexed O'Neill demanded.

"You must be a bat sleeping in a corner for a few hours, and come down in a clean suit," Lipka explained.

"Sleep?" O'Neill replied. "You sleep when you are dead."

9

O'NEILL TAKES MANHATTAN

What's the point of being sheriff if you can't own the town?
—JOHN O'NEILL

O'Neill drove his 1991 Buick Regal from the nation's capital to his new city on the day after Christmas, 1996. About ten miles outside of New York, as he reached the Meadowlands Stadium in Rutherford, New Jersey, where the Giants play, O'Neill could see the outline of New York's stunning skyline. The Twin Towers loomed like enormous signposts telling visitors they had "arrived." O'Neill drove into Lower Manhattan through the Holland Tunnel, which was one of the landmarks Blind Sheikh Rahman had plotted to destroy in June 1993, hoping to kill thousands in the ensuing flood. O'Neill could not help but notice how vulnerable the tunnel remained.

As he did when he arrived for his postings in Chicago and Washington, O'Neill headed straight to his office at FBI headquarters near the World Trade Center rather than check into the hotel room DiBattista had arranged. Once inside the twenty-eight-story federal building, O'Neill took the elevator to a maximum-security section of the twenty-sixth floor that housed the FBI's operations center. The floor was reserved for agents working on highly classified foreign counterintelligence and spy operations. There, in the northeast corner of the building, was his new office.

O'Neill's new title was special agent in charge of the national security division, the second-largest branch in the office, with about four hundred agents under his command. The position not only made him accountable for the office's counterterrorist squads that track radicals and fanatics around the world. His domain also included those highly classified espionage and counterintelligence agents whose mission was protecting U.S. assets from being compromised by foreign operatives while also trying to penetrate the secrets of America's enemies.

Through his large windows, a dazzling view of Manhattan stretched out. Skyscrapers and high-rise apartment buildings appeared as miniature pieces on a real-life urban Monopoly board. O'Neill could see as far north as Harlem, past the Empire State Building and Central Park. Chinatown and Little Italy were nearby, and then the East River, and Brooklyn visible on the other side. If he stood in the right spot in his office and peered up Broadway, he could see One Times Square, the crossroads of the world. Looking west, he saw the Hudson River, and the New Jersey Palisades on the other side, reminding visitors of the famous Steinberg *New Yorker* magazine drawing of New York City, where the Hudson River marks the end of the Big Apple, and everything else on the American horizon appears to be an undefined, colorless canvas.

Since O'Neill was already married to the FBI, New York could be only another paramour, but arguably as intoxicating and alluring as any he had before. It was home to nearly eight million people, thousands of restaurants and bars, hundreds of museums and theaters, and Wall Street with its corporate headquarters, the United Nations, 317 consulates and embassies, nine thousand dignitaries and diplomats, and far more espionage, spying, and foreign counterintelligence activity, if possible, than in the nation's capital. Just as O'Neill loved placing his arms around a friend and giving them his patented bear hug, he threw his arms around the greatest urban metropolis in the world as though she were a gorgeous siren calling his name. He hit jazz joints, the opera, restaurants, and top-shelf saloons filled with celebrities, politicians, and high-rollers all over town. There was First on

First in the East Village, Arté's in Greenwich Village, Saluté and Bruno in Midtown, Elaine's on the Upper East Side, Cité, Kennedy's, and the top of the Rainbow Room on the West Side, and finally Windows on the World atop the World Trade Center.

" 'New York! New York!' So nice they named it twice," he would later exult. "There aren't millionaires here, there are billionaires."

O'Neill decorated his office with a plum-colored upholstered sofa, a coffee table adorned with fresh tulips and art books, and an Impressionist-style painting of the U.S. flag. There was a large credenza for the knickknacks and plaques he had collected from around the world. His large bureau desk was positioned in the corner opposite the door, with his back facing two vast floor-to-ceiling windows that allowed the city to serve as his backdrop.

When he first arrived in New York, O'Neill stayed at the Beekman Hotel—he had yet to befriend the management of the Plaza Hotel—and then moved to an FBI safe house on the East Side. In typical O'Neill fashion, when he started looking for an apartment, he scouted pricey Park Avenue, where rents were the size of his monthly pay stub. He settled instead into a small two-bedroom, one-bathroom apartment in Stuyvesant Town, a complex without air-conditioning that was built for soldiers returning from World War II. Nearby Peter Cooper Village, built for returning military officers, had larger rooms, so he eventually moved there when another two-bedroom opened eighteen months later.

Joe Cantemessa, a special operations expert working on the TWA 800 investigation, installed a separate, super-secure telephone line in O'Neill's Stuyvesant Town apartment—a Stew III security phone unit with top-secret cryptographic features that enabled him to have classified conversations over regular phone lines. The additional phone, which required a key to operate, also offered him privacy when he wanted to make calls that were strictly personal. To decorate the apartment, O'Neill once again chose very basic furniture. Paradoxically, for someone so fussy about his grooming and clothing, O'Neill took little interest in where he lived, so long as it was neat and presentable. After all, he knew he would spend almost all his time at work or out on the town.

John P. O'Neill had arrived. He dumped his Rolodex on the desk of his secretary, Lorraine Di Taranto, on one of his first official days, and handed her a list of people he wanted to meet "ASAP": the mayor, the police commissioner, the fire commissioner, the cardinal, Archbishop John O'Connor, who became a great friend, and a host of other dignitaries and diplomats. He would soon be on intimate terms with movie stars, politicians, journalists, and what some detractors called "the Elaine's crowd," a cozy cross section of New York among whom many government officials worried about news leaks and erroneously laid the blame for them on O'Neill. "I did not like hearing the Elaine's talk," Mary Jo White, then the U.S attorney for the Southern District in New York, acknowledged. "We faceless, nameless government people worry about things being said."

The first people O'Neill insisted on meeting, however, were the agents and NYPD detectives who would be working for him. John told "his people" he understood their sacrifice in New York and that he had always felt his career would never be complete without a stint at the NYC headquarters. "He said unless he spent time in New York, it was as though he would not have experienced the real FBI," said Joseph Billy, then O'Neill's assistant in charge. "He made a point of making that known to his people, that he lived in the city, where everything was happening, while most people bailed out to Connecticut or Pennsylvania. And I was astounded how quickly he took to it."

O'Neill would have it no other way.

"John hit the town with tremendous energy," Billy said. "There was no doubt that after six months he would be part of the fabric of the town and a real New Yorker."

O'Neill immediately began to reach out to various facets of

law enforcement, the intelligence community, and the political side of New York, just as he had done in Baltimore, Chicago, Washington, and overseas. "John O'Neill was about opening doors," Billy said. "He worked twenty-four hours a day. He was tireless. He worked it, and worked it."

Always aware of the "power people" he needed to know, O'Neill believed few were more pivotal to his success in New York than Mary Jo White, who held the office that was arguably the most visible and the most coveted by federal prosecutors. In fact, the Southern District did not cover as large a geographic territory as other offices, including their counterpart across the East River in the Brooklyn-based Eastern District, which covered Long Island and Puerto Rico. In fact, White's jurisdiction did include the Bronx and two counties north of the city. But what made her office so important was the fact it encompassed Manhattan, which seemed to have a connection to virtually every case around the world, and was certainly connected to cases involving both terrorism and espionage.

O'Neill knew White held sway not only with Attorney General Janet Reno, but also with President Clinton. He recalled attending the Rose Garden signing of Presidential Decision Directive 39 in June 1995 that gave the FBI direct authority over terrorist cases. He saw Clinton and Reno emerge from inside the White House accompanied by White, whose office had prosecuted the World Trade Center bombers, Blind Sheikh Rahman and Ramzi Yousef.

O'Neill made one of his first courtesy calls to the diminutive but powerful Manhattan U.S. attorney. "We are joined at the hip," O'Neill assured her. "I will do everything I can to work with you."

"You could almost see it on his face," White remembered. "He wanted to get to know me personally to make the relationship work. We were certainly united in the main mission, which was counterterrorism. John had worked in headquarters with terrorism, building contacts all around the world, and building a coalition to call upon when he needed them to combat a terror plot or gather evidence for a prosecution."

O'Neill brought his extraordinary connections to New York, and then continued to expand his Rolodex as he widened his professional and social circles. He led a steady parade of officials from around the world through White's office in order for everyone to know one another in the event someone needed help. "I think you see the fruits of that still today in a very positive way," White said. "The world coalition in this war against terrorism is the single-most-important thing we have going for us. John O'Neill, probably more than anyone else, built that."

White also liked O'Neill's style. The FBI official standard uniform was a bland dark suit, white shirt, and a plain dark tie, and O'Neill stood out with his manicured nails, silk ties, sharply tailored suits, and expensive leather shoes with tassels. White thought O'Neill was the most polished agent she had seen since Kenneth Walton, the former deputy assistant director, graced the halls of 26 Federal Plaza in custom-made clothes, cuff-linked shirts, and perfectly coiffed blond hair in the early 1980s. "You could see right away that O'Neill was unique," she said.

O'Neill had the good sense to make the Muslim community one of his initial points of contact after arriving in New York in 1997, long before outreach to their neighborhoods was seen as standard. Billy recalled that O'Neill asked for a list of mosques and their leaders, sheikhs, clerics, and holy imams, and then traveled to Brooklyn and Queens regularly to meet with them. He said the FBI was there to help them, not persecute them, in case of a criminal act committed by a few fanatics. "I think it was phenomenal how he would reach out to the Muslim community," Billy said. "We attended prayer services with senior leaders at the Islamic centers shortly after he arrived."

O'Neill's reputation preceded him. Agents who had a similar passion and work ethic welcomed his arrival, and gravitated toward him. Others were concerned. Carson Dunbar, the former joint terrorist task force supervisor, recalled the moment when O'Neill introduced himself. "I'd heard about John O'Neill," he said. "A lot of guys did not relish the idea of working for him. When he walked into my office, I said, 'Gee, you don't have horns,' and John, who was always a bit insecure, replied, 'What do you mean by that?'"

For all his supposed toughness, O'Neill wanted to be loved. After arguing with a girlfriend, he often tried to get back in her good graces: "Just love me, just love me," he would plead. Some colleagues sensed O'Neill's neediness. "He had that basic insecurity to be liked by everybody," Dunbar said.

Though O'Neill was an enigma that Dunbar, like most others, could not solve, Dunbar became a friend and admirer of O'Neill's. "John had rare vision," he said, comparing his ability to think "out of the box" to that of William Bratton, the brash NYPD commissioner at the time, who was credited with driving down crime in New York. "I don't think I saw anyone work as hard as John O'Neill did," Dunbar said. "My secretary once joked, 'You know John was an only child. He has to get his way.' And everything he did was job related."

Kallstrom held a press briefing on January 14, 1997, about the cyberage difficulty the FBI encountered in conducting wiretaps. He revealed to the assembled reporters, most from business and technology magazines, that an astonishing 1,100 telephones were wiretapped or under some kind of electronic surveillance by authorities each day in New York City.

Toward the end of his presentation, Kallstrom briefly introduced his new national security director, who was standing off to the side. I attended the press conference, in my capacity as the *New York Post* criminal justice editor. Afterward, I went over to the refined and distinguished-looking gentleman and introduced myself. Many FBI officials are uncomfortable with the media, fearing that even being seen with a reporter might damage a career. But O'Neill was extremely comfortable greeting me, a journalist he had never met before. We agreed to meet for breakfast before he went to work, at the ungodly hour of 7 A.M., which we did on numerous other mornings over the years.

O'Neill never revealed any information to me that could be described as secret or classified. At best, he steered me to potential stories that were located or substantiated somewhere in the public record. "You know, I can't tell you anything we are doing," O'Neill said. "But I'll always try to help if you are heading in the wrong direction." Of course, it would have been better for me if O'Neill had been willing to be less discreet with his sensitive information, but just having someone in his position willing to take a phone call to shoot down erroneous theories and keep me on the right track was more than I could reasonably expect.

O'Neill's first official day in New York was just two days later—January 17, the six-month anniversary of the crash of TWA Flight 800. Kallstrom had decided to invite the families of the victims to the Calverton, Long Island, hangar, where the doomed jet had been pieced together. Kallstrom had become the point man for the investigation—his face had become widely recognized through the enormous media attention given to the tragedy and its possible ties to terrorism. Kallstrom felt he should meet privately with the relatives to explain the status of the investigation before addressing the waiting throng of media gathering for an update on the half-year anniversary.

"It was snowing and it seemed surreal," recalled Neil Herman. "There was quite a lot of press. And John began to see what New York was really like."

Kallstrom was convinced by then that the crash was an accident, although he was not yet 100 percent certain that a spark in the fuel tank was the cause. Nearly 98 percent of the plane had been recovered. Forensic experts and aeronautical engineers had examined in excess of 1,400 metal tears. More than two thousand chemical swabs had been conducted and analyzed for explosive residue, a monumental reconstruction effort that had cost more than twenty million dollars. The center fuel tank, arguably the most important piece of evidence, had been recovered in a hundred feet of water nearly a quarter mile offshore. The tank showed no signs of scarring or tears from a bomb, and there was not a hint of intelligence suggesting Al Qaeda or any terrorist group was involved.

"The silence was deafening," said Corrigan, the lead investigator. "If it was terrorism, they would want to take credit."

Kallstrom asked O'Neill to write the final report, which was due in a few months. O'Neill agreed with his new boss about the cause of the disaster, but he was in no hurry to close down the investigation without tying up as many loose ends as possible. Pierre Salinger had held a press conference renewing his notions about a missile attack, which revved up the public. The seventy-two-year-old former White House press secretary and ABC-TV correspondent even claimed he had confidential information from his French intelligence sources that the U.S. Navy shot down the 747 jet. His claims only fueled other conspiracy theorists and critics of the U.S. government, who put forward various theories asserting that the military or the national guard shot down the jet while on maneuvers and were now engaged in a cover-up. The most outlandish of these ideas was the allegation that a SAM missile had been fired from the naval carrier USS *Normandy*, bringing down the Paris-bound jet and killing all 230 on board just before the opening of the Atlanta Olympics.

Corrigan had meticulously ruled out that theory, noting that the *Normandy* was 180 miles out at sea, more than eighty miles beyond the SAM's striking distance, that the missile does not emit a fiery plume while climbing, which countered witnesses' accounts of the accident, and that the SAMs, formally called SM-2s, have steel rods protruding from their sides that would have left easily recognizable tears in the skin of the wounded jet. Despite the evidence, the missile theorists persisted in advancing their ideas in the press.

As hard as it was to prove what caused the crash, the FBI was faced with an even more daunting task: demonstrating what did *not* occur. Therefore, O'Neill wanted his final report to go well beyond satisfying questions from professional investigators and government officials. He wanted to close off as many avenues to conspiracy theorists as possible. He summoned Corrigan into his office for a meeting. "John was very formal," said Mark Chidichimo, the head of the office's intelligence squad of thirty agents. "He didn't encourage people to just walk into his office. He scheduled formal meetings. We took him very seriously. He reminded me of a skipper at sea. He was God. He had that kind of charm and bearing. And he remembered everything."

Chidichimo knew of O'Neill's reputation as a tough boss who did not suffer fools. "And his definition of *fools* was pretty broad," he said. But he came to believe that O'Neill was one of the smartest people he had ever met. "One, two, three, 'Here's what we do,'" he recalled. "I never saw anyone with more on his plate and handling it all like John. He could do a phenomenal amount while he had everything in the air, closely examining each one."

Corrigan and O'Neill had never met. Corrigan was a twelve-year veteran of the joint FBI-NYPD terrorist task force who previously worked on the 1993 WTC bombing and was the case agent on the successful investigation into Sheikh Rahman's plot to blow up New York landmarks. Corrigan had been comfortable with Pickard, O'Neill's tall, slender, mustachioed predecessor. "I liked Pickard with his Mr. Peabody look," Corrigan said. "O'Neill was the complete opposite. He was this flashy guy, more flamboyant, with a way with words. We heard he was a tough guy to work for. That you could not go to a meeting with a portion of the information. It was, 'Don't come to the game with three bullets in your gun. You have to be fully loaded.' If you give him a briefing, don't leave anything out."

Corrigan, too, was convinced there was no terrorist or military involvement in the downing of TWA 800. In fact, after putting in six grueling months ostensibly trying to "prove a negative," Corrigan was looking to return to investigating real acts of criminality. Instead, he received a jolt. O'Neill wanted to expand the boundaries of the investigation rather than narrow them. He was developing an "exit strategy"—it was the first time Corrigan had heard those words used in a major investigation. "If you don't put all these pieces to bed, it will come back to bite you," O'Neill told him. "This will become the nation's next 'grassy knoll,'" referring to the theories that claimed Lee Harvey Oswald was not the lone assassin of President John F. Kennedy.

"There were things he asked for that we were not happy with," Corrigan recalled. "He wanted to cover all the bases."

O'Neill's first order of business was to try to obtain a more complete accounting of the military's assets than the joint terrorist task force had compiled. It had already located every military asset within two hundred miles of New York that night, and ascertained their weapons capability, to see if any such asset could have taken down the plane. O'Neill set up a meeting in Washington with H. Allen Holmes, assistant secretary of defense for special operations and low-intensity conflict.

Corrigan and Herman and about fifty top military and intelligence personnel were waiting in Holmes's packed office when O'Neill breezed in. He was a little late because he had stopped at FBI headquarters to lobby for additional funding for the investigation. O'Neill got right down to business, explaining to Holmes and the admirals his strategy about eliminating every possible explanation for the TWA crash—with the exception of an accident. He told the assistant secretary he wanted an accounting of where every naval asset was the night of the crash.

Holmes and the admirals were incredulous and unwilling to comply. Since TWA 800, the navy had been forced to fend off wild speculation about their purported role in what they perceived as an accident. They took offense at allegations that they had perpetrated and covered up the downing of Flight 800. The admiral assured O'Neill that even his most powerful long-range missiles—weapons he was precluded from revealing for national security reasons—were on vessels thousands of miles away from the site of the downing on the plane.

O'Neill was not deterred by their reluctance. He was the FBI head of national security in New York, trying to wrap up the most important investigation facing the United States. He needed to be satisfied with the evidence he would present to an official government inquiry, and even more important, it needed to satisfy the families of the victims. He continued to insist that he needed to know exactly where every naval asset was that night. But Holmes and the navy admirals were not used to being challenged.

"And I suppose you want to know about the Boomers, too?" the irritated Holmes sarcastically asked, referring to his nuclear submarines carrying ballistic missiles.

"Yes," O'Neill fired back. "We need to know that. The fact is, I want to know if there were two guys rowing a navy rowboat in the South Pacific."

The expression on Holmes's face was unforgettable, Corrigan said. "The guy looked at John as though he were thinking, 'You've got to be fucking kidding me.'" O'Neill was not, despite the assistant secretary's reluctance to comply, and because of his tenacity, he eventually received a full accounting of the navy's assets.

O'Neill's "cover every base" philosophy eventually won over the doubting Corrigan, and he became an O'Neill convert. "John's style was, guys locked arms and walked across the football field looking for clues. He wanted every bit of information sucked up. He did not want 'some information.' He wanted 'all the information.'" O'Neill expanded the boundaries of the TWA investigation to the point where the conclusions could deflect any logical question. Ultimately, it was in the interest of the reluctant admiral because it was his agency that came under the most suspicion by the conspiracy theorists. "O'Neill put to rest a lot of questions," Corrigan explained.

International terrorism was not merely a concept in New York City. The city had already been attacked at the World Trade Center, terrorists had been arrested as they were preparing to bomb tunnels and landmarks, and it was certain that New York would be attacked again. On Sunday, February 23, 1997, O'Neill was in his office reading terrorism documents when a Palestinian man from Ramallah got off the elevator on the observation deck of the second-greatest skyscraper in the city, the Empire State Building. He asked several tourists to point out the Statue of Liberty, and announced, "I love Americans and I love America." He then pulled out a .380 semiautomatic handgun and opened fire, killing a Danish man and wounding seven others. As thirty panic-stricken tourists ran for safety, he placed the gun to his head and committed suicide.

Police officer Thomas Verni was one of the first to arrive on the scene. "It was hell on wheels," he said. "Carnage. There were so many victims to attend to. They said they just saw him start shooting people." It was the worst bloodshed at the famed 1931 skyscraper in more than a half century, since a twin-engine B-25 army bomber lost in the fog plowed into the seventy-ninth floor in July 1945, killing fourteen and injuring twenty-six others in a blazing spectacle high over Midtown.

Mayor Giuliani said the dead shooter, Ali Abu Kamal, sixty-nine, had arrived in New York the previous Christmas Eve and traveled to Florida, where he obtained an identity card with a Melbourne, Florida, address that enabled him to buy his weapon in January. Giuliani cautioned the public against speculating that the shooting was the work of terrorists rather than that of a lone madman. O'Neill agreed. But he knew there was a very real possibility that the shooting was an act of terrorism.

Armed with the recent secret debriefings of the Al Qaeda

turncoat al-Fadl, who revealed just months earlier that bin Laden was involved in the Black Hawk Down killings of U.S. soldiers in Somalia, O'Neill became a lone voice warning that bin Laden would continue to seek targets on American soil. "John was the great predictor that bin Laden would continue killing Americans," Schiliro said. "I think even then he was under the impression that UBL would strike here in America, while everyone else was under the impression it would be overseas."

Authorities found a two-page handwritten letter, entitled "Charter of Honour," in a pouch Kamal wore around his neck. There were two versions—one in English, the other in Arabic. "The Zionists are the paw that carried out their savage aggression," wrote Kamal, an English teacher from Gaza. "My restless aspiration is to murder as many of them as possible, and I have decided to strike at their own den in New York, and at the very Empire State Building in particular."

O'Neill's agents ran Kamal's name through their intelligence data banks, checked with foreign law enforcement, and tracked his movement and history back to Israel, without finding any direct connections to a known terror group. In addition, his rambling missive identified three other groups of "bitter enemies" who he said "must be annihilated and exterminated" for misdeeds both political and personal. The enemies included a group of students who, he claimed, attacked him in 1993 because he "didn't agree to their command asking to help them cheat in the final examinations," some students in the Ukraine who, he said, beat his son and stole $250 from him, and an Egyptian police officer who, he said, beat him because of "passport formalities."

O'Neill appeared with Giuliani at a press conference. The mayor said that the authorities believed that whatever demons drove Kamal, he had apparently acted alone. The city breathed a sigh of relief. Photographs of the mayor's briefing, with O'Neill in the background, ran in the next day's papers. O'Neill proudly contacted his mother and his other loves, telling them to get the

New York newspapers. He was now near the pinnacle he had dreamed about in that Atlantic City walk-up apartment just blocks away from the boardwalk and the roiling ocean surf.

Valerie James's son, Jay, was graduating from high school and preparing for the Naval Academy Prep School, so she was now free to take a job with clothing designer Bob Mackie in New York and join O'Neill in his Stuyvesant Town apartment. The dream they shared years earlier in Chicago was now reality. She flew to New York, but quickly learned how small Manhattan apartments can be compared to her three-bedroom house in Chicago.

"I was shocked," she said.

"Val, I couldn't believe it either," O'Neill told her.

James was forced to place most of her belongings in storage.

"But the first months were euphoric," she said. "It was a realization of a dream. It was very great for a while." Her son was not due to report to prep school until May, and he joined them in March for two months. "John always played the daddy with Jay," James recalled.

James was amazed at how wide a network of contacts O'Neill had already cultivated in New York. "He got himself into everything," she said. Kallstrom was no shrinking violet himself when it came to socializing and spreading the FBI gospel, and he introduced O'Neill around. One night he took him to the Friars Club, which was home not only to great comedians, but an array of businesspeople who enjoyed sidling up to law enforcement bigwigs. Another time O'Neill made an appearance with Kallstrom at a Mutual of New York event. The insurance company had a long history of close relations with the New York FBI brass, many of whom joined the company after retiring. It was there O'Neill met Thomas Durkin, the straight-talking, longtime friend and counsel to John Cardinal O'Connor, the archbishop of the New

York archdiocese, which was the most powerful archdiocese in the country.

O'Neill told Durkin how he made it his habit to take St. Patrick's Day off to go to the parade in Baltimore and Chicago, and that he always hoped to have enough "juice" in New York to be invited to St. Patrick's Cathedral. "I thought it was strange he took the day off," Durkin said. "But I told him, your aspirations aren't high enough. Why not come and stand next to the cardinal during the parade?"

O'Neill, the graduate of Holy Spirit High School, was incredulous.

"Why should I ever talk seriously to you?" Durkin joked, extending the offer a second time. This time it was accepted.

A few evenings before St. Patrick's Day, O'Neill went to an Irish social event, also at Mutual of New York headquarters on Park Avenue. He entered the room and immediately spotted an old friend who had started with him as a clerk giving tours at the FBI. O'Neill rushed over to his fellow clerk-agent and tapped him on the shoulder.

"Johnny baby," John Blaha said as O'Neill gave him a trademark bear hug.

They had not seen each other in years. "I'm in town now," O'Neill volunteered as a broad smile creased his beaming face. "I'm an SAC . . . And I guess you can't call me Stinky anymore."

Blaha bounced around the city nightlife as easily as any agent did. He and some of his cronies spent their evenings hanging out at Hurley's restaurant on Fifth Avenue, near Rockefeller Center. Hurley's was widely known for its eclectic crowd of Midtown businessmen, tourists, secretaries, detectives, and writers. It was a wonderful place to spend St. Patrick's Day, one of the great days in New York City, where millions celebrated their Irish ancestry, and most everyone else seemed Irish at least for a day, wearing green and celebrating the day in drink and song. O'Neill asked Blaha if he was going to Hurley's, and whether he could send "a lady" for a pint of beer and some corned beef and cabbage—and if Blaha would escort her inside without waiting in the customary long line of St. Patrick's Day revelers waiting to get inside. He agreed.

On that St. Patrick's Day in 1997, O'Neill went to the cathedral, attended morning mass followed by a reception for a select group of powerful and connected New Yorkers inside the cardinal's residence, and then watched the parade, standing next to the cardinal on the viewing stand outside the fabled church on Fifth Avenue. For the former altar boy, his first St. Patrick's Day in New York was one of the greatest thrills of his life. "The cardinal was absolutely impressed with O'Neill, and his dedication to his job," Durkin said. O'Neill and the Cardinal would become great friends, with O'Neill frequently attending Sunday mass.

Around the corner at Hurley's, Valerie James joined the back of the line, where Blaha overheard her asking if anyone knew John Blaha. "Do you know John O'Neill?" he asked her. She did. "That's how I met Valerie," Blaha said. Although O'Neill rarely spoke about his personal life and appeared to be a single man, Blaha knew O'Neill was estranged from his wife. He always wondered why O'Neill never divorced, especially as he came to know Valerie James. "It's a Catholic thing," O'Neill would say. And Blaha believed that was true.

"How unacceptable would that be in the eyes of the church?" Blaha rhetorically asked. "As much as John liked to think he could walk on either side of the line, when it came to being a religious man, he tried to be one. He pulled out all the stops to meet the cardinal. He attended mass every Sunday. A part of him internally was saying, 'I was brought up in this religious manner that has certain rules of integrity and there are certain things I can't do.'"

But even Blaha has his doubts.

"I once said, 'Why don't you do what's right in this circumstance?'" Blaha recalled, referring to getting a divorce and marrying Valerie. "He would just shake his head."

St. Patrick's Day was unusually pleasant, with temperatures near sixty degrees. But nine days later, the winds howled through the concrete canyons of Lower Manhattan. It was the kind of March day when the chill is raw and begins to cut through your clothes and then through your skin and finally into your bones as the night moves on.

The NYPD and Fire Department responded to a call on a tree-lined Douglaston street. There, in a house belonging to Lester Deily, fifty-one, a technofreak previously convicted of making terrorist threats, Detective Patrick Pogan and other emergency services unit cops found two hundred gallons of gasoline, jet fuel, nitromethane, lacquers, sulfuric acid, aluminum oxide, and other explosive liquids, including shiny thermoslike canisters on the basement floor with a red-and-black computer-generated label that read BIOLOGICAL HAZARD/SARIN GAS. Considering the tragedy that had occurred the previous March in Tokyo, when a religious cult released sarin gas into the subway, and taking into account the global fears about the potential for urban terrorism, the discovery immediately brought a response from ten city agencies.

O'Neill's pager went off about 7:30 P.M. with word that cops were evacuating the neighborhood. He was wearing his nightclub wardrobe when he headed through the Midtown Tunnel and out into Queens. Giuliani, who had a reputation for appearing at every major crime and fire scene, was also en route. So were the police and fire commissioners, and representatives from the city's Emergency Management Services. Heavily armed emergency services unit cops and firemen had shut down the street and surrounded the house.

The NYPD's chief of department, Louis Anemone, with four stars on his shoulders and on the beak of his hat, was standing in the center of the block, which was lit with the eerie illumination of klieg lights. In many ways, Anemone was a lot like O'Neill. He was brash, bluff, a workaholic who started his day at 6 A.M. and did not return home before midnights most nights. Anemone was the highest-ranking officer in the NYPD's thirty-nine-thousand-member force, an army of cops and detectives the size of fifteen military field regiments. He led the NYPD like a field general marshaling his troops, and it was not uncommon to see him donning a helmet and bulletproof vest in the midst of a crisis. People swore Anemone's blood was not red, but NYPD blue. As testimony to his field command vision, one of Anemone's crowning legacies was a crowd-control strategy he developed after three days of riots in Brooklyn's Crown Heights sparked when a young black child was accidentally killed by an ambulance driven by a Hasidic Jew.

O'Neill flashed his FBI credentials as he passed the cops and firemen guarding the yellow crime-scene tape. He typically headed straight for the highest-ranking police official, the one with the greatest number of stars on his shoulder, because he preferred to deal with the highest levels in order to cut right to the chase, a practice that irritated second-tier officials who felt slighted by O'Neill's tendency to bypass them.

Anemone had little patience for his counterparts in the other emergency services. He preferred that the NYPD retain control over all emergency situations without intervention from anyone else. But because of the potential terrorism component of the Deily discovery, an even broader than usual array of personnel from non–law enforcement agencies showed up, including the Department of Transportation and the Department of Sanitation. Anemone saw the unfamiliar figure of O'Neill walking into his tightly controlled area, and didn't know what to make of him.

"This guy comes in dressed head to toe in black—black jacket, black slacks, black socks, black shoes—and he walks straight up to me and says, 'O'Neill, FBI,'" he remembered. "I look at him and I'm thinking, 'This guy doesn't look anything like what you would expect from the FBI.'"

In fact, the last time New York City had an FBI official like

O'Neill was the early 1980s, when the legendary Kenneth P. Walton ran the office, displaying not merely a flair for clothing, but vision when he created the NYPD-FBI joint terrorist task force. Anemone and O'Neill exchanged pleasantries about how it was ironic that they were supposed to meet for lunch later that week, and had never expected to meet under such conditions. But this was New York, where an emergency is always just a heartbeat away.

Mayor Giuliani's white Suburban pulled up, lights flashing, with a cadre of his personal NYPD security. They were soon joined by Thomas Von Essen, the fire commissioner. The mayor also went straight to Anemone for a briefing. "What are we going to do?" he asked. Anemone told the mayor that a six-block area had been evacuated as a precaution, the suspect had been taken to the precinct for questioning, and that he appeared to be an emotionally disturbed person rather than a terrorist linked to an organized network.

"Just the things that they seized at that point would have been enough to ignite that house and maybe half the neighborhood," Giuliani observed.

Anemone explained he was not certain if the drums really contained sarin gas or a harmless substance. Police had not opened the drums because there was a legitimate fear that the gas might escape and contaminate the entire neighborhood. Officials needed to decide what to do with the potentially deadly gas. How could it be safely removed from the neighborhood and tested?

As Giuliani conferred with Anemone, O'Neill stood nearby, quietly watching New York's top officials engage in an animated conversation searching for a solution. The temperature was dipping with each passing minute. It was so cold, plumes of vapor were coming from the mouths of the top brass as they spoke, and O'Neill was standing there in his lightweight evening wear.

"He was freezing his *cojones* off," Anemone recalled. "It was getting cold as a bitch."

Fire Commissioner Von Essen walked over to O'Neill and

offered to provide him with fire department gear from the trunk of his car or from a nearby fire engine. Mayor Giuliani was wearing a fire department coat and hat. But O'Neill did not immediately accept Von Essen's generous offer. He knew that in every city there are turf battles between cops and firemen. New York, for all its cosmopolitanism, was still rife with parochial infighting between the two groups. O'Neill also knew from his days in Baltimore and Chicago that he would need to cultivate closer ties with Anemone than with his counterparts in the fire department. He did not want his first encounter to alienate the NYPD's highest-ranking cop.

O'Neill turned to Anemone, and in a stroke of diplomacy, asked the chief's opinion about donning clothing emblazoned with large FDNY letters on the front and back.

"Hey, Chief. What do you think?" he asked.

"If you wear their gear, we will never talk again," Anemone told him.

O'Neill smiled broadly and nodded his head, knowing he had dodged a bullet.

"And he knew I meant it," Anemone said.

The chief walked over to his car, popped the trunk, and pulled out a flimsy blue NYPD windbreaker. He handed it to O'Neill, who wore the wafer-thin jacket with the letters *NYPD* over his nightclub wardrobe throughout the frigid night.

"What's next?" the mayor interrupted.

The action-oriented Giuliani was growing impatient that the sarin gas container was still in the suspect's house. Jerry Hauer, the head of the city's Emergency Management Service, called in from Florida. Hauer had the mayor's ear when it came to multi-agency emergency responses, much to the dismay of the cops. Before Giuliani became mayor in 1993, the NYPD was unquestionably in charge of emergencies, with a distinguished record of handling every situation. The lone exception to this rule was putting out fires, but the rank-and-file police officers believed with typical bravado they could handle that, too.

But all that had changed under Giuliani. He had created his own office of emergency management, hired Hauer to run it, and was initially impressed with his success at coordinating the cleanup and repair of a massive water-main rupture that flooded Fifth Avenue with thousands of gallons of water. During the previous administration, a similar break disrupted service for months before fresh water was again rushing through apartment faucets. But under Hauer, the water-main and road repairs were completed in weeks. Just months after the successful resolution of the Fifth Avenue disaster, a madman named Stephen Leery set off a fiery gasoline explosion in a packed subway car, killing eight people and injuring dozens more. When Giuliani arrived at the scene of the blast, he received conflicting information about the incident from the officials who had responded from the various agencies. Giuliani was livid at not getting clear, immediate answers—and from that moment on he put Hauer and the OEM in charge of all future events.

Since Giuliani had designated the OEM as the lead agency at emergencies, there had been repeated clashes between Hauer and top police brass. Now Hauer was in Florida calling Giuliani on the telephone. Anemone made a simple tactical decision. "We are on the scene," he said. "The police department will call the shots."

Anemone wanted to move the drums to a safe location where they could be stored in a controlled environment and then opened to examine their contents. The best place, he believed, would be a federal facility in Maryland, Fort Detrick, home to the U.S. Army's medical and biological laboratories. Giuliani's emergency staff called Fort Detrick. They were told the facility was closed, and to bring the drums in the morning.

The mayor was furious. And so was Anemone. None of the

officials wanted to leave the potentially deadly chemicals in a residential Queens neighborhood for one minute longer than necessary. They talked about moving the drums to a warehouse in the city, and someone suggested using a helicopter, but the prospect of an unforeseen mechanical failure and crash, with drums of sarin gas exploding on impact, put that idea to rest.

A frustrated Anemone turned to O'Neill, who barely had uttered a word since he slipped on the NYPD windbreaker, and asked: "Is there anything you can do?" O'Neill pulled out his phone and made a single call to the FBI field office in Baltimore, where his old colleague Gary Stevens was on duty. He told Stevens what he needed and voilà, Stevens arranged for the feds to open Fort Detrick to await the drums.

But O'Neill was not finished. Without being asked, he realized that if Anemone planned to have the sarin drums transported by truck, the vehicle would need police escort in each state as the dangerous cargo crossed from New York, through New Jersey and Delaware, and into Maryland. O'Neill made another call, arranging for state troopers in each state to meet the caravan of NYPD cars and escort the cargo safely along the various turnpikes and highways.

O'Neill turned to Anemone. "We have one problem," he said, with a mischievous smile. "Can you transport it to the New Jersey border?"

"I knew he was the real deal," Anemone said. "He had watched everyone doing their thing. He said virtually nothing all night. He listened. And when we asked, he delivered. It was just not what I expected. All those FBI people look the same. They all take the secret oath. He was different. He was a very easy guy to like. He recruited me to his team, when I thought I would bring him to mine."

That did not mean the two top lawmen always got along. When the Goodwill Games came to the New York area in 1998, the FBI and NYPD were both concerned that the Olympic-style sporting event could be a terrorist target. For months, every law enforcement agency in the region had been planning strategies for the event, with O'Neill and the FBI in charge; Presidential Directive 62, issued in 1995 after the Oklahoma City bombing, gave the bureau supervision over all events of national importance. But there were issues to sort out concerning credentials, transportation, surveillance, undercover agents, and sharing intelligence. Of course, Anemone wanted the NYPD to have ultimate control in New York City. But O'Neill had orders from Washington to station the FBI hostage rescue team in the city. He asked Anemone whether the bureau's HRT could be first responders in the event of a kidnapping or standoff.

"This is New York," Anemone began. "I am not Jack Townsend in Chicago. And I'm not the fucking chief who will roll over. This is our city. My guys do this every day. Your guys, they train and train and train. We train by doing. And you can forget presidential decrees."

O'Neill listened patiently to the plainspoken Anemone, who personified the aggressive posture of the NYPD under Giuliani. This chief was no one's doormat. O'Neill understood how important it was for Anemone to be in charge and to save face. The chief had drawn a line in the sand, but O'Neill had his own orders. After a few seconds of consideration, he leaned forward a bit in his chair and countered, "Chief, you understand, Washington wants this. And I can't be the FBI supervisor who rolls over completely for you."

Anemone came up with a compromise solution. "How about you tell Washington you are in charge, but put the FBI hostage rescue team in a hotel and let us do our work?"

O'Neill thought about the idea for a moment, but said it would not do. So Anemone came up with an even better solution: since the games were spread out over adjoining suburban counties, the NYPD chief proposed, "Let's send them to Nassau County. Those boys will roll over for you in a heartbeat."

O'Neill liked Anemone's plan. He informed headquarters that the NYPD had strong hostage teams with proven track records and that, perhaps, the FBI's experts could be better utilized by supporting the efforts of the Long Island police. And besides, they would be near enough to the city to race into town in the event they were needed. Headquarters agreed with O'Neill's thinking. During the entire three weeks of the Goodwill Games, the Nassau cops had the vaunted FBI hostage rescue team at their disposal. And O'Neill had found a way to avoid losing Anemone—and the NYPD—as an ally.

10

THE MAN WHO KNEW

When bin Laden speaks, we have to listen. They have the capability to strike American soil anytime they choose.

—John O'Neill

Osama bin Laden was inside his Tora Bora mountain fortress in spring 1997 when he received word that the Saudis had put out another contract on his life. Enraged by his efforts to undermine the regime by supplying Stinger missiles to Saudi Islamic militants, the Saudi government worked through the Pakistani intelligence agency, the ISI, to pay mercenaries along the Pakistan-Afghanistan border to knock off bin Laden. But elements in that Pakistani secret authority found out about the plot and tipped off their friends in the Taliban. Bin Laden was alerted to the danger, and moved along with his family to Kandahar, the Taliban stronghold, where bin Laden had recently purchased a home for Taliban leader Mullah Omar, Omar's three wives, and their children.

A month later, bin Laden decided to go public with his mounting radicalism, and summoned CNN reporters Peter Arnett and Peter Bergen to his secret encampment to deliver a devastating message: He could no longer guarantee the safety of American civilians who might get in the way of any attacks, he said. Mothers of American GIs should speak out against U.S. policy, he added, and warned that he would launch more attacks.

"We declared a *jihad*, a holy war, against the United States government because it is unjust, criminal and tyrannical," he said in the interview, which aired on May 12, 1997. "We have focused our declaration of *jihad* on striking at the U.S. soldiers inside Arabia, the country of the two holy places, Mecca and Medina. In our religion it is not permissible for any non-Muslim to stay in Arabia. Therefore, even though American civilians are not targeted in our plan, they must leave. We do not guarantee their safety."

He justified his hostility by criticizing U.S. policy and accusing U.S. officials of hypocrisy in defending the aggression of U.S. allies but condemning others. "The U.S. today has set a double standard, calling whoever goes against its injustice a terrorist," bin Laden said:

> It wants to occupy our countries, steal our resources, impose on us agents to rule us . . . and wants us to agree to all these. If we refuse to do so, it will say, 'You are terrorists.' With a simple look at the U.S. behaviors, we find that it judges the behavior of the poor Palestinian children whose country was occupied: If they throw stones against the Israeli occupation, it says they are terrorists, whereas when the Israeli pilots bombed the United Nations building in Qana, Lebanon, while it was full of children and women, the U.S. stopped any plan to condemn Israel.
>
> At the same time that they condemn any Muslim who calls for his rights, they receive the top official of the Irish Republican Army [Gerry Adams] at the White House as a political leader. Wherever we look, we find the U.S. as the leader of terrorism and crime in the world. The U.S. does not consider it a terrorist act to throw atomic bombs at nations thousands of miles away, when those bombs would hit more than just military targets. Those bombs rather were thrown at entire nations, including women, children and elderly people, and up to this day the traces of those bombs remain in Japan.
>
> Resistance started against the American invasion [in Somalia] because Muslims did not believe the U.S. allega-

tions that they came to save the Somalis. With Allah's grace, Muslims in Somalia cooperated with some Arab holy warriors who were in Afghanistan. Together they killed large numbers of American occupation troops. The hearts of Muslims are filled with hatred toward the United States of America and the American President. The president has a heart that knows no words. A heart that kills hundreds of children defiantly knows no word.

Our people in the Arabian Peninsula will send him messages with no words because he does not know any words. If there is a message that I may send through you, then it is a message I address to the mothers of American troops who came here with their military uniforms walking proudly up and down our land while the scholars of our country are thrown in prisons. I say that this represents a blatant provocation to over a billion Muslims. To these mothers I say if they are concerned about their sons, then let them object to the American government's policy.

Bin Laden ended the interview ominously. Asked about his future plans, he said: "You'll see them and hear about them in the media, God willing."

Bin Laden had by that time established two secret terror cells in Africa, where Al Qaeda loyalists were preparing attacks against two U.S. embassies, which bin Laden believed were gathering information for U.S intelligence. His personal fortune and his contacts and his organizing zeal were all being brought to bear in an effort to use terrorism to inflict pain and force a change in U.S. and Saudi policy.

O'Neill knew this was no idle threat, but Americans were in no mood to heed the warning. They were preoccupied. The end of the Cold War had ushered in a new indifference to the rest of the world. The United States had won. It had no rival in the world, not economically and certainly not militarily. So why worry about some rich Arab making threats and talking about Allah all the time? Even reporters and columnists who might normally have been expected to sound an alarm over bin Laden were busy keeping up with the latest update in the tiresome saga of the Clinton scandals and the media feeding frenzies that perpetuated them. Just that week, the Clintons appealed to the Supreme Court to overturn an order for the first lady to hand over subpoenaed notes to Kenneth Starr, the special Whitewater prosecutor.

Few were willing to face the hard facts the way O'Neill was. He tried to get the message out when he could, and given his polish and eloquence, he had become one of the FBI's most requested public speakers. He enjoyed the feeling of having everyone's attention, and impressing them, just as he had as a kid just out of high school leading tours around FBI headquarters.

His speech to the National Strategy Forum in Chicago on June 11, 1997, stands out as a particular landmark, even though he did not mention bin Laden directly. What O'Neill did that day at the Chicago Athletic Association Continental Room on Michigan Avenue was trace a chillingly accurate picture of the danger posed by Islamic fundamentalism and its potential to unleash a virulent new strain of terrorism on the world. Old ideas had to be updated, O'Neill explained to the spellbound gathering, and old risk-assessment models revised. Resentment against U.S. support of Israel had to be understood in the context of Muslim thinking and had to be factored into our thinking about how twisted and bitter leaders could use this theme to incite their followers to commit depraved acts of large-scale violence.

"At the time of the World Trade Center bombing, the FBI and most of the intelligence community was putting most of its eggs, if you will, in the basket of investigating states that sponsor terrorism," he said. "We still do that. Iran, Iraq, Libya, Syria, Sudan. The World Trade Center case made us painfully aware that there is this new realm that's out there that's growing at a pretty fast pace and that is religious extremism. There is religious extremism in all the major religions of the world. But one that we see growing very, very fast is Islamic extremism, and if you look at the World Trade Center bombers, people that had been charged and convicted, they are Egyptian, Pakistani and Kuwaiti and Iraqis and U.S. persons, all coming together.

These individuals are pretty much identified because of their freedom to move across boarders. They are bound by a *jihad*, a religious belief as opposed to any nation or state. They can quickly assemble and quickly disperse. The other theaters in conflict today include Afghanistan, Southern Sudan, Egypt, Algeria, and we've seen that spill over into France with the Algerian Islamic extremist problem, Bosnia, Chechnya, Kashmir, Mindanao, the tri-water areas down in South America. And when we go back to the World Trade Center case and we look at how things have changed just in the last few years, how the balance of power has shifted. No one is going to attack. No intelligent state will attack the United States in the foreseeable future because of our military superiority. So the only way that these individuals can attack us and have some effect is through acts of terrorism.

The Afghanistan conflict or war, if you will, was a major watershed event. The Jihad and Islamic players came together to fight the Russians. Branches of our government felt that was a noble cause and supported it. They were trained in insurgency. They were trained in terrorist activity, and now, they are back in their various countries around the world with that training and having the network capabilities to know other Jihad players around the world who have the same like mind, the same fundamentalist thinking and the same type of training. Another significant fact about the Afghanistan conflict is the fact they won. They beat one of the largest standing armies in the world at that time, which gave them a buoyed sense of success and that they could take on other countries like the U.S. and be likewise successful.

The liberation of the city of Jerusalem—or the seizure of the city of Jerusalem—was another watershed event in the Islamic cause. It became no longer an issue of Jerusalem being a holy shrine, a holy place of all three major religions of the world. It became no longer a conflict between the state of Israel and the Palestinian people. It became a cause between the state of Israel and Islamic people around the world. So Islamics who are in Indonesia or in Mindanao are also angered by the seizure or the liberation of Israel, depending upon which side you're on.

The assassination of Anwar Sadat in Egypt was another major watershed event. The assassination was by a group called the Egypt Jihad Group, or the Islamic Group. Their cause is to change the form of government in Egypt from a secular form of government as we know with separation of church and state to an Islamic non-secular form of government. That's why Sadat was killed. Reestablishment of diplomatic relations between the Vatican and the State of Israel was another major watershed event. A lot of the individuals in this extreme radical movement cannot understand why the state of Israel and the Vatican would team up together. Why would they get back together again if there was not a movement toward another Crusade and they're ganging up against us because we are Islamic extremists?

It would be a terrible mistake, O'Neill warned, to be lulled into the assumption that these terrorists groups would never take action on U.S. soil.

"Various organizations have a presence in the United States today," he said.

They are heavily involved in recruiting. They are heavily involved in fund-raising activity. We have found in some instances, engagement in small-arms weapons training, independent-tactics training and in one instance, explosive training. They talk across group lines. It's not like the old Mafia type cases or Cosa Nostra cases or organized crime cases where you pigeonhole somebody and you say he's a member of this group, he's a member of this group. You tend to figure out who they may be associated with and all of a sudden, they are talking to all of the different groups at a conference where they are all bound again by the *jihad*, by their religious beliefs and extremism.

Almost all of the groups today, if they chose to, have the ability to strike us here in the United States. They're working toward that infrastructure. Our role is to continue to nick away at their infrastructure, their ability to strike us here in the United States and make it too costly of an effort for them to try to do that. The world is obviously getting smaller. Events that take place in France or in Bosnia, or Chechnya or Kashmir or Addis Ababa can affect us directly in places like Chicago or New York. We tend to say that we're blessed because we have all of those ethnic make ups in our community. In a city like Chicago, there are people who will be on one side of the cause or the other in those countries around the world where there is conflict.

We cannot be isolationist in terms of law enforcement efforts. Our legal attachés assigned overseas continue to grow in number. If an American or an American interest is attacked overseas, if we have the permission of the host government, we will deploy FBI agents overseas to conduct investigations or try to track individuals and bring them back to the United States to stand trial. Last year or over the last 18 months, we've brought back six significant terrorists. Located and captured them overseas and brought them back to stand trial under the rules of law in the United States. So we've been successful in that.

It is very difficult now to try and prove state sponsorship of terrorism. These countries have gotten much better in concealing their involvement through a series of surrogates. So our ability to prove any nation or state is behind their funding or training is especially difficult today . . . We are concerned primarily about the lethality of the attacks that we see. If we compare the terrorist attacks in the mid-1980s to the mid-1990s, they are down by about 500 in total worldwide attacks. But a lot of those attacks were pipe bombs, small incendiary devices. What we see now is a very large series of either sustained attacks or very, very large attacks that try to bring a large number of casualties.

If you are going to engage in terrorist activities for political or social agendas, you want to make it on the news. How many people here will remember that our embassy in Moscow was attacked by a rocket or our embassy in Athens this past year was attacked by a rocket? Very, very few. The only thing that knocked O.J. Simpson off the television, his trial, was the Oklahoma City bombing case. The larger the attack, the more newsworthy they can make it. We are concerned about the lethality of the attacks. Very, very concerned. And we are also concerned now that we have had obviously a lot of conventional types of attacks, but now, we're starting to see unconventional types of attacks like the sarin gas attack that took place in Tokyo.

I think interesting times lie ahead. Certainly we as citizens will be challenged. I know the FBI will continue to be challenged in the years to come. Unfortunately, I cannot predict that no Americans will be injured or killed as a result of a terrorist attack. And in fact, it will happen as long as violence is seen as the way to move along political or social agendas. We will have terrorism as a problem to contend with. Hopefully, working together, we will continue to reduce the amount of terrorism to its possible lowest amount.

The forty-five-minute talk electrified the crowd, and not only because O'Neill obviously knew what he was talking about. This was no mere performance: O'Neill's passion and obsession were palpably real. He could inspire others because he himself was inspired to do all that he could, even when he constantly ran into closed doors and bureaucratic resistance that both frustrated and enraged him. "No one I can think of lived it, breathed it, worried about it, more than John O'Neill," said White. "If ever he confronted anyone who he thought was not taking this seriously enough, he would rattle that cage and make a believer of them."

He could not, however, make a believer of Bill Clinton. This was partly a question of access. Given Clinton's legendary talents as a quick study, the president would have to have been moved if O'Neill had ever had the chance to make a direct appeal about the threat not only to U.S. interests abroad but right here at home. But the White House was hunkered down in crisis mode. Given the almost daily volleys of negative media coverage of the Clinton White House, it may have been inevitable that the administration would be defensive and attempt to get away with a timid, ineffectual approach to fighting terrorism. In the subsequent administration, George W. Bush did not commit himself to truly decisive action until the September 11 attacks rallied the nation behind the need to strike back.

The tragedy was that Clinton let bureaucratic infighting and rivalry get in the way of a clear-eyed look at a problem much more important to the future of the country than a tryst with an intern or its repercussions. Clinton and his sympathizers could complain about the unfairness of what the first lady once called a vast right-wing conspiracy, and subsequent revelations showed the charge was not without foundation, but Clinton and his aides blinded themselves to the very real world of problems demanding imaginative attention and concerted action.

O'Neill grew increasingly exasperated as his warnings about bin Laden and Islamic fundamentalism failed to mobilize the White House or National Security Council. "They don't seem to get it," he told White. Instead, the administration used every conceivable excuse to avoid making the kind of military response needed to stop bin Laden. Worse still, officials were so concerned about being accused of inaction, they actually worked behind the scenes to squelch the sort of inquiries that would have made decisive action a necessity. Sources at the CIA claimed that the Treasury Department, under pressure from the White House, was reluctant even to investigate cash flows to potential terrorists from various Muslim organizations and charities operating within the United States.

"Bin Laden was training thousands of people," Blitzer said. "We knew what was going on. The powers that be at the White House and on the National Security Council, these guys did not think it was as big a problem. Bin Laden kept threatening us and hitting us. It was clear he was coming at us and maybe directly to American soil. The administration thought we could contain them and continue to hunt down fugitives and put them in jail.

"But that was never John's view or mine. We felt we were at war and the FBI was at the point of the spear in this undeclared, secret war. We were trying to do whatever we could to keep things under control and interdict and hunt them down. Why more was not done in terms of taking the battle to these guys, I'll never know."

O'Neill never lost sight of bin Laden's growing menace. Valerie James remembers him coming home to his apartment with videotapes of bin Laden and sitting in front of the television, frequently stopping, rewinding and restarting the tapes, studying the Al Qaeda leader's words and mannerisms. The apartment's fax machine would be printing out information at all hours of the day and night, which O'Neill would pore over, underlining material. It was not long before James's children even became familiar with bin Laden's name from hearing O'Neill mention it so often.

Soon after O'Neill returned from Chicago, his chilling warning of attacks on American soil nearly became reality on a crowded Brooklyn subway train. An Egyptian émigré named Abdel Rahman Mosabbah frantically flagged down two Long Island Railroad police officers in Park Slope, Brooklyn, at 10:30 P.M. on Thursday, July 31, 1997. Using hand gestures because he spoke only fragmented English, Mosabbah indicated that a bomb was about to be detonated in a subway. The LIRR cops immediately radioed the NYPD and the FBI. A translator was rushed to the scene to speak with Mossabah, who breathlessly explained that two Palestinian men with whom he had been living on Fourth Avenue had just completed making bombs and were about to blow up buses and trains because they hated Jews and opposed the American-supported peace process between Palestinians and Israel.

Their target was the B-line train, which ran through a heavily Orthodox Jewish neighborhood in the Borough Park section. According to Mosabbah, the subway attack plan called for the men, Ghazi Ibrahim Abu Maizar and Lafi Khalil, to ride the train into the Borough Park station and leave behind a device packed with nails and attached to a twenty-five-foot cord. As the doors closed, the terrorists would yank the cord and detonate the device, sending shrapnel ripping through the car and into scores of innocent subway riders.

Armed with the tip from Mosabbah, the NYPD laid siege to the block where Mosabbah was staying in a squalid apartment at 248 Fourth Avenue. For the next six hours, police surrounded the building, evacuated about a hundred residents from other nearby apartment houses, and cordoned off a two-block radius around Fourth Avenue. City transit officials also closed several subway lines.

The area had been a focus of terrorist investigations before. Sheikh Omar Abdel Rahman, the radical Egyptian cleric who was serving a life sentence in connection with the plot to blow up the United Nations, the FBI headquarters and other New York City landmarks, attracted followers by preaching regularly at the nearby Abu Bakr El Siddique Mosque on Atlantic Avenue.

Finally, at 4:30 A.M. the following morning, NYPD Chief Charles Kammerdener, the ranking officer on duty that night, made the command decision to launch a predawn raid to catch the suspects off guard while they were asleep. An eight-man team rushed the apartment, broke down the door, and found the two suspects in a rear bedroom. Maizar, awakened by the sound of the cops, jumped out of his bed and lunged at the bomb, trying to hit the detonation switch. But an emergency services lieutenant managed to thrust his hand in front of the trigger. As Maizar fought for the bomb, he and Khalil were shot, but not seriously wounded.

Their arrest came four days before Ramzi Yousef was to go on trial in Manhattan Federal Court for the 1993 World Trade Center bombing. Inside the apartment, investigators found a document that they described as a possible suicide note. It threatened a series of attacks against American and Jewish interests. It also demanded the release of six Islamic militant prisoners, including Sheikh Rahman, Ramzi Yousef, another man who was implicated in the World Trade Center attack, and a jailed leader of the militant group Hamas.

Maizar and Khalil were charged with conspiracy to set off bombs. Maizar had a criminal record in Canada for smuggling immigrants across the border into Washington state. He was once arrested in 1990 in Israel for throwing stones at Israelis during a Palestinian uprising. Khalil, also from the West Bank, had no record. People in his neighborhood recalled him working odd construction jobs and frequently blowing his meager earnings on topless dancers at Times Square strip joints. The two men had met just a few months earlier when they arrived in the U.S.

The feds were not certain what to make of Mosabbah. He claimed to be a teacher in Cairo who had arrived just eight days earlier for a visit. He said he found the apartment on Fourth Avenue through another acquaintance. But the federal agents were suspicious of his account. They recovered his fingerprints from the bomb and in his pockets they found a business card bearing the name of an Egyptian intelligence officer. Mosabbah had explanations. He said he ran to the cops after Maizar boasted he had made a bomb and showed it to him. As for the card, Mosabbah claimed he had kept it as a reminder that the son of the Egyptian officer was one of Mosabbah's students and he wanted to make sure the boy received special attention.

Some authorities did not believe Mosabbah's story. In fact, the Brooklyn U.S. Attorney's Office, which would be prosecuting the case, pressed the FBI to charge Mosabbah as an accomplice. O'Neill had assigned two members of the joint terrorist task force to question Mosabbah. Detective Thomas Corrigan was a lead investigator into the crash of TWA 800, and Detective Louis Napoli worked on the 1993 World Trade Center bombing case and the investigation into Sheikh Rahman. The two veteran NYPD investigators grilled Mosabbah for the better part of three days. His story remained consistent throughout, and Corrigan and Napoli believed he was telling the truth.

They went to O'Neill, who they assumed had already made up his mind to arrest Mosabbah. The detectives thought that like most officials, O'Neill would have caved in to the wishes of the U.S attorney.

"I'm sure you are leaning toward arresting him," Corrigan told O'Neill.

"I am not leaning one way or the other," O'Neill fired back, saying he was waiting to hear from "my people" before he made up his mind.

The two investigators laid out the case. O'Neill listened patiently, and then asked why they believed Mosabbah's explanation about having the business card. O'Neill wanted to know how they ruled out the possibility that Mosabbah was an accomplice who suddenly got cold feet about going along with the plot to bomb the subway. Corrigan said that if Mosabbah was indeed connected to Egyptian intelligence, he would have ditched the card long before he changed his mind about the bombing, and certainly well before he went looking for the police.

O'Neill agreed with their assessment. O'Neill called the Brooklyn U.S. Attorney's Office and said he did not want to arrest Mosabbah. He advised that it would be a mistake to do so because if the prosecutors were later forced to drop the charges, Mosabbah's credibility would easily be attacked by defense attorneys who would argue that the feds did not believe him.

Mosabbah, instead, became the government's star witness at the 1998 trial. The case was so powerful against Maizar that, after the prosecution rested its case, Maizar stunned the courtroom by taking the stand and confessing that he wanted to be a suicide bomber who killed as many Jews as possible. When his guilty verdict was announced, he smiled and then began shouting, "The Palestinian children don't deserve to die!" He then jumped to his feet and began to yell "Allah Akbar!" (God is great.) Khalil, however, protested his innocence throughout and was acquitted of the more serious charges. He was convicted only of carrying an illegal green card.

O'Neill and others were hoping the time might have come to make a much more major breakthrough on the war against terrorism. Mary Jo White's prosecutors were completing their presentation to a secret grand jury that was about to indict bin Laden on charges including involvement in the Black Hawk Down incident. A formal indictment would finally enable the FBI to try to capture bin Laden and bring him back to Manhattan to stand trial. O'Neill had yet to finalize the definitive report on TWA Flight 800 to present to Washington and the American public. Over at City Hall, Mayor Giuliani was embarking on a series of brain-storming sessions on terrorism. He wanted to build a new state-of-the-art emergency command center in the event of a major disaster, such as a hurricane, missile attack, or nerve gas attack similar to the one in the Tokyo subway system. He envisioned a central communications hub that could represent all city agencies and law enforcement and could withstand a nuclear bomb.

Like Clinton, Giuliani sometimes did not want to face the truth. He brushed off the warnings of experts predicting catastrophe. Louis Anemone, then the chief of department, recalled how a disbelieving Giuliani often interrupted the experts and said, "Oh, that could never happen." Giuliani wanted to place the fifteen-million-dollar center two hundred thirty feet above the ground, on the twenty-third floor of 7 World Trade Center—directly across the street from the site of the fatal 1993 terrorist bombing by Ramzi Yousef—even though Anemone and the NYPD argued that it should be located in another borough to make sure government could continue to function if Manhattan were the prime target. "You don't want to confuse Giuliani with the facts, and his 'yes men' would agree with him. It was asinine," recounted Anemone. "In terms of targets, the World Trade Center was number one. I guess you had to be there in 1993 to know how strongly we felt that it was the wrong place." O'Neill agreed but the advice ultimately went unheeded.

O'Neill soon took off for a whirlwind series of meetings in Italy, France, Germany, and England to further cement his relationships with his terrorism counterparts overseas and to compare notes on the globalization of crime. It was his first trip overseas since he delivered his speech in Chicago detailing the burgeoning threat directed toward the United States and every Western ally. The October 1997 trip was grueling, but for someone with

O'Neill's love of travel and nightlife, this type of government-sponsored trip served the dual purpose of allowing him to push forward on his fight against bin Laden while simultaneously inhaling the intoxicating pleasures of a variety of alien locales. He loved being greeted by dignitaries or top police officials at the airports, and these journeys reaffirmed his deeply held feeling that he was at once fulfilling a patriotic calling and his recurring dream as a young boy, when he would lie in bed on Sunday nights in Atlantic City and fantasize about becoming a famous FBI official.

O'Neill saw the trip as an opportunity to take his paramour—at his own expense, of course. But Valerie, still getting used to her new life in New York, declined his invitation. So O'Neill invited DiBattista, who was in Washington looking forward to the time she would join O'Neill in New York. She happily agreed to accompany him. O'Neill would attend bilateral conferences and meetings with station chiefs and other antiterror officials during the day and in the evenings he and DiBattista were invited to top restaurants and clubs by host law enforcement officials in London, Paris, Florence, Rome, and Berlin. In Italy, they even spent a few days in Abruzzi, visiting DiBattista's relatives. "John really liked the people in Europe," Anna said. "He said he would love to live in Europe one day and write a book."

Back in the States, O'Neill went to work meticulously detailing the evidence and conclusions amassed by the FBI for his final report on the TWA disaster. James Kallstrom, the New York FBI boss, went before a packed press conference on November 18, 1997, to deliver the FBI's final conclusions on the crash of TWA Flight 800. The FBI's 485-day investigation cost as much as twenty million dollars. The bureau sent some five hundred agents to the scene, interviewed seven thousand people, and recovered and examined almost one million pieces of aircraft debris, including about 98 percent of the jet, which they meticulously pieced together. The investigators recovered more than four thousand personal effects, took two thousand chemical swabbings, and inspected the decks of hundreds of boats in the vicinity of the crash site.

The FBI also checked more than twenty thousand records of vessels that went under three drawbridges on Long Island near the crash site during the three months before and two weeks after the explosion. "We want people to know we left no stone unturned," Kallstrom said. "In fact, we looked under each stone ten times." He also released the sixteen-minute videotape simulation, created by the CIA at O'Neill's behest, to address the conflicting eyewitness accounts and the lunatic arguments of Pierre Salinger and other critics who argued that friendly fire brought down the Paris-bound jet shortly after takeoff.

The simulation was clearly the most significant part of Kallstrom's presentation. It demonstrated how the explosion caused the front third of the aircraft to separate. As the engines continued to provide thrust, the remaining two-thirds of the craft were lifted another three thousand feet. A little basic physics helped explain what witnesses saw and heard in the summer skies off Long Island. Most reported seeing streaks of light followed by a loud roar and then a huge fireball. This actually made perfect sense. Since light travels much faster than sound, observers saw the flash well before they heard the sound of the center fuel tank exploding. That made some witnesses think the flash caused the explosion. But that was an illusion.

"All the witnesses saw events that happened after the center tank blew up," Kallstrom said. They saw the jet, already on fire and broken in two, shooting upward for twenty seconds after the cockpit and other forward sections fell away. Then the wreckage started a steep descent and the left wing broke off, spilling thousands of gallons of flaming fuel, which caused the fireball. Pieces of the jet began to hit the water forty-nine seconds after the initial blast.

The press conference ended with Kallstrom saying an explosion of gas fumes in the center tank caused the tragedy. He promised to renew the investigation if new evidence warranted it. "If something comes up, we are going to jump into it with both feet as quickly as possible. We are not writing a big 'closed' on it and putting it in some dusty safe somewhere." To this day, no new evidence has surfaced to alter O'Neill's report.

After the final report, O'Neill decided to take a break for the first time in what seemed like years. He rented a four-bedroom house on the beach in Duck, North Carolina, and Valerie accompanied him with her two children. Her son, Jay, had been attending the Naval Academy Prep School, thanks partly to O'Neill's friendship with war hero Colonel John Ripley, who helped smooth the path for Jay's entry. On weekends, Valerie and O'Neill traveled to watch Jay's football games. They also watched the big Army-Navy game, which that year was held at West Point. "We did a lot of family stuff like that," Valerie recalled. "It was a lot of fun."

Several weeks later, the couple celebrated Christmas Eve in typical O'Neill style. They attended midnight mass at Norman Vincent Peale's Marble Church on East Twenty-ninth Street near their apartment—and then went out to a French bistro. "You know John, he always had to be out," Valerie said. Early the next morning, O'Neill left Valerie to drive off to Atlantic City and spend the day with his parents, his estranged wife, and their two children. It was the first Christmas Valerie ever spent alone. O'Neill came home around 10:30 P.M. and they ordered takeout Chinese and ate it in bed before dozing off.

O'Neill turned his attention in the first months of 1998 to getting support from headquarters to expand the Al Qaeda unit dealing with bin Laden and radical Islamic fundamentalist terrorism. But even the indictment of bin Laden did not produce greater interest from Washington to disgorge him from Afghanistan. Nor did the conviction and sentencing of Ramzi Yousef that took place in Manhattan Federal Court. "Yes, I am a terrorist and I am proud of it," Yousef said before he was sentenced to life in prison on February 12, 1998. "And I support terrorism so long as it was against the United States government and against Israel, because you are more than terrorists, you are the ones who invented terrorism and using it every day. You are butchers, liars and hypocrites."

But even so high profile a success for law enforcement could not advance the fight against terrorism without the backing of the U.S. military, and that same month bin Laden upped the ante again. Emboldened by his growing support and stature in the Muslim world, he began a string of public appearances and announced the formation of the World Islamic Front for Jihad against Jews and the Crusaders. Bin Laden was joined by Dr. Ayman al-Zawahiri of Egypt, the head of Egyptian Islamic Jihad, a virulent anti-Western terror group responsible for assassinating Egyptian President Anwar Sadat for trying to make peace with his Israeli neighbors. The group also shot hundreds of tourists in Egypt in its bid to oust the secular government there and replace it with Islamic leaders. Dr. al-Zawahiri's appearance with bin Laden could not have been more menacing. O'Neill believed that if bin Laden could be compared to Hitler, Dr. al-Zawahiri was the Benito Mussolini in this new axis of twisted religious terrorism. And there was another terror leader in attendance, Abu Yassir Ahmed Taha from Egypt's al-Gamma'a Al-Islamiya, which represented the Islamic terror groups in North Africa.

"America has been occupying the most sacred lands of Islam, the Arabian Peninsula," bin Laden began, reiterating his anti-U.S. platform.

> It has been stealing its resources, dictating to its leaders, humiliating its people, and frightening neighboring peoples of Islam. The most evident proof is when the Americans went too far in their aggression against the people of Iraq. Despite major destruction to the Iraqi people at the hands of the Christian alliance and the great number of

victims exceeding one million, Americans are trying once against to repeat these horrifying massacres as if they are not satisfied with the long blockade or the destruction."

Here they come today to eradicate the rest of these people and to humiliate its Muslim neighbors. Although the Americans' objectives of these wars are religious and economic, they are also to serve the Jewish state and distract from the occupation of the Holy Land and its killing of Muslims there. The most evident proof is their persistence to destroy Iraq, the most powerful neighboring Arab state. All those crimes and calamities are an explicit declaration by the Americans of war on Allah, his Prophet, and Muslims.

Based upon this and in order to obey the Almighty [bin Laden concluded] we hereby give Muslims the following judgment: The judgment to kill and fight Americans and their allies, whether civilians or military, is an obligation for every Muslim who is able to do so in any country. In the name of Allah, we call upon every Muslim who believes in Allah and asks for forgiveness to abide by Allah's order by killing Americans and stealing their money anywhere, anytime and whenever possible.

O'Neill was alarmed. He knew bin Laden's public pronouncements would be followed by action; he just did not know where. The explicit threats seemed more than enough of a warning to mobilize decisive action from the Clinton administration, but the White House, mired in the Monica Lewinsky scandal, was unresponsive. "You had to fight his political aides to get his attention," said Jack Caravelli, who worked at the time as a National Security Council director in the White House. "That is just the way it was. Smart government people know that you can only manage one crisis at a time and Lewinsky was always that crisis. The Lewinsky affair just hung over everything. The domestic guys would weigh in on foreign policy decision. Sandy Berger, the national security adviser, would tell the president to take action and focus. But the domestic political advisers had his ear."

The administration did send UN Ambassador William Richard to Pakistan and Afghanistan that April for talks with senior Taliban officials on turning over bin Laden in exchange for UN recognition. But the talks went nowhere. Taliban leaders declined and continued to grant bin Laden the status of "protected guest." Bin Laden was free to operate at will, and he decided to step up his campaign to get out his message about a jihad against America.

He invited ABC correspondent John Miller to Afghanistan for an interview to be broadcast later, and held a press conference in Khost on May 26, 1998, warning of impending attacks against the United States and speaking ominously of "good news coming." Attending that conference was Mohammed Rashed Daoud al-'Owhali, who, like bin Laden, came from a wealthy devout Saudi family, and trained with bin Laden in the Khandan command. al-'Owhali was schooled in kidnapping, gathering intelligence, and operating and managing a cell. He was ready to be a martyr in an anti-American operation and asked bin Laden for a mission.

Two days later, ABC aired its bin Laden interview. "We do not differentiate between those dressed in military uniforms and civilians: They are all targets," bin Laden said, predicting a "black day for America." On June 12, the State Department issued a traveler's warning and increased security at many U.S. government facilities in the Middle East and Asia. But no measures were taken in Africa.

No one ever questioned O'Neill's commitment to his work or his brilliance in mobilizing his people. What put some bureau people off was a sense that his hard-charging style might lead him to make mistakes. Straitlaced, uninspired types forever like to predict that more flamboyant, more imaginative, more passionate individuals like O'Neill can't quite be trusted. When it came to his work, O'Neill never gave his critics or detractors any ammunition to use against him. He was an FBI man to the core, and his work was exemplary.

But given the atmosphere at the bureau in those years, even a seemingly trivial misstep could have important consequences, and what insiders later called the beginning of the end of O'Neill's FBI career actually came when he was off duty. He had planned a weekend drive to Atlantic City with Valerie to visit an old FBI friend, Bernie Murphy, who was working at Bally Resorts on the boardwalk. They planned to drive down in O'Neill's 1991 blue Buick, the same one he used in Chicago and Washington years before. The aging vehicle was always in the repair shop, draining O'Neill of cash. Every time he got behind the wheel of the car, it was an adventure.

Sure enough, barely ten miles out of Manhattan, the car began to chug and coasted to a standstill on Route 3, near the Meadowlands Sports Complex. Stranded near an exit ramp, O'Neill called the AAA for a tow, and when the driver arrived twenty minutes later, O'Neill instructed him to take his aging Buick to a nearby industrial park. As luck, or rather misfortune, would have it, O'Neill's Buick had died just a couple miles away from an FBI garage where he kept his bureau car.

The FBI has strict rules, which it expects will be followed to the letter. Agents are prohibited from using their vehicles for nongovernment business and from having civilians in them at any time. Mostly it's a matter of money. The government fears the potential liability it might face if someone not authorized to be in the car is injured in an accident. Well aware of the restriction, O'Neill avoided breaking the rules by using his Buick for nearly all his travels, both for the FBI and otherwise, and keeping his FBI car in the New Jersey garage, which was actually in a warehouse in a nondescript commercial strip packed with small office buildings and small factories.

The location of the garage was a secret, and a sensitive secret at that. The garage is home not only to agents' cars, but also to a fleet of vehicles the FBI uses in investigations, such as phony telephone trucks and ambulances. O'Neill greeted the mechanic who takes care of the garage, who then allowed Valerie to go inside to freshen up. When she came out of the ladies' room, she volunteered to walk to a nearby diner and use a pay phone to call for a car service to pick them up. She walked two blocks to the diner, only to find that it was closed. Frustrated, she sat on the stoop to decide what to do next. That's when O'Neill suddenly pulled up in his bureau car.

O'Neill was breaking the rules, and he knew it, but here he was, consumed with fighting to save the world from the threat of fundamentalist terrorists. This was such a petty violation, it seemed hard to imagine that anyone would ever know about it, let alone care. But four months later, the garage mechanic became the subject of an investigation. Allegations were made that he was repairing and servicing the personal cars of agents in the warehouse. During his questioning, he mentioned that O'Neill had been there one recent day with a female and she had been taken inside the restricted facility. Unfortunately for O'Neill, the alleged security breach triggered an in-depth internal investigation of O'Neill's actions that day. Valerie and O'Neill were both formally questioned. He was alternately angry, embarrassed, and incredulous that top brass in Washington were treating this technical violation of regulations as though it were a national security leak that held the potential for criminal penalties, including prison.

The timing of the incident could not have been worse. O'Neill's faux pas would have resulted in at most a minor wrist slap under any other FBI director. But that would never be the case in a Louis Freeh administration. His rigid standards went well beyond his approach to investigating the various Clinton scandals. Freeh had instituted an internal FBI policy called "The

Bright Line," triggered when an agent crossed the boundary of professional conduct.

Under Freeh's Bright Line, violations by any bureau employee would be fully investigated and appropriately punished, no exceptions. Some agents and supervisors complained that during Freeh's regime, even minor transgressions never previously scrutinized were sent up for review by the Office of Professional Responsibility. O'Neill prided himself on the fact that none of his agents was ever sent to OPR. "He took care of everything under his command," said Ken Pierneck.

The hard-line policy was actually tougher on supervisors than on agents. As a former agent, Freeh was well aware of how the rank and file took notice when a supervisor was in trouble to see if he was treated with kid gloves. Any hint of leniency could create the impression of a double standard on discipline. Fitting with that severe approach, any mark on the record would remain for three years—and serve as a roadblock to promotion. Freeh and the equally hard-line Attorney General Reno were unlikely to ignore such a blemish, regardless of their respect for O'Neill.

"It was the kiss of death," Pierneck said. "Even if you received your punishment, a slap on the wrist, or a loss of pay, it lingered at least three years. And you could not get considered for anything. It took you out of circulation."

Even close associates of Freeh thought the policy may have gone too far. Schiliro was best man at Freeh's wedding. The two men remain close friends. But Schiliro believes that the tough policy had the unintended consequence of making supervisors more timid, and less likely to take the kind of calculated risks that often make the difference in fulfilling a mission. "Under Freeh's Bright Line policy, if you crossed over it, there was only black and white," he said.

O'Neill might have gotten away with it if he had not allowed Valerie to use the bathroom. But he was found guilty and sentenced to a month off without pay. O'Neill knew this single black mark on his previously unblemished record could derail his dream of a promotion to head the New York office, and he was devastated. "Do you know how that humiliated John?" Valerie asked. "How that embarrassed him? How awful he felt?"

O'Neill hired a lawyer to appeal the ruling, but the finding was upheld. The suspension, however, was trimmed to fifteen days. He was wounded as a professional, and given his mounting debts and responsibilities, he could little afford to lose two weeks' salary. "Lew, this is really going to hurt me," O'Neill confided to Schiliro. "I have expenses. I have a lot of expenses. I have a lot to deal with personally."

It was a crushing blow. John O'Neill did not just work for the FBI; he loved to say, "I am the FBI." He grew depressed, morose, and then paranoid. He felt cut off from everything that mattered to him. "The FBI was what he was, not what he did," said Schiliro. O'Neill was convinced that higher-ups, notably Thomas Pickard, now an assistant director, and Freeh—both men who frowned on agents with the flamboyant lifestyle of O'Neill—would forever use the vehicle mishap as an excuse to bar promotion.

"John got screwed," said Carson Dunbar, then the SAC of administration and the head of the car investigation. "No doubt what he did was technically wrong, but other people would have gotten an oral reprimand."

The problem was not so much the incident, or the bad news it represented for O'Neill's future. The problem was O'Neill's wounded pride, which kept steering him away from reckoning with his own mistake and putting it behind him. Instead, he nursed an increasingly bitter sense of grievance. Like Bill Clinton, he wanted to be liked, and took it personally when people were against him, as if his charm and charisma and flair for his job were supposed to win everyone over. "No one worked harder, and was more successful than John," said Dunbar. "My wife used to say when John talked to you, you always felt that he was truly interested. John could not handle that there were people who did not like him. When you harpoon people, as John was said to do, they want to see you harpooned. But John got so hung up that guys were out to get him, he failed to fully see what his role was. This incident changed him."

Even sensible advice from Schiliro just fueled more paranoia. Knowing how much O'Neill coveted the New York job, Schiliro urged him to apply to take over the New Jersey office when that job came open. That way he would have experience running another office, usually considered a requirement for taking over the all-important New York office. O'Neill would also have time in New Jersey to show his value and put the car incident behind him. But to O'Neill, the idea was unthinkable. New Jersey may have been a two-minute ride away through the Holland Tunnel, but for a Manhattan-loving bon vivant like O'Neill, it might as well have been North Dakota. "Is someone trying to get rid of me?" he asked.

Joe Billy, the assistant terrorism boss, knew the loss of two weeks' pay would be a hardship for O'Neill and his already strained credit cards. Even though Billy had a family of his own and could little afford to be handing out donations, he wrote O'Neill a personal check for $1,500 to help him through the crunch. O'Neill took the check from Billy, but never cashed it. Privately he sobbed over the kindness of Billy's gesture. "Do you believe that fucking guy?" he told Val.

O'Neill's run-in with FBI discipline may have changed him, and may even have led to his eventual downfall in the bureau, but nothing could have kept him from fixating on the danger posed by bin Laden and his message of hatred. Jerry Hauer remembers driving in his car on First Avenue on July 4, 1998, and spotting O'Neill walking on the street in shorts not far from his apartment in Peter Cooper Village. Hauer told his driver to slow down so he could give O'Neill some grief about showing off his knees. "How's it going?" he said. But O'Neill wasn't in the mood.

"My friend's causing trouble again," he said, leaning into the car window.

"Who?" Hauer asked.

"OBL," O'Neill replied. "This guy's a problem."

By then, bin Laden's East Africa Al Qaeda cell was an operational terrorist unit ready to attack. On July 31, al-'Owhali completed a videotape to celebrate his "martyrdom" as a member of the "Army of Liberation of the Holy Lands." He and an Al Qaeda gang rented an unfurnished two-story house and garage surrounded by a high wall and hedge at 43 Rundu Estates, in Nairobi, Kenya. On August 6, the senior terrorist in the plot, Mohammed Sadeek Odeh, a militant Palestinian from Jordan who trained with bin Laden, was told to leave Africa for Pakistan.

The following morning, al-'Owhali carried four stun grenades and a handgun into a Toyota pickup filled with four hundred pounds of explosives. He and an accomplice drove the vehicle through the bustling streets of Nairobi, a city of two million. As the pickup approached the gate of the U.S. embassy, a building he had scouted for months, al-'Owhali ran into an unforeseen problem. The security guard did not recognize his vehicle and declined to let the truck get any closer to the compound.

Al-'Owhali apparently had a change of heart about becoming a martyr. At about 10:30 A.M., he jumped out of the passenger seat, threw two stun grenades at the heroic sentry, and turned and ran. His suicide companion, however, fired his handgun at the windows of the embassy, giving al-'Owhali precious seconds to flee before being hit with the concussion and debris. The huge device took down most of the crowded seven-story embassy, destroyed an adjoining five-story secretarial college, and wrecked a twenty-five-story bank filled with innocent Kenyans, like the security guard, who were not as fortunate as al-'Owhali.

Frank Pressley, a communication expert at the embassy, said

the force of the blast sent him flying across a room and slammed him into a wall. Dazed, he looked up and saw there was no ceiling. "I just could not believe what I saw," he said. "I looked around and I saw like chunks of blood or red kind of meat on the walls. I had lost part of my jaw. I lost a large section of my shoulder. I looked down and I saw bone sticking out of my shirt."

Mary Ofli, a forty-six-year-old examiner who worked in the financial management center on the first floor, later recalled for a Manhattan jury how she found herself on the floor with a thick warm liquid—her own blood—covering her face and upper body. "I was down under chairs and I called to my friends. There was no sign. I knew then that I was alone."

Sam Nagana testified he was in the bank and instantly buried in the rubble. Rescuers took two days to reach him. His legs were partially crushed and he could not walk. He was lucky. A woman pinned nearby died before help arrived.

The devastation in Nairobi was duplicated ten minutes later when a second truck bomb was delivered to the U.S. embassy in Dar es Salaam, Tanzania, several hundred miles to the southeast. Translator Elizabeth Slater said the embassy went pitch black. She was hurled to a corner. Struggling to her feet and down a dusty stairwell, she passed "all kinds of body parts" before finally emerging on the street to encounter yet another horror. "I saw a horribly disfigured guard," she said. "He did not have any skin left and I just wished he would hurry up . . . and die."

In all, 247 people were killed and another 5,000 innocent men, women, and children were wounded. Experts believe the death toll would have surpassed the September 11, 2001, attacks on the World Trade Center had it not been for the heroic security guard who prevented the truck from getting beneath the Nairobi embassy. Fourteen of the dead were U.S. citizens, including a diplomat and his son who was working a summer job. "My father used to say, regardless of where it happens, in Tanzania, in Yemen, in Malaysia or Pakistan, it does not matter," O'Neill's son, J.P., recalled. "Those Americans were doing their duty to help our country. They did not choose to die that day, at the embassy, on a plane, or on a ship. And it shouldn't make a difference that it did not happen on U.S. soil."

But it did. Despite the implications for future bloodshed elsewhere against American interests, the attack was not dealt with in a firm and harsh manner. The Clinton administration's ineffectual salvo simply emboldened bin Laden to step up his violence against the United States, just as O'Neill had warned.

11

"THEY CAN STRIKE ANYTIME"

It was around 4:30 A.M. in New York when the U.S. embassies were bombed. O'Neill was awake at home in his Peter Cooper Village apartment when headquarters urgently rang his encrypted telephone with word of the simultaneous terrorist explosions. O'Neill knew immediately who was responsible. He dialed the operations hot line at 26 Federal Plaza to alert his agents that bin Laden had raised the stakes again. Detective Pat Pogan, a biochemical and mass destruction expert assigned to the joint terrorist task force, had just arrived at his desk.

"The first call was from John O'Neill," he said.

"Patty, what's going on?" O'Neill asked.

Pogan knew O'Neill was the kind of leader who didn't want him to mince words. He preferred the "blunt, honest truth," Pogan remembered, so that's what he gave him.

"There are a lot of dead and injured and it looks real bad from the damage and there are a lot of fires," Pogan said.

"Let everyone know I'm coming in," O'Neill told him. "We have to get moving on this. I know who did this. It's bin Laden."

Lewis Schiliro, then head of the New York office, remembers O'Neill immediately fingering bin Laden. "John said it, minute one," he recalled.

The tragedy was not without opportunity for O'Neill. He didn't need any added motivation for doing his best to hunt down bin Laden, something he had been passionately committed to for years, but as he raced off to work that day, he knew he could have a chance to redeem himself and perhaps even erase the stigma of the car incident. O'Neill was never more in his element than during a crisis.

"Guys were calling from all over and John had a handle on it right from the beginning," Pogan recalled. "He got the right people going. People were talking. Computers and faxes were going and phones were ringing. It was orchestrated chaos and he was the orchestra leader. He was on the phone directing people, with one phone in one hand, another phone in the other. There was no doubt who was in charge."

Once the center was fully operational, O'Neill marched over to see Joseph Billy, then the special agent in charge of foreign counterintelligence in New York. Billy was watching the carnage on television. "You know bin Laden did this," O'Neill told him. O'Neill told Billy he wanted him to lead the first wave of agents from New York to Dar es Salaam, Tanzania.

The FBI has a reputation as an ultrasophisticated law enforcement agency whose agents have access to every state-of-the-art technological gizmo known to exist. But the reality is far more modest. Agents often work in a low-tech, low-comfort world, even on a highly important mission like flying off to Africa to investigate the embassy bombings. The contingent O'Neill sent from New York did not fly to Andrews Air Force Base in Washington to catch a military transport. Instead, they had to take a bus—and not just any bus. They were loaded into a transit bus provided by the NYPD. Not only were they uncomfortable, left to squirm on the cheap plastic seats during the interminable ride, they were stuck in the slow lane. The city had rigged the bus with a governor, which limited the top speed to fifty miles per hour. The drive to Andrews took six hours, and O'Neill was furious when he found out.

"I told him about the governor, and he said, 'Why didn't you take it off?'" Billy remembered. "I said, 'I didn't know how.' I'm telling you if he could have driven the bus quicker himself he would have. There was always a sense of exigency with O'Neill that the trail was getting cold."

O'Neill wanted to fly to Africa and lead the investigation. His New York office had the expertise about bin Laden, and this was just the opening they needed to close in on him. Freeh and his top two deputies were all out of town when the bombings occurred, and that left criminal division head Thomas Pickard temporarily in charge. He was cautious by nature, and according to FBI protocol, the Washington field office (WFO) had primary "extraterritorial" responsibility for incidents in the Middle East that involved American interests. Pickard does not hide the fact that he was uncertain at first about what had happened. "It was early and we were still wondering if it was a gasoline leak or something else in the initial hours of confusion," he said.

Pickard ordered a team of agents from the Washington office to report to Andrews for a flight to Africa. The group was led by Sheila Horan, special agent in charge of the national security division in the WFO, and Kenneth Pierneck, O'Neill's former top aide in Chicago, then the assistant special agent for counterterrorism at the WFO.

"The Washington field office was smaller than New York, but this was clearly a crime against U.S. citizens overseas and the WFO had jurisdiction," said Pierneck, who was eventually the supervisor in Dar es Salaam. "We got out of the chute much faster. But New York had the history with Al Qaeda and the World Trade Center, and they had the best advocate working for them, John O'Neill."

Schiliro told Pickard the New York office should lead the investigation, but Pickard demurred. "We can always change," he told Schiliro. O'Neill was upset. Any time lost in sending his agents was a gift to bin Laden. Even if one shred of evidence went undetected, or one lead went unexplored, it would be an inexcusable failure, given the stakes involved, but O'Neill worried that Pickard's judgment might be clouded by his loyalty to the Washington field office, which he had previously headed. He also wondered if the car incident could be a factor in Pickard's reluctance to immediately trust O'Neill on the Africa investigation.

"John was pissed," Blitzer said. "He was beside himself, calling me every minute."

Fran Townsend, Attorney General Reno's top aide and by then O'Neill's confidante at the Department of Justice, said O'Neill felt personally insulted by the initial snub. He viewed it as a "tremendous slap in the face," she told PBS. "This is the World Series and he's gotten benched. That's exactly how he felt about it. He was very, very upset about it, and bitter."

Even the intervention of Mary Jo White could not move the FBI brass. She used her influence with Reno and the White House to push for giving the case to the New York office. It was far better equipped to handle the investigation, she argued, and was better versed in collecting evidence for a successful prosecution. She still thinks it was the wrong decision. Bureaucratic caution may be unavoidable, but the bottom line is that the investigation "lost a little bit in those early days," she said. "If the New York agents had been running it, we might have moved a little faster," she said.

Patricia Kelly was the regional security officer in charge at the U.S. embassy in Nairobi, and she was also the sister of FBI agent Kathy Kiser, O'Neill's old friend in Baltimore. Kelly was in Washington for a ceremony marking her elevation to special agent in charge of all diplomatic service protection when her husband called and woke her up to relay the bad news. "Patricia, you need to go to CNN," he said. "The embassies in Kenya and Dar es Salaam have been bombed.'"

Wiping sleep from her eyes, Kelly jumped out of bed and turned on CNN and saw the first shocking images of thousands of injured people screaming and running for their lives or being rushed to local hospitals. As the camera scanned the destruction, she could barely recognize the buildings she knew so well. Structures she had walked through hundreds of times were ripped to pieces, trapping scores of people, including her friends, in mountains of debris.

Kelly could not believe her eyes. She knew that regions of Africa were dangerous places, rife with crime, and that individual countries were corrupt and unstable, and that borders between the countries were extremely porous. Would-be terrorists and criminals could move freely around the continent. But U.S. intelligence had gleaned no hard information about any imminent attack on the African continent. The CIA had incorrectly theorized that bin Laden's recent threat of "good news to come" would result in violence in the Middle East, not Africa.

Kelly's hotel phone rang again. She expected to hear her husband's voice again, but instead it was a State Department official ordering her to grab some clothes, hail a cab, and get to Andrews Air Force Base. "We have a plane ready to go," she was told. Kelly arrived at Andrews to find that FBI supervisor Sheila Horan was already on board with about thirty FBI agents, primarily evidence recovery specialists, crime-scene experts, and explosive technicians. The military plane was airborne by 10 A.M. with this first wave of agents seated on the hard, steel seats, eating boxed lunches they bought out of their own pockets.

The plane touched down to refuel at an air-force base in Rota, Spain, but a cockpit fire forced the agents to change planes. The diplomatic security officers and agents finally arrived two and a half days later, having traveled eight thousand miles from Washington, D.C. When they arrived in Nairobi, Kelly was in for a fresh shock. The devastation had been miniaturized on the small screen of a television in her Washington hotel. Here the true-to-scale devastation was overwhelming. "It was just horrible," she said. "I could hardly recognize the interiors of buildings that I knew."

Kelly was a detail-oriented security official, but even she felt lost. Many of her familiar reference points had been obliterated.

The embassy was so badly damaged that she could barely instruct rescuers where to go. "It was difficult to know where things had been," she recalled. "It was total devastation. Body parts were everywhere. The scene was gruesome."

Joe Billy had a similar impression when he arrived in Dar es Salaam. "The destruction went for blocks," he said. "Terrible. Unbelievable. Phenomenal destruction. You had to be there to believe it."

Kelly immediately established a perimeter of agents around the Kenya embassy and a safe zone for rescuers to enter and leave. She dispatched a team of agents to protect the ambassador and to remove any classified documents they could recover for transportation to the makeshift embassy she had established at the U.S. Agency for International Development, fifteen miles away in the suburbs. "It was very dark and very eerie," she said.

More order was gradually established as Marines arrived by military transport to take up positions around the bombed embassy and provide additional protection at the temporary mission. Hour by hour, Kelly learned which friends were among the dead or missing. Soon she stopped asking. "We did not really want to know the answer after a while," she remembered.

The FBI, with Horan in charge in Nairobi, began securing the crime scene, communicating with the local cops, establishing protocols for examining evidence, and trying to investigate leads. Imagine the complexity of organizing an investigation of this magnitude on America soil, and multiply that a hundredfold in a foreign country so far removed from a First World level of sophistication in medical care, law enforcement, and security. Factor in the scorching heat and the ravenous mosquitoes and you have the makings of an investigative nightmare.

The FBI and African authorities quickly determined that a "victim" in a hospital had wounds consistent with those that would be sustained while running away from the blast. That suggested he had been involved. How else would he have known to run away? The patient turned out to be Mohamed Rashed Daoud al-'Owhali, the terrorist who had asked bin Laden for a mission when they were together in Afghanistan. Al-'Owhali's arrest, made within days of the Kenyan blast, was the first major break in the case.

Meanwhile, authorities in Pakistan stopped a man traveling from Kenya through Yemen with phony travel documents that did not even bear his photograph. That passenger was Mohamed Sadeek Odeh, who had trained in bin Laden's Afghanistan camps and had tutored Al Qaeda supporters involved in the Black Hawk Down murders in Sudan. O'Neill ordered Joe Billy to fly from Kenya to pick Odeh up from the Pakistanis, who appeared to be motivated mostly by healthy self-interest and a desire to keep a possible cold-blooded terrorist out of their own country, not any desire to help the U.S. investigation. Billy hurried off to Dar es Salaam to fetch Odeh for questioning before the Pakistanis had time to change their minds about releasing him.

O'Neill kept up-to-date on the investigations through daily conference calls over secured satellite feeds, which usually involved Reno, Freeh, and Pickard as well as himself. But sometimes the feeds could not accommodate an additional tie-in to New York, leaving O'Neill out of the loop and feeling like a caged animal. "He hated getting anything secondhand," Mike Rolince said.

Just days after the FBI arrived, there was a threat against another embassy, this one in Koala, Uganda, where a large glass-and-steel structure stood isolated and vulnerable with many American diplomats inside. The FBI needed to know whether the dangerous chatter they were hearing related to bin Laden or to local tribal strife. So an order was given—without O'Neill's knowledge—to shift a group of agents from Dar es Salaam to Uganda to investigate this new threat. O'Neill was livid, and not only because he was kept out of the loop. He strongly believed that the families of his agents should never hear about an investigation's shift to another country from a television news report. "If we move an agent from New York," O'Neill barked at Mike Rolince, "we have to call their family. We can't have them watching CNN and see their loved ones on TV." Rolince never forgot the lesson O'Neill taught him about always remembering the families, even in the pitch of a battle.

One week into the investigation, O'Neill believed the FBI had overwhelming evidence that bin Laden was behind the attack. This included the so-called happy talk that had been picked up via satellite eavesdropping of bin Laden and his Al Qaeda members exulting over the bombings. Armed with that information and the arrests of al-'Owhali and Odeh pointing to bin Laden, O'Neill appealed to Freeh that the jurisdiction should be shifted to New York. "John was getting information every day that UBL cells in Nairobi and Somalia were behind the attacks," Schiliro said. But Freeh told O'Neill he had to wait.

The delay left O'Neill even more frustrated than before. The investigation was the biggest terrorism case in U.S. history. With a few suspects already in custody, O'Neill believed the case could not only be successfully prosecuted, it could lead the FBI directly to bin Laden. Keith Weston of Scotland Yard's terrorism division said O'Neill was so anxious to get bin Laden that he discussed leading a raiding party into Afghanistan to capture the Al Qaeda leader. "John wanted to go door by door and cave by cave to get him," Weston said. "And we would have followed him because that is how much respect we had for him."

O'Neill was stuck cooling his heels in New York partly because of a basic clash of visions of how an FBI agent should go about his business. He and Freeh clearly had great respect for each other, but in some ways they could not have been more different. Freeh was a devout Catholic. He was a family man with six children. He believed in strict discipline as an end in itself and kept an eye on mavericks. O'Neill was everything Freeh was not. He sported cravats, custom suits, Gucci shoes, and semitransparent silk socks. He wore a nine-millimeter revolver strapped to his ankle. He threw himself into his work and threw himself into his other passions, too. He hit popular nightspots and rubbed elbows with rich swells and celebrities. He smoked fine cigars and sipped Chivas Regal. Director Freeh, by comparison, worked off his energy by running. O'Neill and Freeh were two patriots united in their quest to protect the United States, but at a time when Freeh and all of Washington were consumed by an atmosphere of scandal, the differences in personal style between the staid director and the flamboyant bin Laden hunter seemed to O'Neill to take on an increased importance.

O'Neill would not have cared about Clinton's infamous dalliance with an intern if the resulting scandal had not compromised the president's ability to deal with what O'Neill saw as clearly the most pressing challenge to U.S. security since the end of the Cold War. He hoped Clinton would do the right thing, even as he spent far too much of his time worrying about how to manage a crisis he brought on himself with his reckless unzipping. So when Clinton announced he would address the nation on August 17, 1998, the same day he became the first president to testify before a federal grand jury, O'Neill and his team held out for an optimistic interpretation. Maybe the former Arkansas governor would at last take the necessary steps and lash out at bin Laden with effective military force.

O'Neill had been at his post on the top level of the FBI's bustling command center virtually without sleep since the bombing occurred ten days earlier. He worked nonstop, fielding calls from FBI supervisors in Africa and other points throughout the Middle East and providing direction and support to more than five hundred agents in what was now the largest investigation ever mounted by the United States outside its borders.

The bustling command center came to a halt that evening when a voice said, "Ladies and gentlemen, I give you the president of the United States," and images of President Clinton filled the three giant screens, interrupting live feeds from the Africa disasters. O'Neill and the roomful of investigators paused to listen anxiously to their commander in chief, hopeful that the president's emergency announcement would mobilize the vast power of the U.S. to strike against bin Laden. There was a sense of unanimity within the room that Clinton would at last detail how the power of the United States would descend upon the terror leader.

But President Clinton instead spoke of an issue that was far more personal. Appearing florid and contrite, Clinton stared into the television camera and quickly confessed that he had an intimate relationship with twenty-one-year-old White House intern Monica Lewinsky. Clinton had angrily insisted for seven months that he "did not have sex with that woman, Miss Lewinsky," but now he admitted that he had misled—some would say lied—to the American public.

The president had taken to the airways to head off the obvious furor that would envelop him when his secret testimony about the Lewinsky affair became public. His advisers had urged him to use words like *apology* and *sorry*, but Clinton was too annoyed at what he perceived as Starr's prying into his private life to capitulate completely. The president concluded his five-minute appearance by saying, "Our country has been distracted by this matter for too long and I take my responsibility for my part in all of this. That is all I can do. Now is the time—in fact, it is past time—to move on. And so tonight I ask you to turn away from the spectacle of the past seven months, to repair the fabric of our national discourse and to return our attention to all the challenges and all the promise of the next American century."

O'Neill shook his head in dismay, and not because he frowned on Clinton's personal life. O'Neill's own life was every bit as complicated as Clinton's appeared to be. But his affairs never sidetracked his devotion to "the mission" of combating threats from bin Laden and a host of other global terrorists. Clinton had allowed his personal life to take his focus away from the mission.

Inside the FBI command center in New York, the frustration and disappointment felt by O'Neill and the roomful of agents was palpable.

Freeh had still not relented and let O'Neill take over the mission. But the director decided to fly to Africa to visit the crime scenes himself and rally his agents, just as he had previously gone to Saudi Arabia after the OPM-Sang and the Khobar Towers bombings. Freeh asked Schiliro to join him, and Schiliro jumped at the opportunity to spend time with the director and lobby him on O'Neill's behalf. "I thought it was a great chance to be alone with Freeh and make the case that New York should take over the investigation," Schiliro recalled.

The two FBI officials arrived in Dar es Salaam on August 21 and were met at the airport by Billy and Pierneck in an armored Suburban that had been brought in a few days earlier for a visit by Secretary of State Madeline Albright. Freeh and Schiliro were given a whirlwind tour of the damaged embassy and conferred with their agents on the scene, and then in the late afternoon they took off for a one-hour flight to Nairobi, Kenya. Their plane had just lifted off when President Clinton emerged from seclusion on Martha's Vineyard to interrupt scheduled programming with another emergency announcement. Once again his image filled the screens behind O'Neill's podium in the FBI command center in New York.

"Today, we have struck back," Clinton said. In a surprise announcement, he revealed he had just authorized a strike of seventy-five Tomahawk missiles fired from American warships and submarines in the Red Sea and Arabian Sea. One strike was against one of bin Laden's training camps in Afghanistan, and the other was against a pharmaceutical plant in the Sudan that U.S. intelligence sources had identified as a chemical-weapons facility manufacturing "VX," a deadly nerve agent. The assault was the most formidable American military offensive ever undertaken against a private sponsor of terrorism. The president called the synchronized attacks an act of self-defense against imminent terrorist plots, and said he considered them to be retaliation for the twin African bombings.

"Let our actions today send this message loud and clear: There are no expendable American targets. There will be no sanctuary for terrorists," Clinton said. He then cut short his vacation and headed to Washington for a conference with his national security team in the White House situation room.

The attack was precisely the kind of stern military action O'Neill had been advocating all along. But he did not rejoice. Instead, he became visibly enraged. He immediately came to the conclusion that Clinton launched the attack to try to deflect attention from the Lewinsky scandal and his own impending impeachment. O'Neill's suspicions were based on inside knowledge. He and a few people inside a tight circle of national security officials knew that the intelligence Clinton was using to support the positions he attacked was old. In fact, it was as much as a year out-of-date, not nearly fresh enough to justify the launch of a surgically precise air assault.

"If they were going to use the information, they should have used it when we gave it over," O'Neill fumed to Detective Louis Napoli of the joint terrorist task force. "Don't they have anything better to do? And why didn't they confer with us before they did something like this?"

O'Neill soon learned that he was not the only major FBI figure the White House had failed to notify. Amazingly, the White House had also failed to inform Clinton's nemesis, Freeh, about the strikes. The FBI director was furious, and not just because he wanted to be in the loop. His agents were stationed in two heavily Muslim countries that were loaded with bin Laden sympathizers. The agents had been given no warning whatsoever, and were unprepared for a potential retaliatory strike that could have come in the wake of the missile attacks.

"Freeh was pissed," said Schiliro. "We had agents on the

streets, exposed and wearing FBI jackets, and the White House was firing missiles. What better targets for reprisals than the FBI?"

Clinton and Freeh had by this time developed an openly adversarial relationship. Under Freeh, the bureau investigated a long list of ethical and potentially criminal scandals involving Clinton and his wife. After dealing with the controversial real estate deals known as Whitewater, the Travelgate scandal involving the White House Travel Office, and allegations of campaign law violations, Freeh had come to shun political niceties when it came to Clinton and the White House. Clinton came to distrust Freeh, and their relationship grew so frosty that Clinton stopped inviting his FBI director to top-level briefings, and ultimately, even declined to say publicly whether he had any confidence in Freeh.

The director would normally have been advised of such military action as the retaliatory strikes. Given the fact it was his agents working on the front lines, he would have been notified in order to ensure their troops were protected in the event of any "blowback." Instead, the FBI agents and military personnel on the ground in Africa were forced to scurry to prepare for possible retaliation. FBI supervisors suddenly had to locate each of their agents and make certain they were protected. Pierneck recalled getting a phone call in Dar es Salaam, and then turning on CNN to get the news, which prompted him to order SWAT teams to take up positions at the weakest points on the compound's perimeter and prepare to evacuate his troops if the threat level increased.

"It caught us by surprise," said Billy. "We did not know how far-flung the military operation would be. We just knew the U.S. was striking out at another Muslim country. I don't know why we were viewed as unimportant."

Freeh and O'Neill would soon grow even more irate over the White House handling of the missile strikes. Even though neither

FBI official had been trusted with the sensitive information that a missile strike was being prepared, U.S. officials tipped off the Pakistanis. This might have sounded to some like a mere diplomatic courtesy, necessary to gain permission to fly the missiles in over Pakistani territory. But in fact, anyone familiar with Pakistan knew that sharing such information with the ISI, Pakistan's intelligence agency, was highly risky. The ISI had ties to the Taliban regime, which they had helped put in place.

Few insiders realized at the time that the ISI immediately shared the confidential U.S. military warnings with their friends, the Taliban, who in turn warned their distinguished guest, bin Laden. "The attacks were doomed from the start by the U.S. government," a U.S. intelligence official recalled. "The White House was just afraid of what the Pakistanis would say, what the Chinese would say, what the Russians would say. We gave the Pakistanis four hours' notice to be nice, and they of course told bin Laden. If we wanted to kill him, we could have. But no one wanted to send in a ground operation."

Clinton said the strike on the Al Qaeda training complex in Khost, Afghanistan, just inside the border with Pakistan, was designed to pulverize "one of the most active terrorist bases in the world." His advisers said there may have been a broader meeting of bin Laden and his upper echelon from the Egyptian Islamic Jihad and the Armed Islamic Group taking place at the camp around that time. Sandy Berger, the national security adviser, traced the timing of the strikes to "credible information" that there "may have been a meeting of some of bin Laden's organizations." William Cohen, the secretary of defense, later amplified the justification for the strikes. "We'd be derelict if we did not take action intended to cause sufficient damage to disrupt them for some time," he said.

Coming three days after the televised Lewinsky admission, the missile strikes were greeted cynically by some congressmen, who made comparisons to the recently released satirical movie *Wag the*

Dog, starring Robert De Niro and Dustin Hoffman. The film's fictional president, entangled in a sex scandal, creates a fake war and his devilish spinmeister hires a Hollywood producer to manufacture war images to distract the public from the president's personal and political woes. Defense Secretary Cohen responded stonily at a press briefing when asked about any comparisons to the movie. "The only motivation driving this action today was our absolute obligation to protect the American people from terrorist activities," he said.

But the question remains: How much did domestic political calculations have to do with the timing of the cruise-missile attacks? The scandal atmosphere unquestionably magnified the influence of Clinton's domestic political advisers, who had little grounding in world affairs. These advisers might even have made a good faith effort to grapple with what to do about bin Laden, but they lacked expertise—and were inclined instead to look for the quick fix.

"There is a saying in government that it is impossible to manage two crises at the same time, and they were managing Lewinsky," remembered Jack Caravelli, a director with the National Security Council in the White House at the time and a top CIA official. "The Lewinsky affair hung over everything. The domestic policy guys would weigh in on foreign policy decisions, to protect Clinton's political assets, but they had no clue what was really going on in the world."

Clinton knew he had to respond to the murderous twin embassy attacks, but there was a reluctance among his advisers to use military power. They worried about whether the public would support a forceful military action, and what the reaction might be in the event of American casualties. As so often was the case with Clinton, he decided on a compromise that satisfied no one. He would take military action, but only military action that was largely symbolic. Firing missiles from a distance would display a measure of force while limiting the risk to American servicemen and women.

"The missile response was limp-wristed," Caravelli said. "It was almost weaker to respond that way because you do not drive the spear of fear into your enemy. Either you find a way to hurt them or not, because what message are you sending?"

A clear message was sent that the United States was at most interested in limited strategic responses that held little risk to Clinton's popularity at a time when Americans enjoyed the comforts provided by a roaring stock market and a misplaced sense that they were safe from any terrorist attacks. As a result, the U.S. missile strikes had no appreciable military impact. Bin Laden was unhurt since he had been living for months about two hundred miles south of the site of the attacks, using a fortified and heavily guarded hilltop near Kandahar as his base. Taliban leader Mullah Mohammed Omar proudly declared bin Laden to be safe and said no injuries were sustained by his organization, but more than a dozen Afghanis were killed by the bombs that fell on the Zhawar Kill A-Badr complex. As for the pharmaceutical plant in Sudan, the facility turned out to produce little more than cheap medicines for impoverished Muslims. Sudanese officials decried the attack as "a criminal act" and vowed to rebuild the demolished facility and make it larger than before.

In the end, the Tomahawk strikes had the opposite effect from what Clinton intended: they elevated bin Laden's mythic stature as an unbeatable David fighting yet another Goliath. The attacks emboldened his army and garnered him even more support for his jihad against the United States from disaffected Muslims and anti-American fanatics.

"It was fucking stupid," said James Kallstrom, former assistant director in New York and an ex-Marine. "It was clear there was no gumption to do anything about this. We saw the war happening, yet our government would not address a thing."

Clinton did consider more concerted military action. He asked Joint Chiefs of Staff chairman General Henry H. Shelton about sending a small contingent of Special Forces into a bin Laden camp. "You know, it would scare the shit out of al Qaeda if suddenly a bunch of black ninjas rappelled out of helicopters into the middle of their camp," Clinton said, according to *The Age of Sacred Terror* authors Daniel Benjamin and Steven Simon, the director and senior director for counterterrorism on the NSC staff during Clinton's second term.

General Shelton, however, told the president such a raid could not work. The authors suggest the encounter demonstrates that Clinton wanted to take stronger action against Al Qaeda, and possibly he did. But the trouble was, Clinton seemed to be operating in a world far removed from the realities on the ground. It's highly questionable whether a small U.S. force could really have inspired fear in battle-tested mujahedeen. Then again, it was also true that the U.S. military establishment often gave presidents pessimistic views of what could be accomplished, eager to avoid the trap of having politicians put them in a position to fall short and repeat the painful experience of Vietnam. Clinton's relations with military leaders had always been strained, going back to the flap over gays in the military during the first days of his administration.

Most damning of all was Clinton's failure to seek out the best information on how to strike back at his target effectively. The rationale for retaliation largely rested on the work of O'Neill's agents. Secretary of State Madeline Albright and CIA Director George Tenet argued that the evidence gathered in Africa and the Middle East by the FBI—primarily by O'Neill's agents—demonstrated that bin Laden and Al Qaeda were responsible for the U.S. embassy bombings and that decisive action was warranted. Yet even though the White House and NSC used the evidence gleaned by the FBI in Africa as the foundation for launching the missile strike, they failed to notify the bureau of their plan, which prevented the White House from learning from the likes of O'Neill—the national security chief in charge of the Al Qaeda squad—that the White House targets were out-of-date.

That failure doomed the attack. If accurate intelligence had been used, and Pakistani leaks avoided, bin Laden might have seen his operational capability hindered in some way. And even though Cohen insisted the point was never to target bin Laden himself, an attack on the right place at the right time would have at least had a chance of hurting or killing bin Laden. Instead, the attack made the United States look ineffectual and weak-willed and may in fact have emboldened bin Laden to ratchet up his campaign to kill Americans.

"The president's response was ridiculous, a disgrace," said Kenneth Maxwell, assistant special agent in charge of counterterrorism. "You can't think about diplomacy or wrist slaps with people whose purpose is to destroy you and your way of life."

President Clinton flew off to Ireland after the failed missile attack, trying to appear presidential while putting an ocean between him and his problems back home. Behind the scenes in Washington, his brain trust hunkered down to prepare another countermeasure. But it was not against Al Qaeda. It was to deflect attention from the imminent release of Kenneth Starr's so-called Sex, Lies, and Videotape report about Clinton's affair and whether he had tried to cover it up. The report would contain hundreds of pages of explicit information that Congress would consider as evidence for a possible impeachment of Clinton.

Late that Labor Day, as President Clinton was stumping donors in Orlando, Florida, and apologizing for his sexual transgressions, O'Neill received word that the Pakistanis had grabbed four more suspects crossing their borders. The FBI already had al-'Owhali and Odeh in custody in Africa. O'Neill immediately turned to Detective Napoli, who had been on the Al Qaeda squad since its inception and had worked on the 1993 World Trade Center bombing case and the investigation of Blind Shiekh Rahman and the plot to be blow up New York City landmarks. "Louie, you are on your way to Pakistan," O'Neill told him.

Napoli spent the next twenty-four hours traveling to Pakistan and, after the exhausting flight, met up with the Pakistani ISI agents holding the suspected terrorists. Napoli thought the Pakistanis would be as accommodating as they were when FBI supervisor Joe Billy arrived from Dar es Salaam to take Odeh into U.S. custody. But they had apparently decided they no longer wanted to risk being perceived as helpful to the Americans. Instead of allowing Napoli to question the suspects, the Pakistanis stonewalled. They told him they would accept questions only in writing. The wily NYPD detective smelled a setup, but diplomatically accepted the challenge and stayed up an entire night meticulously writing down basic investigative queries: How did the suspects travel? How were they financed? Where did they come from?

The Pakistanis made him wait almost a week for a reply. Even then, the answers finally produced were insulting rather than illuminating. "I would ask how the suspect got to Pakistan and the answer would be 'On a plane.' Then I'd ask, 'How did they purchase a ticket?' The answer came back, 'With money,'" Napoli remembers. "They were playing a game and it was a complete waste of time."

O'Neill was not about to sit still when one of his people was being treated like a fool. He called as many of his Washington contacts as he could, trying to find a way to put leverage on the Pakistanis to cooperate, but got nowhere. He ordered Napoli home, both of them deeply frustrated to have him return virtually empty-handed. But O'Neill already had new plans for Napoli. Back in New York, he found O'Neill still going at full throttle in the command center, staying up hours after everyone else went home. "We would say, 'Why don't you go home?' But he would go upstairs and write, read, or be on the phone, spearheading and developing leads to send people to different countries," Napoli said. "I have been all around the world and in all kinds of cities, but I never met anyone like John O'Neill."

O'Neill understood the importance of the recent appearance of Dr. al-Zawahiri, a leading Egyptian terrorist, at bin Laden's side. A year earlier, terrorists shot and killed fifty-eight tourists outside the Luxor, an Egyptian tourist site. O'Neill's contacts in Egypt shared intelligence on the shootings that led him to believe that Egyptian radicals were going to be active participants in a new round of terror strikes. Napoli was one of the most knowledgeable JTTF members about Egyptian terrorist organizations, and O'Neill wanted him back in that arena. But the veteran investigator and terrorist hunter was not pleased at being yanked off the biggest terrorist case in American history. He had worked on the bin Laden squad since 1995 and resisted the change in assignments.

"I need you there," O'Neill told him, making it clear there would be no discussion of the transfer. "There was no deterring him," Napoli recalled. "He wanted someone with institutional knowledge, and he said, 'Louie, I don't care.'"

Around the same time Napoli returned from Pakistan, Patricia Kelly's relief arrived in Nairobi and she was ordered back to the United States, where she was needed to assume her new role as worldwide head of diplomatic service protection. Kelly's office was on the thirty-fourth floor at 26 Federal Plaza, eight floors above O'Neill's. He was always the first official to personally greet his own agents when they returned home, and he took the same approach with Kelly, even though she was with another agency. He heard she was in his building, and made a point of stopping by her office to introduce himself. He made a lasting impression in his tailored gray suit and fancy leather shoes. "You're Kathy's sister," O'Neill greeted her. "I've known her for years. Welcome to New York."

"John was always so immaculately attired and very crisp," she said. "He was always smiling, courteous, happy to see you." Kelly quickly began to rely on O'Neill for candid analysis of the credibility of threats against her diplomats and their facilities around the world. "I would ask if he thought something would impact on my mission," she said. "And he would always look into the sources, and get back to me and say, 'It's nothing to worry about, it's not from a good source. Don't worry about it.' And I could count on him."

Kelly had a lot in common with O'Neill. She did not suffer fools lightly. Nor did she tolerate employees who were not devoted to their extraordinarily important mission. "John expected people to be as hardworking as he was," she said. "I see myself that way. What we are involved in is too important not to give it your full attention. Once you knew the rules, you'd love O'Neill to death and would follow him anywhere."

Napoli did that in accepting his transfer, and soon found himself pleased he had. There were developments regarding al-Zawahiri and Blind Sheikh Abdul Rahman that caused the FBI's Egyptian squad to be as active as the bin Laden team. O'Neill ran into Napoli in a hallway of 26 Federal Plaza, and told him, "You see? I told you there was a reason for putting you there. Do I finally get a smile out of your face now that you have something to work with?"

Even in the best of circumstances, building a solid case against terrorist suspects can be a strategic nightmare. Overseas it becomes even more difficult. Language and cultural barriers have to be overcome, and obtaining sophisticated equipment to secure and dig through a crime scene can prove as immense a problem as tracking suspects from one Third World country to another. Governments often stonewall investigators the way they did Napoli in Pakistan. And although the investigators are working in a foreign country, they have to be mindful that they are still operating under the umbrella of U.S. law. Suspects must be given their Miranda rights against self-incrimination to ensure that any statements they make will be admissible and survive defense challenges in American courts. The same standards apply to taking witness accounts, which often require meticulous translations, which can be difficult especially in the case of rare dialects. Searches and seizures of property have to be conducted by local authorities with an eye toward whether the evidence can be used in court. All these factors explain why federal prosecutors are dispatched overseas to work closely with the FBI to ensure that the evidence secured will pass American standards of jurisprudence.

The federal investigation in the African bombings provided a road map for any eventual military action. It defined the structure and organization of Al Qaeda and identified its leaders and key soldiers, determined how highly sophisticated they were, and where they operated, right down to the locations of their training camps in Afghanistan. During the course of the investigation, four of bin Laden's followers were quickly tracked down and taken to the United States, while another two dozen were identified as having connections to the devastating bombings. Mary Jo White credits O'Neill with the successful investigation and the substantial discoveries about Al Qaeda. "I can't overstate it," she said. "John O'Neill in the investigation of the African embassy bombings created the template for all international terrorism investigations."

NEW YORK, NEW YORK

O'Neill and Joseph Dunne, the NYPD first deputy police commissioner, in Times Square for the anxious New Year's Eve activities for the millennium 2000.

12

SO NICE THEY NAMED IT TWICE

Since becoming head of the national security division in New York in 1997, O'Neill had taken to Manhattan like an olive to a martini glass. He would sit around Bruno with friends and colleagues unwinding from work, and ask, "Are we having fun yet?" The popular piano player, Danny Nye, would regale the audience with a personalized rendition of the time-honored Irish song "Danny Boy," changing the lyrics to "Oh, Johnny Boy." Some evenings O'Neill would stand around the piano near closing time, call Anna DiBattista, and have Nye sing one of their songs, Van Morrison's "Brown-Eyed Girl," Rod Stewart's "Have I Told You Lately," or "A Time to Say Goodbye."

New York encouraged O'Neill's penchant for lavishly entertaining visiting agents and dignitaries. But the FBI was niggardly when it came to expenses, and was always on the lookout for possible corruption or padding. As a result, O'Neill rarely put in for reimbursement, often picking up the tab for an entire night's entertainment. This exacerbated the debts he was incurring through his support of his wife and children and his own high-end lifestyle. O'Neill became a wizard at juggling credit cards and taking advantage of fluctuating interest rates.

His personal life remained as complicated as ever. While living with Valerie James, O'Neill had been telling DiBattista for more than a year that they would be together. He said either he would get another promotion and move back to Washington, or she could eventually move to New York. DiBattista was comfortable in the Washington area, with its less frenetic pace, and in no hurry to move to New York. She did not share O'Neill's passion for the high life, nor was she impressed with the famous people whose names O'Neill sprinkled into conversation. But she was no homebody. Once he challenged her to name four restaurants in Washington that stayed open past 11 P.M., and she did, which irritated O'Neill.

DiBattista had a hard time believing everything O'Neill told her. She had grown more impatient to marry by the start of 1999, and suspected that he was hiding aspects of his life. She never went to his apartment when she visited New York, and to explain why he didn't want her coming over, O'Neill claimed that he had translators living with him. She had her doubts, and would ask him, "You're the boss, why do you have to have them in your apartment?" But he would stare into her eyes and give her his most sincere assurances, and she went along with it. Sometimes when she complained about their inability to make plans and stick to a schedule, he bristled and reminded her that when they met he explained he was involved in "national security" and that meant they would sacrifice a normal life, including many holidays together.

O'Neill used the same excuses when Mary Lynn Stevens and others came to town. O'Neill was by this time spending less quality time with Valerie James, and she began to talk about breaking up. She felt O'Neill was no longer the man she met years earlier in Chicago. He had changed. He was distant. He was enamored of meeting important people in New York. He enjoyed his nights out—without her—and he was returning home later and later when he went out. In short, she believed their dream of sharing a life in New York was not happening. Things became so shaky that she spent one night sleeping at a friend's without telling O'Neill where she was staying.

O'Neill was angry and frantic when he could not find her. He called Valerie's adult children seeking their support in convincing their mother to stay with him. He even suggested they seek counseling, which they started to attend in April—even though O'Neill surreptitiously continued to see DiBattista, Mary Lynn Stevens, and others.

Sometimes DiBattista would threaten to end their relationship, and again, O'Neill was adamant they remain together, just as he had been with Valerie James. Considering how consumed O'Neill was with his job and his expanding social network, he could have viewed a split with James or DiBattista as a way to streamline his complicated life. But instead, he vigorously resisted any such efforts. He asked for undivided love, without judgment. "Just love me, just love me," O'Neill would say.

His resistance to ending any relationship was no doubt partly the reflex of a willful man used to getting what he wants and never shy about putting up a fight rather than giving up. But interviews with the women who shared parts of O'Neill's life make it clear that they satisfied deep and important needs in him. As confident and brash as he could be, he needed their approval and emotional support to overcome his basic insecurities. Even after he made masterful presentations at the highest levels of government, O'Neill would surprise his colleagues with an almost puppy-doggish need to be reassured that that he had performed well.

"John always wanted to be thought of as being close to perfect," Richard Clarke, the former National Security Council official, said. "At the end of any meeting, he would hang around saying, 'How'd I do? What can I do better next time? What am I doing wrong?' Of course he was doing nothing wrong. He was doing everything spectacularly well. But he always wanted to do better. He always needed that reassurance."

Despite his bluff manner, O'Neill was known inside the FBI for the compassion he showed to "his people" whenever there was a personal crisis with them or their family. When Detective Thomas Corrigan's brother, also an NYPD officer, was diagnosed with brain cancer in June 1998, Corrigan held a fund-raising event at Gaelic Park in the Bronx that attracted an overflow crowd of four thousand people. O'Neill showed up unannounced with a two-thousand-dollar donation from the Federal Law Enforcement Foundation, one of many organizations in which he was involved. He obtained a similar donation for a Philadelphia agent with cancer. When Patricia Kelly's husband was stricken with kidney cancer, O'Neill was constantly asking what he could do to help. And when a fire ravaged Detective Pat Pogan's home in July 1999, O'Neill was angry that he had not learned of the blaze until months later.

"Why the fuck don't I know this?" he barked at Pogan. "One of my guys' house burns down and he is living in a trailer and I don't know about that!" Just in time for Christmas, O'Neill got another check from FLEF, and raised more cash passing the hat around the office, all of which turned a potentially disastrous holiday for Pogan's family into one filled with gifts. "I wish I could have gotten it sooner and there was more to it," O'Neill said, putting his arms around Pogan. "You deserve a lot more."

O'Neill's largesse extended overseas. When the wife of a Scotland Yard investigator became ill with cancer, O'Neill arranged for her to be flown to New York, and pulled a doctor he knew out of an operating room to set up admission at a top hospital. He did it a second time for the wife of another Scotland Yard detective. And there was Grammy night, 1999, when singing sensation Macy Gray was in her hometown, Chicago, to perform for the televised event. The singer contracted a throat infection and was considering pulling out of the show. Sony music executive Thomas Mottola, then still a close friend of O'Neill, called him in New York. O'Neill rang Jerry Hauer, the New York City director of the Office of Emergency Management, who in turn telephoned the chief of otolaryngology at Northwestern University in Chicago, who abandoned a black-tie affair to help the stricken singer. And the show went on.

That was O'Neill.

He was the first supervisor to congratulate someone on the

birth of a child, a marriage, or a promotion. He was always first to greet agents returning from dangerous assignments. And every month, someone in his office seemed to get a birthday cake with candles from O'Neill. "John never hurt anyone, even people he clashed with or agents who worked for him that might deserve it," Donlan said. "He loved people."

That June, the job as head of the Newark office became available, as Schiliro had predicted. But O'Neill officially declined to submit his name for consideration, even though it would have given him the valuable experience of running a bureau office, which would have bolstered his chances of rising to the FBI's highest ranks. Instead, he chose to gamble with his future. He banked on the superlative job he was doing as national security director in New York and on his leadership in the embassy bombing investigation being enough to earn his next promotion and help him overcome the blemish of the "car incident."

At about the same time, Louis Freeh promoted Thomas Pickard to assistant director, making the Queens native the number two official in the bureau. This must have annoyed O'Neill, both because he and Pickard had started as FBI clerks and because he believed Pickard was against him. John Lewis then retired from the job of assistant director in charge of the national security division in FBI headquarters in Washington. O'Neill wanted Lewis's job because it would mean promotion into the highest levels of the FBI. He lobbied hard, but the position went instead to Neil Gallagher, then the deputy director of the criminal division in Washington and a former section chief for counterterrorism.

O'Neill was deeply upset. He believed Freeh and Pickard used the car incident to pass him over unfairly. But no one close to him noticed any change in his drive and passion, and he remained the same determined executive he had always been. He began to look forward to the following year, when Schiliro, the head of the New York office, would be eligible for retirement. O'Neill believed that would be his chance for the promotion he desired. But as both Kenneth Pierneck and Schiliro correctly observed, under Freeh's Bright Line policy, O'Neill's mistake the previous summer with Valerie James would likely remain a roadblock for him for the requisite three-year period. While murderers, rapists, and mobsters can sometimes win parole and absolution for their crimes, clemency for agents was rare at the FBI.

NYPD chief of department Louis Anemone also retired in June. Anemone had been the poster boy for Giuliani's aggressive policing, but he became the scapegoat in the aftermath of the tragic police killing of Amadou Diallo, an unarmed African immigrant gunned down by four street crime unit cops in a dark vestibule outside his Bronx home. The officers opened fire when they thought they saw Diallo reaching for a gun, but later discovered that Diallo was actually pulling out his wallet.

Anemone's successor was the popular chief Joseph Dunne. True to form, O'Neill visited Dunne to introduce himself shortly after the promotion. Despite his disappointment that Gallagher had been promoted over him, and his lingering annoyance about the troubling car incident, O'Neill was still O'Neill. The lavish professional courtesy that O'Neill, a high-ranking fed, extended to Dunne surprised the police chief as it had Anemone and other police officials at the NYPD and also in Baltimore and Chicago. Although Dunne had heard from Anemone that O'Neill was "an honest broker," he was still suspicious when O'Neill said he viewed his job as supporting the NYPD. But O'Neill won him over. "He pledged his full one hundred percent assistance, and it was true," Dunne said.

O'Neill provided Dunne with as much sensitive information as he could, including details of confidential terrorist investigations, and worked hard to encourage the NYPD to feel like a partner instead of being left to sit back and wonder about the movements of federal agents through its streets. "He didn't give me a wink, and say, 'Don't worry, I'll give you everything,' when he would not," Dunne remembered. "He was always careful about what he told me, but he promised he would try to keep me in the loop even though there were times he would have to say, 'I can't say a thing.' But he gave us what we needed to ensure that we were prepared for a threat."

That cooperation paid off during the August 1999 outbreak of the West Nile virus. O'Neill and his team were immediately concerned that the deadly infection might have been caused by infected mosquitoes unleashed by terrorists, but soon discounted that possibility. When the city's top cops began to head out to Queens to investigate, O'Neill called Dunne and said he wanted to ride along with him. "He wanted to know everything that was going on," Dunne recalled. "I said I was going out to look for bugs."

Dunne briefed O'Neill during the drive, and the man known even among local law enforcement officials as the "bin Laden freak" assured Dunne that there was little chance the outbreak was the handiwork of terrorists. "I doubt this is something they would deliver this way," O'Neill correctly advised. He understood that terrorist organizations prefer to limit variables and take action with the guaranteed result of killing people, spreading fear, and making their point. Unleashing mosquitoes and waiting to see whether they might infect victims was not the style of terrorists who could detonate a bomb and have an immediate impact. "They would want something more precise and effective," O'Neill explained.

The upcoming anniversary of the embassy bombings in Africa the previous August 7 aroused fears of another attack. On August 5, the State Department issued a blanket warning to U.S. citizens all over the world about possible terrorist action surrounding the anniversary. By then, federal prosecutors in New York had indicted seventeen suspects, including Osama bin Laden and seven others, who were at large as the United States policy remained trying to capture them and bring them to justice. The U.S had also spent millions hardening security around its embassies and other government facilities abroad. The havoc the terrorists had wrought was never far from the minds of O'Neill and his counterparts.

On the anniversary of the attacks, on Saturday, August 7, more than 250 people, including Attorney General Janet Reno and CIA Director George Tenet, as well as families and friends of bombing victims and State Department staff wearing commemorative blue ribbons, joined in the ceremony held in the State Department's ornate Benjamin Franklin Room. O'Neill was there, shaking hands with the families and assuring them the FBI would bring the killers to justice.

But President Clinton did not see fit to attend that day. He was in Little Rock, Arkansas, raising $250,000 for Vice-President Al Gore's campaign, which was more than a year away. Sandy Berger, the national security adviser, read a statement from Clinton to the mourners in Washington: "Working with our friends abroad, we have tracked down, arrested and indicted key suspects, and we will not rest until justice is done."

Four days later, the White House made an announcement that deepened concerns that Clinton was indifferent to the fight against terrorism. Clinton had decided to commute the sentences of sixteen Puerto Rican separatists, many of them members of a Puerto Rican national independence terrorist organization known as the Armed Forces of National Liberation, or FALN. The group was allegedly involved in more than 130 bombings in the United States in the late 1970s and early 1980s, killing dozens of people and wounding hundreds more in New York, Chicago, Boston, and Los Angeles. None of those granted clemency had been directly involved in any deaths, but were instead convicted of seditious conspiracy and possession of weapons and explosives.

The White House hoped the move would go relatively unnoticed, even though the FBI and every other law enforcement agency privately lobbied against it. But those being pardoned by Clinton were hardly dupes or innocents on the periphery of the terrorist group. One was Dylcia Pagan, wife of the FALN bomb mastermind, William Morales, who had escaped from a hospital ward, fled across the country, and was captured in a bloody shoot-out in Mexico. Although President Reagan asked for Morales's extradition to the U.S., the Mexican authorities instead handed him over to Cuba, where he remains to this day. Other freed FALN members were working directly for the founder of the organization when captured.

The clemency did not go over well at the FBI's New York office, which had been bombed by the FALN along with police headquarters on New Year's Eve, 1982. Several agents who worked on the FALN investigation were still on the job in O'Neill's division. The public outcry was swift and vocal, and extended from families that lost relatives in the FALN bombings to law enforcement officials to politicians. They blamed Clinton's decision on bald political calculation. Many believed the president hoped to curry favor with the huge Puerto Rican voting population in New York, where his wife, First Lady Hillary Clinton, planned to mount a run for the United State Senate, although she had never lived in the state. Those suspicions were fueled by the fact that the Clinton administration had rarely granted clemency. Up until he pardoned the FALN members, Clinton had granted just 3 out of 3,042 applications for clemency filed since 1993. Now he had granted 16 for members of a convicted terrorist organization, and he compounded the insult by issuing the decree just days after the anniversary of the worst attack against American interests overseas.

"It's to help Hillary get the Puerto Rican vote," said Joe Connor, who was nine years old when his father, Frank, was killed along with three others on January 24, 1975, when a powerful FALN bomb destroyed historic Fraunces Tavern, the site of President Washington's initial inaugural address in Lower Manhattan. "There is no other possibility. To say these people are nonviolent is ridiculous. It made me feel good that members of this organization had been put away for a long time. Why release terrorists? Why?"

Among the critics of Clinton's move was none other than his wife, Hillary, who made a bizarre public statement calling on her husband to rescind the decision. She questioned her husband's assertion that the convicted terrorists could be counted on to renounce violence, a condition of their release. "I believe the offer of clemency should be withdrawn," she said at a press conference in Albany, New York, a few days later.

It was yet another low point in the sideshow atmosphere of the Clinton administration, and O'Neill was appalled. How could the president free terrorists while simultaneously justifying a battle to end terrorist acts overseas? If Clinton was concerned about terrorism and sending a message to bin Laden and the rest of the world that he was serious about combating the threats, all he had to do was ignore the FALN requests. While it often seemed difficult to get the White House to spotlight bin Laden, it was clear to O'Neill that people involved in Democratic politics and concerned with the Hispanic vote in New York obviously had no such problem getting Clinton to focus on the jailed FALN terrorists.

Many in Congress shared O'Neill's outrage, and soon Congress moved to probe the presidential grant of clemency. As part of its inquiry, Joe Connor's brother, Thomas, appeared before Congress on September 21, 1999, and warned that the greatest threat to the nation came from international terrorism. He argued that the U.S. should be leading the war on terrorism, not freeing those convicted of it.

"On the eve of the next century, the threat of global terrorism is greater than it has ever been," he warned, sounding themes O'Neill had raised in Chicago and elsewhere. "And right now the President decided to offer clemency to 16 members of one of the most violent organizations ever to wage war against the U.S. government from within our own borders. There never was a pacifist wing of the FALN, and not one member has ever expressed remorse."

Connor claimed Clinton's move "endangered America" because it subverted the will of the court, and that the president's explanation for freeing the convicted felons "insults" the intelligence of the America people. "Terrorists of any nationality should never be granted clemency if this country is to be serious about stopping terrorism," Connor said. He ended his remarks by predicting that lightning wouldn't strike him twice—that the next attack on American soil would probably not kill him or anyone else in his family.

He was wrong. Although he and his brother narrowly escaped the attacks on the World Trade Center in 2001, they lost two relatives: a cousin who is the son of their late father's brother, and a husband of another cousin.

O'Neill could no longer entertain hopes of a promotion and imminent return to Washington, where he and DiBattista could have pursued their relationship more seriously, so now he began to persuade her to move to New York. He regaled her with tales of the splendor of the city and of the powerful circle of friends and acquaintances he had made, from Cardinal O'Connor and Sony music executive Tommy Mottola, to Elaine Kaufman and Robert De Niro. "He begged me to come up," she said. New York was the greatest city in the world, O'Neill told her, and he was the sheriff who owned the town. Of course she could not move in with him because of the translators who continued to live with him in Peter Cooper Village. Instead, he and Anna looked for an apartment for her in Manhattan, but found that rents were too high.

DiBattista's search for an apartment finally ended in September when she selected a lovely apartment in nearby Fort Lee, a bedroom community just across the Hudson River on the New Jersey Palisades near the George Washington Bridge. O'Neill began squiring DiBattista to restaurants and certain events, but he rarely spent an entire night with her. As always, his work got in their way, but that was something she had to live with. He was "married" to the FBI, and there was always a crisis somewhere, often right in New York.

A few days later, on September 6, O'Neill flew to Virginia Beach, Virginia, for an antiterrorism conference along with Detective Thomas Corrigan from the joint terrorist task force. They spent two days discussing various threats from around the world with federal agents from the Naval Criminal Investigative Service, and then they caught a flight back to New York. Corrigan recalled making small talk with his boss. He mentioned the speculation among the rank and file that O'Neill might become the next head of the FBI's New York office. O'Neill was curious about the consensus opinion, but he downplayed the likelihood of such a promotion. O'Neill, for no apparent reason, looked at his watch and suddenly announced, "You know, today is my son's birthday."

Corrigan recalled the sympathy he felt for his overworked supervisor. "I felt bad for the guy," he said. "He was so driven and so good at what he did. But he sacrificed a lot. It was a spring back to reality." O'Neill landed in New York and reached out to his son. The pace of his work was relentless, but he loved it.

On October 31, 1999, at about 1:30 A.M., EgyptAir Flight 990 took off from JFK International Airport bound for Cairo. About twenty minutes into the flight, the Boeing 767 aircraft suddenly began to plunge from the sky, crashing at 1:52 A.M. into the ocean sixty miles south of Nantucket Island, Massachusetts, killing all 217 people on board, including 167 Americans and 14 EgyptAir crew members. O'Neill was once again the first supervisor to arrive at the command center. He telephoned the home of Thomas Donlan, then supervisory agent of the reactive squad

Christine Shutz, John O'Neill's high school sweetheart and future wife.

O'Neill was a member of his high school track team.

O'Neill's FBI class at graduation, 1976. J. Edgar Hoover, who at the time was director of the FBI, is at center left in the front row.

Mary Lynn Stevens with the tuxedoed O'Neill. She began dating O'Neill in 1989 and she remained unaware until his death that he was involved with anyone else.

O'Neill enjoying a night out in Rome with Anna DiBattista and Italian federal agents.

Ramzi Yousef, the mastermind of the 1993 bombing of the World Trade Center that killed eight people and injured thousands more. O'Neill, on his first day as the FBI section chief for counterterrorism, coordinated Yousef's capture in Pakistan in 1995, and prevented Yousef from carrying out other horrific plans to blow up American jets in midair and assassinate the pope.

O'Neill with FBI director Freeh (center) and Special Agent John Lipka *in Saudi Arabia following the Khobar Towers bombing.*

O'Neill (second from right) pictured with FBI director Freeh (center) *and other federal agents in Saudi Arabia in 1997 while on another mission to Dhahran to enlist support from the duplicitous Saudis.*

On March 26, 1997, O'Neill attends a press briefing held by Mayor Rudolph Giuliani outside a Queens home where canisters of supposed poisonous gas, possibly deadly sarin, and other hazardous materials were found. The discovery forced the evacuation of the neighborhood.

James Kallstrom, then head of the FBI's New York office, stands in front of the reassembled TWA Flight 800 jet that was culled from the ocean and pieced together on a giant metal frame, November 11, 1997.

O'Neill (left), Louis Freeh, and Kenneth Maxwell survey the reconstructed TWA Flight 800 plane.

Al Qaeda leader Osama bin Laden in Spring 1998, when he publicly issued a fatwa *warning that he would attack Americans and that "good news was coming."*

On January 26, 1998, U.S. president Bill Clinton denied allegations of a sexual relationship with former White House intern Monica Lewinsky during a White House event unveiling new child care proposals. Insiders say Clinton was distracted by the scandal and failed to heed warnings about bin Laden.

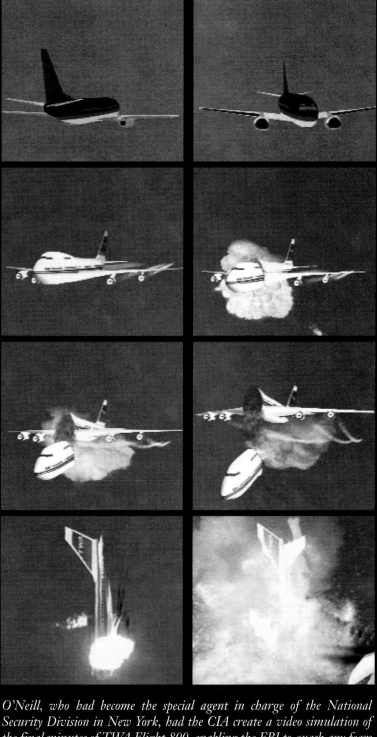

O'Neill, who had become the special agent in charge of the National Security Division in New York, had the CIA create a video simulation of the final minutes of TWA Flight 800, enabling the FBI to quash any fears that the disaster was a terrorist event.

On August 7, 1998, bin Laden truck bombers destroyed the U.S. embassies in Dar es Salaam, Tanzania, in Africa (pictured here) and in Nairobi, Kenya, killing 247 people and wounding 5,000 more.

Manhattan U.S. Attorney Mary Jo White and Lewis Schiliro, the head of the FBI's office in New York, announce the indictment of Osama bin Laden on November 4, 1998, for the bombing of two U.S. embassies in Africa that killed 247 people and injured more than 5,000. O'Neill led the investigation that resulted in bin Laden's indictment.

The giant crystal ball dropped at midnight in Times Square ringing in a safe New Year 2000 after O'Neill, federal agents, and police captured several bin Laden terror suspects who were planning to disrupt millennium celebrations around the world.

O'Neill attending a grave City Hall press conference with Mayor Giuliani after a Palestinian national shot eight people, one of them fatally, on the observation deck of the Empire State Building on February 23, 1998, after yelling "I love America!"

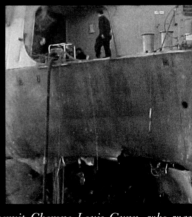

U.S. Navy Signalman Seaman Recruit Cherone Louis Gunn, who was among the seventeen sailors killed when bin Laden suicide bombers attacked the USS Cole *in Aden harbor in Yemen on October 12, 2000. His father later credited O'Neill with giving him and the other families of the victims hope that the case would be solved and suspects brought to justice.*

A gaping hole mars the port side of the USS Cole *after a bomb exploded and killed seventeen U.S. sailors and injured thirty-six others. The U.S. began to refuel in Yemen to improve its relations with this desert country, despite warnings about terrorism.*

Barbara Bodine, the former ambassador to Yemen who clashed with O'Neill and refused to allow O'Neill to return to Yemen to head the investigation into the bombing of the Cole. It was the first and only time a State Department official has denied an FBI official country clearance.

O'Neill in Rome during his first major swing through Europe to meet with law enforcement and counterterrorism experts in 1997.

O'Neill chatting with his friend Elaine Kaufman at her fabled restaurant, Elaine's, on Manhattan's Upper East Side in 2001.

O'Neill enjoying a laugh inside his office at 26 Federal Plaza on his last day of work for the FBI, giving his trademark hug to Robert McFadden, a special agent with the Naval Criminal Investigative Service, whom he met in Yemen.

*The South Tower collapsed in ten seconds, killing O'Neill and thousands of
other innocent victims.*

O'Neill's crushed 1991 Buick was discovered in the garage of the World Trade Center and removed to the Fresh Kills landfill in Staten Island to be cataloged along with the myriad of remains recovered from the September 11 rubble.

On September 28, 2001, the casket of John O'Neill, former special agent in charge of the National Security Division of the FBI in New York City, is carried from St. Nicholas of Tolentine Church in Atlantic City, New Jersey. O'Neill died just days after beginning his new job as head of security for the World Trade Center.

O'Neill's mother, Dorothy, and his estranged wife, Christine, leave St. Nicholas of Tolentine Church after O'Neill's funeral, which attracted more than one thousand mourners, including a galaxy of law enforcement officials, foreign service personnel, diplomats, Wall Street executives, restaurateurs, and the media.

With Manhattan and the Brooklyn Bridge serving as a backdrop, O'Neill and his longtime paramour Valerie James, with whom he lived in New York from 1996 until his death. The couple first started to date in Chicago in 1991.

handling domestic terrorism leads, and ordered him to get into the office. Donlan, who became the case agent, arrived at around 4 A.M. By then, O'Neill had compiled a list of orders, starting with a review of the manifest of passengers and crew on the plane, then contacting the FAA and NTSB to learn if they heard anything from the pilot before the crash that could explain the disaster. He contacted the CIA to see if there had been any "happy talk" from potential terrorists, the coded conversations that might signal their involvement. "John was absolutely brilliant," Donlan said. "I never saw him make a mistake."

The crash occurred on a Saturday night. By Monday morning the FBI had zeroed in on the copilot, Gameel Batouti, as a possible suspect. The NTSB and FAA said they heard commotion in the cockpit as it plunged toward the ocean and that someone repeatedly said in Arabic, "I rely on God." Donlan had already dispatched agents to the Pennsylvania Hotel near Madison Square Garden, where the crew had been staying. He was hoping for cooperation from the hotel, but hotel officials often refuse to allow anyone to be interviewed until lawyers are contacted.

This time the FBI got lucky. Hotel employees regaled them with stories about Batouti's odd behavior. They claimed he drank heavily, and often sat in the lobby in his pajamas shining a red laser penlight at women's breasts as they passed by. He tried this on some El Al stewardesses and narrowly avoided being beaten up by other El Al employees. "John just said, 'Let's look hard at the copilot,'" Donlan recalled.

The FBI continued to explore other theories, but Batouti attracted increasingly more of their attention. O'Neill and Donlan quickly learned that he had recently been passed up for captain. Flight 990 was supposed to be his final international journey. Flying for EgyptAir was "his life," friends told the FBI. They also said that Batouti loved coming to the States, mostly to let loose and party. The copilot's daughter lived on the West Coast and suffered from cancer, and some people speculated that might also have contributed to a distressed mental state, although her ailment was not life-threatening and was being treated. One more damning piece of evidence seemed to complete the puzzle: the EgyptAir official who made the decision not to promote Batouti was also on Flight 990.

"Initially you think it is terrorism unless proved otherwise," Donlan said. "But there were a lot of complaints about the copilot's behavior, plus the guy he probably hated the most was on the plane."

EgyptAir would not publicly confirm any aspect of the case that indicated the copilot committed suicide and took the plane with him. For three weeks the FBI and O'Neill operated their command center. Every evening at 9 P.M., they held briefings with the other agencies involved in the investigation, ranging from the FAA to the navy, which was involved in the salvage and search for survivors and bodies. One evening, Schiliro asked O'Neill to conduct the briefing. In seven short minutes, O'Neill magically provided a meticulous overview of an airtight case. But since the FBI was not the lead agency, they could only present their evidence to the NTSB, which was in charge of making the final determination as to the cause of the crash.

It took more than two and half years before the NTSB issued its findings on the disaster. They concluded that the copilot used a ruse to get inside the cockpit during takeoff, despite regulations barring him from being there at that time. He then seized control of the aircraft, shut off its power, and fought with the pilot when he tried to regain control. Batouti uttered the phrase "I rely on God" a total of eleven times as he fought to take down the plane. Yet to this day Egyptian officials continue to resist any suggestion that an employee was involved in the disaster.

Once it became clear there was no terrorist involvement in the crash, O'Neill reduced the FBI's role in the probe and, several weeks after the crash, shut down the command center. It was now November, a wonderful season to be in New York. The city was adorned with all the lovely decorations of the holiday season. O'Neill and Valerie spent Thanksgiving together, while DiBattista went home to Maryland to visit her family under the impression that O'Neill was visiting his parents in Atlantic City. On December 1, 1999, he and Valerie went to the Christmas tree lighting ceremony in Rockefeller Center.

The holiday season also brought fresh fears of an incident connected with the arrival of the millennium. The FBI and NYPD faced mounting threats that ratcheted up everyone's fears for New Year's Eve. The city and federal committee meetings that O'Neill attended had become weekly events. O'Neill's intelligence agents were reporting increased chatter to the effect that Al Qaeda was planning a stunning attack for the millennium.

The monumental task of protecting New York City fell as much on O'Neill as anyone. And the undertaking extended well beyond Times Square, which was the most widely known tourist spot. Extraordinary fireworks displays were planned for Central Park in Manhattan, Prospect Park in Brooklyn, and Flushing Meadow Park in Queens. O'Neill and other law enforcement officials faced a dizzying array of logistical puzzles and potential headaches: How would they go about getting people out of the areas if there was a problem? What if there was a bomb? Or chemicals? What were the protocols for dealing with the various substances? Which agency would be the lead? What role would the FBI play?

O'Neill was concerned about the FBI being directly involved in responding to any hospital where victims would be treated. The problem was his realization that during a vast attack with heavy casualties, first responders from the medical community rarely recognize that victims are also witnesses to the crime and can be vital assets in bringing culprits of criminality to justice. O'Neill wanted agents to work side by side with the doctors, nurses, and paramedics to obtain crucial first-person accounts that could be pivotal to solving the crime and capturing suspects.

"Some teams respond to a hospital, triage a patient, and forget to get the law enforcement investigators in to debrief the victims or witnesses at a hospital," said Dunne.

And if the threat of terrorists and a possible Y2K computer meltdown were not enough, the contract for the city's transit workers ran out at midnight, December 31, 1999, and the workers already were threatening to walk off their jobs as the ball was dropping at Times Square—something they had done once before on New Year's Eve.

13

THE VOICE OF GOD

Fog shrouded the town of Port Angeles, Washington, on the night of December 14, 1999, as the last ferry arrived from Victoria, British Columbia. Traffic was light, and U.S. customs agents at the remote Olympic Peninsula port of entry quickly processed the thirty-five cars arriving from Canada. The last car to roll off the ferry, a steel-blue Chrysler 300M, eased forward and stopped at U.S. Customs Inspector Diana Dean's booth. The car had already cleared one checkpoint, and the driver handed Dean documents that identified him as Benni Antoine Norris of Montreal.

Dean was puzzled. The driver could have taken a direct route south from Vancouver, arriving in the United States via the main border crossing at Blaine, Washington. Instead, he detoured hours out of his way to take the ferry down from Victoria Island. Dean noticed that his hands were shaking, and despite the damp chill of the Northwest fog, he was sweating noticeably. She asked him to get out of the car and open the trunk, and he bolted and sprinted toward the nearby town, disappearing into the fog. Two agents gave chase, lost him for a moment, and then spotted him under a car. Again he ran off, making it six blocks before the agents tackled him outside the Wonderful House of Chinese restaurant.

Dean searched his car and found ten large bags of whitish powder in a spare-tire well, and two jars of a honeylike liquid packed in sawdust. She assumed the suspicious materials were drugs. Only later did she learn she had intercepted the makings of one or more powerful bombs. Customs also confiscated four homemade timing devices, maps of Washington, Oregon, and California, and another identification card with a different name than Norris. Tattered scraps of paper were found in the driver's pockets with three New York City phone numbers and a single word: *Gani*.

The arrest sent shock waves throughout the U.S. government and right up to the White House. Overseas intelligence had warned the United States and numerous other countries to prepare for possible millennium attacks, and the fresh discovery only heightened fears of an attack during the worldwide round of celebrations. But the White House and the Justice Department decided to keep a tight lid on the arrest, hoping the Algerian man captured with the powdery substance would turn out to be a dope dealer rather than a terrorist. The last thing the Clinton administration wanted were alarmist stories about millennium terrorist threats, so they decided to keep the information confined to a small network of federal officials. They made this decision even though they knew with near certainty that the powdery substance was an explosive material, and had tentatively identified the suspect as Ahmed Ressam, an Algerian with ties to a terrorist organization, the Armed Islamic Group.

U.S. Commissioner of Customs Raymond Kelly knew his agents had prevented a potential attack, and he wanted to hold a ceremony the following day to honor them for capturing the suspected terrorist. Kelly believed the attention paid to the incident would serve a twofold purpose: it would bolster morale among the agents who guard the nation's borders, and it would alert the public to watch for suspicious people and activities as the millennium approached. But the White House disagreed. It ordered Attorney General Reno to tell Kelly to cancel the ceremony, which he did reluctantly.

By the following morning, customs agents received confirmation from Canadian authorities that the driver of the car was indeed Ressam, who had lived in Montreal for the past five years, committing petty thefts and working as a grocer. He had unsuccessfully sought political asylum from the Canadian government, claiming he was tortured and falsely accused of terrorism in his native country. Ressam had been under surveillance by the Royal Canadian Mounted Police as a suspected member of a Montreal-based cell of the Armed Islamic Group of Algerians, who were opposed to their country's military regime and were also active in France. The powder found in his car was positively identified as dynamite.

Agents determined that a "Benni Antoine Norris" had reserved a room at the Best Western Loyal Inn near the Space Needle for a couple of days following his entry into the United States. That fit with the expected pattern of attacks planned to disrupt the millennium celebrations that would circle the globe, starting in Sydney, Australia. But as concerned as customs and FBI agents were about the fate of the fifty thousand revelers who were expected at the Space Needle for New Year's celebrations, they were even more worried about what they did not know: Were other bomb carriers on the ferry with Ressam? Did they slip through customs? If so, what were their targets?

"That is what frightened us," recalled Fran Townsend, Reno's chief of intelligence policy and review, and a confidante of O'Neill's. "We believed for the first time they were really planning to hit us on our own soil, and that scared the life out of us."

The FBI Strategic Information and Operations Center in Washington was on full alert, and the CIA and the National Security Agency mobilized all their available resources. Agents and prosecutors appeared before the ultrasecret federal Foreign Intelligence Surveillance Court to obtain approval for phone taps and search warrants in the interest of national security. U.S. diplomats invoked international mutual legal assistance treaties to enlist the cooperation of Canada, France, and any other country that might have information about Ressam or other millennium terrorism plots. Kenneth Maxwell, then the FBI special agent in charge of operations in New York, recalled receiving communications from overseas intelligence officials who strongly suggested several plots were under way in the United States.

"But no one knew what the targets were," he said. "We did not want to take a chance. With our open borders there had to be other players."

In the White House and National Security Council, officials were "screwed with fear to the ceiling," another official said.

But the White House had still not alerted the public about the Ressam arrest. O'Neill was frustrated. He wanted information about Ressam's belongings and the contents of his car and needed raw intelligence about his background from sources in Washington and overseas. O'Neill felt that every second lost in a major investigation was serious, and he had always urged his men and women to react to the situations as though their mother's life depended on it. He was at a loss to explain why the White House and the Justice Department wanted to sit on information, and once again he witnessed politics impeding the war on terrorism.

"John would say, 'I might have a piece of the puzzle and the new information might have lit the bulb,'" said Raymond Powers, the NYPD chief of operations in charge of coordinating the millennium coverage. "He always spoke of the need to communicate. He shared everything he could within the law."

The NYPD had already launched "Operation Archangel," the highest state of alert, as the millennium approached. Ressam's capture intensified concerns that bin Laden or other Middle Eastern terrorists might disrupt the dropping of the ball. What better target than Times Square on New Year's Eve? Besides destroying a powerful symbol of the American people and their traditions, such an attack would send a message that for the next thousand years, Islamic fundamentalism would do battle with American power, just as bin Laden had vowed.

Finally, two days after Ressam's arrest, the nation was suddenly blanketed with news of the bomb-smuggling attempt and its worrisome ties to the millennium. The appearance of a terrorist cell on American soil, as O'Neill predicted years before, reinforced the notion that President Clinton's ineffectual attack on bin Laden a year earlier had only emboldened the terror leader. Airports around the country heightened security measures, which included an order that Christmas packages be unwrapped, delaying tens of thousands of passengers. Hundreds of extra border agents were rushed to points of entry around the country, and hundreds of investigators from every law enforcement agency were enlisted to chase down leads on the evidence recovered from Ressam and his Montreal apartment. French authorities then disclosed that Ressam was linked to the "Roubaix Gang" of extremists responsible for deadly bombings and other attacks in Paris in the 1990s, and that he apparently trained in bin Laden's camps in Afghanistan, news that only heightened fear of other attacks.

"We are taking extraordinary efforts in the government to act based on the incident out in the Pacific Northwest," Clinton said in a new conference at which he finally spoke of Ressam and asked the public to be on the lookout "if they see anything suspicious."

National security adviser Sandy Berger convened meetings in the White House basement, gathering the so-called Principals Committee of senior law enforcement, military, and intelligence officials to keep on top of the terrorist threat and provide regular briefings to Clinton. "We knew something was out there . . . we were not sure where," one official recalled. "We felt like we were in a dark room, trying to find the light switch."

Once O'Neill received the hard information from Seattle, he discovered that the men they sought were just across the Brooklyn Bridge. The scraps of papers found in Ressam's pockets contained the name Gani, and a phone number in the 718 area code, which corresponded to four of New York City's five boroughs. Agents then traced Ressam's phone calls to a building on Newkirk Avenue in Flatbush, Brooklyn. Wiretaps were set up so agents could eavesdrop and record phone conversations. O'Neill quickly

assembled a team of agents that provided round-the-clock surveillance on the Newkirk Avenue apartment building and on anyone who might visit the apartment. The agents wanted to identify
any suspicious persons and track their movements and contacts
with any possible accomplices. They operated on the premise that
this was a terrorist cell in Brooklyn—and wondered how many
other bin Laden Al Qaeda sleeper cells might exist under their
noses.

O'Neill and his staff were joined by Chief William Morange,
head of the NYPD's special operations division, which included
emergency services personnel. Morange and his cops met with
O'Neill and a group of JTTF members at an old NYPD narcotics
division office located near Prospect Park, a few blocks from the
building under surveillance. They used the run-down police facility as their command post, and for the next three days, O'Neill—
the man who never needed sleep—did not close his eyes.

Antiterror troops in Montreal determined that "Gani" may
have been a reference to Abdelghani Meskini, an Algerian
national who had lived on and off in Montreal for five years and
who had a record for credit-card fraud and check kiting. Meskini
was one of a number of suspected Algerian terrorists who had
moved to Canada and occasionally came under police surveillance
because of his contact with other suspected terrorists. He spent a
year in Afghanistan, where he received advanced training in the
use of explosives, and flight records showed that Meskini had
flown to Seattle just before Ressam was captured. He abruptly
returned the day after Ressam's arrest.

Meskini landed in America in January 1996 by jumping out of
the anchor hole of a vessel pulling into Boston Harbor, according
to Isabelle Kirshner, his former lawyer in New York. Once
Meskini swam ashore, he disappeared into the Algerian community and got involved with ATM, check, and credit-card fraud,
and also waited tables. He later moved to Montreal, where he
lived off the largesse of the Canadian welfare system. There he

befriended another Algerian, Mokhtar Haouari, a shopkeeper who gave him money and spiritual guidance. By the time Meskini returned to Brooklyn, he had become religious and politically engaged. After the African embassy bombings, Meskini talked of visiting bin Laden's camps with the goal of becoming a martyr. Haouari called Meskini just days before Ressam planned to cross the border into the United States. He told Meskini that Ressam was an important player, and that Meskini should assist him in the Seattle plot.

"This is the guy," Haouari said. "He has been to the camps. This is important. This will set off a great flame."

Although O'Neill had been denied the chance to go to Africa a year earlier to confront bin Laden's henchmen, now he believed he was face-to-face with some of bin Laden's operatives on his home turf in New York City. Within twenty-four hours of establishing the surveillance on Newkirk Avenue, O'Neill received an update from his Jordanian counterparts, who said they had smashed another bin Laden cell that planned to blow up an embassy and several tourist hotels filled with Americans in order to disrupt the millennium. The Jordanian agents believed these planned attacks were meant to coincide with attacks in the United States. As he sat there less than two days after Ressam's arrest, listening to wiretaps as heavily armed lawmen and surveillance teams patrolled the area, O'Neill could only speculate what horror these followers of bin Laden had planned for America. Their anti-American and anti-Semitic rhetoric was coded, but easily interpreted. "It was hardcore Muslim rhetoric," a source close to Meskini said. "'We will bring America to its knees. Jews are dirty, gutter-sucking dogs,' and the like."

Once Newkirk Avenue was put under surveillance, other locations quickly followed. Wiretapped phone calls to and from the building provided leads to several other locations in Brooklyn and Queens. Cops raced to those addresses and placed the callers under surveillance. One location was a Brooklyn travel agency.

Another was the Long Island City address of a taxi driver who had direct connections to several suspects caught crossing the Vermont border the day after Ressam was captured. Another was that of a Jewish businessman who lived on Ocean Avenue—it turned out his cell phone had been cloned.

O'Neill's agents listened as Meskini received an overseas call informing him of Ressam's arrest. This was only two days after Meskini had returned from Seattle to his Newkirk Avenue apartment. "Change your phone number, beeper and cell phone. Throw them away," the caller told Meskini. "A lot of things are going on. Leave the place. Leave everything."

Meskini tore up a Seattle plane ticket and some ATM slips, and tossed them into a trash bin. Federal agents staking out the house walked across to the garbage and retrieved the incriminating ticket and later pieced it back together as evidence. Every time Meskini emerged from his apartment, he was followed by federal agents and NYPD detectives, which forced O'Neill to add personnel at an expanding universe of locations. The action became so intense that the NYPD had to use helicopters to follow the suspects. No one wanted to let anything fall through the cracks in the investigation.

On the third day of being camped out at the narcotics offices in Brooklyn, O'Neill and the agents and cops were again feasting on stakeout staples—McDonald's burgers and fries—when an all-points bulletin was issued 2,500 miles away, in Texas, after a gas-station attendant reported to police that a group of Middle Eastern men were traveling in a van loaded with cardboard boxes. The attendant became suspicious because of the news of Ressam's arrest in Seattle. The FBI located the last owner of the van, who said she had just sold the vehicle for cash to a group of Arabs who said they sold Korans for a living. She was embarrassed that she had not realized who the Arabs might be, in light of Ressam's recent arrest.

The FBI began tracking the battered blue van across dusty

Texas highways, and grew concerned as it traveled east and then made its way up the East Coast through Virginia. The FBI lost the van somewhere near Washington, D.C., and at that point they issued the APB. O'Neill's command had monitored the radio frequency carrying BOLA (which in law enforcement parlance stood for "Be On the Lookout for A") updates on the blue van filled with Middle Eastern men, until the FBI reported they had not seen the van since it neared Washington, D.C.

A day later, Meskini emerged from his home and walked to a nearby Middle Eastern restaurant on Atlantic Avenue. The agents followed and set up surveillance as Meskini settled into a seat at the back of the restaurant. As they watched the terror suspect fumble with a menu, the mystery blue van suddenly pulled up in front of the restaurant. The license plates matched the alert issued to all law enforcement. The situation immediately grew more tense. Agents waited and watched, hearts pounding and adrenaline pumping.

Even cool and calm O'Neill was on edge. Could this be a rendezvous of members from two terrorist cells? O'Neill immediately ordered fresh teams of agents and cops to wait near the restaurant in case they had to move swiftly, but he told them to hold off because he wanted to ensure that any attempted interdiction took place with minimum risk to the public. If the men simply returned to their vehicle, O'Neill preferred to follow them in order to see if they would lead them to other conspirators.

Half an hour later, the Arabs emerged from the restaurant, climbed back into the van, and pulled away, unaware of the teams of lawmen on their trail. The surveillance lasted two days as agents and detectives watched the van drive all around the city, yet never stop anywhere for long. The van would pull off to the side of the road in the evening so the passengers could sleep. "I would hear hourly from John," Dunne recalled. "He'd say, 'Hey, what is with the fucking van?'" The tension in the command post was rising as the blue van from Texas again wound its way through

Brooklyn toward Flatbush. "They were driving around the city for two days without stopping, and never getting out," Dunne recalled. Meanwhile, the clock continued toward New Year's Eve and O'Neill wondered how long he could wait before moving in on the van.

Finally, O'Neill decided to stop the van after it showed up once again at the restaurant near Meskini's apartment. If it was transporting bombs, it did not make sense to continue to allow it to drive through crowded New York streets simply to allow the FBI time to obtain more intelligence. O'Neill had criticized the CIA for similar actions since he first became section chief of counterterrorism in Washington in 1995. The intelligence community usually preferred to leave suspects in the field to get more intelligence, a practice that O'Neill and other legendary FBI bosses like Ken Walton decried. As Walton used to say, "There comes a point when you have to act."

So O'Neill did.

He ordered SWAT teams and bomb technicians to join the van surveillance team. Using unmarked cars and a big Suburban, the FBI followed the van as it pulled away from the restaurant. O'Neill hoped the van might end up stopped in a street where they could cut it off and swoop down with teams of armed agents, bomb-sniffing dogs and technicians, but where it would have the least exposure to the public. "We didn't want *Live at 11*," Maxwell said. "No Cecil B. DeMille production." The FBI needed to surprise them, and if there were explosives, needed to make sure no one would be hurt.

The teams trailed the suspicious vehicle for about fifteen minutes, with each turn dutifully reported over the radio to O'Neill, who was watching from another trailing vehicle. Suddenly the blue van from Texas made a sharp right onto a side street and pulled into a convenience-store parking lot bordered by an empty lot and no homes. "It was perfect," Maxwell recalled. O'Neill gave the green light. The teams of agents finally pounced on their quarry.

The driver got out of the van and was stunned to see he was being surrounded by a small army of heavily armed agents. They whisked him off to one side as another cadre of agents and dogs rushed up to the rear of the van and swung the back door wide open. The agents climbed into the van and meticulously opened one box and then another, only to find that the boxes contained recordings of the Koran on compact discs. The driver had come halfway across America to sell the CDs to mosques in Brooklyn, and he and his colleague slept in his van rather than stopping at a hotel or apartment because they had no money. And why did they stop at the restaurant at exactly the moment when Meskini was eating there? "They heard the restaurant just had good food." Maxwell laughed. "It was pure coincidence. There was no connection at all to Meskini."

The mood of intense anticipation and suspicion was immediately deflated. O'Neill, Dunne, and Maxwell and the others understood the humor of the situation, but they were still frustrated. Law enforcement was doing its job perfectly—but at the end of the day, they had nothing to show for it but a few more sleepless nights. Meanwhile, the clock was ticking toward the New Year, and so was the explosive fuse attached to Mayor Rudolph Giuliani.

New York's millennium celebration, which as usual was to be broadcast around the world, was the centerpiece of a special global event to introduce the year 2000. The mayor of Seattle already had called off the celebration at the Space Needle in the days following Ressam's arrest. But Giuliani had vowed that no terrorist threat or arrest would stop the Big Apple revelry. The ball would descend on Times Square as it had since 1906, the feisty former prosecutor and tough-talking mayor insisted. Not even World War II prevented New Yorkers from basking in its glow, and in the hope it symbolized for the New Year. Giuliani was not going to allow any interruption in New York City's annual display of pomp and circumstance, and he claimed his NYPD had the resources to ensure everyone's safety.

Other knowledgeable officials weren't so sure. James Kallstrom told reporters at the time that the last place he would be on New Year's would be Times Square. "I would avoid major events," he said. "I wouldn't let [my kids] go to some huge event like dropping the ball in Times Square. The prudent thing at the turn of this millennium is to celebrate by yourself or with your family." Kallstrom meant that it did not make sense to take chances if you did not have to. But his remarks infuriated Giuliani.

"Rudy was pissed," said Lewis Schiliro, who was then head of the FBI's New York office.

Giuliani argued that there was no reason to avoid the Times Square celebration, and he laid out the plan devised by Dunne and O'Neill. "We live in a dangerous time and a dangerous world, but everything is being done that can possibly be done based on the information we have," the mayor said. He said he could not guarantee everyone would be absolutely safe—"Nobody can give that to you, with regard to terrorism or anything else," he said—but he insisted the city would be as safe on New Year's Eve as it is on any other day. "I think everyone but Jim Kallstrom is coming," he added.

Privately, Giuliani was concerned enough to push both his cops and the FBI to handle the still-unresolved matter involving Meskini, Ressam's suspected accomplice in Brooklyn. Giuliani informed Police Commissioner Howard Safir that he wanted all loose ends like Meskini taken care of. "With Safir, the attitude was nothing could disturb the millennium," Schiliro recalled. "There was a fair amount of pressure from City Hall to resolve the situation before New Year's. When you deal with Rudy it had to be resolved in enough time for New Year's Eve and negating the threat."

Law enforcement had certainly not forgotten Meskini. For nearly two weeks, FBI agents and detectives had him under surveillance. They were monitoring his telephone conversations, which were laced with incriminating terrorist chatter. In one conversation, he said that he and his Algerian associates would rise up and "punish America." And O'Neill was still vigilantly watching his quarry. When he left the command post, he returned to his office at 26 Federal Plaza, where he would read reports and send a flurry of e-mails to his agents to make sure that every possible avenue was pursued. "I came in and there were twenty-seven e-mails from him," said Maxwell, who knew little about O'Neill's personal life. "I told him maybe he should get a girlfriend to take up some of his time."

On Christmas Day, 1999, O'Neill dined at home with Valerie James. The following day, they went to see Tchaikovsky's *Nut-cracker Suite* at Lincoln Center, but O'Neill's pager went off at least twenty times. His agents had recordings of Meskini speaking with someone in Arabic, revealing that he, Ressam, and others were part of a well-organized cell. Meskini also said he went to Seattle to meet Ressam, who was supposed to leave the Chrysler in a parking lot with the keys in the ignition, and then "walk away from it." The plot was devised, he boasted, so that each conspirator did not know the tasks of the others, in order to limit the information they could reveal if captured. Meskini also bragged that there was a "Big Flame" coming for America.

"The closer we got to January first, our biggest fear was bin Laden, who could blow the shit out of us," Maxwell said.

Finally O'Neill told Maxwell, "Let's take this thing down." He and the NYPD decided to invade Meskini's home in a predawn raid on December 30, barely twenty-four hours before the first of the New Year's Eve revelers were expected to arrive in Times Square. O'Neill and the NYPD brass set up a staging area in Prospect Park around 4 A.M. As usual, O'Neill arrived an hour before everyone else. They had obtained floor plans and schematics from the Department of Buildings for Meskini's building, but no one knew what to expect inside. Plans called for sixteen FBI SWAT operatives to tiptoe up two narrow flights of stairs to Meskini's apartment. A battering ram would be used to knock down the door. The agents hoped he could be surprised and easily subdued.

James Roth was the FBI's legal counsel at the time. He recalled O'Neill asking him to show up to ensure that none of Meskini's rights were violated, and that, if the FBI confiscated items from his apartment, it would be done pursuant to their warrant, so that any incriminating evidence gathered or statements made by Meskini would be admissible in court. Despite the urgency and danger of the impending tactical maneuver, O'Neill was not a man to overlook small details.

Before he launched the initiative, O'Neill began walking among his troops in the park in the freezing night air, making last-minute preparations. He checked with the squad leaders to double-check that everyone knew their tasks and was in place. He continued to review assignments down to which hostage rescue teams would be used in the event Meskini took a civilian prisoner, and which bomb squad members would be called upon in the event explosives were found.

Just before giving the green light for the raid, O'Neill walked over to Sal Emilio, an Alcohol, Tobacco and Firearms agent who admits he joined the JTTF "kicking and screaming" in 1995 because he did not want to link up with the FBI. Emilio was milling around in a separate staging area in the back of a Seventieth Precinct annex in the park when O'Neill found him. "O'Neill was giving briefings, mostly updates on what was happening and what everyone's assignments were," Emilio recalled. "He was breaking down roles we were going to have."

The veteran ATF agent believed his role would be in support. But O'Neill had a different idea. Exactly as he had done in Baltimore and Chicago, where he blended lawmen from various agencies to work together in one unit, he turned to Emilio and told him he would be driving Meskini to 26 Federal Plaza after he was taken into custody. Emilio was pleased that O'Neill would give someone who was not from the FBI such a pivotal responsibility rather than a small job on the periphery of the investigation.

"The FBI generally trusts their own," Emilio said. "But John was different. He barked out a lot of orders and a lot of people did not like that, but he got things done. And he did not snub anyone."

Before Emilio joined the JTTF, he believed FBI bosses thought "the only good agent was an FBI agent." But O'Neill showed an appreciation for all agents and cops, and never walked past a colleague without acknowledging him, whether he was with the bureau or not. To Emilio, O'Neill seemed to be a refreshing surprise. "Maybe he wanted to be Italian," Emilio joked, referring to O'Neill's wise-guy wardrobe and the way he would always give Emilio his trademark hug and kiss on the cheek when they met.

At last, as dawn approached, nearly two hours of standing in the cold ended when O'Neill gave the order to move in. The SWAT teams raced up to Meskini's apartment, knocked down the door, and grabbed the half-asleep suspect. He was handcuffed and brought downstairs. Roth raced into the apartment to witness the seizure of evidence. "The apartment was a pigpen," he said. Meanwhile, agents led Meskini to the street. There was no shooting, no hostage was taken, and everything went smoothly.

Emilio was two blocks away when the first agents and cops stormed into Meskini's apartment. "And then O'Neill got on the radio and said, 'Come on in,'" Emilio recalled. Since he was a munitions expert, there was no reason for Emilio to arrest people, and he had never taken a prisoner into custody. Now he found himself placing one of bin Laden's followers in the backseat of his car. "Don't make it hard," Emilio told Meskini, who appeared weak from fasting during the holy Ramadan period.

As Emilio drove off with Meskini, O'Neill was standing near

Maxwell. He pulled out his phone and turned and said there was someone who wanted to speak with him. Maxwell asked who it was and O'Neill replied, "Janet Reno." Maxwell thought O'Neill was joking, but he grabbed the cell phone and put it to his ear. To his amazement, it was the attorney general.

"Hello, Madame General," said Maxwell as O'Neill stood by with what Maxwell remembers as a "shit-eating grin" on his face.

"I just want to thank you and the members of the task force and police," she told him. "I know you guys have spent a great deal of time in advance of Christmas and New Year's and I want you to know how much the president and I appreciate it."

Maxwell hung up with the attorney general and handed O'Neill's phone back to him. By the time the conversation ended, Emilio was pulling into 26 Federal Plaza, where Meskini would be questioned over the next eleven hours as the New Year beckoned. He told the feds he had approached Haouari in Montreal and asked him if he could become a martyr for bin Laden and the Al Qaeda cause. Haouari instructed him to go to Seattle and meet a man named Abu Reda, a "very important brother," with contacts in both London and Afghanistan. Meskini said his job was to deliver cash to Reda (who was Ressam), to assist him as a translator and guide, and to drive him around to "meet with people" as far away as Chicago. Initially, Meskini cleverly chose not to mention the "Great Flame" and "Great Fire" to avoid implicating himself in the horrific millennium plot, which FBI agents heard on their wiretap.

Finally he admitted that Ressam was coming to commit terrorist acts, and that he had been told that Ressam was "on an important mission" in the United States to "light the fire," a source explained. Meskini claimed that when he returned to New York, he was still unaware that Ressam had been caught.

Using telephone logs seized in the case, and relying on some leads from Meskini, agents fanned out across seven states in a last-ditch effort to head off the feared millennium attack. They tagged more than forty people with ties to Ressam and Meskini in six states: California, New York, Massachusetts, Tennessee, Texas, and Washington. With only twenty-four hours until the millennium, O'Neill and thousands of agents worked around the clock to try to ensure that the brilliant work by Customs Inspector Diana Dean was not wasted, and that they had in fact disrupted a terror attack on American soil. O'Neill was confident they had. Yet he still did not know any more about what the potential target might be than he had when Ressam was arrested more than two weeks before.

Law enforcement officials live by the maxim that you are only as good as your last case. And while the Meskini affair ended successfully in his arrest, the fear remained that other cells might still be operational and plotting an attack. New York City's millennium celebration still needed protection, and it was not a moment for O'Neill to rest on his laurels. As he often said, unlike Hall of Fame baseball players, he could never strike out, even once. In the end, the NYPD and FBI's jointly orchestrated millennium plan was as well designed and as well thought out as was humanly possible.

Streets would be cleared of all furniture, mailboxes, and benches—any object that could be used to hide a bomb would be removed. Manhole covers were sealed. Starting in mid-December, the FBI checked the lists of guests booking rooms in the city's hotels for the New Year's Eve celebrations around town. Deliveries to all hotels, restaurants, and buildings within the central Midtown area were cut off by midafternoon on New Year's Eve. Cops were placed on twelve-hour tours, and virtually no one was given the night off. An "A team" of special-weapons officers was positioned on several rooftops to survey windows and potential snipers. Explosive experts and trained bomb-sniffing dogs would canvass the area and the adjacent buildings in the Times Square area.

On New Year's Eve, there was a blanket of NYPD blue cover-

ing New York City. Metal-detecting wands would be used on revelers as they arrived in Times Square, and backpacks would be
examined by hand. The crowd would then be ushered through
ever-narrowing checkpoints, where they trickled past cops, giving
the authorities a final opportunity to inspect them and winnow
out any suspicious characters that might be terrorists. Once inside
the "Frozen Zone," the throng, like cattle, was steered into
penned areas from which they could not move.

The NYPD security level that night was already on
"Archangel," its highest state of alert, that incorporated the most
far-reaching response plan of any police department in the nation.
This level of alert called for police scuba divers in the water near
the United Nations, a cordon of heavily armed cops stationed at
armories, officers combing subway tunnels, and one hundred officers on standby who were trained to use gas masks and suits in the
event of a biological or chemical attack. The NYPD's five helicopters would be in the air, utilizing surveillance cameras to zoom
in on small objects. Nearly eight thousand cops were scheduled to
cover Times Square alone. The FAA banned aircraft within a
three-mile radius of Times Square below an altitude of four thousand feet, beginning at 6 P.M. on New Year's Eve. And if there
were a terrorist strike, every cop in the city would be called upon
to respond. (The plan's highest level of action—condition
"Omega"—called for lightning action minutes after any incident.
Thousands of New Yorkers would be stopped and questioned,
and entire sections of the city shut down.)

Party planners had designed events to keep New Year's Eve
celebrants entertained during the long hours leading up to the
stroke of midnight when the eight-hundred-pound crystal glass
ball dropped. They decided to set up huge television video
screens and loudspeaker systems at various locations around
Times Square that broadcast images and sound throughout the
evening. "I was concerned about something explosive getting
inside Times Square, or a crackpot sticking automatic weapons

out of the window," said Dunne. "If you have a kook, or one desperate person there to inflict harm on someone, the question was, 'How could we react? How do we get the message out to the crowd if it is a terrorist event?'"

The answer was "The Voice of God." The NYPD and FBI decided that in the event of an attack or other emergency, they would need to address the crowd to provide instructions or calm any panic, so they decided to tap into the event's vast speaker system. It would only take the trip of a switch to transform the network of speakers into a huge public-address system for the authorities to use. Hundreds of thousands of people might hear Giuliani—or Manhattan South commander Alan Hoehl—booming through the ten-square block canyons surrounding Times Square, letting people know what had occurred, whether it was serious, and if so, what they had to do to ensure everyone's safety. "We had the speaker system up and we felt we could pull the plug if something happened, to get the message out," Dunne said.

As the millennium approached, the U.S. intelligence network continued to pick up traffic that indicated bin Laden was planning several attacks. But the NYPD was confident that it had developed the best possible plan for dealing with any incident, which they felt was all that could be asked of them. Even with all these preparations, O'Neill remained ill at ease. He was convinced bin Laden had trained and financed a worldwide network of "sleeper cells" ready to attack America. He was concerned that bin Laden's followers would raise more money and recruit more fanatics to the cause, who would then be "activated" and transformed into assassins. O'Neill worried that even the NYPD's rigorous preparation could not avert or fully anticipate how or where bin Laden and his group might strike next.

O'Neill's instincts were again on target, but he could not possibly know the full breadth of bin Laden's terror plans for the millennium. His Jordanian friends had reported that bin Laden planned bombings of embassies and tourist hotels filled with

Americans. That night, O'Neill's concerns about the New Year's celebration persisted as he headed toward Times Square. He was working his cell phones, but he also decided to take Valerie's son, Jay, with him to watch the ball drop. O'Neill showed up in a suit and a long black cashmere overcoat as the first of nearly 500,000 people began to filter through the police checkpoints into Times Square. He was joined by Dunne. "Without sounding too cocky, I was concerned, but I knew we did everything we could, and were prepared in the event anything bad would happen," said the equally confident Dunne, who brought his family along with him to Times Square to celebrate the millennium.

Dunne sensed that O'Neill did not think a terrorist attack would occur, because of the sharp-eyed work of a Seattle customs agent and the follow-up work by the FBI and of the JTTF. "But it was a nervous night," Dunne said.

The millennium celebration proceeded around the world in one-hour intervals. At 11 A.M. New York time, the New Year was celebrated with a spectacular fireworks display in Beijing, China, and then from the bridges of Sydney, Australia. "As time clicked, there was no Y2K problem," Dunne said. "Computers around the world from the Far East were not having a problem. There were no terrorist incidents." Fears of power failures eased, but the officials were pleased they had positioned generators in hospitals and ESU and fire trucks in Times Square that could provide light if there was an outage.

At 5 P.M. New York time, Italians celebrated at the Vatican in Rome, then the Eiffel Tower became a fountain of sparkle and color, followed by England's enormous fireworks show over the Thames. The crowd at Times Square watched each successive New Year's countdown, as midnight moved west through the time zones. At each locale, as midnight approached, there were no terror-related incidents—and O'Neill and his colleagues continued to hope those uneventful results would bode well for New York City.

At 7:15 P.M., O'Neill's cellular phone rang with a call from his pals at Scotland Yard. Their New Year's Eve worries had subsided. "Everything is okay on my watch," said John Bunn, the detective chief superintendent. "I am passing it off to you now." O'Neill and Dunne wandered the crowd, more comfortable because there had been no incidents in Europe, which often provided easier targets for Middle Eastern fanatics.

But at 9 P.M., the FBI picked up a report of a bomb threat. Standing now at the command post at West Forty-first Street, below the ball, O'Neill again got on his cell phone. "Joe, the information comes from a field agent in the south, through an informant, and I don't think it has much credibility," he told Dunne.

A half hour later, the FBI stopped a man in a Bronco SUV, his gun rack filled with weapons, heading toward New York. "John just started working the phone again to verify the accuracy and track down the lead," Dunne said. "He was able to. The guy was just a Southern cracker."

At about 10 P.M., just thirty minutes after the arrest of the man in the SUV, a new and frightening report came over the secure federal and police radios—a man wrapped with explosives at a hotel. "It's not good for your indigestion," Dunne said. "You just say, 'Oh brother, if this is for real,' and you think, 'How are we going to handle this?' We have to think about what to do if he succeeds." O'Neill quickly called his agents at various city hotels and concluded that the report was not true.

As midnight approached, O'Neill and Dunne and Jay James strolled to One Times Square, and then to West Forty-second Street and Broadway. The rest of the world was safe, and the crowd in unison began the countdown to the millennium. Ten. Nine. Eight. Seven. O'Neill pulled out a cigar, cut the end, and fired it up, blowing smoke as the crowd chanted down from seven to one. As the ball lit up the sky above him, Dunne turned to O'Neill and the two tough lawmen shook hands, congratulated each other, and then embraced. "I felt great," Dunne said. "It was over. We said how great it was working with each other. We got it done. We made it. We were still here."

Dave Kelley, the assistant U.S attorney in Manhattan in charge of counterterrorism and organized crime cases, was in his office with fellow prosecutor Pat Fitzgerald anxiously counting down the hours toward midnight. Kelley and Fitzgerald were intimately involved in the millennium investigation, just as they had been in the African bombing cases and virtually every other terror prosecution overseen by their boss, Mary Jo White. After London passed without a hitch, the two federal prosecutors left their office about 10 P.M. to get something to eat as O'Neill and Dunne kept the vigil in Times Square.

"There was a feeling something was going to happen and there was John running around feverishly to make sure that did not happen," Kelley said. "John O'Neill worked six weeks and lit up a cigar at midnight. There were few people that night that deserved it more."

In the SIOC command center in Washington, where O'Neill first helped capture Ramzi Yousef, the mastermind of the 1993 bombing of the World Trade Center, Attorney General Reno, her top aide, Fran Townsend, and the FBI brass breathed a sigh of collective relief that New York and the entire East Coast had made it through the New Year's celebration without any terrorist incidents. O'Neill called the SIOC and was put on a speakerphone, exuding pleasure at the job well done. He got off the speakerphone and paged Townsend, with whom he had become extremely close during the past two years, working cases jointly and spending long hours dissecting the subtle nuances of their respective professional lives. They both said how relieved they were with the day's events. "You've gotten through at New York," she said. "But I'm not going home until we get through L.A."

O'Neill hung around Times Square for another hour and a half to make sure there were no incidents across the country.

Finally, he went up to Elaine's at about 2 A.M., where maître d'
Giovanni Adamo sat him at table three on the right, near the
door. O'Neill sat sipping a Scotch and smoking a cigar. Everyone
who knew him and had wandered in for one last cocktail posed
the same question to him. Is it safe? "Of course it is," O'Neill said.
"If it weren't, I wouldn't be here."

Shortly after 3 A.M., when there was no longer any danger,
even on the West Coast, O'Neill telephoned Townsend. She was
driving home from the headquarters command post and just turning onto her street when her cell phone rang. She immediately
knew who it was. Who else would be calling at that hour? "I'm
calling you to say congratulations," O'Neill said, "because you
wouldn't take it at midnight. We are through it. We're going to be
okay."

14

THE BRIEFCASE INCIDENT

O'Neill caught a few hours' sleep on New Year's morning and was back in his office by noon. The end of one millennium did not mean he could let up on his private war on terrorism. Meskini had finally confessed to O'Neill's agents that he was involved in a millennium terror plot that was designed to coordinate a "Great Flame" against America, just as O'Neill predicted years before. The question was where. Although several targets were obvious, the FBI began to believe the target was neither the Space Needle in Seattle nor Times Square in New York. All the evidence pointed instead to an attack in California. Maps found in Ressam's and Meskini's belongings and other clues indicated the target was Los Angeles International Airport, a thriving hub far away from the better-protected targets in New York or Washington, D.C.

O'Neill's counterparts in Jordan, the same lawmen he had wined and dined over the years in New York and Beirut, provided him with the clearest perspective yet on bin Laden's diabolical millennium campaign. The Jordanians now believed the attacks planned in the Middle East would include simultaneous bombings of hotels owned by Americans and Israelis, a U.S. consulate, and several tourist sites popular with Westerners. They also had evidence of a plot to blow up a U.S. warship in bin Laden's homeland of Yemen. They did not know which ship was targeted, but they believed the plot was imminent.

The tip from his Jordanian counterparts put O'Neill on a collision course with Barbara Bodine, U.S. ambassador to Yemen, a strong-willed career Foreign Service officer who underestimated the terrorist threat in Yemen. Bodine had bravely survived the siege of the U.S. embassy in Kuwait during the Iraqi invasion in 1991. Her posting in Yemen was to be her final overseas assignment, and she wanted to make her mark before her scheduled departure in late 2000. She staked much of her credibility on her belief that Yemen, an arid nation composed of warring tribal factions that trace their roots to biblical times, was showing signs of progress.

The State Department had considered listing Yemen among the countries that harbored terrorists. The small country had more weapons within its borders than inhabitants, and maintained strong ties to bin Laden, who traces his ancestry to Hadramout in the south. In many respects, Yemen remained a Third World nation, and its current government had come to power following a civil war in 1994 that had briefly united warring tribes and deposed the previous communist regime. The relatively new administration of President Ali Abdullah Saleh was fragile, and owed a large debt to various tribal warlords.

Yet Bodine, known for her "my way or the highway" attitude, not only believed that there was minimal terrorist activity in Yemen, she further argued that President Saleh had taken strong measures to guarantee there would be none. She also lauded President Saleh's efforts to provide women with basic freedoms that had been denied under Muslim law. Bodine lobbied the U.S. to relax its hard-line stance. Given Clinton's eagerness to establish lasting peace between the Israelis and Palestinians before he left office in January 2001, in part to improve his legacy, the administration found it useful to improve relations with Yemen. Having another moderate Arab ally in the turbulent Middle East peace process could pay dividends.

As worthy as the goal of Middle East peace was, Bodine underestimated the security concerns. The White House ultimately agreed with Bodine's assessment, and the military began to allow American warships to refuel in the port of Aden. The presence of the U.S. armed forces served several purposes: it pumped money into Yemen's struggling economy, and signaled better diplomatic relations between the U.S. and the Yemeni government.

But the U.S. decision about terrorist activity in Yemen did not square with reality. In the years following the Afghan victory over the Soviets, mujahedeen warriors returning from the battlefields were offered jobs in Yemen, which retained strong ties to bin Laden and Al Qaeda. O'Neill's agents and the CIA uncovered evidence of irrefutable connections between Yemen and bombings in the Middle East. The FBI demonstrated that the plan for the 1998 U.S. embassy bombings in Africa was financed and carried out by a bin Laden network that ran through his ancestral homeland. Several Yemeni nationals were believed to be directly involved in the attacks. And Dr. al-Zawahiri, head of the Egyptian Islamic Group and by then bin Laden's deputy, had a makeshift base of operations in Yemen.

A more clear-eyed assessment would have told Bodine and others in Washington that the sight of huge American warships in Yemeni harbors would inevitably provoke anger among anti-Western radicals in Yemen and neighboring Saudi Arabia. To them, the u.s. painted proudly on the sides of ships carrying bomb-laden American fighter jets through Mediterranean waters could not help but unleash seething resentments. The U.S. presence off the shore of bin Laden's homeland would not go unanswered by the Al Qaeda leader, who had vowed to cleanse the region of the American infidels.

U.S. officials did not know it at the time, but on January 3, a group of Al Qaeda fanatics drove a trailer with a twenty-foot skiff into the surf of Aden Harbor. Fortunately, the small vessel laden with 350 pounds of explosives listed to one side and sank. The attack had been planned for the twenty-seventh day of Ramadan, the day the Koran was revealed to the prophet Muhammad. The target was the USS *Sullivan*, named after seven brothers who died in World War II on an American carrier. It refueled without incident and sailed off to join a fleet enforcing the embargo of Iraq.

O'Neill had repeatedly cautioned that law enforcement could not afford to miss a single threat because lives were at stake, but that morning in Yemen, luck played the decisive factor, rather than any American diplomat, lawman, or intelligence operative.

The FBI would later learn that the millennium strategy was orchestrated by bin Laden's chief of operations, Abu Zubaida, who had brought the plan to bin Laden for final approval in the months before New Year's Eve. Less than two weeks after the botched attack on the USS *Sullivan*, several of the plotters flew to Malaysia to attend a top-level Al Qaeda meeting to discuss the next wave of assaults against America. Among those attending the January 20 terror summit were Khalid al-Midhar and Nawaf al-Hazmi. They arrived from the West Coast of the U.S. and would later be among the men who hijacked the plane that struck the Pentagon on September 11. Also present was Ramzi bin al-Shibh, who had been a roommate of September 11 mastermind Mohammed Atta in Germany.

U.S. officials pressed Malaysian authorities to conduct surveillance of the meeting after learning of it through information gathered in Yemen with wiretaps initiated by leads obtained in O'Neill's investigation of the Africa embassy bombings. O'Neill recognized that many bin Laden terrorist paths converged in Yemen. Malaysian intelligence monitored the meeting, taking clandestine pictures of those in attendance. Since no laws were broken, the Malaysians could only watch, and not intervene, as plans to attack the USS *Cole* and the World Trade Center were being developed.

The Malaysian photos were given to the CIA, but they did not provide them to the FBI and O'Neill, who had a "rogues' gallery" of Al Qaeda terrorists in his office in Manhattan. On it, a maze of arrows connected suspects and attacks that all led to bin Laden. O'Neill kept a set of charts in his apartment so he could connect the dots at all hours. He also spent time at home studying videos of bin Laden's public statements, always looking for any revealing details about his dangerous adversary, whose eight-by-ten inch photo sat on his desk. "He just had hundreds of books, many about bin Laden, with underlined passages running through them," Valerie James remembered. "Even my grandson knew who Osama bin Laden was."

The Al Qaeda flowcharts constructed by O'Neill and his squad were enhanced by information gathered through relationships with investigators around the world. John Bunn, then the detective chief superintendent of Scotland Yard, had such admiration and affection for the charismatic O'Neill, he said he would die for him. George Andrew, a former FBI counterterrorism official with his own international contacts, was deeply thankful to O'Neill for tapping his network on his behalf.

Andrew retired from the FBI in early 2000 and was working as director of security for Seagram when terrorists threatened to bomb the company's theme park near Barcelona if it did not meet ransom demands. Andrew needed information to provide to Seagram chairman Edgar Bronfman, who was considering shutting down the park but did not know what to do. Company officials in Spain had been unable to glean any solid information from the few contacts they had. Andrew thought the FBI's legal attaché stationed in Spain might be helpful, but the legat confessed he had little contact with Barcelona's tight-lipped local police.

As a last resort, Andrew called O'Neill, his old former colleague from the FBI's Baltimore office. O'Neill said the Spanish ambassador to the United States was his drinking buddy, and that the federal police chief in Spain was also a friend. "Let's see what we can get done," O'Neill said. "Let me make a call, and I will make the introduction and you can talk to him."

In minutes, Andrew was talking to Barcelona's chief of police, who informed him that several suspects had already been arrested, and there was no longer any danger to the park. He picked up the phone and personally delivered the good news to Bronfman, who was amazed at Andrew's power to obtain such delicate information from his office in Manhattan when people in Europe had been unable to learn anything.

"I felt like the cat's meow," Andrew said. "The businessmen were saying we should shut down the park, and I was getting details and saying, 'Do not shut it down.' I was really impressed with John. I marveled, actually."

Sometimes O'Neill's prodigious knowledge of how things really worked enabled him to suggest simple solutions that others overlooked. That was the case when he testified before the National Commission on Terrorism, which was created by Congress in 1998 after the Africa bombings to examine the failure of the intelligence community and was chaired by J. Paul Bremer. O'Neill did not recycle old arguments for the board, complaining of a lack of federal agents or poor cooperation from foreign countries. Instead, he zeroed in on a significant obstacle that could be easily solved: "We need more translators," he told the commission. "There is a lot of information that we simply can't get to."

John Lewis, the former FBI national security division boss at headquarters in Washington, sat on the panel and heard O'Neill's testimony. He recalled how the members were both surprised and impressed by O'Neill's insights. "In retrospect, the issue about the translators was one of the most interesting comments before us," he said.

Another of the panel's specific recommendations was that President Clinton designate the U.S. military—not the FBI or the Federal Emergency Management Agency—the lead organization in responding to a catastrophic terrorist attack on U.S. soil. O'Neill had advocated this change in command structure after the African embassies were bombed in 1998. The commission also recommended giving more freedom to the CIA to undertake direct operations overseas, and streamlining FBI guidelines to make it easier for them to launch an investigation. These, too, were O'Neill's suggestions.

Although the commission adopted O'Neill's recommendations, none were implemented by the Clinton administration. Yet again, O'Neill was disappointed that an opportunity was lost to change the bureaucratic culture and marshal more resources for his war on terrorism. "They just don't get it," he would say.

O'Neill's frustration with the Clinton administration's inadequacy in fighting international terrorism always centered on his conviction that Clinton had let his turbulent personal life interfere with the mission of being president and commander in chief. O'Neill believed he would never let this happen to himself, but that spring he found out he was human after all. For the first time, he displayed the strain of juggling the complexities of his frantic work schedule and his relationships with as many as four women.

On April 25, 2000, O'Neill was driving home in his bureau car after attending a game at Yankee Stadium in the Bronx when he discovered his Palm Pilot was missing. Panicked about the possibility of losing the device, loaded with a myriad of contact numbers, he called Yankee Stadium security. He said he was with the FBI and might have accidentally dropped his Palm Pilot from a pocket. A guard hurried to where O'Neill had watched the game, and soon found the device under his seat. O'Neill was relieved and immediately returned to the stadium to retrieve it. The temporary loss of a Palm Pilot might be relatively insignificant to many people, but not to O'Neill. Many of his closest friends say the lapse by the usually flawless O'Neill showed the strain on his mind.

A few weeks later, Schiliro announced his official retirement as the assistant director in charge of the New York office. The job O'Neill had coveted for so long was finally open. Overseeing the FBI's flagship office had been his dream since he was a boy imagining himself as TV's Inspector Louis Erskine. The ADIC position would not only give him more authority for his fight against bin Laden, it would also keep him in New York City, which by now was his other mistress. " 'New York, New York,' so nice they named it twice," O'Neill liked to say, evoking the song made famous by Frank Sinatra. The thought that he might become the top FBI official in New York City was too sweet to envision. For a few brief weeks, he became acting ADIC until a successor for Schiliro was chosen.

A panel of top FBI officials considered two candidates for the job, O'Neill and Barry Mawn, a former air-force officer who had risen through the FBI ranks and in 1980 became the first cosupervisor of the newly created joint terrorist task force. Mawn had gone on to run two of the FBI's largest field offices. He was in charge of the Newark, New Jersey, office when the Unabomber killed his final victim, Thomas Mosser, an executive with the public relations firm Young & Rubicam. Mawn was boss of the field office in Boston, where he handled the probe of the EgyptAir crash and dealt with the fallout from the sensational scandal involving the state senator's brother, James "Whitey" Bulger, a murderous mobster who compromised several FBI agents before disappearing.

O'Neill lobbied fiercely for the post. It is difficult to assess the extent to which the infamous car incident and O'Neill's love of nightlife influenced the decision-making process, but both were assuredly factors. Reno, Freeh, and Pickard all claimed in the end it was Mawn's résumé that tipped the scales in his favor, but clearly the decision hinged on more than résumés. "It was close, but Mawn's résumé was a notch above John's and he had a few more years' experience," Pickard said. "And there was no baggage."

O'Neill could rub people the wrong way, and that translated to murmurings within the bureau that he was not a team player. But that charge was both unfair and absurd. His penchant for stating strongly held opinions was based on his belief that an honest sharing of views would lead to the best possible solutions. The mission, not niceties of social discourse, was always his top priority. "He was very strong-willed, and he was very opinionated, and didn't sort of roll over on something he felt strongly about very easily," said Fran Townsend, the attorney general's aide. "I think people misinterpreted that as him not being a 'team player.'"

When Freeh made the final decision, he simply circled the name of his selection on the list of candidates, initialed the choice, and handed the paper to Pickard for Reno's final approval. As in biblical times, as it was written, so it was done: Barry Mawn became the new head of the FBI's New York office.

O'Neill was devastated. Once again, he was denied a promotion, and this time he lost out on his dream job. But he kept quiet about it, except to loved ones. "I never heard any disgruntlement, no sour grapes, from John," Pickard said.

For a few weeks before Mawn took over, O'Neill continued as acting head of the New York office, and one afternoon Freeh stopped by to discuss a New York case with him.

"Let's go into your office," Freeh suggested.

"That's not my office and I don't sit there," O'Neill said. "I only wished it would be permanent."

O'Neill showed no bitterness toward Mawn, either. The two were both attending seminars at Quantico shortly before Mawn took over, and O'Neill took the opportunity to reach out to his new boss. Just as he had done in Chicago, when he shared drinks in his apartment with Agent Kenneth Pierneck to map out an attack plan on the city's gangs, O'Neill brought a couple of beers up to Mawn's room. O'Neill pledged his loyalty and asked in exchange that Mawn support his national security division. Mawn had heard about O'Neill's hard-charging style. Who in the bureau hadn't? But he came to respect O'Neill's passion. "Supporting John O'Neill turned out to be more than a full-time job," he joked, referring to O'Neill's endless requests for manpower and financial support for his various investigations.

If O'Neill was licking his wounds, few people knew it. He appeared totally occupied with the trials of Africa suspects, the aftermath of the millennium case, and a number of other important classified espionage cases. He was also racing against a July 2000 deadline to complete his division's important annual field report, which outlined every counterterrorism and counterespionage case in New York. The report, generally about two hundred pages, provided an overview of his division as it entered a new fiscal year and helped determine future funding levels.

As he neared the final stages of its preparation, O'Neill attended an agency retirement seminar in Florida. It was a session he felt he could do without. In fact, he perceived it as an annoyance. He was a chronic workaholic who never gave a thought to fiscal responsibility in his day-to-day life, much less saving for a retirement he never imagined.

"John was never about money," Valerie James said. "He liked people who had it, but he was never about it himself. He never had anything himself."

O'Neill was in debt, still helping to pay off the monthly mortgage on his estranged wife's home as well as underwriting his global networking and funding his own New York lifestyle. He had told Grant Ashley in Chicago in 1994 that he would never live long enough to retire, and now, in July 2000, he was being asked to attend a dreary retirement session just as he was preparing the report that would provide resources for his pursuit of the world's most dangerous terrorists and spies. But in typical O'Neill fashion, he decided if he was given lemons, he might as well make lemonade. He took his annual report with him to finish at the tutorial. And since he was already in Florida, he decided to spend a few extra days there with Valerie James and vacation in the Keys.

O'Neill arrived in Orlando for the seminar. He sat in the back of the conference room so he could fine-tune his report and ignore the presentations. As he was working, his pager began to vibrate. O'Neill did not know it at the time, but just as the car incident had derailed his chances at promotion, this page would produce the most devastating moment of his career. And not because it was bringing news of another huge terrorist attack or major capture. No, when O'Neill went out of the large conference room to answer the page, he left behind his briefcase, which was filled with classified information and an outline of virtually every national security operation in New York. He returned minutes later, but the briefcase was gone, along with his laptop.

O'Neill panicked. He instantly realized the gravity of the situation. FBI agents are forbidden by federal law from removing classified information from any FBI facility. Certainly agents sometimes take work home that they should not take—but it is a major violation of FBI policy and, depending on the circumstances, could be a violation of law. This new violation dwarfed the error O'Neill had made in bringing Valerie to the secret garage where FBI vehicles were stored.

He knew that if his briefcase fell into the hands of foreign agents or enemies of the country, they would have information about every case the FBI was working on under O'Neill's command. They would have enough details to interfere in those cases with potentially lethal results. It would take a year or two to fix the damage caused by the missing information. "The annual reports contain strategic plans that show what we are doing and what we are trying to do with terrorism and counterintelligence," explained Thomas Pickard, then the FBI deputy director. "They do not say who, but they give our game book. Everyone's hair was on fire."

O'Neill felt sick, and not only because of what it meant to his career. He had sacrificed many years of his life and a marriage to protect the United States, and the idea that he could have harmed national security was devastating. He immediately called the local police and then Mawn to report the theft. He also telephoned Neil Gallagher, the head of the national security division, to tell him. "You know how much I care about this program and these investigations and what we have accomplished," O'Neill told Gallagher. "I'm sick at the thought I could have compromised them."

Freeh was notified. So was Reno. Fortunately for everyone except O'Neill, the briefcase was located a few hours later in another hotel. A petty thief who was unaware of the true value of the documents must have been disappointed to find little more than paper in it. All that was missing were O'Neill's silver cigar cutter, a lighter, and his Montblanc pen. Fingerprint experts soon determined that the only people who had handled the documents were from the FBI.

O'Neill was two and a half hours late to meet Valerie that afternoon to go to the Keys. She was reading a book and drinking an iced tea when he walked into the Belle Harbor Hotel near Miami where she was staying. "He was white and shaking," she recalled. The ashen O'Neill told her what had happened. "He looked like a kid, someone you wanted to put your arms around," she recalled. But she also did not fully grasp the importance of the briefcase incident right away. Valerie was an extremely busy professional woman in her own right. She had grown a bit weary of the roller-coaster life caused by O'Neill's job, since it kept getting in their way as a couple. At the time, she felt that the FBI was once again challenging the viability of their relationship. "We had just come off the car thing, and his job was again interfering with our lives," she said.

Valerie expected his bosses to be understanding, just as her own supervisors would be if she had briefly misplaced something important. After all, it had been found intact. "I just thought he was being paranoid," she recalled. But O'Neill told her she was being naive. This latest problem was much bigger than the car incident, he told her, and soon she came to understand the gravity of the situation. She told him, "John, you work for an organization that eats their young." She believed his career was over.

Valerie was not far off the mark. A slim possibility remained that some foreign agent could have stolen the documents, copied them, and left the originals behind. The FBI's Office of Professional Responsibility immediately launched an investigation of O'Neill to determine whether any criminal charges should be brought against him. If none were, there would still be an internal probe of his conduct to determine if he violated FBI guidelines and should be punished.

Fran Townsend almost didn't recognize O'Neill when he called to give her the bad news. His voice was so tight with fear that he had trouble talking. "He knew . . . this was going to be a federal case," she said. "This was going to be a big deal in terms of the bureau, and it was going to be used to hurt him."

O'Neill paced the floor all night. In the morning, he and James returned to New York after spending barely a day in Miami. Once again, the timing of the transgression could not have been worse. It was difficult enough to expect leniency under Freeh's Bright Line policy even under normal circumstances, but both the FBI and the Justice Department were reeling from criticism over two recent security violations. One involved Wen Ho Lee, the analyst in the Los Alamos laboratory who was falsely suspected of leaking nuclear secrets to the Chinese. In the other, former CIA director John Deutsch had lost his security clearances and become the subject of a Justice Department investigation for mishandling classified material after he placed classified documents on unclassified computers in his home. Deutsch's transgression later required a pardon by President Clinton.

Clearly there would be no pardon for O'Neill, given the heightened tension in the bureau. Nor would he expect it. "John understood what he had done, and if he were alive today, he would be the first to say he should not have taken the papers," Gallagher said. "He did it in a rush. He felt it was important."

O'Neill faced a criminal inquiry even though it was obvious to everyone that he harbored no criminal intent. The lone reason for the so-called briefcase incident was O'Neill's slavish devotion to his work, even at a retirement seminar he did not want to attend. If no criminal charges were filed, then the matter would go to OPR or to the security countermeasure section for internal discipline. Mawn believed O'Neill deserved only a letter of reprimand or censure, and felt the matter should be ended quickly. But that was rarely the case with an OPR investigation. O'Neill was pressed to answer endless questions about his movements and his reason for taking the classified documents to Florida. The OPR probe haunted him for nearly a full year, well into 2001, like a slow death by a thousand cuts. It would haunt him to his grave.

"WE'RE DUE FOR SOME-THING BIG"

O'Neill arrived in Aden airport in Yemen to head the investigation into the bombing of the USS Cole in which seventeen sailors were killed and thirty-six others wounded. The first words that are visible upon leaving the airport include "bin Ladin," the family that built the airport and nearly everything else in Yemen and Saudi Arabia.

15

THE TIP OF THE SPEAR

Osama bin Laden was back on Al Jazeera on September 22, 2000, this time wearing a dagger in his belt, a traditional Yemeni symbol, in this case signaling an impending battle. The videotaped statement showed him flanked by two Egyptian militants, Dr. Ayman al-Zawahiri and a son of jailed Egyptian Sheikh Omar Abdul Rahman, who was serving a life sentence in U.S. federal prison for ordering the bombings of a myriad of New York City landmarks. Bin Laden vowed new attacks on the United States to win Rahman's release from American custody.

"Enough of words!" bin Laden declared, just as he had done in 1998 before attacking the U.S. embassies in Africa. "It is time to take action against this iniquitous and faithless force that has spread troops through Egypt, Yemen and Saudi Arabia." As bin Laden spoke, Abdul Rahman's son could be heard in the background, chanting, "Forward to shed blood! Forward to shed blood! Forward to shed blood!"

The broadcast of bin Laden's latest threats happened to come just one day before the joint FBI-NYPD terrorist task force's twentieth anniversary party. If times had been calmer, the gathering might have been publicized. Newspaper and television reports might have described the successes of the unit formed by the legendary FBI supervisor Kenneth Walton. Instead, details of the celebration remained a closely guarded secret. The event would attract top law enforcement officials from seventeen separate agencies, including prosecutors who played roles in the arrest and conviction of every major terrorist from Ramzi Yousef to Blind Sheik Rahman to the millennium bomb suspects.

The guest list made the event a terrorist's dream target. So did the location. Organizers chose the Windows on the World restaurant, located atop the World Trade Center, the very symbol of American imperialism that had already been attacked by terrorists in 1993. The irony of the choice—and the danger of it—was not lost even then on the event's planners or their three hundred guests. Still, despite their collective impudence in thumbing their noses at the growing threat and holding the soiree in the Twin Towers, security was extremely tight.

O'Neill attended the affair with Valerie James, and appeared at ease all evening long, almost as though he didn't have a serious care in the world. Detective Pat Pogan introduced O'Neill to his wife as the miracle man who saved their last Christmas with a gift of funds after their home caught fire, and O'Neill joked: "Yeah, your husband's lucky he got that. He doesn't do anything to deserve that much money. It should've been half." Then he put his arms around Pogan and added, "He's one of the best detectives."

Only a select few knew about the embarrassing OPR inquiry into O'Neill's recent loss of his briefcase, and the shadow it cast could not interfere with the mood of camaraderie and festivity in the air. The people who worked closest with O'Neill recall how he remained steadfast, consumed by the latest bin Laden tape and the danger it posed to American lives somewhere in the world. O'Neill devoted his attention that week to meetings designed to decipher exactly where his nemesis bin Laden might strike.

Intelligence gathered in the Middle East warned of an impending Islamic attack on an American warship, but there was no information on what type of vessel or when and where the attack would take place. Naval officials had more than three hundred ships around the globe to worry about, and felt the threat was too unspecific to alter their deployments in the Persian Gulf region, even though there was already a stark rise in violence in Israel.

The USS *Cole*, one of the navy's newest and most sophisticated warships, was on medium level alert when it sailed into the harbor outside the port of Aden in southern Yemen to refuel. Only a handful of sailors armed with rifles were posted as sentries on the deck. The 457-foot-long ship, with a crew of 297 sailors, dropped anchor in the modest port as a part of the continuing program pushed by Ambassador Bodine to soften the U.S. image in the Persian Gulf and improve relations with this troubled desert nation.

In the weeks before the *Cole* sailed into Yemeni waters, Bodine and the State Department persuaded the White House that diplomacy was working, the Yemeni government was moderating its position toward the United States, and American warships would be safe docking there. O'Neill knew better. He considered the State Department recommendations to be at best naive. Along with his FBI colleagues and a handful of like-minded experts at the CIA and naval intelligence, he believed the evidence indicated that American ships in Yemen were extremely vulnerable to an Al Qaeda attack.

It might not have looked that way to anyone who saw the *Cole* on the morning of October 12, 2000. Gleaming and sleek as it sat on the Red Sea waters, the *Cole* boasted a powerful radar system, long-range cruise missiles, and air defense weapons that made it seem almost invincible. A handful of sailors were at work scrubbing its decks, and the majority of the crew was below, dining in the mess hall. At about 11:15 A.M. (3:15 A.M. in New York), a small skiff with two Arabs on board came slowly across the harbor toward the fueling facility where the gigantic warship was moored.

None of the sailors on deck thought twice when the skiff glided within twenty feet of the *Cole*. One of the Arabs waved, and some of the sailors waved back. Then the other Arab stood up and saluted. Suddenly there was a flash and a tremendous explosion. Several hundred pounds of the synthetic explosive known as C-4 had been detonated, making a bomb twice as powerful as the device detonated by Timothy McVeigh in the 1995 Oklahoma City bombing. The blast tore a forty-by-forty-foot hole in the reinforced-steel side of the warship. The suicide bombers were obliterated—only a few of their teeth were recovered.

The bomb triggered a raging inferno and instantly crippled the massive destroyer. Seventeen sailors in the mess hall were killed when they were speared or pinned by bomb-twisted metal. Another thirty-nine were seriously injured, including Kathy Lopez, who was badly burned while working in the ship's oil lab. Lopez was determined to survive for the sake of her children and her husband. Despite her pain, she and Robert McTureous managed to jump into the rushing water inside the *Cole* and swim out through the hole in the side of the ship, away from the flames engulfing them.

A makeshift triage center was quickly set up on the *Cole* flight deck to treat the bloodied survivors. Medics raced to the wounded, and military helicopters were dispatched from other ships nearby in the Arabian Gulf to evacuate the most seriously injured to waiting planes for flights to Ramstein, Germany, where the U.S. maintains a military base with a sophisticated hospital. The U.S. Navy ordered its ships in the region to close ranks around the wounded *Cole*, which was taking on water and in danger of sinking.

The U.S. attempt at détente with the Yemeni government had turned into a nightmare. O'Neill knew right away that the attack was no simple act, like crashing a truck bomb through a barricade: the terrorist group responsible for this bombing had orchestrated its plan carefully and expertly. It had to have obtained advance knowledge on the ship's refueling stop, as well as gained an intimate understanding of the procedures involved in the process.

The complicity of one or more Yemeni officials had to be considered likely.

There was no serious talk of a U.S. military reaction to the *Cole* attack. The election was less than a month away, and Clinton was still hoping to create a legacy by ending the violence in Israel. The president decried the attack "as despicable and cowardly," and linked it to his peace initiative, calling for an end to "bloodshed" and a "return to dialogue," and warning that if the *Cole* terrorists intended "to deter us from our mission of promoting peace and security in the Middle East, they will fail, utterly."

O'Neill knew the attack on the *Cole* bore all the earmarks of an Al Qaeda operation. He believed it was more likely designed as part of bin Laden's collective plan to wage jihad than any desire to thwart Clinton's peace initiative in Israel. To suggest that the bombing was an attempt to derail the president's diplomatic efforts in Israel struck him as a politically expedient analysis.

O'Neill's lingering anger about never going to Kenya and Tanzania to hunt down bin Laden was well known among FBI insiders. The probe into the blast that struck the *Cole* would be different. "The assumption was New York and John would be going and taking over the investigation," recalled Kevin Donovan, then associate special agent in charge of the New York criminal division and now the head of the New York office.

Nearly five years had passed since O'Neill identified bin Laden as America's greatest threat. Now he would have an opportunity to lead the manhunt for bin Laden in the country in which bin Laden's father was born. O'Neill believed he had to be there in Yemen, taking on a mission that would place him as close as any FBI terrorist hunter could get to face-to-face combat with a terrorist mastermind—and a man who had long ago emerged as his personal adversary.

Not everyone agreed that O'Neill should go to Yemen. Several of his detractors argued against sending him, suggesting he was too brash for such a diplomatically sensitive investigation. But Freeh and Mawn felt differently. They believed O'Neill's knowledge and single-minded focus were precisely what was needed to spearhead what promised to be the most difficult investigation ever mounted by the FBI—an inquiry that would place their agents in the most hostile environment in which they had ever traveled. In fact, the way the FBI hierarchy saw it, there wasn't anyone better equipped than O'Neill. He had created the template for all international terrorism investigations, he had unique expertise concerning bin Laden, and he had the determination— and if all else failed, the O'Neill charm—to persuade the Yemenis to work with the United States.

But what O'Neill did not know was that there was an even more formidable, unexpected foe awaiting him in Yemen: Ambassador Bodine, a fifty-two-year-old career diplomat who would insist upon controlling virtually every aspect of the U.S. response to the *Cole* attack. Bodine took an immediate and strong dislike to O'Neill, and seemingly worked to hamper some of his initiatives. Rather than going out of her way to be cordial and cooperative, as one might expect from an official whose assurances of safe sailing in Yemeni waters helped bring the *Cole* to Yemen, Bodine instead dug in her heels. According to FBI officials in Yemen at the time, Bodine often seemed to be outright hostile to O'Neill, when her anger may have been better directed at helping him find the terrorists who had murdered Americans.

At 6 A.M., Friday, October 13, 2000, O'Neill and his people set out from 26 Federal Plaza in a van with lights and sirens blaring, heading toward Washington, D.C., and a C-17 military transport plane waiting for them on the tarmac at Andrews Air Force Base. A contingent of rapid-deployment communications and hostage rescue teams were already aboard, and when the nearly one hundred FBI agents and support staff boarded the plane, the transport was filled to capacity. Gary Fitzgerald, who had been to Africa and a number of other cities in the course of his years with the JTTF, grabbed one of the last canvas jump seats and pulled on the safety straps. He sat down on O'Neill's left, with their backs facing the fuselage.

"We felt a little trepidation," he recalled. "Everything was running through our minds."

O'Neill was all business. He talked about the obstacles they might face and the equipment they would need to accomplish their mission in Yemen, where the FBI had never sent a full complement of agents. He was concerned about establishing lines of communication with the ambassador, the U.S. military, and Yemeni officials. "We were bouncing things back and forth," Fitzgerald said. "How many people do we have? Can we get them in? Where are we going to billet? What were the communication capabilities within the country and to D.C.? He even talked about the availability of potable water and force protection."

The temperature in the plane dipped below freezing, forcing Fitzgerald to put on more sweaters to fend off the chill. O'Neill remained in his sport jacket. About halfway into the first leg of the flight, the agents were sold small packaged sandwiches and fruit, which they paid for out of their own pockets to the military personnel on board, who were de facto flight attendants. "Nothing but the best for our boys," Fitzgerald recalled.

O'Neill would have liked to get to Yemen as quickly as possible, but according to one Navy source, Bodine had used her influence to have the FBI agents' plane held up in Ramstein. It was the first of many stop signs the ambassador would throw up in the way of O'Neill and the investigation, but the delay in Ramstein turned into a positive, since victims of the *Cole* blast had been sent there for medical treatment. By the time O'Neill's plane touched down, agents from the Naval Criminal Investigation Service (NCIS) were already at the Ramstein hospital. The NCIS is a small and little-recognized agency that provides protection and intelligence for the navy. Because the NCIS has agents stationed around the world, many of them fluent in foreign languages, their special agents often are the first American investigators to arrive in a country when there is an emergency or an attack. They were at the Ramstein base organizing the safe arrival of the wounded from the *Cole*.

O'Neill realized the stop provided an opportunity for him to gather critical eyewitness accounts about what happened to the ship. "We have to do this before we get to Yemen," he told Donovan. "This way we will have something real solid for when we arrive in Yemen. Maybe it will also keep us from turning in a wrong direction that would lead us astray."

Instead of cooling his heels at the airport and waiting for the plane to be refueled, O'Neill rounded up his agents and rushed off to the hospital to try to interview survivors of the blast. "John O'Neill had a sense of purpose," Donovan said, recalling how O'Neill even ordered his bomb technicians to the hospital to examine the sailors' clothing for explosive residue.

O'Neill was confronted with a grim scene when he and his team arrived at the hospital. Scores of wounded U.S. sailors were lying in beds or walking the hallways in bathrobes. Most of the men and women looked amazingly young, like teenagers. O'Neill was reminded of his own children. And as a super-patriot, he was proud to witness the sailors' willingness to make such an enormous sacrifice for their country. Tears welled in his eyes for a brief moment. He fought back the emotion in order to continue his work.

O'Neill went with NCIS investigator Kenneth Reuwer to the intensive care unit and saw petty officer Kathy Lopez, the thirty-one-year-old sailor who escaped the raging inferno inside the *Cole* by jumping through the hole in its side. Lopez looked like a mummy. She had suffered serious burns from the tips of her toes to the top of her head and was completely covered in bandages. Reuwer avoided interviewing Lopez, not wanting to disturb her recovery, but stopped by simply to let her know he was praying for her.

Before he left, Lopez motioned for him to come nearer. The NCIS agent moved closer to the wounded sailor's bed, but he could not make out what she was trying to say. He thought she must be in terrible pain, and summoned a nurse, who leaned over Lopez and placed an ear against her lips to hear what she was murmuring. Lopez then made a gurgling sound, as though she were trying to speak. The nurse understood her remark and turned to Reuwer.

"Get them!" Lopez had told the nurse.

O'Neill was overwhelmed. He left the ICU committed to telling everyone in the *Cole* response party about the brave petty officer's words. "I want everyone to tell that story to all the investigators," O'Neill said. "This is what should inspire all of us working on this case."

Another sailor provided perhaps the most important eyewitness account for O'Neill before he arrived in Yemen. At the time of the blast, a nineteen-year-old rookie sailor was standing on the deck of the *Cole* looking down at the small skiff just before it exploded. He told the FBI that one of the two Arabs was waving fruits and vegetables at him, giving the false impression that they were friendly locals selling their wares. The sailor watched the Arabs as they waved and saluted, thinking they were harmless peddlers hoping for a greenback in exchange for fruit.

But suddenly their seemingly innocent salutation turned into a bolt of lightning as the boat blew up, sending hot shrapnel into the young American sailor even before he realized what had happened. So just eight hours after leaving New York, O'Neill had already gathered hard eyewitness evidence that beguiling suicide bombers had attacked the *Cole*. Most important, the sailor's account directly contradicted the initial claim made by Yemeni President Ali Abdullah Saleh that the blast appeared to be an accident that occurred inside the *Cole*. President Saleh was desperate to avoid an international incident. With no survivors on the skiff, he said the case should be quickly closed, and the sooner the better for his fragile government, which existed in an even more precarious geopolitical environment than the Saudi Arabian monarchy. President Saleh did not want to appear to be sacrificing his citizens' rights to the foreign power of the United States and the FBI, which had long been trying to prove allegations that numerous terrorist groups operated out of Yemen, including Hamas, the Palestinian Islamic Jihad, and the Egyptian Islamic Jihad.

One federal official described Saleh's predicament quite succinctly. "He could not be seen rolling over for the United States and Western dogs when his country was overwhelmingly an Islamic fundamentalist state with ties to bin Laden." Nothing would have been better for Saleh than for the *Cole* tragedy to be just that—a horrible accident. "Yemen does not have any terrorist elements," he insisted.

O'Neill knew differently. By the time he accompanied some of his people to the Ramstein airport, where they boarded the C-17 for Yemen, he knew that bin Laden had been involved in yet another deadly attack on Americans. "John had a clear-cut explanation of what had occurred at the *Cole* and he had a mission," Donovan said. With the gurgling sounds of petty officer Lopez still fresh in his mind, O'Neill sent his agents off to Aden while he stayed in Germany to meet with U.S. military officials and oversee the debriefing of more survivors.

France was among the countries that refused to allow the C-17 with O'Neill's people to fly over its airspace, despite the need to get to the crime scene as soon as possible, so the trip began with a short detour to bypass France, and ended with a larger one to fly around Saudi Arabia, which also declined the U.S. overflight request. A good eight hours had passed by the time the C-17 landed at the cinder-block arrivals building at Aden Airport. Before the plane could even taxi to a halt, Jeeps mounted with machine guns approached and a standoff began.

The Yemenis insisted they had to inspect every piece of American equipment before allowing it into the country. Negotiations dragged on for several hours, leaving O'Neill's team to sit baking in the stuffy transport plane with the desert heat outside hitting 115 degrees. The FBI agents were finally allowed to disembark, but only after surrendering their weapons and unloading each piece of cargo and equipment. Once the Yemeni customs agents and presidential police had inspected the equipment, it was passed along a conveyor belt and the FBI agents had to reload it onto flatbed trucks that were to be driven to their hotel. Embassy personnel hired several trucks, drivers, and helpers to assist the agents for about $150.

Agents who had arrived a few days earlier from Washington brought heavily armed vans and cars to escort the caravan of flatbeds as it moved past concrete buildings pockmarked by large-caliber bullets fired during the civil war ten years earlier. The ordeal of maneuvering armed motorcades through the winding streets of Aden would soon become known as "doing a movement." There were "movements" to travel to the harbor to meet boats that shuttled agents to the Cole. There were "movements" to the palace for meetings with Yemeni officials. There were "movements" to get pizza and "movements" to get Coca-Cola. Routes were always varied to minimize exposure and risk.

O'Neill had warned his team that Yemen would be the "most hostile environment the FBI ever operated in," and planned to billet his people in a hotel on the outskirts of town that was relatively easy to defend against would-be attackers. But shortly after O'Neill's group arrived at the hotel after the grueling and exasperating day of travel, they found out they would have to move again. Ambassador Bodine had decided she wanted all U.S. assets based in a single hotel. She ordered O'Neill's agents to join the other U.S. personnel who were staying at the centrally located Aden Hotel. For the second time in a day, the agents loaded all their equipment onto flatbed trucks. It took about twenty minutes through the dusty, winding roads to reach the Aden, which, by comparison, was a four-star hotel. But it was packed, and there were not enough rooms for all the agents. O'Neill's people were forced to billet four to a room while others slept on the dining room floor on inflatable mattresses.

The U.S. contingent took over several floors of the hotel that they dubbed the "Third Deck." For anyone to gain access to the Third Deck, they had to pass through a special team of highly disciplined antiterror Marines who were led by a twenty-five-year-old captain. In addition, another two dozen Marines, all as young as the sailors O'Neill had greeted in Ramstein, were positioned on the roof and in hallways, guarding agents who had previously arrived from Washington as well as the first contingent of personnel from a naval fleet antiterrorism support team and a State Department federal emergency support team that already were shuttling back and forth to the *Cole*.

O'Neill arrived two days after his people with a small contingent of agents. He was met at the airport by an Arabic-speaking FBI agent, who explained to the Yemenis greeting O'Neill that he was the equivalent of a general. They were impressed, and helped him from the plane. On the way out from the airport, O'Neill spotted a billboard that was startling, if not really unexpected. The sign was for the construction company that had built the airport, which announced its name in large, bold letters: THE BIN LADEN GROUP. The family of the terrorist mastermind built pretty much everything in Yemen, just as it had in Saudi Arabia. O'Neill shook his head at the sight of his archenemy's name looming in the parched Yemen desert. It was a reminder of just how complicated and dangerous this assignment would be.

"Yemen is a country of eighteen million citizens and fifty million machine guns," O'Neill later quipped when assessing the risk of operating inside the country. The abundance of weapons, combined with the terrorist risk and possibly hostile population in bin Laden's home country, necessitated the elaborate security procedures under which the U.S. contingent was forced to work.

O'Neill did not even take time to go to his room and unpack, once he arrived at the Aden Hotel after his day of travel. Instead, he went straight to the top floor of the eight-story hotel to meet the top U.S. officials in charge of the case. As he came out of the elevator, he spotted Mike Dorsey, the special agent in charge of the NCIS Middle East field office, overseeing agents in twenty-three countries.

"You must be Mike Dorsey," O'Neill said, then made clear he wanted good teamwork with the NCIS. "I want to assure you this is a joint investigation. I want you to know that we could not have done any of this without you and your quick response. We will be joined at the hip. Everything the FBI knows or learns will be shared with you."

O'Neill then slid his right arm around Dorsey's shoulder and neck, and gave him one of his trademark hugs. Dorsey was taken aback by the touchy-feely gesture, but he was also pleased that the new FBI boss recognized his agency's pivotal role in helping launch this difficult and dangerous investigation. "He wanted to get right to the folks who were working," Dorsey said. "It showed his genuineness."

Dorsey introduced O'Neill to Admiral Mark Fitzgerald, who had flown to Yemen from his command center in Tampa, Florida, and Fitzgerald in turn introduced him to Ambassador Bodine, who had driven down from the northern capital city of Sana. They all exchanged pleasantries about how everyone looked forward to working together, but there was no mistaking a certain stiffness between Bodine and O'Neill from his first day in Yemen. Shaking hands, O'Neill was very formal. The two had actually met before, back in Washington, when Bodine headed the State Department's counterterrorism program, but might as well have been meeting for the first time.

O'Neill, perhaps tired from the long flight, made a mistake and pronounced "Yemen" as if it rhymed with "Cayman."

Bodine instantly corrected him, right in front of all of the others.

"It's Ye-men," she announced coldly.

It was neither the first time nor the last time Bodine would correct someone on their pronunciation of "Yemen" and "Yemeni," an understandable urge for an ambassador who took pride in her awareness of the cultural sensitivities of her host nation. Nevertheless, as one participant in the meeting remembered, the relationship between Bodine and O'Neill was "chilly from the outset."

But for Dorsey, that first meeting was reassuring. He had worked on the African bombings and had trained at Quantico in a program spearheaded by O'Neill. Called the Supportive Crisis Incident Response Group, it was a multiagency response strategy developed after the 1998 embassy bombings in Africa. Before O'Neill arrived in Yemen, Dorsey had worked closely with Tim Caruso, an FBI supervisor who led an early contingent of FBI agents from the Washington field office. He was concerned that the investigation could be hurt by a change in FBI leadership, even if the shift involved someone of O'Neill's reputation.

But O'Neill quickly dispelled any concerns. "It was evident that he was an extreme professional and very gracious," he said. "John made a point, coming over to me, the investigative side of the house. He made an effort not to snub a colleague."

Dorsey, a former narcotics detective in Norfolk, Virginia, who had spent twenty years with the NCIS, had been to Yemen before. He and his fellow navy investigators had risked their lives working as part of an effort to find and destroy land mines that had been planted during the country's civil war in the early 1990s. After hearing about the *Cole*, Dorsey and five colleagues boarded a P-3 antisubmarine prop plane at their base in Bahrain and took off for Yemen to begin to organize the U.S. recovery and investigative efforts.

O'Neill headed off to the room he shared with Donovan and spent the next two hours discussing the fledgling investigation on the phone with Washington and New York and with his agents. He then grabbed a few hours' sleep on one of the room's two single beds. Thirty members of the hostage rescue team were not as fortunate. They bivouacked on the floor of a banquet room while other agents were packed into hotel rooms, forced to sleep on damp floor mats.

At 4 A.M., only hours after arriving at the hotel, O'Neill made the first of his daily predawn calls to FBI Director Louis Freeh and Attorney General Janet Reno. At 6 A.M., shortly after dawn, he joined Dorsey and a few other agents in the lobby to get his first look at the *Cole*. They took a thousand-yard trip in a small boat to a refueling dolphin, where the crippled U.S. warship was moored. O'Neill and Dorsey, both of them making their maiden voyage to the *Cole*, climbed a ladder alongside the gigantic vessel and ascended to the flight deck.

The scene was even more horrific than they had imagined. Dead sailors whose bodies had been pulled from the wreckage were lying on the flight deck covered in American flags. Federal agents were standing among them, examining and photographing their bodies and processing their belongings in as dignified a manner as possible. Many of the less seriously injured sailors were still being treated on board. Everywhere O'Neill looked, there were the young brave faces of American sailors, still stunned at the loss of their friends and comrades and at the toll the attack had taken on their vessel. "We could not avoid the emotions," Dorsey said. "They were just seventeen-, eighteen-, nineteen-, twenty-year-old kids. They were pretty shell-shocked."

The *Cole* was without power and faced the very real danger of sinking. Sailors who had somehow escaped injury in the blast were literally living outdoors on the aft deck. But as tragic and surreal as the scene was on deck, it did not compare to the horror inside the belly of the ship. O'Neill and Dorsey descended into what used to be the *Cole* mess hall. The temperature increased with each step down, ultimately topping 110 degrees. The smell of acetylene torches was everywhere. So was the odor of decomposing bodies. Shipyard workers and engineers flown in from the

States were working feverishly to free the dead, who were pinned and crushed by twisted steel. "The blast forced steel to collapse on people," Dorsey recalled.

Evidence recovery experts tried to gather remains, but had to perform their grim task without further compromising the structural integrity of the ship. O'Neill and Dorsey pushed farther down into the bowels of the vessel, carefully avoiding walls of jagged metal that were jutting out like sharp knives all around them. Finally, they reached the cavernous hole in the side of the *Cole.*

"Even though we had gotten reports on what it looked like, John and I were amazed," Dorsey said. "We were literally looking through the ship. It's not a natural thing for a ship to be open to the sea. Looking down twenty feet, you could see divers swimming around the jagged metal. There were the remains of bodies hanging overhead. One sailor was crushed against a bulkhead. He was nearly impossible to extract. The emotional reaction was powerful. Even agents who had been around other horrible crime scenes were overwhelmed."

For the first time, O'Neill was witnessing bin Laden's destructive handiwork up close with his own eyes. These images of death and pain were not photographs beamed to satellites and broadcast on television screens behind him at the command post or on CNN. Along with the gurgling request from Petty Officer Lopez to "get them," the horror on the *Cole* only served to strengthen O'Neill's already intense determination to dismantle Al Qaeda.

But he knew it was not going to be easy. The level of hostility against the FBI agents and military personnel working in Yemen was extreme. Some Yemeni citizens were reportedly handing out flyers urging sympathizers to kill Americans, specifically FBI agents. "We knew the environment was dangerous," Dorsey said. "We were in bin Laden's backyard. You could feel the atmosphere."

Gunshots were often heard at night. Marines with night vision goggles who were standing guard at the hotel reported spotting shadows outside their boundaries. They believed the movements in the dark were terrorists or terrorist sympathizers conducting surveillance for a possible attack. "If they bombed the hotel, they could take out the ambassador and the senior delegation from many U.S. agencies," Dorsey said. "They were certainly looking for an opportunity to hurt us."

Radar aboard one U.S. military plane taking off from Aden Airport recorded that an infrared locking device from a land-to-air missile had zeroed in on its fuselage. "We believe someone on the ground was going to shoot it down," Donovan said. The threat level was so intense, the military went to its highest alert, Delta Con.

That put Ambassador Bodine in a tough position. She had staked much on her assessment that there was minimal terrorist activity in Yemen, and now it fell to her to try to smooth the way for O'Neill and his team to investigate the mass killing against a backdrop of strong anti-American sentiment. She viewed Yemen as a struggling democracy overshadowed by oil-rich monarchies in the Persian Gulf, a Muslim nation that was moderate in comparison to its neighbors; in Yemen, women had the right to vote. She had built bridges to the Yemenis and didn't want to see her work amount to nothing. She prided herself on the understanding of the political and cultural nuances of Yemen. There was probably no way for Bodine to reconcile her duty to expedite the U.S. investigation with her desire to continue to reach out to the Yemenis, but she made clear she was going to try.

A career diplomat, Bodine was smart and confident, that rare type of government official who attended meetings in Washington alone instead of with an entourage of aides. Known as a diplomat who operated with a steel hand inside a velvet glove, Bodine had earned a reputation for toughness while serving as the deputy chief ambassador in Kuwait. When the U.S. embassy fell under siege during the Iraqi invasion in 1991, Bodine remained in the embassy until the bitter end, helping hundreds of others to escape before finally departing after 137 days, which earned her the secretary of state's Award for Valor.

After the Gulf War, this Phi Beta Kappa from the University of California at Santa Barbara served as acting coordinator for counterterrorism and then was named ambassador to Yemen by President Clinton on November 5, 1997. Yemen was to be her final posting overseas before returning home, and she hoped that improved relations between the U.S. and Yemen would prove to be her final achievement. Bodine was practically packing her bags to leave for a university position at her alma mater, UCSB, when the *Cole* was bombed, but her stint was suddenly extended indefinitely.

The State Department's office of counterterrorism cabled Bodine at the outset of the *Cole* investigation, spelling out what her priorities were. Foremost was the safety of American personnel, followed by the importance of assisting the investigation. The least important aspect, she was told, was maintaining a relationship with the Yemeni government—and only then in order to achieve other, more important objectives.

But the ambassador seemed more concerned about preserving her relationship with the Yemeni government than in assisting the FBI, an attitude attested to by more than a dozen law enforcement, naval, and intelligence officials present at that time in Yemen. After just a few days in Aden watching agents arrive from America, Bodine was concerned about the size of the FBI force. She wanted their presence kept to a minimum—perhaps to just a handful of agents—to avoid inflaming tensions with the Yemeni president and his citizenry.

Bodine said she was concerned that a large, heavily armed U.S. "footprint" marching around a small country like Yemen might damage the relationship she had brokered between the U.S. and the fledgling democracy—and might harm her bridge-building between the two countries. Rather than push hard for the FBI to utilize every weapon in its arsenal to find the terrorists, Bodine seemed to see the FBI presence largely through the eyes of the Yemenis, who viewed them as an invasion force. "Try to imagine if a military plane from another country landed in Des Moines and three hundred heavily armed people took over," she would later explain to the *New Yorker*.

But the FBI contingent of one hundred agents mostly consisted of doctors, photographers, crime scene investigators, evidence recovery specialists, bomb technicians, and communications experts. Only about thirty would actually be involved in the investigation on the mainland, and that number would easily be scaled back depending on the cooperation level of the Yemeni government. Nonetheless, since the *Cole* bombing constituted another act of war against America by bin Laden, O'Neill believed it was prudent to have enough resources from the start rather than having to wait for their arrival.

By all accounts, Bodine saw things much differently—and was anything but diplomatic about it. She made it perfectly clear to O'Neill that she was in charge in Yemen and that anything he wanted to do would have to be cleared by her. There were no subtleties in her message. Ambassadors and State Department officials almost universally try to keep some distance from law enforcement and military procedures because they lack expertise. But not Barbara Bodine.

"From the moment I walked in the door, she said, 'I am in charge of everything,' and 'This is the way it is going to be,'" O'Neill later told Patricia Kelly, the head of U.S. diplomatic security.

O'Neill had a reputation for not easily bending, but in this case, he was willing to try. He had worked with State Department officials before and understood their responsibilities. He had no trouble accepting that the ambassador was the top U.S. official in any foreign country, directly representing the president of the United States. Even before he landed in Yemen, O'Neill said he would gain nothing by having a strained relationship with the ambassador. He planned to keep Bodine fully briefed on his investigation, which was in his interest as well as hers. "There was nothing in it for him to cross swords with her," said Fran Townsend, then Attorney General Reno's head of intelligence policy and review.

O'Neill was pragmatic and wise enough to realize he could only be hurt by tangling with Bodine, and anything less than a professional relationship between them would imperil the criminal investigation. He had little reason to expect that she would become another obstacle in his path, and assumed that after she came to better understand his mission and what he needed to accomplish it, she would cooperate with him. If all else failed and tensions between them surfaced, he figured he could always fall back on his magnetic Irish charm to smooth over any differences. He was badly mistaken.

If anything, Bodine disliked and distrusted O'Neill even more with each passing day. Some people came to believe her personal animus toward O'Neill adversely influenced her judgment. Kevin Donovan, now the head of the FBI's New York office, recalled attending numerous meetings with O'Neill and Bodine where the ambassador tried to suffocate O'Neill's initiatives to promote her own.

"John would go to a round of meetings in the morning and another round at night with the ambassador," he recalled. "She was hard on him. Hard on his opinions of what needed to be done. Hard on the type of cooperation we needed. She insisted, 'This is my country,' and she was in charge."

Bodine justified her animosity toward O'Neill by claiming he had promised early on that he would have only a handful of investigators on the case. When another wave of agents arrived in the immediate aftermath of the attack, with portable generators and other emergency equipment, the number increased. Bodine was angry, and her lack of expertise in law enforcement may have played a role in her misunderstanding of how many agents were needed to provide initial support and crime scene work at the *Cole*.

"Barbara Bodine thinks she is a law enforcement expert and she thinks she knows everything there is to know," said a U.S. official in the Office of Diplomatic Security who worked closely with her. "No ambassador inserts himself or herself that deeply into an investigation. You are supposed to go to her for help and she is supposed to go to the host government and say, 'Americans died on your shores, and you have to help.'"

But the size of the FBI presence was not her only point of contention with O'Neill. Bodine also claimed O'Neill failed to consider the delicate political environment. "Her basic complaints were that he was insensitive to the Yemenis," Donovan recalled.

O'Neill might not have been as sensitive as Bodine would have liked. He could be gruff and single-minded, especially in the middle of an investigation. But if Bodine sought to portray him as a provincial American with little knowledge of the region, she was badly mistaken. In fact, O'Neill was probably the FBI's single greatest student of the Persian Gulf region. Agents and audiences at lectures were held spellbound by the way he was able to intelligently link investigative analysis with history and geopolitical nuances. He not only connected the dots about bin Laden long before many in government had even heard his name, he was way ahead of most officials—including State Department diplomats— in recognizing where Al Qaeda was headquartered and in which countries it operated. He was aware that Yemen allowed Al Qaeda cells to operate with impunity in its borders.

He was right and she was wrong. But she not only derided O'Neill's years of knowledge and understanding of bin Laden and Al Qaeda, which would have been questionable enough, she actually resorted to claiming that the Yemenis disliked O'Neill and did not want to work with him. This could not have been further from the truth.

Several top Yemeni law enforcement officials privately criticized Bodine to the FBI and the NCIS. They often told O'Neill that they wished they could meet with him alone because Bodine often addressed them in a condescending and abusive manner, according to FBI and Naval Criminal Investigative Service officials. The idea that Yemeni law enforcement and military officials would side with an American FBI official—and not the practiced diplomat—was hardly surprising to those who knew O'Neill.

"John was a master at developing rapport with foreign counterparts," said David Kelley, the assistant U.S. attorney in charge of terrorism and organized crime cases in New York, who was in Yemen handling the *Cole* investigation for U.S. Attorney Mary Jo White. "I thought the Yemeni counterparts really liked John and respected him."

Kelley says he thought O'Neill bent over backward trying to reach out professionally to Bodine. "John O'Neill had conducted countless investigations and knew better than anyone what was necessary," he said. "He was always rational, always reasonable, and always cordial and professional."

O'Neill and Bodine even clashed over the danger faced by American agents and military in Yemen. Perhaps because Bodine had survived the siege in Kuwait, she never perceived the threat as being as serious as it appeared to the FBI, the NCIS, the CIA, and the military, even though she was thoroughly briefed on all their intelligence. Or she may have been overly concerned about offending the Yemenis.

To O'Neill, providing for the safety of his people was a top priority, just as it was in Africa two years earlier or on the streets of Brooklyn or Chicago. When he pushed for permission for his people to carry long weapons for defensive purposes, Bodine denied the request, insisting the agents remain armed only with handguns and insisting they keep them hidden. "She wanted no weapons shown at all," Donovan said, quickly pointing out that Yemen was—and remains—home to open-air markets where powerful automatic weapons and even rocket launchers are sold. "The citizens are better armed than the government," O'Neill observed.

Just how far the ambassador would go out of concern about

offending the Yemenis became clear just days after the *Cole* attack. She insisted agents avoid wearing any clothing with the FBI insignia, but curiously, she also requested they purchase and wear State Department T-shirts she'd had printed up featuring the U.S. flag as part of the logo, along with the Yemeni flag. One afternoon, Bodine arrived at the Aden Hotel for a meeting and spotted two female agents wearing shirts tucked into their slacks. Bodine marched over to the women, one of whom spoke Arabic, and, in extremely undiplomatic tones, excoriated them in public about the role of women in Yemeni culture. "In Yemen, we don't wear our shirts in," the ambassador said, claiming that the agents' formfitting American garb showed off their figures and this could be insulting to the Yemenis. Then Bodine reached over and pulled one agent's shirt out of her slacks.

"Cover your butt," she barked, according to an FBI official.

"The ambassador was a raving lunatic," said Gary Fitzgerald, the veteran JTTF detective. "She pulled the shirt out of the pants of one agent and dressed both of them down in public in the hotel about the social mores of the country, and told them that it was not appropriate for women to have their physical attributes exposed."

O'Neill was not happy about the episode. There were a number of protocols and personality quirks he would have to accept from the ambassador, but he was not going to sit still for her harshly addressing his agents in public. O'Neill believed in respect. Just as he demanded respect from Lipka in Washington and Ashley and Pierneck in Chicago, he would request it from Bodine. He told the ambassador that there was a chain of command in the FBI. If she had problems with any of "my people," in the future she should come to him and he would take care of the matter. "Listen, don't manhandle my agents," he added.

On the face of it, O'Neill's decision to stand up for his people was a reasonable, professional response. But Bodine was the ambassador. She lived in a protected embassy in Sana and stayed in her own comfortable room in Aden with all the trappings that a top U.S. official enjoyed. She was not used to being instructed on how to behave, especially as the highest-ranking American in Yemen. Nevertheless, she could have acknowledged her own possible faux pas. Instead, she seemed to take O'Neill's request for professional courtesy as an insult and the confrontation only hardened her opinion of O'Neill.

Most perplexing, despite her lambasting of the female FBI agents for their trespass against Yemeni culture, Bodine returned to the hotel the following evening wearing a tight-fitting pant suit, directly contradicting her own edict and giving the clear impression that the rules applied to everyone but her, according to several U.S. officials and agents.

It sent a sour message to the agents now stationed in the command post on the eighth floor, which had to be protected day and night by Marines. Visitors to the command post were routinely patted down, and maids and hotel staff had to pass checkpoints to get into the FBI's secure area. Rooms were constantly swept by bomb-sniffing dogs. Communications experts detected listening devices on several occasions, which forced O'Neill to change his meeting places. "Of course they [the Yemeni security apparatus] were spying on us," Detective Gary Fitzgerald of the JTTF recalled. "They would not allow anyone to do anything on their own. Their president was caught between a rock and a hard place. He had fundamentalists on one side and he could not be seen as rolling over for the West and the United States."

Saleh was a volatile army commander who had sided with Iraq and Saddam Hussein during the first Gulf War. His officials promised to cooperate, but never delivered on their pledge. Instead they stonewalled. Like the Pakistanis and the Saudis, the Yemenis scheduled meetings for midmorning, postponed them a few hours, and then delayed them once again until late at night, leaving FBI officials frustrated. O'Neill would shuttle from investigative meetings to the *Cole* and back again to meet with the ambassador and the Yemeni officials, always trying desperately to win permission to conduct interviews with possible suspects and eyewitnesses, and to visit the sites where the bomb was built and where the skiff was launched.

"We were up and eager and the meetings would not materialize," Kelly said. "We were constantly waiting for the green light. Kids were killed and we were trying to solve it, but it would not happen."

But Bodine always seemed to side with Saleh over the FBI. The Yemenis refused to allow the U.S. to conduct interrogations or even be present when they were done, and the agents could not travel freely in Aden to investigate leads or speak with possible witnesses. They would not even allow FBI sketch artists to interview witnesses. "She was not an investigator or a criminal investigator," Fitzgerald said. "She had no concept of forensic science, which John had a master's degree in, and what it takes to get a prosecution. In fact, she was a roadblock, always asking the U.S. investigators, 'Why do you do this or that?' and then frequently saying, 'You cannot.'"

O'Neill was beside himself, worried that the trail of the suspects was growing colder. But he cautioned Donovan and the other agents to be patient and respectful of the ambassador and Yemeni officials. He continued meeting with his Yemeni counterparts, hoping that face-to-face contact would ultimately enhance the U.S. relationship with them. This was not easy, because Yemen's law enforcement community is a complex mixture of four agencies. Each branch had to be dealt with whenever O'Neill had a request. Ultimately, all decisions on what the FBI could or could not do had to be brought to the president or his aides by the presidential security officers. The answers were rarely quick or direct, which only added to the agents' frustration, considering the urgency of the situation. The investigation was difficult enough, with divers in the water and engineers trying to keep the *Cole* from sinking, and the threat level was a constant concern. When an answer finally came back, it was almost immediately counter-manded. "Today they'd give permission, tomorrow they'd say, 'Nope,' " Fitzgerald said.

On October 16, the FBI managed to dredge the bottom of the harbor near the *Cole*, but the Yemenis refused to sift through the sand or allow the FBI to use their facilities to search for evidence and remains. Many of the United States' investigative techniques puzzled the Yemenis. "Their idea of investigations was from watching 'Quincy,' " one investigator said, referring to the television show starring Jack Klugman as a forensic medical examiner. The Yemenis did not understand the value of the mud at the bottom of the port, but they understood the value of the American greenback. When the U.S. offered a one-million-dollar payment for their help in shipping the mud to another country to be analyzed, the payoff was accepted.

16

FACE-TO-FACE WITH THE ENEMY

Six days after the *Cole* attack, President Clinton spoke in Norfolk, Virginia, at a memorial service for the fallen sailors. To the great frustration of O'Neill and other law enforcement officials who hoped Clinton would at last launch a strong military action against bin Laden, the president steered his talk toward thoughts of peace. Clinton's mind was still on his increasingly unsupportable hopes of brokering a lasting Middle East peace. Clearly a decisive reaction to the threat posed by bin Laden was beyond him, despite the loss of American life.

"Their tragic loss reminds us that even when America is not at war, the men and women of our military still risk their lives for peace," Clinton said. "[Terrorists] can take innocent life. They have caused your tears and anguish, but they can never heal, or build harmony, or bring people together. That is work only free, law-abiding people can do. People like the sailors of the USS *Cole*. To those who attacked them, we say: You will not find a safe harbor. We will find you, and justice will prevail. America will not stop standing guard for peace or freedom or stability in the Middle East and around the world . . . The lives of the men and women we lost on the USS *Cole* meant so much to those who loved them, to all America, to the cause of freedom. They have given us their deaths. Let us give them their meaning. Their meaning of peace and freedom, of reconciliation and love, of service, endurance and hope."

Despite the assurances that the culprits would "not find a safe harbor," Clinton's political calculus did not allow for a forceful response. First, there was the issue of whom to attack, since the FBI had been held back in gathering hard evidence. And there was no chance Clinton would take military action against bin Laden, since the administration was still smarting over its failed strike in Afghanistan. But no doubt the most important factor was Election Day, which was just two weeks away. Too much was at stake at the polls for Clinton to order a politically risky military strike.

A major breakthrough finally came in the investigation, but too late to force Clinton into action. A twelve-year-old boy told Yemeni police that on October 12, a bearded, bespectacled man gave him about one hundred Yemeni riales (less than a dollar) to watch a car and boat trailer that launched what turned out to be the bomb-laden skiff. That information quickly led Yemen investigators to the terrorists' abandoned car, a Nissan with four-wheel drive, and the boat trailer.

O'Neill soon scored a breakthrough of his own. His frequent meetings with General Homoud Naji paid off when the Yemenis gave O'Neill and his investigators access to four key locations, including the observation post the terrorists set up so they could look down on the harbor as the attack was taking place and videotape the explosion. The Yemenis also showed the FBI two suspected safe houses used by the bombers, including the one in which the bomb was built.

One was a bungalow located in Little Aden, a small peninsula across the bay from Aden in an area of villages built for British colonial officials and inhabited now by refinery workers. Besides the cinderblock walls already in place, the terrorists erected new corrugated iron fences at least ten feet high to block the house from the street. A set of rust-colored steel gates with sharp spikes guarded access to an area behind the house where the men had prepared the white skiff and the bomb. The other house, more modest and private, was five miles away in a neighboring district called Madinat ash Shab. Three more safe houses were quickly discovered after the FBI teams began gathering evidence, including phony identification documents issued by a Yemeni official in Lahej, twenty-five miles to the north.

O'Neill persuaded the Yemenis to allow them to visit the marina where the skiff was launched. The boat ramp, near a bridge linking Little Aden Peninsula to the city, gave the attackers a perfect launching point. It was miles from Aden's main waterfront, in a relatively quiet residential neighborhood near a power plant and an oil storage depot, yet it had a clear view of the entry to the harbor from open sea.

The FBI determined that the attack boat circled the *Cole*'s bow from the west, then slowly skirted the ship's port side as the two men on board waved to the sailors. The *Cole* had been moored in the harbor for less than two hours when it was struck, which meant the terrorists knew its precise movements in advance. The American and Yemeni investigators camped at the marina, setting up a cluster of dark green tents where they sifted debris for clues to the suicide bombers. As O'Neill stood in the hot Mediterranean sun examining the crime scene, a telephone nearby rang. Bob McFadden, an NCIS expert on Middle East intelligence, answered it.

"There's a phone call for Mr. O'Neill," McFadden told him. O'Neill stood up, took the phone, and smiled at McFadden. "My father is Mr. O'Neill. I'm John." Then he put his arm around McFadden, whose sweaty brow left a water mark on O'Neill's clothes.

One of the first suspects picked up by the Yemenis admitted training in Al Qaeda camps in Afghanistan and obtaining the skiff. One of the ringleaders, Abd al-Rahim al-Nashiri, left Yemen a day before the assault. Another suspect was supposed to videotape the attack, which would have provided valuable propaganda footage for bin Laden's media operation, but never showed up. There were false rumors he overslept.

The Yemenis provided mug shots of the suspects, and O'Neill

faxed them to agents debriefing an Egyptian informant who had provided early warnings of a planned Al Qaeda attack on an American warship. The informant quickly identified the suspects as known bin Laden associates, providing further evidence to warrant military action against bin Laden in Afghanistan. Even President Saleh finally reversed his position and admitted the *Cole* bombing had been a terror attack. Moreover, he revealed that two men who had used one safe house spoke with Saudi Arabian accents, which meant they were either Saudi or from the same Hadramout province as bin Laden. He also told the FBI that a fake driver's license had been issued to a second suspect from Hadramout.

The progress was encouraging, but not encouraging enough to justify the upbeat reports on the investigation Ambassador Bodine gave to reporters. "It's going very well, it's expanding," she said. She even suggested that a break in the case was near. But other U.S. officials in Yemen cautioned against such a rush to closure. They knew their mission was to break "the broad jihadist network" that had declared "holy war" against the United States, not just to round up a few simple foot soldiers. O'Neill and the NCIS believed that if Bodine had allowed the FBI to push harder with the Yemenis at the start of the case, they would have learned of the twelve-year-old informant and the safe houses much sooner.

President Saleh's disclosure of the possible terrorists' ties to bin Laden dramatically increased the threat to Americans in the region. Yemen was home to as many as sixty-thousand militants who fought the Soviets in the 1980s as allies of the United States, Pakistan, and Saudi Arabia. There were an estimated sixty million Kalashnikov rifles in Yemen, and some tribal chiefs were reportedly so heavily armed that they parked Soviet-era tanks in their courtyard with the end of the barrel facing out.

On October 26, President Saleh announced that one of the suicide bombers was an Egyptian and that Yemeni officials had picked up several other conspirators—Yemenis, Egyptians, and Algerians—who assisted in the bomb plot. Saleh said the perpetrators were with the Islamic militant group Egyptian Islamic Jihad and had fought in Afghanistan against the Soviets and returned to live in Yemen, where despite his efforts to rid the country of terrorists, some pockets remained, "dressed in Yemeni clothes." The Egyptian Islamic Jihad is the virulent anti-Western organization headed by Dr. Ayman al-Zawahiri, who had become bin Laden's second in command—and appeared with bin Laden in the September video threatening American troops.

In all, the Yemeni authorities rounded up sixty people with direct or indirect links to the bombing, including forty from outside Yemen. One man was a carpenter who confessed to helping build a false wood floor to conceal the explosives in the skiff. A man from Somalia, just across the Gulf of Aden on the Horn of Africa, was accused of taking money, buying the car, and registering it under his name. But the FBI was still not given direct access to the suspects.

Meanwhile, threats against the FBI agents in Yemen had become so intense that O'Neill asked Washington for permission to remove his people from the mainland. Mike Dorsey of the NCIS told O'Neill he had decided that he had to return to Bahrain to prepare his family to leave in the event of an attack there. It was the first time in the nearly two weeks the two had spent working together that either of them mentioned their loved ones rather than their mission. "I told John I would stay here forever, but I have a wife and family in Bahrain, and the threats there were as serious as in Yemen and we needed to get ready," Dorsey said. O'Neill told him to take care of his family. "We need to have you safe and in a position to respond again if there is another incident."

But Ambassador Bodine lobbied the State Department to block any departures by FBI agents. She did not agree with the experts' assessment of the threat level and felt that the shift could be seen as a slight to the Yemenis. She thought it might be seen as a suggestion that they could not provide adequate security. Earlier she had complained about the size of the FBI footprint, and now she was resisting its reduction, despite the fact that any such redeployment was a law enforcement decision largely outside her diplomatic domain.

"It was zero cooperation with her," said Gary Fitzgerald, the veteran joint terrorist task force detective. "Nonstop butting in."

FBI Director Freeh consulted with the military and various intelligence agencies before ultimately siding with O'Neill. On October 27, the FBI reduced its footprint. Most of the agents returned to the United States. A few dozen remained, but they retreated from the Aden Hotel to the USS *Tawara* and the USS *Duluth*, which were positioned near the crippled *Cole*. McFadden remembers that morale nose-dived when the agents were moved offshore and their investigation appeared to grind to a complete halt.

O'Neill did what he could to rally his people. The day they moved to the ships, he called all fifty agents into the Tawara mess hall and provided a thirty-minute briefing on the investigation and what he had learned from Washington that day during his conference call. O'Neill said he knew he had a reputation for being a bull-in-a-china shop agent who wanted quick results, but assured the agents that he understood that the FBI and the NCIS were working in a difficult environment, and patience was required. He promised them that time would eventually be on their side. Then he cranked up the O'Neill eloquence a notch and closed by telling them how proud he was to be serving with all of them on such an important mission.

"He wrapped it up with 'God Bless You,' and 'God Bless America,'" said McFadden, who now serves as NCIS division chief in the counterterrorism department. "You could feel the goose bumps. We were a tough audience, but when he delivered the speech, it came across as sincere, and I can tell you how we felt: it got to you in a good way."

The FBI's decision to leave the mainland deeply irritated Bodine. Once they were gone, she temporarily refused to allow them to return. In fact, she actually denied clearance for their shuttle boats or helicopters to land ashore to continue the probe. O'Neill waited several days until the threat level had subsided, and then negotiated a partial return of the FBI to the mainland.

But he refused to return to the centrally located Aden Hotel, which he viewed as an easy target. Instead, he billeted his people in the Golden Maher, a five-star hotel with a swimming pool and a view of the harbor. The hotel had been bombed before when U.S military briefly stayed there in 1995. But from a security standpoint, it was an improvement. There was only one entrance and the first checkpoint was secured by a combination of Yemeni police and Marines. A second checkpoint was manned only by U.S. military personnel, who used bomb-sniffing dogs to inspect arriving vehicles. For exercise, the agents ran back and forth across the small two-hundred-foot beach just beyond the hotel's plush rear lawn. The grass was watered every day from the bay, but the harbor water was so polluted that it smelled worse than a cow pasture.

Throughout these machinations, the wounded *Cole* had sat in Aden Harbor with its gaping hole on display for all to see. Finally, on October 30, the ship was taken out to sea on the back of a Norwegian transport ship, the *Blue Marlin*. As the *Cole* left the harbor, headed for dry dock in Pascagoula, Mississippi, and more than $150 million in repairs, the skeleton crew on board blasted "The Star-Spangled Banner" over the ship's loudspeakers followed by an in-your-face song by the rapper Kid Rock called "American Bad Ass."

In mid-November a suspect in the *Cole* bombing told Yemeni authorities that the Islamic militants behind the attack had tried to bomb the USS *Sullivan* in January, but aborted the assault when the explosives-packed skiff foundered near the beach. The information was shared with O'Neill, confirming to him just how widespread and sophisticated the millennium plot had been. It also supported O'Neill's belief that bin Laden's network would continue to assault American interests.

The Yemenis trusted O'Neill enough to bring him to the site where the botched attempt on the USS *Sullivan* had occurred, and they revealed they had several other suspects in custody for the *Cole* bombing. But they said they could not provide the FBI access to the detainees. O'Neill lobbied Bodine to press for direct FBI access to the suspects, but their appeals went nowhere.

Bodine was busy trying to get rid of O'Neill. She cabled her supervisors at the State Department saying that she was having problems with him. At first she accused him of insubordination, contending that the Yemenis did not get along with him, and complained about his general lack of understanding of the delicate diplomatic situation. Soon her missives began to take on a nastier, more personal tone.

Eventually, Director Freeh was forced to send O'Neill's boss, Mawn, over from the New York office to see if he was causing trouble and alienating the Yemenis, as Bodine kept claiming. It took Mawn only a few days to report back that O'Neill was doing a superlative job, particularly under such extraordinary conditions. Even President Saleh's personal security officers liked O'Neill. In fact, they admitted that they preferred dealing with O'Neill alone, without the ambassador. They said they would not object if the FBI had a thousand agents on the ground in Yemen.

Mawn concluded that the only person who had a problem with O'Neill was Bodine. "The ambassador's view was, 'We don't need U.S. military and Jeeps and planes here,'" Mawn said. "We tried to explain that we start big and then scale back. But she didn't care. She was more of an advocate for the Yemenis than for the U.S. She saw us more as a threat to diplomacy." Mawn's opinion of Bodine was shared by a number of other top officials, who all believed that Bodine may have "gone native," a term that implied she had become too close to the host country's officials to view the FBI's role clearly. O'Neill was pleased by his boss's vote of confidence, but he was privately hurt that Freeh had questioned his stewardship. He felt he was being stabbed in the back by the ambassador and needlessly targeted for investigation by the head of the FBI.

O'Neill continued to work at full throttle for several weeks, rarely sleeping. He started his day with 4 A.M. conference calls with Reno and Freeh, ran meetings with his agents and the Yemenis throughout the day, and huddled at night for updates before grabbing a couple hours of sleep. "John was like an Energizer Bunny, he just kept going and going and going," Fitzgerald said. "He was driven, by duty, honor, and country, a sense of right and wrong."

Some evenings he would sit in the hotel lounge with a few agents, smoking a cigar and discussing bin Laden. Pat Patterson, a supervising agent in charge of the violent crime squad in Los Angeles, was sent to Yemen because he had expertise in dealing with a recent Alaska Air crash off the coast of California, and was experienced in deep-water recovery and salvage operations. He and O'Neill spent several evenings speculating about what bin Laden's next target might be. The conversation invariably turned to the World Trade Center, which O'Neill believed would be attacked again. "I thought it was unlikely they would hit a target a second time," Patterson said. "But John was convinced of it. He said, 'No, they definitely want to bring that building down.' He just had that sense and was insistent about it."

O'Neill left Yemen two days before Thanksgiving, wrapping up what was supposed to be his initial tour of duty after seven frustrating weeks. Despite some breakthroughs, the FBI had for the most part remained on the outside looking in. Before he left, he made a point of shaking hands with all the agents and soldiers he could, thanking them for their work and sacrifice on behalf of their country. He flew home to New York feeling that he would probably never return to Yemen as long as Bodine was the ambassador.

O'Neill had dropped twenty-five pounds during his time in Yemen, and Valerie James could not believe how thin and tired he looked after he got off the plane. "He appeared emaciated and absolutely exhausted," she said. Yet despite his exhaustion and physical condition, he went straight to his office at 26 Federal Plaza.

The bad blood with Bodine continued to bother O'Neill back in New York. He remained a gentleman when asked about her anywhere in the vicinity of 26 Federal Plaza, shrugging his shoulders and saying, "What are you going to do?" But in more private moments, he revealed how disturbing he found her hostility. "She really hated me, Pat," he told Patricia Kelly, the head of diplomatic security. O'Neill prided himself on winning people over, but Bodine disliked him from the outset without ever giving him a chance to prove himself, he told Kelly. "I felt awful. The minute I walked through the door, it was like she wanted me to know, 'I am in charge of everything. And this is the way it is going to be, don't even bother to explain.'"

O'Neill tried to take pleasure in reconnecting with New York. On November 29, he and James attended the tree-lighting ceremony at Rockefeller Center, a tradition for them. The next week, they attended Sony music chairman Tommy Mottola's wedding to Mexican singer Thalía Sodi, which attracted celebrities from Robert De Niro to Jennifer Lopez. O'Neill had often dined with Mottola, visited his sprawling compound in Bedford, New York, for holiday season parties, and sailed on his 157-foot yacht, once with De Niro. O'Neill felt so close to Mottola, he believed Mottola might hire him after he retired from the FBI.

There were persistent rumors that O'Neill had used his relationship with Archbishop John Cardinal O'Connor in the months before Mottola's wedding to help Mottola obtain an annulment from his pop-star wife, Mariah Carey, and permission for Mottola to be married inside the city's most famous chapel, at Fifth Avenue and Rockefeller Center. The truth was much different, as a church insider recently explained. Mottola, it was decided, did not need an annulment from Carey because the singer was Episcopalian, and therefore the Catholic Church never recognized their union. Permission for the use of St. Patrick's Cathedral was obtained largely from New York City Police Commissioner Howard Safir, who was even closer to Mottola than O'Neill.

Valerie James recalled being at a Christmas bash at Mottola's with Safir, who suddenly looked past her and blurted out, "Oh my God, Val. There's Michael Jackson." Safir intervened on Mottola's behalf with Monsignor Anthony Della Villa, the rector of St. Patrick's, who made the arrangements for Mottola's wedding. Safir and his wife, Carol, attended the Mottola wedding and the lavish reception that followed at the Regent Wall Street, where singers Gloria Estefan and Donna Summer performed. Yet for reasons only Mottola knows, he never spoke with O'Neill again after the night of his wedding, leaving his former friend puzzled and hurt.

That holiday season Valerie told O'Neill that she needed a vacation and had decided to spend two weeks with her son, Jay, skiing in Val d'Isère, France, starting December 17. She asked O'Neill if he wanted to join them, fully aware that his work might once again prove an obstacle. She made it clear that she and Jay were going for the holiday, even if he had to work. O'Neill decided a skiing trip would be both enjoyable and rejuvenating, given the stress of recent months. They planned to return on December 31, in order for O'Neill and Jay to again spend New Year's Eve together in Times Square.

But before he left for Europe, O'Neill had dinner with DiBattista and exchanged Christmas gifts. Because she collected Barbie dolls, O'Neill gave her a Barbie music box along with a set of pearls he had brought back from Yemen. He also managed to see his close friend Fran Townsend and present her with an identical set of pearls from the Middle East. He presented James with a diamond-and-emerald bracelet after they arrived in France, where they skied and relaxed before moving on to Belgium, where O'Neill spent Christmas Day sipping cognac, cigar in hand. James thought O'Neill joined her and Jay in Europe to have some time to assess where his life was heading. He was thinking about leaving the FBI and changing his life "to be a little different kind of person, perhaps a 'Mr. Family Man,'" she said.

Two days after Christmas, O'Neill's deputy, Jay Manning, left for Aden to head the investigation. Waiting in Cairo for a connecting flight to Aden, Manning was keenly aware that everyone milling around him knew he was a representative of the U.S. government, thanks to his passport. As he stood on the hot tarmac waiting in line to board the puddle jumper, a couple ahead of him appeared to be having trouble with the agent over their passports. The male passenger pulled out some cash, gave it to the gatekeeper, and both were personally escorted onto the plane. Manning could only imagine what a terrorist might accomplish under such lax standards.

Once he took his seat on the broken-down Russian-made aircraft, with its frayed wires dangling overhead, a uniformed man emerged from the cockpit after takeoff, embraced two unsavory-looking male passengers, and escorted them into the cockpit. Manning braced himself for his adventure to take a turn for the worse. But he arrived safely in Aden, wrapping up nearly two days of travel. He was greeted by a dozen agents and taken to a small room where Ambassador Bodine was waiting to meet him. The FBI supervisor walked up to Bodine and introduced himself in a forthright manner.

"I'm on John O'Neill's staff, and I'm going to be the new on-scene commander here," he said.

"That man will never come back to this country, ever again!" the ambassador fired back.

Manning was stunned. He expected a certain amount of tact

and grace from an ambassador. "I barely set foot in the country, and this woman goes off on me," said Manning, now the FBI's assistant special agent in charge of foreign counterintelligence in Washington. "It was literally the first thing she said, right off the bat. And she's supposed to be a diplomat! I thought diplomatically she might say, 'John and I did not hit it off, but I am glad you are here.' But she hits me over the head with it."

Soon Bodine was saying something even more shocking. "The Yemeni people love you," she insisted. "They are so glad you are here. You will get full cooperation."

Manning knew that wasn't true, based on what he'd been told by the FBI, the NCIS, the CIA, the military, and many of Bodine's own colleagues in the Foreign Service. "Everything I heard was that they wanted to kill us," Manning said. "Intelligence reports every day contained threats against Americans and warnings that Yemen was a dangerous place where everyone carried guns, and weapons were traded regularly."

Manning was struck immediately by how much Bodine appeared to be ignoring reality. "This woman is wearing rose-colored glasses," he thought at the time, and his intuition was quickly confirmed. He left the airport in the company of a heavily armed FBI SWAT team, U.S diplomatic security forces, and local secret police in a "movement" of six SUVs. Like O'Neill before him, he was shocked to the see the name bin Laden prominently displayed on a billboard outside the airport. As his procession drove through the winding streets of Aden, past buildings pockmarked by bullets, he could feel the tension mount.

Suddenly a truck darted out from behind a blind curve, cutting off their caravan. Everyone in the U.S. contingent grabbed their weapons and braced for an attack. "I waited for the sound—*phoom*—like a missile launching," Manning recalled. "We were thinking we'd be hit with a rocket-propelled grenade, or antitank weapon." But their rush of adrenaline quickly subsided when the driver of the truck put it back in gear and harmlessly drove away.

The incident illustrated how nervous all the Americans felt while working in Yemen.

O'Neill, Valerie, and Jay flew back from France on New Year's Eve, arriving at 4:30 P.M., just in time to unpack, change, and make it to Cibo's restaurant for dinner with Joseph Dunne, his wife, and Dr. Gregory Fried, the renowned NYPD surgeon, and his wife, Anne, before heading to Times Square for the dropping of the ball. O'Neill stood beneath the huge Tiffany glass ball, with confetti raining down on him, and thought about Manning in Yemen, ringing in the New Year with a group of agents and young Marines, drinking soft drinks, eating pizza, and watching a local belly dancer.

Manning had the feeling during his entire monthlong stint in Yemen that his agents were vulnerable to attack at any moment. He speculated that the only reason they had not been assaulted was that the government had convinced the fundamentalists and tribal warlords that the price of another attack might be too high for everyone. But the Yemenis continued to do little to help the investigation. They pretended to be friendly partners, but still restricted access to suspects. "When we tried to conduct interviews there were very strict rules," Manning said. "They had to be present, and would have to ask the questions we had. There were concerns about the credibility of the answers."

O'Neill came up with an idea in early January to solve this problem. He suggested bringing the Yemeni officials to Washington. The Yemenis did not grasp certain fundamental aspects of American forensic investigations, including why O'Neill was interested in retrieving hats, toothbrushes, and garments worn by possible suspects in order to obtain DNA for analysis and comparisons. A quick tour of Quantico and the FBI laboratories would help them understand the FBI's investigative requests. Some officials lobbied against offering this olive branch. "I personally said we should not bring them until we get some information," said Stephen Corbett, an NCIS supervisory special agent who had arrived from Hawaii to join Manning as a supervisor on the case.

But O'Neill insisted, and the move was approved. President Saleh himself flew to Washington on January 10 and was given a tour of the FBI and its laboratories. Soon after he returned to Yemen, the FBI and NCIS were finally given the information that two suspects in custody had direct knowledge of the *Cole* attack and had trained in Afghanistan. One admitted taking an oath to die for bin Laden. Two other suspects said they provided false documents, but had no knowledge of a plan to attack the *Cole*. Other suspects, including two Yemeni nationals who had arrived from Afghanistan and Saudi Arabia, had links to the Africa embassy bombings. The flow of information quickly dried up, but at least the FBI had made some progress in the difficult investigation. "If it had not been for O'Neill's suggestion, I would still be waiting for information," Corbett said.

Manning was packing his belongings on January 22, 2001, preparing to leave Yemen and return to the States, when he received an urgent call from agents in Sana. An armed gunman had hijacked a jet carrying Ambassador Bodine to a meeting with Army General Tommy Franks, the commander in chief of the U.S. Central Command who was making his second visit to Yemen since the *Cole* attack. Also on board were U.S. military and political attachés from the embassy, and a Yemeni protocol official. Manning instantly feared the hijacking might be the work of Al Qaeda. He called Mawn in New York. "Holy shit!" Mawn said in his Boston accent, recognizing the international ramifications of a U.S. ambassador falling into the hands of terrorists.

The hijacker warned that he had a bomb and fired two shots in the air during the hour-long standoff, which ended when he was overpowered by crew members after the 727 was diverted to Djibouti. Bodine and the other ninety passengers were released unharmed. The suspect turned out to be an Iraqi, Mohammed Yahya Ali Satar, and a supporter of President Saddam Hussein.

Yemeni officials vowed a full-scale investigation into faulty airport security that allowed the gunman to bring a weapon onto the plane.

For Manning, the incident demonstrated just how lawless, dangerous, and "unsecured" Yemen was. But Bodine, who had been battle-tested in Kuwait, downplayed the entire incident, dismissing the hijacker as a disturbed man in need of help. "She was making excuses and apologizing for the hijacker," Manning recalled. Another agent said Bodine went so far as to tell the FBI it didn't need to investigate the hijacking at all.

Freeh and Mawn discussed sending O'Neill back to Yemen to jump-start the stalled *Cole* investigation. O'Neill wanted desperately to return to Aden to guide the mission, and since FBI policy always called for the rotation of supervisors, Freeh could send him back without explanation. The director planned to do just that, but Bodine was still stewing about O'Neill and continued to insist—as she had told Manning—"that man will never set foot again in Yemen."

O'Neill kept himself busy pursuing leads on the *Cole* bombing with his contacts in other countries. He and John Klochan, the ASA of foreign intelligence who had served in Yemen in November, headed off to Baku, the capital of Azerbaijan, and then to Amman, Jordan. The Jordanians had one of the best intelligence-gathering networks in the Middle East, and O'Neill wanted to get as much information from them about Al Qaeda as he could.

Klochan, a mild-mannered, cerebral-looking supervisor, was astonished at the entourage of Jordanian officials that showed up at the airport to greet O'Neill with hugs and kisses, surrounded by a phalanx of heavily armed officers in late-model Mercedes Benz cars. "They absolutely loved him," Klochan remembers. "They were opening doors, carrying our belongings. I had never been treated like that before. They clearly saw John as 'Mr. Terrorism' in the U.S. They looked at him as the pinnacle, number one."

O'Neill was careful about clearing all his meetings with the

U.S. ambassador to Jordan. Klochan recalled one afternoon when a Jordanian official requested a meeting with O'Neill that had not been officially scheduled. O'Neill would not agree until he had notified the ambassador to ensure O'Neill would not appear to be sidestepping the chain of command. "He knew that was protocol," Klochan said.

The pace left him begging O'Neill for sleep. He and O'Neill would attend meetings with the Jordanians during the day, and head out at night with about twenty of their hosts and their hosts' wives for an evening of barhopping and dining out at lesser-known locales. "When you're traveling all you want to do is hit the hay," he said. "But John liked dining out. 'We can go here, we can go there,' he'd insist. It was a rush for him. He was so energized."

By the time O'Neill returned to New York, Ambassador Bodine had made an extraordinary decision: she had issued an edict officially declaring that she would not give clearance for O'Neill to Yemen. This was the first time in U.S. history that an ambassador had seen fit to bar an FBI agent from entering a foreign country to do his work.

"That's bullshit!" Mawn yelled into the phone when the State Department advised him of Bodine's action. "He is the head of our division. We need him to go back."

But Freeh ultimately did not back up O'Neill, even though Bodine's unprecedented action was an affront not just to O'Neill's professionalism and dignity but to the professionalism and dignity of the entire FBI. Freeh did not have the time to fight with incoming Secretary of State Colin Powell. He planned to retire in June, and was focusing his priorities on a smooth transition with the newly installed Bush administration.

"We decided we would not start the third world war over this, regardless of who was correct," Mawn said.

But others were not afraid to point the finger at Bodine. "John is a very diplomatic person," said Fitzgerald, the veteran joint terrorist task force detective who was among the first wave of U.S. investigators into Yemen. "His forte is being diplomatic and schmoozing. The fact it got to that point tells you something about her."

O'Neill was deeply disturbed, and not so much by Bodine. What bothered him was that Freeh and the bureau did not defend him. The FBI's authority to lead the investigation was established directly by presidential edict. O'Neill thought Freeh should have taken the matter to the president himself—not for O'Neill's sake, but in the interest of preventing ambassadors with limited knowledge about investigations from dictating how the FBI should handle investigations and who it would appoint to head its international probes.

Privately, O'Neill felt abandoned by the bureau. The past two years had been tough. He had suffered two serious setbacks of his own making, and been passed over for promotion when Mawn was given the top position in New York. Finally, Freeh had failed to support him in the latest and most important investigation—a case involving bin Laden, whom O'Neill had recognized back in 1995 to be the head of a global terrorist network committed to attacking America. O'Neill actually began to contemplate the unthinkable: life after the FBI.

Nearly six months after the attack, the families of the victims of the *Cole* bombing had little hope that the terrorists would be caught and brought to justice. But O'Neill tried to bolster their spirits, and became a one-man source of support, e-mailing them and offering assurances that the FBI would not fail them. "If it weren't for John O'Neill, I would have lost all faith," confessed Louis Gunn, father of slain U.S. Navy Signalman Seaman Recruit Cherone Louis Gunn.

Meanwhile, another round of Yemenis came to America for formal tours of Washington, D.C., and O'Neill insisted they visit New York as well. Besides the obligatory tours of 26 Federal Plaza and the U.S. attorney's office, O'Neill took charge and squired them to his favorite nightspots, just as he had done with African officials before the embassy bombing trial. O'Neill traveled with the Yemenis in a motorcade, in deference to how they were accustomed to traveling at home. He also arranged a breathtaking helicopter tour around the city and a visit to the United Nations. "To say they were impressed was an understatement," McFadden recalled.

One night, O'Neill took them to one of his favorite Middle Eastern restaurants in midtown, the Cedars of Lebanon, which featured belly dancing, and another time he took them to Cité, near Rockefeller Center, where they stuffed themselves on huge steaks. One marveled at the portion size, and asked, "Now, where do we find the human meat?" joking about picking up women. O'Neill laughed and said they were on their own in that department. By the time the Yemenis left New York, they were wearing new suits and eating out of O'Neill's hand. "General Naji was saying, 'We have to cooperate further,'" recalled Corbett. The Yemenis even looked forward to Bodine's departure in August, because they assumed her successor would permit O'Neill to return. But that was never to be.

Around Easter, the *Cole* investigation entered another frightening period because of an increase in threats. The remaining FBI agents in Aden were withdrawn to Sana, where they could be protected inside the ambassador's compound and have access to Yemeni investigators based in the capital city. But agents were still sleeping on floors, and the threat level only increased. "We continued to get intelligence that other attacks were being planned," Mawn said. "The drumbeat was louder and louder."

Extra diplomatic security officers were brought in to bolster protection, but Bodine still refused to allow the FBI to carry rifles and shotguns along with their nine-millimeter handguns, even though her own security personnel were now carrying them. Finally, the danger to the agents reached such an extreme, O'Neill began to weigh pulling the FBI out of Yemen for safety reasons. Yemeni police said they had arrested several suspects plotting to attack FBI agents and other U.S. investigators. Eight terrorists planned to scale the embassy wall and fire rocket grenades. Bodine dismissed the threat. "How much damage can three grenades do?" Bodine asked, according to Mary Galligan, then the FBI on-scene commander. "They can do a lot of damage if it involves people," Galligan replied. The FBI commander had occasional disagreements with Bodine. But at O'Neill's urging, Galligan always respectfully began any expression of dissent with, "Ambassador, I recognize that you are the highest ranking American and I recognize your position, but . . ." O'Neill asked his agents if they felt safe, and they told him they did not. They were not alone in that threat assessment: the Fifth Naval Fleet had also sensed a growing danger and retreated, while Marines in Jordan canceled exercises.

"You can't dismiss the intelligence," Maxwell recalled. "The FBI is not cowardly. But we do not send people anywhere without providing responsible protection."

The FBI was about to conduct crucial interviews of participants in an important meeting a few days before the *Cole* attack, which they believed was attended by suspects in the bombing, but O'Neill felt the safety of his people took precedence. Seventeen sailors had lost their lives in the *Cole* bombing, and he did not want to risk any more casualties. So the interviews with possible "Last Supper" participants would have to wait. "We can come back to do the investigation," he told Corbett.

Bodine was furious. She felt it was unconscionable for the FBI to consider pulling out. She was also under pressure from the State Department to make things work with the FBI, so it would be embarrassing to her if the FBI were to depart. In recent days, she had become uncharacteristically tough on Yemenis, demanding that they provide the FBI with access to suspects and documents. She was so abrasive, she insulted the Political Security Office director, General Domash. "He said he did not want to talk to her anymore, because he felt he was being yelled at," Corbett recalled. Bodine, who thought the FBI agents were whiners, then ordered the FBI to leave at least a few agents in Sana.

But Freeh was not going to back down. The State Department told the FBI it could not protect them, the military attaché was saying the FBI should leave, and the Defense Department raised its threat level to Delta Con. Despite all this, Bodine was saying, " 'Let's have a party!' " said Mike Rolince, who was in charge of the Washington field office's counterterrorism program. On Father's Day, June 16, 2001, O'Neill gave the decisive order for the FBI to pull out. Bodine was livid. She insisted she was the only one who had the authority to order an FBI pullout, and told the embassy's heavily armed Marine guards and diplomatic security personnel to block FBI agents from leaving. So about twenty agents found themselves face-to-face with Marines who refused to unlock the entrance of the embassy compound. "What are you going to do? Shoot us?" an agent with Mary Galligan, the on-scene FBI commander, demanded. Bodine wanted Galligan to leave at least two agents behind, but Galligan nixed that idea. "We arrived as a team, and we leave as a team," she said. The bizarre standoff lasted several hours, while a caravan of military vehicles waited to take the agents to the airport. Finally, the ambassador was ordered by her superiors to release the agents from her compound, and the FBI departed Yemen completely. The FBI team flew sixteen hours before finally landing at McGuire Air Force Base in southern New Jersey the following morning. When they disembarked at about 6 A.M., they found O'Neill standing on the tarmac, dressed perfectly in a suit and looking as fresh as a daisy, waiting to greet them with a compliment of other agents to drive them home. "I am glad you're safe," he announced, before personally shaking the hand of each agent and doling out his patented bear hugs.

A few days later, another bin Laden videotape surfaced. He claimed credit for the attack on the *Cole*, declaring, "We thank God for granting us victory the day we destroyed *Cole* in the sea."

The video contained images of the ship over which red lettering proclaimed THE DESTRUCTION OF THE AMERICAN DESTROYER *Cole*. Also on the hundred-minute tape, bin Laden's ranting image was superimposed over pictures of dying children in Iraq. He insisted, "More than a million die because they are Muslims." He referred to President Clinton as a "slaughterer" of Muslim civilians. He implored Muslims ruled by "allies of Jews and Christians" to come to his camps to train for attacks on Americans so they "can taste the bitter fruit" Muslims have tasted for centuries. The tape also showed what was to become the most widely seen footage of bin Laden, showing him kneel and fire automatic weapons with hooded terrorists in the Al Farouq camp in Afghanistan, followed by shots of his Al Qaeda members running a gauntlet of physical challenges in a desert obstacle course, and then invading makeshift apartments, firing weapons or tossing exploding grenades into bedrooms and living rooms.

Bin Laden and his top aides made an impassioned speech about Muslims being killed in Chechnya, Kashmir, Iraq, Israel, Lebanon, Indonesia, and Egypt, accompanied by graphic video of war victims and violence. "Arab rulers worship the God of the White House," bin Laden asserted at one point as pictures of the Saudi royal family rolled by. He explained that the attacks on the U.S. embassies in Africa were designed to destroy U.S. intelligence-gathering capability on that continent. And as for the *Cole* bombing, he rejoiced that his "brothers in Aden hit the *Cole*. They destroyed this destroyer which, when you see it moving through the water, makes you frightened. She had the illusion she could destroy everything and then this small boat bobbing in the waves collided with the destroyer. When the collision happened, it was the beginning of the war. If you don't fight, you will be punished by God," bin Laden said, exhorting Arabs to come to Afghanistan for training for holy war. "The victory of Islam is coming," he vowed. "And the victory of Yemen will continue in the name of God."

Each previous bin Laden tape had been followed by an attack. In this most recent appearance, bin Laden wore a traditional Yemeni warrior's sword in the sash around his waist, once again offering a clear indication that he was preparing for battle. O'Neill feared an attack with mass casualties was imminent, he just did not know where. As he had warned in his Chicago speech four years earlier, he was certain Al Qaeda was heading for a strike on American soil.

17

FORCED OUT

O'Neill began to think seriously of retiring from the FBI and leaving the war on terrorism to others. His two transgressions, particularly the briefcase incident, would probably keep him from further promotion, and he was demoralized that the FBI had not backed him against the State Department when Bodine barred him from Yemen. The stodgy bureaucracy had finally beaten him down. O'Neill began to look for something new, but he felt devastated at the thought of leaving the job he loved.

"I don't think I'm going anywhere in the bureau," he confided to his friend Jerry Hauer.

"How many body blows does somebody have to take?" he asked his close friend and colleague Fran Townsend.

O'Neill's decision to jump before he was pushed could not have come at a worse time in the war on terrorism. He was the FBI official most capable of "connecting the dots," and at this moment the "dots" connected up to something ominous. Even CIA Director George Tenet was frantic with concern about Al Qaeda mounting a major terrorist operation against unidentified U.S. targets. "It is highly likely that a significant al Qaeda attack is in the near future, within several weeks," he warned in an intelligence summary to national security adviser Condoleezza Rice on June 28.

Yet O'Neill, a principal architect of the war on terrorism, was being forced out of the FBI. He was starting to look for a suitable position in the private sector that would utilize his vast experience and provide him with enough cachet to continue to be acquainted with Fortune 500 executives, the archbishop of New York, the literati at Elaine's, and celebrities from Robert De Niro to Vincent Curatola from TV's hit series *The Sopranos*. Such high-level positions are rare in the corporate world, but Jerry Hauer maintained a vast array of contacts as the former head of the city's Office of Emergency Management, and he helped O'Neill job-hunt. "John loved the bureau, but he was frustrated, and I think he decided to try to make money," said Hauer. "I told him I would keep my ears open."

That same month, Larry Silverstein, president of Silverstein Properties, a vast real estate company, took over the proprietary lease of the World Trade Center from the Port Authority of New York and New Jersey, which had completed construction on the two 107-story towers in 1973. When Hauer was the city's OEM director, he had many dealings with Silverstein's company and was also a friend of its president, Jeff Wharton, who told Hauer that Silverstein was looking for a top-level candidate to revamp security at the World Trade Center complex. Hauer called O'Neill, but he said he was "not quite ready."

"The scope of the job at the WTC was interesting, but he was looking for something more worldwide," Hauer said. O'Neill had always hoped Mottola might hire him for a global security position with Sony, but that offer never materialized. Searching for other candidates, Hauer telephoned Kallstrom to inquire about the backgrounds and work ethic of several other FBI supervisors. "I don't understand why John's not taking this job," Kallstrom said. "It's good for him."

A few days later, O'Neill telephoned Hauer. He had changed his mind, and he asked for an interview. With Hauer acting as go-between, O'Neill met with Wharton and Silverstein. "They loved John," Hauer recalls.

The other leading candidate for the position was Alan Hoehl, a three-star chief in the NYPD who had earned a reputation for policing the prestigious Manhattan South police borough that ran from the Hudson River to the East River, and from ninety-seventh Street down to the southern tip of Manhattan. His beat included every trophy building on the Manhattan skyline, and virtually every other valuable piece of real estate in the city. But Hoehl was reluctant to take the position. "I'm not sure I can do this yet," he told them, thus eliminating himself from consideration.

Although Silverstein was seeking a top-level executive to serve as his security director, he was even more insistent that the selection be in place by the first week of September, when his firm would assume control of the buildings. He was extremely impressed with O'Neill and his accomplishments. But O'Neill had yet to make a final commitment. After all, he had often boasted, "I am the FBI." The decision to leave an agency he had long dreamed of joining tormented him. Yet it was comforting to know there was a lucrative position available for him so he could make a soft landing after leaving the bureau.

Secure in the knowledge that there would be life after the FBI, O'Neill felt he could take a vacation with Valerie, a break that would allow him to contemplate his future. He suggested they visit Saudi Arabia, since he was a friend of King Abdullah and they would be treated like royalty there, and then continue on to Europe. But he had also received an invitation to speak in Madrid before the Spanish Police Foundation. The organization was seeking insight on how the FBI coordinated its efforts with the many different police agencies in the United States. In light of the growth of terrorism and the creation of the European Union, law enforcement agencies throughout Europe were seeking ways to synchronize their operations. O'Neill was invited to speak because the top lawmen in Europe knew he valued teamwork and personal contacts. So O'Neill accepted the invitation, and planned a two-week holiday around the speech. Valerie and her son, Jay, accompanied him.

O'Neill told DiBattista he would be traveling on business, and said he regretted he could not take her along on one last trip before he retired. But she was also tired of O'Neill's job, and of his inability to spend time with her. She was also thinking about leaving New York, a city whose glamorous nightlife she had never loved the way O'Neill did.

He also telephoned Mary Lynn Stevens in Washington. He assured her that she was the "most important person in his life," and told her he wanted her to consider moving to New York now that he was planning to leave the FBI to join the private sector. He estimated that he would need about six months to work everything out, and that he was seeking guidance from the church. "He knew I would never come to New York and relocate unless it was to be married to him," Stevens said.

On June 26, several days after his interview with Silverstein and his conversations with his girlfriends, O'Neill left for Paris with Valerie and Jay. The FBI's permanent legal attaché was away at the time, and they used his apartment near the Arc de Triomphe for a week, visiting museums, gardens, and restaurants. "It was simply lovely," recalled Valerie.

On July 5, they flew to Marbella on Spain's Costa del Sol, where they joined FBI agent Mark Rossini, who was staying at the home of a friend, and in turn graciously welcomed O'Neill, Valerie, and her son as guests. Valerie remembers that she and O'Neill were a bit reluctant to settle into the home of someone they did not know—until they saw it. Rossini's friend owned a ten-bedroom compound, with a full wait staff, a tennis court, and an Olympic-size pool. Sitting on the veranda, they could see Morocco across the Strait of Gibraltar.

O'Neill, a history buff, sat by the pool each afternoon reading *Making Patriots*, by constitutional scholar Walter Berns, who wrote: "Patriotism means love of country and implies a readiness to sacrifice for it, to fight for it, perhaps even to give one's life for it." It was one of O'Neill's favorite books, and every few minutes he would stop and read passages aloud to others lounging in the sun. "He kept reading segments to us, over and over, to the point

where people said, 'Yeah, John. Can't we just enjoy the afternoon?'" Valerie said. "But he wasn't deterred. He read that book
over and over and over."

For the first time in years, she said, O'Neill seemed relaxed.
Three days after arriving in Spain, he was sitting on the veranda
sipping coffee when he pulled out a cigar and lit up. Rossini, who
was sitting with him, noticed that O'Neill began to grin as though
he had a secret. "What are you smiling at?" Rossini asked. O'Neill
paused before answering, and then pointed to his watch, all the
while continuing to smile like the Cheshire cat. It was about 4 P.M.
in Spain, and 10 A.M. in New York.

"I'm K.M.A.," O'Neill finally told him. "It's my K.M.A. Day."
In the parlance of the FBI, K.M.A. was an abbreviation for "Kiss
My Ass." At precisely 10 A.M. on July 8, 2001, O'Neill celebrated
his twenty-fifth anniversary as an FBI special agent, which meant
he could instantly retire with his pension. It was an exhilarating
moment for him, Rossini recalled. They went out to celebrate,
first to dinner, then to a popular discotheque that, like most dance
clubs in Spain, did not open until 11:30 P.M. O'Neill, the polished
agent who boasted that he had appeared on *American Bandstand*,
got up on top of one of the club's loudspeakers and shimmied and
shook the night away until closing time, around 7 A.M.

"John was speaking about retiring and said he had 'some feel-
ers' out," said Rossini, adding that O'Neill was feeling "disre-
spected" by management. "His superiors were not listening to
what he was saying, and they did not understand his vision."

At the precise moment that O'Neill was in southern Spain
lighting the cigar that marked his K.M.A. day, a steely-eyed,
thirty-three-year-old Egyptian named Mohammed Atta was landing at Madrid Airport. Atta was already taking lessons in a flight
school in southern Florida. He arrived in Spain from Miami, via
Zurich, where he had purchased a knife in order to test whether it
would go undetected through the airport magnetometers. It
passed through undetected.

Atta was masterminding a plot to attack the World Trade Center with hijacked commercial jets, a variation on a concept developed years before by Ramzi Yousef and his uncle, Khalid Shaikh Mohammed, who also helped design the attack on the African embassies. Atta was enlisted to hijack planes after exploring the purchase of crop-duster planes that he proposed to strip bare, load with bombs, and crash into his target. But he abandoned that plan when he realized it was too expensive and too difficult to accomplish.

Atta arrived in Spain to attend a string of important face-to-face meetings he scheduled with terrorist collaborators. He stayed overnight at the Hotel Diana Cazadora near the airport, and the following morning, on July 9, only four days after O'Neill's own arrival in Spain, Atta rented a car and headed off to the northeastern city of Tarragona, near Barcelona, where he met up with others involved in the plot. They included Marwan al-Shehhi, a cousin of Atta's who also was taking flight lessons in Florida, and Ramzi bin al-Shibh, a Yemeni from the same Hadramout region as Bin Laden. Al-Shibh was supposed to fly one of the planes, but he was refused entrance into the United States. Both men had arrived in Spain that morning. Also in attendance were Khalid al-Midhar and Nawaf al-Hazmi, who had both attended the mysterious meeting in Malaysia, in January 2000, and who were already living in the United States on student visas, attending flight training schools in the West.

As Atta drove off to rendezvous with his fellow Al Qaeda members, O'Neill, Valerie James, and her son packed their belongings and flew to Madrid. They stayed in Madrid as guests of the Spanish authorities. The next morning, on July 10, O'Neill delivered his twenty-page speech entitled "Meeting the Crime Challenge: Cooperation and Teamwork in a Multi-Police Environment." After the speech he took questions about how the world's various police entities could best cooperate in international investigations. O'Neill and James remained in Madrid for another week after the speech, using the hotel as a base for day trips into the countryside.

On July 16, a day before Valerie's birthday, they flew back to New York, and on the flight, Valerie was leafing through a new edition of *Time* magazine, where she noticed an article about how the FBI's investigation of the *Cole* bombing in Yemen was bogged down. The piece referred specifically to the tension between Bodine and O'Neill, but was slanted in favor of the State Department, which made it seem planted. She skimmed the article and provided O'Neill with a brief synopsis. He didn't want to hear about it. He slammed his seat as far back as it would go, and asked Valerie to inform the flight attendant that he would not be dining on the flight.

Upon his return to work in New York, he tracked down Anna DiBattista, who was traveling in Dallas. O'Neill repeatedly told her how bad he felt about going to Spain without her. A few days later, he flew to Washington for meetings about the *Cole* investigation. He lunched with Frank Ciluffo in Washington, an old friend who studied international threats for a Washington think tank called the Center for Strategic and International Studies. O'Neill liked to talk to Ciluffo to get his "out of the box" view of diplomacy and international affairs. Ciluffo and O'Neill discussed the *Time* article, which Ciluffo felt was clearly slanted in favor of Bodine. "I've been called worse," O'Neill said.

He had been—and often. O'Neill, like many charismatic figures, inspired great loyalty in many of his followers, and also triggered less positive reactions in people who were put off by his swagger and brusque manner. He had more than his share of enemies at the bureau. Some of them would derisively refer to him— behind his back, of course—as the "Prince of Darkness," because he frequently wore dark clothes and stayed out until near sunrise.

FBI Director Freeh had recently met with Bodine to discuss the situation in Yemen, but he had decided not to waste time trying to convince her to allow O'Neill back into the country when he knew she would not permit it. He left it to Rolince and others to try to change her position. In the first week of August, O'Neill sent Maxwell and Rolince back to Sana to meet with the ambassador and broker the terms of an FBI return to Yemen. Their plane landed at 2 A.M., but even before they reached the hotel, there was news about their arrival on state-sponsored television. The fact that they could not arrive undetected only heightened their concerns about safety.

Rolince heard gunfire everywhere. The signs of poverty were clearly visible, and many people seemed to be under the influence of the native plant leaf, Khat, which, when chewed, is intoxicating. He was familiar with the possibility of violence because he had been in Yemen in December 1998 when sixteen tourists were kidnapped by a group calling itself the Islamic Army of Aden-Abyan, which was later linked to Al Qaeda. The kidnapping ended in a shoot-out between police and the Islamic Army of Aden-Abyan, and four died when the hostages were used as human shields.

"We went in order to set up a protocol for conducting an investigation when an American citizen is involved," Rolince said.

Bodine seemed eager to establish that she wasn't viscerally opposed to all FBI agents, only O'Neill. Rolince and the others found her extremely obliging and personable. Maxwell felt it was because Bodine was "under a lot of pressure" from Colin Powell "to make it work this second time around." It was in her interest to do so, because her tour of duty in Yemen was drawing to a close. She therefore preferred to see the return of the FBI on her watch. "She was most accommodating," Maxwell recalled. "Everything was terrific. She had a limousine drive us around. She even toasted us at dinner."

But the FBI insisted on three points before agents would return. First, they wanted the ability to travel anywhere and follow leads without interference. Second, they wanted documents, such as transcripts of interviews and telephone logs, handed over from Yemeni investigators. Finally, they wanted to bring at least fifteen agents in to Yemen. Bodine acquiesced to most of the FBI's requests, but stood her ground on one point: the FBI agents must not brandish long weapons in the capital city of Sana. O'Neill, informed of the agreement, graciously suggested that it should be implemented before Bodine departed at the end of the month.

Back in New York, Maxwell passed O'Neill in the hallway and was asked how the trip went. Maxwell dryly replied that Bodine was "a delight." O'Neill smiled and gave his pal the finger.

For weeks, O'Neill had been telling Valerie James that their life together would be different once he left the FBI, that in fact they would finally be "normal." She believed that meant they would finally marry. But he was also telling Mary Lynn Stevens that she should move to New York and get a job, which to her meant that O'Neill was finally willing to take what she thought was their "exclusive" relationship to the next level, i.e., marriage. Then on Monday, August 6, he met Anna DiBattista for lunch at the Porto Rosa restaurant in Midtown.

DiBattista had just returned from a four-week work trip through the Southeast and Texas, and O'Neill had promised her a New York weekend filled with restaurants and theater. But DiBattista had other plans. She'd had time to think on her trip, and had made the decision to break up with him. DiBattista had long harbored doubts about the relationship. Every time they went out to a restaurant, she had the feeling he had been there before, with other women. She was no longer willing to pretend to believe he lived with "translators." She was sure O'Neill was living a double life, she was not enamored of the "beautiful" and "powerful" people O'Neill found enthralling, and she missed Washington, D.C.

"I'm leaving," she told him. "I don't want to be here anymore. I know the FBI is everything to you, your love. So it's over."

O'Neill's reaction was typical—and still astounding. Rather than accept the breakup as a way to simplify his life, he begged DiBattista not to leave him, just as he had done so many times before. In fact, the only women he willingly broke up with were the ones who demanded marriage. "No, I don't want that," he insisted. "I'll make this work. Please don't go. Give me until the end of the year." But DiBattista was adamant. She told him she had already looked at a condominium in Washington, D.C. He went "ballistic," she said, and accused her of being deceitful. "How could you do this behind my back?" he demanded.

Three hours after he left DiBattista's apartment, he telephoned her. "Contrary to what you think, I do love you," he told her. "All I want is for this to work." O'Neill once again succeeded in getting through to her. "He always had the words," she said. So she softened her hard line. "Love is blind," she later observed. He telephoned her again that night, telling her again that he loved her, and she agreed to see him again that Sunday for dinner at her Fort Lee apartment.

O'Neill finally worked out a property settlement with his wife of nearly three decades. Christine O'Neill signed an agreement on August 8 that granted her child support and ownership of their Linwood home, while O'Neill would keep his pension. So he was potentially free to marry one of the women he had been dating for years—but which one? He arrived at DiBattista's apartment for dinner on August 12 uncharacteristically attired in shorts, a cotton shirt, and Nike slip-ons. Once again, he insisted she should remain in New York and that their life would again be solid. "Just give me a few more months because these people [the translators] need time to wrap things up."

O'Neill was getting ready to accept Silverstein and Wharton's offer of what he said was three times his $125,000 FBI salary. His readiness to make the move was spurred in part by his disgust with the drawn-out Office of Professional Responsibility investigation into the briefcase incident. By mid-August, Silverstein was insisting that if O'Neill was serious about the offer, he would have to tender his resignation from the FBI and sign an agreement to start work no later than the first week of September 2001.

O'Neill agreed. The special agent who used to boast "I am the FBI" finally made the decision to leave the bureau. When he informed Pickard of his decision, he told him, "It's time. I have a great job offer." Pickard felt that retirement was perhaps the best avenue for O'Neill to take, but he also knew O'Neill was FBI from his underwear out, and a born warrior. "I felt his heart was not in it," he said. "I said, you could always pull [your retirement papers] back."

"Nah, this is a great opportunity," O'Neill answered. "More money than I ever thought someone would pay me—and they came after me."

O'Neill would finally know financial comfort after years of living paycheck to paycheck and maxing out on his credit cards. Not only would he get a huge raise, he was also owed a year's unused sick pay, since he had used only a handful of sick days during his thirty-one years with the bureau.

Grant Ashley, the FBI buddy from his Chicago days fighting drug dealers, called O'Neill to confirm the rumor, and congratulated him. Ashley, a former CPA, offered his former boss some wise advice about getting rid of his hefty debt load. He urged O'Neill to adhere to a conservative financial plan by placing pension money and his new salary into a diversified portfolio of mutual funds in order to protect his financial future—a future John once told him he would never live to see.

O'Neill's retirement brought an end to the seemingly endless OPR investigation. No criminal charges were lodged, and his departure brought a halt to any further inquiry into whether he should face any internal discipline. O'Neill would walk out of the FBI with his head held high. He felt he had reached the finish line with no more enemies to stand in his way. He was wrong.

Only days after O'Neill accepted his new job, the *New York Times* contacted the FBI press office in Washington about a tip they had received. Reporters David Johnston and James Risen had been told the FBI was investigating the serious security breach represented by O'Neill losing a briefcase filled with top-secret documents. The reporters had very specific financial information that could only have come directly from O'Neill's file or from an FBI official with firsthand knowledge of his private affairs. O'Neill certainly had enemies, but whoever had leaked the information was particularly cruel. Were they out to hurt his reputation? Were they out to prevent him from getting a job? Or did they want to portray him as a security liability to ensure he could never replace Richard Clarke on the National Security Council, as was sometimes rumored?

Some insiders pointed the finger at Pickard, the straitlaced agent who admired O'Neill but frowned on his nocturnal activities. Pickard flatly denied the allegation, and insisted he would take a polygraph to prove it. He even publicly stated that the *Times* was free to say whether he was the source. Pickard said he believed O'Neill was the victim of "one of those little vicious personal attacks" that occur within the Beltway.

O'Neill supporters also suspected Dale Watson, the head of terrorism in Washington, who had leapfrogged over O'Neill at the bureau although his résumé was not as strong. Watson, for his part, also denied involvement. "I don't leak bureau information," he told the *New Yorker* magazine. Some people pointed fingers at Clarke himself, suggesting the wily NSC official was a student of Machiavelli. But most people viewed Clarke as one of O'Neill's strongest enthusiasts.

Ambassador Bodine also had ample motive for the leak. She made no secret of her deep dislike for O'Neill, even calling him a "liar." She could have obtained the sensitive financial information from an FBI ally. Bodine declined to be interviewed for this book.

The source of the damaging story will likely never be known. But its timing could not have been worse for O'Neill. "Call me 'Black Cloud,'" he used to say. Not only was the public airing of his briefcase incident a major embarrassment, but he feared its disclosure might force Silverstein to reconsider the job offer and renege on their handshake deal. Deeply distressed, O'Neill called Mawn. "The FBI has been everything to me. I gave my all to it," he told him, adding that he couldn't believe his exit would be so unfairly tarnished, and his golden job parachute lost to an unkind rumor. He also called Hauer, who reassured him, "Look, I don't see that it is a problem."

Mawn, Pickard, John Lewis, Neil Gallagher, and John Collingwood all spoke with the *Times* reporters, trying to kill the article or at least put the story in context. They discovered that the reporters had been given other uncorroborated and untrue pieces of information about O'Neill. Clearly someone was trying to use leaks to cast him as a man living beyond his means and therefore vulnerable to having his loyalty compromised by foreign counterespionage efforts. Mawn and the other FBI officials told the reporters that O'Neill's reputation did not deserve to be ruined by anonymous leaks. They pointed out that the briefcase incident was nearly a year old, and the bureau was convinced that no security breach had occurred. Besides, they argued, O'Neill was only days away from retiring. What was the purpose of publishing an embarrassing article about an official with O'Neill's long and distinguished career a year later, and days from his retirement?

The reporters' justification for going with the story was largely the scandals involving Deutsch and Wen Ho Lee, which had prompted the FBI to take a hard line on the missing briefcase in the first place, along with the big story of FBI spy Robert Hanssen. So the paper of record would not mark O'Neill's retirement by preparing an article that lauded his uncanny ability to connect the dots, and his visionary warning about the danger Osama bin Laden and his Al Qaeda network posed to Americans abroad and at home. No, the one substantive article about O'Neill the *Times* would run during his lifetime would portray him as a threat to national security—the very security he worked to enhance, the very security he had for years warned was in drastic need of overhaul.

O'Neill's fears about losing his new job even before he started proved to be unfounded. Several of the same people who talked to the *Times* also talked to Silverstein to preempt the negative publicity and to assure him that no matter what the *Times* reported, O'Neill was an unsung American hero. Silverstein did not need their guarantees. O'Neill had impressed him from the moment they met. Despite the bad timing of the *Times* article, they still wanted O'Neill as their first director of security at the World Trade Center.

In its August 19, 2001, edition, the *New York Times* published its first story on John P. O'Neill, bearing the headline FBI IS INVESTIGATING A SENIOR COUNTERTERRORISM AGENT. The first sentence declared, "The FBI has begun an internal investigation into one of its most senior counterterrorism officials, who misplaced a briefcase containing highly classified information last year." To balance the article, the reporters quoted Mawn, Kallstrom, and Mary Jo White praising O'Neill's heroic efforts in fighting terrorism. In what some would see as a disingenuous attempt to distant themselves from complicity in a smear campaign, the reporters quoted Kallstrom's claim that "people were seeking to damage his reputation, perhaps because he has been mentioned for a national security job at the White House, a job he never sought."

O'Neill was particularly concerned about the reaction of his mother. His FBI career and professional image meant as much to her as it did to him. Dottie O'Neill read every article that ever mentioned her son, and was of course very upset about the *Times* story. Later that day, O'Neill called her. He started the conversation as he always did: "Hi, Mom, this is your son. I love you." He tried to convince her that everything would be all right. He was the dutiful son trying to placate a concerned mother, but she was not completely convinced.

Three days later, on August 22, 2001, O'Neill was back at his desk for his last day at the FBI. He turned on his computer and began typing an e-mail to Lou Gunn, whose son had died on the *Cole*. Gunn often said he and the other families would have long ago lost hope had it not been for O'Neill.

By now you may have heard that I am retiring from the FBI after thirty-one years of what I believe was loyal and dedicated service," O'Neill wrote. "Today is my last day. I want you and those USS *Cole* family members you are in contact with, to know that the FBI has and will continue to work hard on the investigation in Yemen and wherever else the case takes them. There has been an assessment team, which was in Yemen in early August, and an advance team is about to depart to Yemen within the next week. The FBI will be back in Yemen with full resources by early September if all goes well.

In my thirty-one years of government service, my proudest moment was when I was selected to lead the investigation of the attack on the USS *Cole*. I have put my all into the investigation and truly believe that significant progress has been made. Unknown to you and the families is that I have cried with your loss. All Americans share your pain. I will keep you and all the families in my prayers and will continue to track the investigation as a civilian. God bless you, your loved ones, the families and God bless America.

A crowd of seventy-five agents and staffers gathered around O'Neill's desk that afternoon for coffee and a cake that said *Happy Retirement*. O'Neill gave a brief thank-you speech, telling everyone how much he appreciated their efforts. When he started to say how much he loved them and the FBI, his eyes began to fill with tears. "I won't be far away," he insisted. "Just a few blocks away."

"Everyone else got teary-eyed, too," his longtime assistant Lorraine Di Taranto said. "As much as he pretended to be a tough guy, John was a very sensitive man. The bureau was everything to him."

O'Neill spent much of the rest of the day on administrative paperwork related to his retirement. Mike Rolince called O'Neill around 5:30 P.M. to thank him for helping him out through the years, especially with recent issues in Egypt and Saudi Arabia. At the end of the day, around 6 P.M., O'Neill telephoned Fran Townsend.

"What in the world are you still doing there on your last day?" Townsend asked him. "What could conceivably keep you there?"

He read her the e-mail to the fallen sailor's father.

"I wanted to make sure that you were the last phone call from my desk, given all the cases we had worked on together," O'Neill replied. "And the other thing, the real reason I'm still here, is there was a piece of paper, and I am determined that it will be my last official act in the FBI."

"What is it?" she asked.

"I just signed the authorization to send the agents back into Yemen," he said. "I wasn't leaving here until I did it, because I promised that we would send them back. When I pulled them out, I had to, but I was determined to be the one who signed the piece of paper to send them back."

O'Neill walked out of 26 Federal Plaza knowing that he was going to work in a building with even more breathtaking views of the city he loved. Painful as it was to leave the FBI, he was relieved to be moving on. He started his new job at the World Trade Center the next morning, and in typical O'Neill fashion, wanted to get off and running on his new "mission" of preventing the Twin Towers from being attacked by bin Laden and Al Qaeda, and having the buildings and their tenants well prepared to deal with any eventuality.

That same morning O'Neill started his new job, the CIA

cabled the FBI, informing them that they had known for months that two suspected Al Qaeda terrorists, Nawaf al-Hazmi and Khalid al-Midhar, who had been spotted at the infamous Malaysia meeting in January 2000, were at large in the United States.

This was the type of intelligence failure that O'Neill had railed against throughout his career. The FBI launched a frantic search for the two terrorists, but the addresses the men had given to the INS when they entered the country were false, and they were never located. Al-Midhar had been in the country so long—and obviously felt so comfortable being here—that he had his visa renewed in July 2001. Al-Hazmi felt so comfortable in America, he was listed in the phone book for several months, the FBI later determined.

One of O'Neill's most trusted agents, Stephen Baumgart, a former air-force top gun who accompanied O'Neill to Yemen, requested the use of "full criminal investigative resources" to hunt al-Midhar, but he was prevented from tapping into all areas of intelligence. FBI officials at headquarters claimed that because al-Midhar was technically not under criminal investigation, certain information could not be shared with the field because of the wall between intelligence and prosecution. Baumgart responded by firing off an e-mail to FBI headquarters that warned, "Someday someone will die and the public will not understand why we were not more effective and did not throw every resource we had at certain problems."

There had been equally disturbing developments within the FBI itself in the weeks before O'Neill's departure. Five days before he retired, agents in Minnesota arrested a Moroccan national, Zacarias Moussaouri, on immigration violations after a flight school instructor grew concerned that Moussaouri was only interested in learning how to steer a plane, not how to take off or land. FBI agent Coleen Rowley attempted to get her superiors in Washington to permit her to search Moussaouri's computer files, just as O'Neill, years earlier, had successfully sought access to

Ramzi Yousef's computers. But Rowley was beaten back by bosses who downplayed the significance of Moussaouri's possible ties to Islamic extremists. Another agent, Kenneth Williams, wrote to headquarters from the Phoenix, Arizona, office to say he was concerned about Middle Eastern men who were taking flying lessons in his area of the country. The information was never developed further—although it would later be shown to be critical.

Each of these pieces of information was handled in a manner diametrically opposed to O'Neill's vision and managerial style. In Baltimore and Chicago, O'Neill had argued that every case be handled as though it was a life-or-death emergency. When he took over the section chief's position for counterterrorism in FBI headquarters, he brought a CIA official into the FBI to try to expedite the flow of information between the two agencies. During the millennium scare, he became visibly upset at the White House for withholding information after suspected terrorist Ahmed Ressam was captured in Seattle. And in Yemen, he tirelessly tried to bridge the gap between Ambassador Bodine and the Yemenis to expedite the investigation into the USS *Cole* bombing.

O'Neill had no contact with any of these disturbing pieces of information—these dots that were left unconnected during his final days at the FBI. He had been marginalized in the bureau, and no longer played an integral part in the antiterrorist effort he had launched in 1995. It is impossible to know with any certainty what might have happened if O'Neill had still been on the job and fully engaged in the fight against bin Laden, instead of heading out the door. But it's clear that if any of these miscues—the Moussaouri request, the so-called Phoenix letter, or the information about the two unaccounted-for suspects from the Malaysia meeting—had been handled in "O'Neill fashion," they might have led to the exposure of bin Laden's plan to attack the World Trade Center before it was too late.

During his first few days at his new job, O'Neill barely had an office to call his own. He was using various security rooms while his own office on the thirtieth-fourth floor was being completed. But he managed to do what he usually did when he had a new mission to tackle: he threw himself into learning everything he could about the Twin Towers. He immersed himself in discovering what security systems were already in place, and what the WTC would need in the future—what state-of-the-art systems would stop robberies and drug dealing as well as the threat of terrorism.

O'Neill was in his office on August 29 when he heard from Ken Maxwell that FBI agents had returned to Yemen, barely in time for Bodine's departure the following day. "The cooperation we got in the next thirty days was more than in the prior ten months," Rolince noted. "There was instant cooperation when we got back. We had video conference calls. The Yemenis immediately asked for more people. We were getting access to information, information the Yemenis said they never had."

If that information had been obtained at the outset of the *Cole* investigation, several suspected terrorists who met with Mohammed Atta in Spain would have been identified and perhaps his plot would have been unearthed. "It might have made all the difference," Rolince would later ruefully reflect.

18

Whenever John was around, it was a major event, right up to the way he died in the major event of all events.
—KEVIN GIBLIN, CURRENT FBI CHIEF OF TERRORIST WARNINGS

Leaving the FBI presented O'Neill with an immediate surprise: rather than suffering or brooding over the break with his past, he found a level of contentment and self-satisfaction he had never imagined. He still worked hard and played hard, melding the two in inimitable O'Neill style. The challenge of crafting a world-class security apparatus for the world's most recognizable skyscrapers had him fired up in a fresh, new way. As always, he consulted his network of contacts to gain the kind of expertise that would enable him to look for out-of-the-box solutions. He planned to meet with his old friend Raymond Powers, former NYPD chief of operations, to discuss the various security techniques and technologies powers he employed at Rockefeller Center as head of security. Powers suggested the following Tuesday morning, September 11, but as fate would have it, O'Neill had a conflicting appointment. They decided on the following Monday morning instead.

Early Wednesday evening, O'Neill dashed off to Chimia to meet his friend Robert Tucker, a former special assistant to Queens District Attorney Richard Brown, who now owned a security company. "He must have asked me a million questions that night," Tucker said. "I was flattered. John was a guy who knew the international universe better than anyone, and he's picking my brain about the security-guard business."

The next night, O'Neill and Hauer ended up at Bruno, where Jeff Wharton, his new boss, and DiBattista joined them. "He wanted me to meet the guys he was working with," DiBattista said. Wharton excused himself around 10 P.M., and Hauer left for Elaine's, giving O'Neill a chance to "pour his heart out" to DiBattista about their shaky relationship, she remembers.

"You're going to have it all," he told her. "I know I haven't been good to you. You've put up with a lot. We'll get married."

He insisted they take a vacation together when he returned from a "business excursion" he had scheduled to Canada later that month. Actually, this "excursion" was really a trip to Italy with Mary Lynn Stevens to take cooking classes together. And yet O'Neill talked about going to Puerto Rico with DiBattista at the end of September. She was starting to think perhaps O'Neill's new career might really mean a fresh start for them, but then a wealthy businessman O'Neill knew came over to say hello. Once he was back at his table, O'Neill told DiBattista his friend was married, but also had a longtime mistress who was forcing him into a divorce that would cost him millions.

The encounter brought DiBattista back down to earth. It reminded her that O'Neill was far more interested in people who had money and fame than she was, and that he remained enthralled by New York nightlife and all that went with it. Also, O'Neill said the businessman had attended the Marine Corps Law Enforcement Dinner the previous year, when O'Neill was honored and received a plaque from Janet Reno that was presented by her aide, Fran Townsend. DiBattista had not been invited, and it bothered her. Now she wondered why a businessman O'Neill barely knew attended the event when she had not. She held her tongue all through dinner, but as they were leaving, O'Neill sensed something was wrong and insisted on knowing what it was.

"Why was that couple at the Marine Corps dinner and not me?" DiBattista demanded. "You were there. Your son was there. Your parents were there. Why wasn't I there? I am supposed to be your girlfriend. You supposedly can't live without me. This relationship is insane."

O'Neill tried changing the subject and saying there was something wrong with her for reacting so strongly. Then he tried downplaying the slight. But her anger was not assuaged. Out on the street, they were still arguing, and DiBattista speculated that the reason she had not been invited was because O'Neill had taken another woman to the event.

"Are you accusing me of being with another woman?" O'Neill shot back, doing his best to sound offended that she could possibly imagine such a thing.

The fight grew more heated, and O'Neill cruelly brushed aside her hurt feelings. They each went to their own homes and O'Neill called to apologize the next day, Friday, September 7. "We're going to work out," he told her. But he also said he did not have time to see her again until Monday. He said he had to work, but did not mention he planned to attend a wedding at the Plaza Hotel with Valerie James, and fly to Chicago with her on Sunday.

Around noon on Friday, O'Neill went to lunch with Richard Dienst, a highly regarded lawyer whose firm had handled cases for the Port Authority cops who police the World Trade Center. Joining them for lunch was Robert Von Etten, the PA's former security chief of the World Trade Center. Walking back to their respective offices afterward, O'Neill and Dienst began to discuss the recent flare-up of violence in Israel, and O'Neill laid out his vision for how to bring peace to the region. Instead of spending billions of dollars each year on weapons for Israel and its enemies, O'Neill suggested the money should be spent on housing and infrastructure for the Palestinians, who live in shantylike camps. This would not only improve the quality of their lives, it would provide the Palestinians with a tangible stake in the region.

"The only solution is to build middle-income housing that is good or better than anything around them, so they have an interest in wanting to stay and protect it," he said. "We spend billions of dollars supplying the Israelis and the Arab nations with guns and supplies and tanks and satellites and aircraft. But we have to give them an interest in something that is their own. They want what everyone wants—a home, schools, and decent place to live."

Dienst, an ardent supporter of Israel, loved the clearheaded logic of a world where the Palestinians and Jews could prosper and live in peaceful coexistence. He gave O'Neill a hug and watched him walk away toward the Twin Towers.

Across from Brooks Brothers, O'Neill ran into his friend Rodney Leibowitz, a dentist who also worked with the NYPD. O'Neill complained to Leibowitz that security at the Towers was medieval. Even though the complex received bomb threats every day, the telephone system did not feature caller identification. O'Neill also mentioned he might be taking a vacation by car, but did not mention the destination. Leibowitz, aware that O'Neill's 1991 Buick Regal was not ideal for road trips, offered him his Mercedes convertible to use "with Valerie."

"No," O'Neill told him. "It's not going to be who you think it is."

That evening, O'Neill drove up to a restaurant at First Avenue and East twenty-first Street to meet Maxwell so he could sound him out about leaving the FBI and coming to work with him. O'Neill was late, but breezed into the restaurant, sat down, and announced that he could not stay very long, so he would have to get right down to business. He told Maxwell that Silverstein had given him a wide berth in selecting his own people at the World Trade Center, which was beset with petty robberies, open drug use, and other concerns, including terrorism. "I would like to bring you on as my number two, my deputy director for security," O'Neill said.

Maxwell was a twenty-year veteran of the war on terrorism, dating back to the early 1980s, when the FALN and Weather Underground organizations committed more than 120 bombings, including the NYPD and FBI headquarters in New York. He was eligible to retire and had been thinking about a career change. There was no doubt he admired O'Neill's intelligence, dedication, and style, and the offer represented a substantial raise, so he indicated he wanted the job. He told O'Neill he needed the weekend to discuss the proposal with his wife, Vetta, who was also an FBI agent. The two friends shook hands and O'Neill took off.

That Saturday, O'Neill and Valerie attended the wedding of Teddy Lebb's daughter at the Plaza. O'Neill and Valerie danced virtually every number, and O'Neill appeared not to have a care in the world. As he wandered the room meeting old friends, he stopped to talk with his old boss, Lewis Schiliro. "I feel like a huge burden has been lifted from me," O'Neill told him. Schiliro could not help but notice a dramatic change in O'Neill. "For the first time, I saw someone who was relaxed," he recalled. "John was smiling and he was dancing away."

O'Neill told Lebb that he was going to buy a diamond ring, presumably an engagement band, for Valerie James. "You know that I have put this girl through hell, and I'm getting her the biggest diamond," he bragged. O'Neill and James flew to Chicago on Sunday so James could take care of some business there, and returned to New York in time to catch a late dinner at Kennedy's, a West Side restaurant owned by their friend Roy Bernard.

On Monday, September 10, O'Neill went over to Rockefeller Center to meet with Powers, and planned to brief Silverstein and Wharton about security at the Trade Center directly afterward. They met on the plaza because there was a *Today* show fashion segment being shot outdoors. Powers recalled that O'Neill was so intent on their conversation, he barely paid any mind to the semi-nude models gathered for the segment. Instead he peppered Powers with security questions. He was particularly interested in new screening techniques for visitors to a building, and they discussed a new technology that allowed companies to assign confidential passwords to visitors so they could obtain access to the building.

The two men spent nearly two hours on the sidewalk discussing security procedures until the conversation shifted to Osama bin Laden, and Powers commented that it was ironic O'Neill had taken a job at a building that had already been attacked by Islamic fundamentalist radicals. Just as he had told Agent Pat Patterson in Yemen in October 2000 and just as he had reiterated since 1995 to any official in Washington who would listen, O'Neill said he was sure bin Laden would attack on American soil, and expected him to target the Twin Towers again.

"We were kidding about it," Power said. "I told him, 'You were a target all those years, and now you're a target again.'"

"It's going to happen," O'Neill said, turning serious. "And it looks like something big is brewing."

The two lawmen shook hands and agreed to meet for lunch on Friday. O'Neill arrived back at his office about an hour later, and Maxwell called him to say he had discussed the job offer with his wife, and he wanted to accept, but there was one final obstacle.

"I thought money wasn't an issue?" a surprised O'Neill replied.

"No, it's not the money," Maxwell said. "I don't want to do all the work and watch you just do all the schmoozing."

O'Neill burst out laughing, and they made plans to meet on Friday to celebrate Maxwell joining the team.

Wharton, the president of the World Trade Center, remembers being impressed that day with the security concept O'Neill presented to him, and his plans to hire senior law enforcement professionals with broad experience here and abroad. "It was comprehensive and it was visionary," Wharton said. O'Neill had previously asked Wharton if he could hire his twenty-nine-year-old son, J.P., as a computer technician. Wharton had already given his consent, which pleased O'Neill, who hoped to make up for all the time he had spent away from his son while he had been with the FBI. Later that afternoon, he went to Wharton again to make sure there was no problem hiring J.P. "These are your people," Wharton told him. "I have full confidence in you and whatever choices you make."

O'Neill's son was scheduled to take an early train from Delaware the following morning to meet with his father and hook up his computer equipment, which was sitting in boxes on the floor. Now O'Neill could look forward to telling his son he had the job. He phoned DiBattista to try to smooth things over, and assured her that everything would be all right, but she continued to insist that O'Neill should "go find the life" he wanted without her. It seemed the more she wanted to end their relationship, the more O'Neill insisted on making it work. Next he called Robert Tucker to suggest they have a drink at Windows on the World.

As O'Neill sat in his office watching the sun set over the Palisades on the New Jersey side of the Hudson, Mohammed Atta, the leader of the bin Laden plan to hijack planes, drove into the parking lot of a Comfort Inn in South Portland, Maine, in a rented blue Nissan Altima with Abdulaziz al-Omari in the passenger seat. The two terrorists had driven from south Florida during the past several days, completing the final stretch from Boston while O'Neill was meeting with Wharton about World Trade Center security.

Atta had left eight other hijackers behind in a downtown Boston hotel. Two other teams of bin Laden terrorists were also in position, one group staying in a hotel near Newark Airport and another in Laurel, Maryland, not far from Dulles Airport. On their last night, the hijackers were supposed to read handwritten instructions that Atta had distributed, which told them to shave excess hair from their bodies, to read certain passages of the Koran, and to remember that the most beautiful virgins, "the women of paradise," awaited the martyrs of Islam. "When the confrontation begins," Atta's instructions read, "strike like champions who do not want to go back to this world."

Atta and al-Omari checked into Room 233, and then headed out to a seafood restaurant and a Pizza Hut. After dinner, they withdrew money from a nearby ATM and drove a short distance to a nearby Wal-Mart, where at 8:35 P.M. they purchased four box cutters, each costing $1.84, that they planned to use the next morning during their attempt to commandeer a jet and, as O'Neill had predicted, carry out "something big."

By the time Atta had left Wal-Mart, O'Neill and Tucker had stopped off for a drink on the 107th floor of the South Tower, and headed to Elaine's for dinner with Hauer, but before they left, O'Neill called Mary Lynn Stevens to discuss the trip they planned to take to Assisi, Italy, on September 23. "We decided to talk on Wednesday because with John, things were always canceled at the last minute," she said. O'Neill and Tucker went down to the garage, where in 1993 Ramzi Yousef had blown a hole six stories deep. Tucker had been an aide to Queens DA Richard Brown at the time of that attack, and talked with O'Neill about the devastation it caused as they climbed into O'Neill's Buick. They drove to Tucker's 2001 BMW, which was parked on Vesey Street, and O'Neill looked at it admiringly. "I should probably get a new car now," he said.

At Elaine's, O'Neill ate a lavish meal of pasta and steak and drank his customary Chivas with a twist. "The dinner was fit for a king," Tucker recalled. At one point, they discussed bin Laden. "We're due for something big," O'Neill repeated. O'Neill told Elaine he was attending a dinner party there that Friday with Gary Schweikert, the vice president and managing director of the Plaza Hotel, where O'Neill had placed many foreign contacts. O'Neill arranged for Elaine to prepare a surprise chocolate cake for Schweikert's wife's birthday. He gave her a big hug and a kiss as he left.

They went to the China Club and found a long line outside, but O'Neill gave a hug and kiss on the cheek to someone and inside they went. "He was doing the O'Neill shuffle," Tucker said. The group was rushed right into the VIP section upstairs, and soon the dance club was packed. "John showed me around like it was his home," Tucker recalled. Because Tucker was twenty years younger than O'Neill and Hauer, he said he felt like he was out with his two fathers. Yet at 1 A.M., Tucker was the first to say he was tired and had to go home. O'Neill and Hauer stayed another hour.

O'Neill arrived home at about 3:30 A.M. to find Valerie James sitting at the computer playing solitaire, upset that he was home late again. She had been out for dinner with a Nordstrom's client at the Red Cat Restaurant, and when she arrived home around 10 P.M. she expected O'Neill to be there since he had promised to meet her, either at the restaurant or the apartment. So much for his big promises that his days of coming home late were over. Knowing she was angry, O'Neill slipped his arm around her as she sat moving cards on the computer screen. "You are really good at that, babe," he said, trying to turn on the charm. "Good Johnnie was bad," he told her. But James would have none it, and she cursed as she continued playing solitaire. O'Neill knew better than to persist, and he went to bed, followed soon after by James. It was 4:30 A.M.

Atta and al-Omari were awake in Room 233 in Comfort Hotel in Portland at that time. They knelt on a prayer rug and, for a final time, prayed toward Mecca, seeking Allah's blessing to fulfill bin Laden's *fatwa* "to kill Americans." They then drove to the Portland airport for a flight that connected with American Airlines Flight 11 at Boston's Logan Airport. Security procedures were less rigorous at the smaller airport, where Atta knew they stood a better chance of getting the knives through checkpoints. If all else failed, he wanted to make sure that at least he and al-Omari would fly one plane to the target. The connection was so tight that any delay in Portland would have caused them to miss the flight they planned to hijack.

September 11, 2001, was Primary Day in New York. Voters were turning out on a clear, beautiful morning to choose a successor to

Mayor Giuliani, who was completing his second and final four-year term. O'Neill and James woke up after just a few hours' sleep, and James was combing her hair when O'Neill walked up to her, put his arm around her waist, and said, "Babe, please forgive me. I fucked up. It will not happen again." Normally she would have refused to speak to him for a few days to make a point. But this time she sensed a new sincerity from him. "I forgive you," she said.

O'Neill insisted she wait for him to drive her to work, and she agreed, then tapped her foot impatiently as he pulled out a blue suit, and a blue shirt, and held up a blue tie, asking her opinion on whether there was too much blue for one outfit. Valerie told him he looked fine. He returned the compliment, telling her, "I love that suit on you." As they drove toward the Flower District, O'Neill laughed about being able to drive her to work after years of being prohibited from having civilians riding with him in his bureau vehicle. All the irony of the "car incident" was with them that morning, she recalled.

It was now 8 A.M., and American Airlines Flight 11 took off on time for Los Angeles, piloted by Victor Saracini, a boyhood friend of O'Neill's who had grown up just eight blocks from him in Atlantic City. On board were another ten crew members and eighty-one passengers, including Atta, al-Omari, and two other bin Laden followers, who were about to execute the plot Atta had finalized in Spain. Just minutes after takeoff, Atta and his henchmen began to stab several crew members and passengers who resisted their attempt to hijack the plane.

Betty Ong, an American Airlines flight attendant, telephoned the reservations line in Boston, and was patched through to American's operations center in Fort Worth, Texas. Nearly hysterical, she told the manager on duty that four men had stabbed two flight attendants, that one was dead, and that they had slit the throat of a passenger before storming the cockpit. The command center checked the flight's path and saw it veer erratically to one side and then the other, presumably until Atta had taken complete control of the doomed plane. Above Albany, he veered south, apparently to follow the Hudson River to New York City and the unmistakable target of the World Trade Center towers. He switched off the flight transponder and disappeared from the radar screens of the flight controllers, who had no idea where the hijacked plane was heading.

At 8:13 A.M., O'Neill pulled up in front of a flower shop so James could pick up a bouquet to take to her office. They were still joking about the "car incident" when he kissed her good-bye and headed downtown to a meeting. Later, he planned to meet with his son. It would take O'Neill about twenty minutes to arrive at his reserved spot in the Trade Center's lower parking garage.

At 8:14 A.M., United Airlines Flight 175 took off from Logan bound for Los Angeles with six crew members and fifty-six passengers aboard, including Marwan al-Shehhi, who had been with Atta in Spain, and three other bin Laden supporters. At 8:21 A.M., American Flight 77 left Washington's Dulles International Airport heading for Los Angeles. On board were six crew members and fifty-eight passengers, including Khalid al-Midhar and Nawaf al-Hazmi, who were also with Atta in Spain when O'Neill was there for his speech on fighting global terrorism and celebrating his "Kiss My Ass" anniversary. And at 8:42 A.M., United Flight 93 departed for San Francisco from Newark International Airport with thirty-eight passengers and seven crew members.

At 8:43 A.M., Amy Lynn Sweeney, an American Airlines attendant on Atta's flight, called Michael Woodward, a flight services manager at Logan, and calmly described the hijackers as four Middle Eastern men, some wearing red bandannas. The plane suddenly swerved to the right following the Hudson River downtown along the West Side of Manhattan.

"What's your location?" Woodward asked her.

Sweeney peered out a window into the clear blue sky, and said she saw water and buildings.

THE MAN WHO WARNED AMERICA *366*

"Oh my God," she said. "Oh my God."

O'Neill was in his office on the thirty-fourth floor of the South Tower when Atta accelerated the plane to its maximum. It roared south over Lower Manhattan, picking up speed before slamming high into the North Tower, killing everyone on board, propelling flaming wreckage and a massive fireball through the building's upper floors, and showering the streets below with the shattered ruins of the jet and the building. O'Neill would no doubt have felt the earthquakelike shock to the building, and witnessed the wreckage and the body parts cascading past his windows. From inside the building, he immediately called his son, J.P., who had taken a later train to New York than originally planned. Thankfully, J.P.'s wife, Lina, had allowed him to oversleep, or he would have been in the towers with his father.

"My father said he was okay, and he was going out to check the damage," said J.P., who looked out from his train and saw a huge plume of smoke filling the sky. "I love you," O'Neill told his son before hanging up. O'Neill's son says that at 8:50 A.M., his father received a call from his estranged wife, Christine. He told her he was all right, even as the New York skyline was darkened by the massive amount of smoke billowing out of the top floors of the North Tower where Atta had crashed his hijacked jet.

Just thirteen minutes later, as the world watched in horror on television, United Flight 175 from Logan banked toward the Twin Towers. Al-Shehhi was now in command of the plane. "Just stay quiet and you will be okay," he told the passengers. "If you try to make any moves, you'll endanger yourself and the airplane. Just stay quiet." At 9:03 A.M., he crashed the plane into the South Tower, killing everyone aboard and unleashing another massive fireball.

By then, O'Neill had reached the concourse level, where he helped shepherd a group of children from a day-care center to safety in the plaza. There he caught his first glimpse of the horrible aftermath of the collisions. He knew immediately the attacks were without question the work of his nemesis, Osama bin Laden. He called agent Pat Patterson, who served with him in Yemen, where the two had had argued about whether the Twin Towers would be attacked again. Patterson had left his cell phone at home that day, and his wife answered O'Neill's call. He told her he would catch up with her husband later, but never reached him.

"I believe he was calling to say, 'I told you so,'" Patterson said.

Scores of O'Neill's former colleagues in the FBI and the NYPD were among the first investigators and rescue workers to respond to the burning World Trade Center after Atta's plane hit. Many were nearly killed by falling debris from the second plane's impact on the South Tower. Joe Dunne, who was then the first deputy police commissioner, was on crutches from a broken foot and made his getaway "literally running for my life" as huge pieces of steel and concrete fell around him. "It was just a matter of luck I was not killed then," he said.

Ken Maxwell, the FBI counterterrorism boss who had just agreed to retire to become O'Neill's deputy, arrived at Liberty and Church to meet Mawn as the South Tower was hit. The first thing he noticed were several unconscious people nearby who had been struck by falling debris. He spotted a huge plane part, which, because of his experience with the crashes of TWA Flight 800 and EgyptAir, he immediately recognized as a piece of a Boeing cowling. "That's no commuter plane," Maxwell told Mawn.

The first person Maxwell recognized in the chaos was the tall figure of Joe Dunne, waving his crutches to get his attention. "Do you know we are under attack?" Dunne asked Maxwell.

"Yes," Maxwell said. "Where is everyone?"

"I am telling them Church Street and Vesey Street."

When they reached that intersection, Mawn and Maxwell found a group including David Kelley, the assistant United States attorney in charge of terrorism who had worked with O'Neill in Yemen.

"Has anyone called the military?" Maxwell asked, which

prompted Mawn to call Robert Cordier, the special agent in charge of the FBI's criminal division, who assured him that air force F-16s had been scrambled.

Wreckage continued to rain down around them. Dunne asked if anyone had heard from John O'Neill. Mawn told him he heard that O'Neill got out, but had gone back into the towers to assist in the evacuation and to get a better view of the damage. Suddenly another jet came roaring overhead, but this time it was an U.S. fighter jet. "We're at war," Dunne said.

Maxwell, Mawn, Kelley, and the NYPD brass recognized the danger they were in and started walking north, away from the burning tower. Dunne went off to meet with Mayor Giuliani and Police Commissioner Bernard Kerik while Mawn spoke to the Department of Defense and FBI Director Robert Mueller.

Valerie James was in her office arranging flowers when her phones started ringing off the hook. People were concerned about O'Neill: her children called looking for her, and her brother called warning her that once again O'Neill would be working for the next several months during the investigation. "Oh my gosh, I know," Valerie said, never thinking for a moment that something terrible might have happened to him.

Finally, at 9:17 A.M., O'Neill called. She breathed a sigh of relief, and started to sob.

"Are you crying, babe?" O'Neill asked her. "Val, it's terrible. There are body parts everywhere."

O'Neill said he feared his boss Jeff Wharton might be dead, and expressed concern that he would lose the job he had just started, and told her how much he needed the position. "They are going to need you more than ever," she assured him. She then telephoned her children to tell them that she had heard from O'Neill.

Anna DiBattista, who was driving to Philadelphia to meet a Windham Hotel customer, also began receiving calls from friends and family shortly after the first plane hit. They encouraged her to telephone O'Neill, but she resisted. She knew better than to disturb him in a crisis. He would be fully immersed in whatever the emergency required of him. "No," she said. "He will call me."

But her attitude changed when the second tower was struck. She dialed O'Neill's cell at 9:29 A.M. He could not have sounded calmer. "Honey, I'm safe, I'm fine," he reassured her. "I've been in and out of the building."

She urged him to get out and leave.

"I can't," he said. "I'm helping people and doing things. I love you. I'll be okay."

He started to describe the carnage he was witnessing, but the cell-phone connection failed and the line filled with static. The last thing she heard was O'Neill promising to call her later.

Fran Townsend tried to call O'Neill after the first plane struck, but couldn't get through. She tried again after the second plane hit, but again had no luck and left a voice-mail message. O'Neill paged her later with a message saying he was all right. "As ironic as it is that this happened after he left the bureau," she later said, "it wouldn't have been John O'Neill not to start to work. You couldn't be John O'Neill and stand outside and watch everybody else. It wasn't the man; it wasn't the person."

At 9:40 A.M., O'Neill arrived at the city's makeshift command center in the lobby of the North Tower. He was still immaculately dressed with a handkerchief in his front left pocket. But the back of his jacket had a dusty white smudge. He joined top members of the fire department at the command center, including Chief Peter Ganci, First Deputy Commissioner William Feehan, and Father Mychal Judge, the department's most senior chaplain.

Falling glass and debris crashed outside the revolving doors of the lobby facing out to West Street as O'Neill made phone calls and emergency personnel awaited further orders. Battalion Fire Chief Raymond Pfeifer was standing next to O'Neill, and asked if anyone had heard from the NYPD-FBI joint terrorist task force. O'Neill smiled as he realized that the chief was unaware that he was standing next to someone who knew more about fighting terrorism than almost anyone in the United States of America.

At 9:43 A.M., hijacked American Flight 77 crashed into the Pentagon, outside Washington, D.C., killing all 64 on board. One of the building's five sides collapsed, claiming the lives of another 125 people.

For the next five minutes, O'Neill remained in the lobby of the North Tower as hundreds of the tower's tenants streamed out of the building. O'Neill was as calm in the FDNY command post as he had always been at the FBI's command posts during previous crises, whether it was capturing Ramzi Yousef, orchestrating the African embassies bombing investigation, or leading the manhunt for the planners of the USS *Cole* attack.

Wesley Wong, an FBI agent who had known O'Neill since they had teamed up on the Chinese gang case in Baltimore, was also at the FDNY command post. Wong, a special operations communications expert, had arrived shortly after the first plane hit the North Tower. "As I crossed the circular driveway, a fireman yelled, 'Watch out! Run!' And I looked up and saw a man in business clothes falling down toward me from about fifty stories up," Wong recalled.

"It was surreal. He was wearing navy-blue dress pants, a white dress shirt, and black shoes. He looked like he was in his late thirties or early forties. I saw him midtower. He just had his arms out and he was just coming down. I ran toward the lobby through the windows, which had been shattered."

O'Neill asked Wong if he knew if the Pentagon had been hit. Wong called FBI headquarters and confirmed the attack. Still calm, O'Neill moved away from the command post to get a clear view of the damage to the towers. As he left, Wong called out to him, "Hey, John, I owe you lunch because I missed your going-away coffee."

O'Neill smiled.

"I'll call you when this is over," he said, disappearing down the corridor. It was 9:49 A.M. O'Neill was heading toward the South Tower.

Sixteen minutes later, at 10:05 A.M., the top floors of the South Tower began to collapse. Mountains of concrete, steel, and debris came crashing down, causing each successive lower floor to cave in with pulverizing force and filling the canyons of Lower Manhattan with a smothering black cloud. The falling debris killed most of the FDNY brass that had been with O'Neill at the North Tower command post, because they had gone outside into the plaza.

Wong discovered the body of FDNY chaplain Judge when he and a group of firefighters managed to find their way out of the lobby through the blackened haze. The group included Chief Pfeifer, whose brother, Kevin, a fire lieutenant, did not survive. "I just thought I would never see my kids again," Wong recalled.

By the time the South Tower collapsed, O'Neill's son had made his way south to Greenwich Village from Pennsylvania Station, running through the pedestrian-clogged streets of Manhattan, which were now open only to emergency vehicles. J.P. managed to get as far downtown as St. Vincent's Hospital, where scores of doctors were waiting—ultimately in vain—for survivors. J.P. was standing there when he watched in horror as the 108-story skyscraper where his father worked started to crumble. He prayed that his father was safe, although he knew his father would have to be in the thick of the action. Several cops told him that any news about survivors would be available at the First Precinct, the local precinct for the Trade Center, and J.P. began to make his way farther downtown.

Valerie James heard screams from an office across the hall and raced over in time to see the second tower collapse on television. "Oh my God, John's dead," she declared, slumping down into a chair. Her friends and coworkers told her not to think such a thing.

Mary Lynn Stevens, who had spoken with O'Neill twice a

week for more than twelve years, was in her office in Washington, D.C., at the time of the attack. Like DiBattista, she did not try to call O'Neill. "When I knew he would be overwhelmed with work, I always left him alone," she said. "When I saw the collapse, I knew he was gone. I knew he would have to be in the middle of that." But DiBattista remained hopeful. "In my heart of hearts, I thought he was alive," she said. "That is how invincible I thought he was."

Maxwell said he felt the rumble of the towers and instinctively started to run along with a group of people. Because he was a former basketball star from Fairleigh Dickinson University, Maxwell felt he could outdistance the falling skyscraper. But he could not, and he dashed into a lobby as the *whoosh* of crushed cement and steel whizzed past him. He remembers that everything went dark, and that he believed he was going to die.

After a few minutes, sunlight began to shine through the blackness. "I thought we had a lot of dead people outside," Maxwell said as he removed soot from his mouth and nostrils. He was alive, and through the opaque air he able to see David Kelley, the terrorist prosecutor O'Neill worked with in Yemen, who was covered with ash. "He looked like something out of the movie *The Night of the Living Dead*," Maxwell said.

"Have you seen Barry [Mawn]?" Maxwell asked Kelley about his boss.

"I think he's dead," Kelley replied evenly. "I think he laid down behind a truck. I think he's dead."

The two federal officials headed off toward Federal Plaza to the FBI command center. "We get paid to manage a crisis," Maxwell said. "But there was just a feeling of helplessness."

Dunne made it to safety in the basement of 75 Barclay, where he joined Mayor Giuliani and Police Commissioner Bernard Kerik, who had near death experiences of their own. "Everyone heard a roar, and it just continued and continued and the room was shaking and filling up with dust," Dunne said.

Thirteen minutes after the South Tower collapsed, the North Tower gave way, vanishing from the skyline at 10:28 A.M. Maxwell was near Chinatown when "the noise started again," he recalled. Again he ran for his life as a second huge dust cloud enveloped him.

O'Neill's son was making his way down to the First Precinct on lower Hudson Street, in the shadow of the collapsing North Tower. He watched helplessly from the steps of the station house as the second tower came down and saw cops and firemen assisting people as they emerged from the smoke, washing their faces from open hydrants. "I was witnessing the best of humanity, and the worst of humanity," J.P. remembers.

He wanted to make his way toward the fallen towers, but feared he would only get in the way of the rescuers. He decided to remain on the steps of the First Precinct, hoping for news of his father, though he feared the worst. "My father could have survived, but that was not the kind of guy he was," J.P. said.

Maxwell made his way to the FBI command center at Broadway and Reade Street. "I think Barry's dead," he said. But moments later, he found out Mawn had arrived safely a few moments before him. "Don't you ever leave my side again," he later scolded Mawn. Despite the enormous sense of helplessness, the two FBI bosses started counting heads and then immediately launched the investigation into the attack. They obtained a list of passengers from airline flight manifests and began to check out every person aboard the four hijacked planes. These were O'Neill's men and women, and they knew bin Laden was behind the attack.

Valerie James began calling the FBI, frantically looking for news about O'Neill. Maxwell told her he would let her know the moment he heard anything, but he did not want to provide her with false hope. "I tried to give her updates, but there was no news," he said.

As the hours passed, scores of O'Neill's friends, colleagues, and acquaintances from around the world called his cell phone. By the day's end, there would be two hundred messages on his voice mail. One of them was from Tucker. "I hope you overslept like I did. There is a disaster in your building, and I want you to know about it."

Mark Chidichimo, who manages the FBI's intelligence squad and its analysts in New York, went into O'Neill's old office, which was now used by his successor, Joseph Billy, and still a hub of action. "Valerie called. She asked if I heard anything from John. She was panicky and upset." O'Neill's son also called. Chidichimo put J.P. in touch with his mother, who had also called and was concerned because she knew J.P. was going to meet his father.

Jerry Hauer, who had been at a doctor's office when the towers were hit, went to CNN to give a live interview, and then to Silverstein's Midtown headquarters. His phone was also ringing with people looking for news about O'Neill. At Silverstein's office, he learned that in addition to O'Neill, Doug Karpiloff, the Security and Life Safety director for the Port Authority, was missing. Silverstein and Wharton were all right, but in a state of disbelief. Although Silverstein watched a billion-dollar investment crumble, his primary concerns were the staff and employees and whether they had gotten out. "Larry was absolutely devastated," Hauer said.

In Washington, D.C., Kathy Kiser, an FBI agent who had worked with O'Neill years earlier in Baltimore, had gotten an oil change on her car before finding herself stuck in traffic on New York Avenue. By coincidence, September 11 was also her mother's birthday. A woman told Kiser that something terrible was happening in New York and she turned on the television in time to see the second plane hit the South Tower.

In nearby Baltimore, Agent Gary Stevens, another colleague from O'Neill's first posting, knew when the tower collapsed that John was dead. "I knew John would never be standing on the sidelines. That was not John. He was going to be where he thought he should be."

Jack Caravelli, O'Neill's boyhood friend who had gone on to be a director of the National Security Council at the White House, was in his office at the Department of Energy, where he was in charge of tracking weapons of mass destruction. He was watching the events on television, hoping O'Neill had escaped, when a hijacked jet slammed into the Pentagon across the Potomac River. He was now forced to flee for his own safety.

Detective Louie Napoli, the JTTF Egyptian terror expert whom O'Neill sent to Pakistan in search of African bombing suspects, was right under the North Tower when it was struck. His first concern was for his son, who worked at the tower. His son always ran late for work, which he had fortunately done yet again, but Napoli could not know this. "The second plane came and it hit and body parts are everywhere, and I got tired of looking down, and I looked up and people were jumping from the building." His son was safe, but Napoli was right in harm's way. "I thought maybe I would get killed." He said he asked everyone if they had heard from O'Neill.

"He chased bin Laden all over the world and bin Laden caught up with him," he said.

At 11 A.M., New York Governor George Pataki declared a state of emergency and postponed the primary elections. Mayor Giuliani ordered Lower Manhattan evacuated and urged all city residents to remain at home. No one was to come into New York unless they were involved in the emergency response.

At 1:04 P.M., President Bush, from a Louisiana air base, vowed to "hunt down and punish those responsible for these cowardly acts." At the FBI's SIOC Command Center in Washington, D.C., where O'Neill helped capture Ramzi Yousef in 1995, Special Agent Kenneth Pierneck, who had served with O'Neill both in Chicago and Africa, stood near the podium in the large room that only hours earlier had been silent. Now it was teeming with more than 250 agents running in every direction, sharing information with one another and their counterparts around the globe.

Moments after the president's statement, Pierneck made his own announcement over the SIOC loudspeakers to a somber and hushed audience. "I have some sad news to share," he began. "John O'Neill, who was a personal friend and someone known to many of you, was last seen in Building Two when it collapsed, and is believed to have died. His body has not been recovered. We will let you know more as we know it." Pierneck barely finished speaking before he became overwhelmed with emotion. "The bureau forced out the foremost, most knowledgeable person on terrorism," he reflected later. "It was tough fighting back the tears."

In New York, the FBI began holding conference calls among the fifty-six special agents in charge across the country to share information already being gathered. Even at this early stage of the investigation, various offices were tracking the hundreds of passenger names provided on the airline manifests. Yet someone seemed to ask about O'Neill during every call.

At the time of the attacks in New York, Thomas Dolan, one of O'Neill's most loyal supervisors, was in Yemen with Stephen Corbett and Bob McFadden, both from the Naval Criminal Investigation Service. They were in Yemen planning to question the participants in the so-called Last Supper meal that took place before the October 2000 attack on the USS *Cole*. "John kept saying bin Laden would strike America and it would be big," said Donlan. He wondered what had happened to O'Neill, and he worried about the safety of his two brothers, who were New York firemen.

At around 2 P.M., J. P. O'Neill was still sitting outside the First Precinct waiting for news. A cop came outside and suggested he have something to eat or drink, so J.P. ordered a Diet Coke. "I just kept looking at the towers lying there," he recalled. His wife called and asked him to come home because she feared there could be further attacks, but there were American F-16s flying overhead, so he told his wife he was probably in the safest city in America and that he wanted to stay the night.

He went uptown to Valerie's office, where they stayed together for a few hours before heading off to Keane's Steakhouse nearby, where they had Caesar salads for dinner. The shaken James told J.P. that she believed O'Neill was gone, but his son did not want to hear such a dire prediction. When they emerged from the restaurant, which was one of his father's favorites, the city was desolate. "There was not a single person on the street. No one," J.P. said. "I looked in both directions. It was eerie." Everyone, except rescue workers, was home watching television. When they got to Valerie's apartment, they watched television, still "in utter disbelief" about the tragic events of the day.

That evening, they watched President Bush tell the nation that "these acts shattered steel but they can not dent the steel of American resolve." Numb with grief, the two of them tried to get some sleep, hoping the following day would bring a miracle.

On September 12, the country awakened still in shock. J.P. and Valerie as well as her own children, who referred to O'Neill as their father, held out hope that he was still alive. O'Neill's son went to a friend's house in Brooklyn, eventually making his way back to his own family in Delaware, where he picked up his infant son and hugged and kissed him like never before.

With the help of the FBI, James tried to get permission to go to Ground Zero. She wanted to look for O'Neill, but the streets around the smoldering ruins were closed to everyone. She even tried to contact Hauer, hoping that his connections from his former job as the head of the mayor's Office of Emergency Management would allow her to gain access to the downtown site, which was essentially a huge, frozen crime scene off limits to anyone without a badge. "I told her there was no way," Hauer said. Among those who called offering other types of support was Robert De Niro, the actor, whom she and O'Neill had met through Sony chairman Tommy Mottola.

Mary Lynn Stevens had sometimes asked O'Neill how she would know if anything happened to him, and he would laugh and tell her she would read it in the papers. As the images of the destruction filled her television, Stevens knew her "boyfriend" of twelve years was among the thousands lost forever. That morning, she paged O'Neill a final time, punching in their secret code, "5-8-8-8," which spelled out "LUVU."

Anna DiBattista, who had spent a sleepless night at her home in Maryland, watched ABC anchor Peter Jennings report that O'Neill, the former FBI national security chief in New York, was missing in the World Trade Center. "I let out a scream," she said.

In Yemen, a group of government officials and American investigators held an emotional meeting. Agent Robert McFadden, from the Naval Criminal Investigation Service, recalled that one Yemeni official was near tears at learning O'Neill was probably among the dead. He had trouble speaking when he asked if they knew the circumstances surrounding "Al Aqh's"—Brother John's—final moments. "He had to pause when he spoke," McFadden recalled. The Yemeni position on assisting the United States immediately changed, he said, partly because of their affection for O'Neill, whom they knew personally, and because of President George Bush's clear declaration that the countries needed to decide whether they were "with the U.S." or "with the terrorists."

Meanwhile, the scene at Ground Zero was barely controlled chaos. Firefighters and police were already searching for survivors in the rubble, hoping to find their own lost brothers and sisters. But their task was nearly impossible because of the fires, the smoke, and the constant fear that remaining sections of the tower and nearby buildings might collapse.

The FBI shifted its command center to a secret garage warehouse on the Lower West Side. A high-ranking NYPD official who was never a big supporter of the JTTF arrived and immediately announced that the NYPD could solve the Twin Towers case quickly, with just a handful of Brooklyn detectives. His insensitive remark drew incredulous stares from the roomful of agents and detectives who had traveled the world hunting bin Laden and other terrorists over the years.

Although the focus of the media and the American public mostly centered on the stunning loss of life and the rescue operation, another, subtler set of concerns preoccupied representatives from the law enforcement agencies that had had offices in the towers. These officials had well-founded concerns about finding their important documents and equipment. The Drug Enforcement Administration wanted to find the records of cases they had built against drug dealers, while CIA operatives came to the crumbled towers to get into secure safes that had held stacks of classified information and documents in a phony office they had set up. The most closely guarded secret in the towers was kept by the Secret Service, which was concerned about a Stinger missile, secretly stored there, which was used to protect the president in the event of an attack when he visited New York.

The FBI was concerned about finding the black boxes from the jets and quickly identifying the bodies recovered on the streets, speculating that they probably came from the jet and might include some of the hijackers. Their investigative haste to find evidence did not sit well with some NYPD personnel, who, like Lieutenant Eugene Whyte, felt that the primary focus should be locating survivors and ensuring that the victims were properly handled so that the medical examiner could conduct positive identifications.

The NYPD established a makeshift morgue staffed with seasoned investigators at the medical examiner's office on First Avenue to handle the grim and exacting task of cataloging the dead. First Deputy Commissioner Dunne gave specific orders to notify him every time a member of the uniformed services was found. That edict applied not merely to New York City personnel, but included O'Neill and Leonard Hatton, a forty-five-year-old FBI bomb technician and father of four from Ridgefield, New Jersey, who had worked on the 1993 World Trade Center bombing and, along with O'Neill, on the African bombings and the attack on the USS Cole. Hatton had rescued civilians from the towers, and it was later found that he perished when he returned to provide further help.

On Thursday afternoon, two days after the collapse, Valerie James felt an inexplicable need to go down to a storage shed that she had rented for O'Neill after he had left the FBI. He had needed the additional space because there was no room for all his police emblems, placards, photos, and other personal effects in their apartment. Perhaps Valerie thought that by handling his belongings she would somehow feel closer to him. She asked her children to go with her and lend support, but they refused at first. That evening, they went together to the Manhattan Storage office on First Avenue, near the apartment she and O'Neill shared. After opening the shed containing his belongings, she received the second greatest shock of her life.

There among O'Neill's personal property was a large box containing letters and cards from many women. There were photographs of Anna DiBattista, and scores of personal greeting cards and letters from Fran Townsend. There were even letters from O'Neill's old flame, Anne, in Baltimore. In this mound of letters, cards, and pictures, James also found a prepublication manuscript of Carol Higgins Clark's novel *Fleeced*, which featured on its cover a picture of the World Trade Center. Clark, she would later learn, was another close friend of O'Neill's.

Valerie also found a leather-bound diary in which O'Neill had meticulously detailed his emotions and thoughts on a regular basis, along with sets of three-by-seven index cards that contained other thoughts and correspondences that were written in a secret numerical code. A shattered James sat on the floor and began reading the letters and cards aloud in the cold storage room. Neither she nor her grown children could believe what she was reading. As she read a passage or note, her emotions ranged from sadness to fury. O'Neill's private thoughts and notations were just too much to bear.

"I was reading, reading, reading, and everyone was in shock," James recounted. "There was a lot of crying and rage and anger." After hours of facing the terrible fact that the man she lived with had betrayed her, she returned home, and tried in vain to sleep. Her children later told her she had cried in her sleep.

FBI officials, who later learned about O'Neill's personal writings, sent agents to Valerie and John's apartment to examine O'Neill's possessions and ensure that his private papers and effects contained no classified secrets.

Newspaper and magazine stories about O'Neill's disappearance in the towers mentioned that he lived with James. It was then that the other women in his life—the ones who also believed they were his only love—learned that their relationship was not exclusive. These other women were as shaken at this revelation as James was when she discovered the stack of letters and cards hidden in O'Neill's storage shed.

DiBattista, for example, found out about James that morning from friends and family in Chicago who saw James quoted in her hometown newspaper, the *Chicago Tribune*. Anna telephoned the reporter to tell him he must have gotten his facts wrong. As far as she knew, O'Neill and James had dated in Chicago, but had not seen each other in years. The reporter insisted his sources were accurate. She then telephoned O'Neill's son, who politely denied any knowledge of James to spare DiBattista's feelings.

Mary Lynn Stevens learned about O'Neill's death just as he had predicted she would, from news reports. But while she was prepared to hear of his death in prominent media reports, she did not expect to later discover "from three national magazines that John had other loves."

The following night, Friday September 14, Gary Schweikert,

the vice-president of the Plaza Hotel, his wife, Jacqui, and eight friends kept their dinner appointment at Elaine's. They felt that O'Neill would have wanted it that way. "His memory was very dear," Schweikert said. "We were still in shock, but we felt he was that kind of special person who would want to be there in spirit." After their meal, Elaine surprised them with the chocolate cake O'Neill had so thoughtfully ordered for Jacqui's birthday the day before he died. "It was difficult," Schweikert said. But the cake was eaten, "and thoroughly enjoyed."

A week later, on Friday, September 21, firefighters digging through shattered concrete, twisted steel, and other assorted wreckage discovered a body in a mass of debris at the corner of Liberty and Greenwich Street. The body was about twelve feet beneath the surface in a pile of wreckage that extended almost ninety feet into the base of the South Tower. The victim was wearing a suit. A rescuer reached into a pocket and found a wallet containing O'Neill's identification. His American University graduation ring was on his left hand. Most of the victims of the attack were never recovered, and many mourners were left to bury only a piece of a loved one. O'Neill's body was intact. He had suffered a fatal blow to his chest and head and a minor burn, but he was otherwise unhurt. The look on his face reflected the shock of the event: O'Neill had predicted an attack on the Trade Center, but he could not have envisioned that the building would collapse and that he would ride a mountainous wave of debris from his thirty-fourth-floor office.

Charles Campisi, NYPD's chief of internal affairs, whose office was in charge of the recovery of the victims, now believes that O'Neill must have tried to make his way up to his office on the thirty-fourth floor, since his body was recovered nearer the top of a pile of rubble. It took rescuers months before they found police officers and firefighters in the same pile of debris who were in the lobby at the time of the collapse. "We believe John rode the debris down," he said.

O'Neill's body was gingerly lifted from the debris, and an American flag was placed over him. A phalanx of cops and firemen then carried his corpse to a waiting ambulance for the ride to the morgue. The NYPD detectives working at the site had established a protocol for handling the remains of every victim, regardless of size or type. With each discovery, police officers at Ground Zero radioed ahead that a body had been found. But with O'Neill, as with the recovery of every one of the 403 deceased members of the uniformed services, the protocol was different.

As O'Neill's body was being driven up First Avenue, police officers and other personnel at the morgue stepped outside to solemnly greet his body, much like a funeral cortege for a head of state or an honored military official. They formed two lines, each standing at attention. Detective Michael Fabozzi remembered standing with dozens of colleagues, and saluting O'Neill's flag-draped body as it was removed from the ambulance and carried into the morgue. Detective Sergeant Christopher Cincotta and Detective John Cantwell notified Commissioner Dunne that his friend had been recovered, and Dunne came immediately to pay his respects to O'Neill.

The medical examiner, Dr. Seymour Hirsch, determined O'Neill died from "blunt trauma" and "fractures to his skull and torso." Dr. Hirsch classified O'Neill's death as "a homicide," just as he eventually did for the other 2,822 World Trade Center victims.

Valerie James received a call from Jerry Hauer asking what arrangements she would be making for O'Neill. She explained that since O'Neill was technically still married, the authorities would have to contact his wife, Christine, or his parents.

O'Neill's son called DiBattista, who was still praying for a miracle. "Are you sitting down?" J.P. asked her. "There's something I have to tell you."

The FBI agent who had chased bin Laden for years was now a victim of the very attack he had sought to prevent. "It is beyond ironic that John, who was probably the one person in the United

States that knew more about Osama bin Laden and Al Qaeda than anyone else, died in the rubble of the World Trade Center," said Robert "Bear" Bryant, the former FBI deputy director, recalling again how he first heard the name bin Laden from O'Neill in 1995.

A funeral service was held a week later, on September 28, in O'Neill's hometown. It was in Atlantic City that a young boy had dreamed of being a heroic special agent with the Federal Bureau of Investigation. Residents lined the streets of the city and his casket was part of a procession that ended at the regal St. Nicholas of Tolentine Church, where O'Neill had served an altar boy almost forty years earlier. When the limousine carrying O'Neill's family arrived, his mother emerged and was helped along by John Heanon, who was now a detective sergeant in the Atlantic City Police Department. "Why my Johnny?" the crestfallen Dottie O'Neill repeatedly asked Heanon. "I should have died that day," she said. O'Neill's father appeared shaken by the loss of their "pride and joy."

Several of O'Neill's dearest friends, including Jay Manning and Kenneth Maxwell, served as pallbearers, helping hoist his casket up the steps of the church as a U.S. Army helicopter hovered above. A few yards from the entrance, near the rectory, someone had placed an Atlantic City Beach Patrol lifeguard stand, which evoked images of the teenage O'Neill working summers as a lifeguard while attending Holy Spirit High School.

As his casket rested near the altar, flanked by the flags of the United States and the FBI, bagpipes played "God Bless America." More than a thousand mourners packed the church, representing the wide range of O'Neill's friends. There was FBI Director Louis Freeh and a legion of top law enforcement officials, military personnel, cops, members of foreign intelligence, and agents who had joined O'Neill in his war on terrorism. Fran Townsend, Mary Jo White, and Joseph Dunne were among the government dignitaries at the service, which began with the playing of bagpipes. But there were also friends from the media, restaurateurs like Elaine Kaufman and Roy Bernard, and a collection of acquaintances from Wall Street, the diplomatic community, and the security industry.

O'Neill's complicated personal life made the tragic ceremony even more difficult for certain mourners. O'Neill's parents took seats in the front pews along with his wife and two children, but the grieving James and her two children had to slide into seats a few rows back. A crying Anna DiBattista insisted on sitting with John Lipka and Mike Brooks at a dignified distance from the front, to avoid causing more trauma for the others.

"When Fran Townsend came in the church, she sat right near the front row with Mary Jo White," James would later recount. "And then Anna DiBattista came in. We already knew from John's letters. But it was still a shock, nonetheless."

Patricia Kelly, from the Diplomatic Security Service, and her sister, Kathy, from the FBI, were together in the eleventh row, paying their respects to a former colleague and friend of many years. Like everyone else there, from Bryant, to Neil Gallagher, to Maxwell, to Manning, they knew little, if anything, about O'Neill's complex personal life. To them, he had always appeared to be in love with the FBI and to be a patriot. "Why else did he give twenty-one hours of every day to his work, and just three hours for everything else?" David Kelley, the antiterrorism prosecutor, asked rhetorically.

Barry Mawn, the FBI head in New York City who was scheduled to eulogize O'Neill, was prohibited by the stodgy FBI rules from flying to Atlantic City in an FBI plane because he was taking his wife, a civilian. Instead, they flew with Dunne in an NYPD helicopter. Mawn spent a considerable part of the eulogy dismissing the "briefcase incident" especially when it was measured against O'Neill's decades of service and in light of his efforts to prevent the very attack that claimed his life. Mawn pointedly added that O'Neill's death had prompted the Yemenis to work more closely with the U.S. investigators.

Mayor Giuliani was not there, having remained in New York to handle the aftermath of the attack, but his chief counsel, Dennison Young, told the audience that the American public would "never know how much they owe John O'Neill." James Kallstrom lauded O'Neill as "a patriot, a hero, a tireless worker and leader in our fight for public safety and our national security. When it came to fighting terrorism, John *was* the FBI," he said. "And John knew all too well what the general public knows today: We are at war with evil."

On his desk, O'Neill had always kept a photograph of John Cardinal O'Connor shaking hands with him in front of St. Patrick Cathedral on St. Patrick's Day. O'Connor had signed the picture with an inscription: "For a loyal friend and impeccable patriot with many thanks for many things. God Bless you." Thomas Durkin, a lawyer and counsel to the late archbishop, was the last to speak about O'Neill, and he reminded everyone that O'Neill was not only an FBI official, but also a man who loved people and life.

The most moving moment came when O'Neill's son, J.P., reached into his pocket and pulled out a letter his father had written to his first grandchild when he was born in May 2001—a grandson whose photograph had a prominent place among the many photos, plaques, and awards in O'Neill's office. O'Neill's letter to his grandson spoke of respecting parents and having a love of God, family, and country.

"You have been born in the greatest country in the world," J.P. began, his voice bravely masking the pain and difficulty he was feeling inside. "It is well to learn the ethnic backgrounds of your parents, to love and cherish the ancient folklore. But never, never forget, you are an American first. And millions of Americans before you have fought for your freedom. The Nation holds all the terms of our endearment. Support, defend and honor those whose duty it is to keep it safe."

By the time O'Neill's son finished reading the note, the hushed cathedral was filled with the sounds of people sobbing or choking back tears. FBI National Security Director Neil Gallagher said he "went to pieces" during the reading, and it took him nearly a week before he could even discuss the letter. The funeral had such a powerful impact on him that he eventually decided to retire to spend more time with his own family.

"The note to his grandson probably said as much about John as anything," notes Jack Caravelli, O'Neill's boyhood friend who went on to work at the CIA and in the White House. "There was not a word in that note that was not from the heart. And as for terrorism, he gave his life to show he was right all along."

Joe Billy, who had served in Africa and had been with Director Freeh when Clinton launched his retaliatory strikes at bin Laden after the embassy bombings, brought his eleven-year-old son to O'Neill's funeral. "I wanted my son to see someone who was a good man and who dedicated his life to preventing such things as the World Trade Center attack," said Billy, who succeeded O'Neill at the FBI in New York. "I wanted to show my son that there was evil in the world, but that there are people who are good and there are people who appreciate what they do."

Billy knew O'Neill was not a perfect man, but a flawed and complicated one, especially in relation to the women in his life. But Billy believed that whatever his flaws, O'Neill "cared for all of his girlfriends, I know he did, and he gave something to each of the women. And they were probably better off for it."

Mary Lynn Stevens only learned about the discovery of O'Neill's body and the funeral plans the day before he was buried. She had been in Italy attending the cooking classes she and O'Neill had signed up for together. She went to Italy because she felt O'Neill would have wanted it that way, but she never expected his body to be recovered so quickly. Before boarding the plane in

Bologna to return home, she retrieved her messages and learned that he was definitely dead. She thanked God that his body was found, but was "heartbroken" at the harsh reality that he was gone and she could not attend the service. She found consolation in knowing that her absence might spare others further discomfort. "Perhaps God decided that I was to do my mourning alone," she later wrote in her condolence note to J.P.

The two-and-a-half-hour service ended with the playing of the mournful Irish ballad "Danny Boy," which O'Neill loved, and which now could be heard over loudspeakers through the streets of Atlantic City. When his body was carried from the chapel, a police honor guard lined up in the middle of Pacific Street and saluted his flag-draped casket.

The long funeral procession drove to the Holy Cross Cemetery in May's Landing escorted by a dozen motorcycle cops. The limousines passed firefighters in full dress, saluting O'Neill's hearse as it moved slowly past their firehouses. Hand-painted banners saying THANK YOU, JOHN, FOR ALL YOU DID decorated the streets, and as the procession disappeared into the cemetery, the army helicopter continued to hover above the cathedral as the sound of the bagpipes again filled the air. "John would have loved this," Agent Gary Stevens said. "This was the big show."

EPILOGUE

I saw John O'Neill at Elaine's just five days before he died at the World Trade Center. O'Neill had dinner with about ten people that night, sitting center stage at one of the restaurant's coveted large tables near the front, across from the crowded bar. At the end of the evening as he was leaving, O'Neill came over to say good night and arrange to have dinner with me.

He surprised me with a question.

"Where do I get my reputation back?" he asked, referring to the recent article in the *New York Times* about the infamous briefcase incident. Even then, weeks after its publication, O'Neill was still upset by the story's appearance. I told O'Neill I would write about his upcoming retirement party, to which hundreds of important people from inside and outside the world of law enforcement were to be invited.

O'Neill smiled and threw an arm around my neck, giving me his trademark hug and a kiss on the cheek, and then he was gone out the door onto Second Avenue. O'Neill's desire for the retirement party to erase the blemish on his reputation indicated the extent to which his professional lapses still haunted him. After all, he had devoted his life to integrating his professional and personal lives—his "day job" and his "night job"—into a cohesive force that would help him accomplish his missions. He had performed his job as an FBI agent with flair and panache, but he wanted to be remembered as a serious and successful law enforcement agent, not someone known merely for stylish eccentricity, or more seriously, for a careless breach of protocol. Yet O'Neill was both: he was a serious and successful—even prescient—law enforcement agent, and he was also a flawed man who led a tangled personal life, a complex figure whose unorthodox approach to his job and miscues led to his exit from the FBI, his one great love.

How does one explain a life so rich in paradox?

After O'Neill's death, when Valerie James opened the storage shed that held the evidence of O'Neill's complicated love life, it was devastating for her to be confronted with the fact of his deception. Like Pandora's box, the unearthing of O'Neill's secrets raised more questions than it answered. O'Neill conducted his personal affairs as though he were James Bond, using elaborate codes to organize his lives with different women.

But since O'Neill was in fact a government agent who had held some of the top classified positions in the United States during his time at the FBI, it is fascinating to uncover his almost inexplicable need for secrecy and control in every aspect of his life. O'Neill was both the bright and shining counterterrorism warrior who wanted his patriotic reputation burnished and maintained after his retirement, and the man who had played cloak-and-dagger for so long, he did not know how to prevent the duplicitousness of the spy game from leaking into his personal life.

With his ability to see into the mind of darkness, and perhaps around corners as well, O'Neill worked tirelessly and imaginatively to marshal the resources of the United States to close in on bin Laden and his Al Qaeda network. Years before most Americans had ever heard of bin Laden, O'Neill was reading book after book on Islamic fundamentalism and accurately forecasting that the United States would have to revise its thinking and rally itself for a long, costly war on terrorism. He warned that this war would take years to fight and require single-minded resolve, if America were to avoid a catastrophic attack on U.S. soil that could claim hundreds or even thousands of lives.

O'Neill's warnings were prophetic, but not prophetic enough

to save his own life or those of the other September 11 victims. O'Neill fell short in his battle against bin Laden partly because even given his fondness for twenty-hour workdays, his genius for international networking, and his creativity in studying a problem until he found original solutions, O'Neill was all too human. His FBI career would unravel in part because of two lapses that showed his sense of mission could on occasion make this most thorough and precise of men susceptible to error.

But no one who knew John O'Neill well believes these lapses were what ultimately led to his undoing. That was much more complicated, like the overall failure of U.S. intelligence to avoid major setbacks in a war that not enough people recognized as a war. O'Neill could have weathered these small storms if his visionary pursuit of bin Laden and redefinition of the threat posed by terrorism had received more emphatic support from cautious, procedure-oriented higher-ups, all the way through the FBI, the National Security Council, and the White House. But O'Neill's endless socializing earned him more than his share of enemies, and his can-do, direct style inspired panic and fear in stuffy bureaucrats who adhered to a motto of "Big cases, big problems; small cases, small problems; no cases, no problems."

O'Neill's flaws were part of what made him the best weapon the bureau had in its most important challenge in generations, and it was up to the people in power at the FBI to make use of that weapon and bring it to bear against sworn enemies of America and the American way of life. That failure is a failure that will haunt the bureau and U.S. law enforcement for years to come. "O'Neill was saying we are at war, and we had to get aggressive if we wanted to prevent a large-scale attack," a top antiterrorist official who worked at the CIA said. "But no one wanted to listen to John O'Neill."

FBI brass were not the only ones to fool themselves during those years when O'Neill was trying to rally the fight against the rich Saudi-born terrorist. The Clinton administration and the

American people had been sleepily complacent. President Clinton had been elected in 1992 on the strength of his focus on the economy, as immortalized by this campaign phrase "It's the economy, stupid." And the economy had roared through the 1990s. Stock markets spiraled ever upward. Americans felt wealthy, giddy, and insulated from the rest of the world's woes. There were all too many distractions, junk-TV obsessions from the O. J. Simpson trials to the Clinton scandals; but none of that can ever excuse the American failure to see itself as part of the rest of the world.

John O'Neill never made that mistake. He was a visionary patriot who sounded the clarion call about bin Laden's jihad against the United States. A larger-than-life figure with his own flamboyant style, O'Neill was a swashbuckling agent with slicked-back hair, manicured nails, a penchant for high-end restaurants, and a millionaire's wardrobe. He reached across boundaries, both within U.S. law enforcement and internationally, to forge relationships with top terrorism fighters all over the world, earning a level of loyalty and respect few men could match.

"I would die for him," said John Bunn, detective chief superintendent for Scotland Yard.

O'Neill had helped capture the mastermind of the 1993 World Trade Center bombing, coordinated the 1995 Oklahoma City investigation that led to the arrest of Timothy McVeigh, played a decisive role in the probe of the crash of TWA Flight 800 in New York, and was a point man in the separate investigations into plots to blow up New York City landmarks, U.S. commercial planes, and two deadly bombings of U.S. military assets in Saudi Arabia. O'Neill's work in the African bombing case is widely credited among law enforcement officials with creating the template for all future international terrorist investigations.

At the outset of the new Bush administration in January 2001, the president espoused a foreign policy based on "humility" rather than military strength, with the focus decidedly not on terrorism. Bush's new attorney general, John Ashcroft, went so far as to dismiss an FBI request to allocate fifty million dollars to enhance the bureau's antiterrorism programs, insisting on highlighting white collar crime targets and drug dealers instead.

But the destruction of the World Trade Center shocked the United States out of its decade of complacency and awakened the nation to the warning O'Neill had delivered in a speech five years before: the single greatest threat to national security was international terrorism. As a result, many of the remedies advocated by O'Neill have come to pass both in the United States and abroad.

On October 7, 2001, President George Bush ordered the type of harsh military action to destroy bin Laden and his Al Qaeda camps in Afghanistan that O'Neill had advocated since the two bombings of U.S. embassies in Africa in 1998. Although bin Laden managed to elude capture, the ruthless Taliban that had ruled Afghanistan with an iron fist and provided cover for him and Al Qaeda was driven from power and a nascent democratic government was installed in its place. Afghan women, arguably among the most oppressed in the world under Taliban rule, were no longer mistreated, and instead were allowed to show their faces in public and attend school again. "Today we focus on Afghanistan," Bush said, "but the battle is broader."

More than a year later, President Bush demonstrated just how extensive his war would become. Bush held a meeting at the White House in December 2002 with the president of Yemen, Abdullah Saleh, who offered to help reconcile America's disagreements with Saleh's longtime ally Iraqi president Saddam Hussein, with whom Saleh had sided during the Persian Gulf War in 1990–1991. Invoking an Arab proverb that cautioned the American president against taking military action against Saddam Hussein, the Yemeni president warned Bush that if he were to put a cat into a cage, it could likely turn into a fierce lion. But Bush was unmoved.

"The cat has rabies," Bush sharply replied, "and the only way to cure the cat is to cut off its head." Bush's bluntness startled Saleh, but it reinforced the U.S. position that the days of Middle Eastern duplicity and fence-sitting were over, and that Arab leaders would have to decide whether they were on the side of the United States or they supported the terrorists.

President Bush's point had its desired effect. Soon unmanned American predator planes, with the permission of the Yemeni government, were flying over sovereign Yemeni territory searching for the Al Qaeda leaders O'Neill had warned about. They were found traveling in a car that was subsequently destroyed by a CIA guided missile. Bush then made good on his promise to cut off the head of the cat—this time without complete United Nations support—by leading a coalition of troops into Iraq that toppled the dictator's regime. This invasion directly led to the capture of one of the architects of terrorism in the 1980s, Abu Abbas, the head of the Palestinian Liberation Front, who had been a fugitive since he orchestrated the hijacking of the Italian cruise ship the *Achille Lauro* and the murder of a wheelchair-bound elderly American passenger, Leon Klinghoffer, who was thrown overboard. Within weeks of the end of fighting in Iraq, the U.S. began to pull military personnel from bases in Saudi Arabia, where they had been stationed since the 1991 Gulf War, enflaming the anti-American passions of the virulent terror movement led by bin Laden.

The vast worldwide law enforcement network that O'Neill helped forge with his dynamic personality had coalesced into a united global effort against bin Laden, Al Qaeda, and the other terror organizations. Although they could not completely prevent further bloodshed—183 people were killed in two nightclub bombings in Bali on October 12, 2002, the second anniversary of the attack on the USS *Cole*—those endeavors quickly resulted in the breakup of terror cells in England, Spain, Italy, Germany, Yemen, the Netherlands, and the Philippines just as other waves of attacks were set to commence. Several of bin Laden's top operatives and advisers were captured. Ramzi bin al-Shibh, a ring-leader of the World Trade Center attack, was caught in Pakistan on the first anniversary of September 11. The agents believe bin al-Shibh's capture was somehow a gift from O'Neill to energize them just as they were growing frustrated and weary. Many say how much they still miss O'Neill. "John was not just a manager, he was a leader," said Mary Galligan, now the inspector in charge of the "PentBomb" case.

Abu Zubaida, the Al Qaeda operations chief and Khalid Shaikh Mohammed, the mastermind of the attacks on the African embassies and the Twin Towers and the uncle of Ramzi Yousef, the convicted mastermind of the 1993 WTC bombing, were also caught. These Al Qaeda leaders, along with nearly six hundred suspected terrorists, were taken into custody and imprisoned at the U.S. military base in Guantánamo Bay, Cuba, where their debriefing sessions continue providing information in the war on terrorism.

In the United States, President Bush ordered the creation a Department of Homeland Security to bring together nearly 170,000 employees from twenty-two agencies in what would become the largest bureaucratic reorganization of governmental responsibilities since the founding of the Department of Defense after World War II. The mission of this new cabinet-level agency was comprehensive and mirrored recommendations made by O'Neill: improving security along the nation's borders; revamping the Department of Immigration and Naturalization, which was unable to locate thousands of registered immigrants that investigators need to question after September 11; toughening airline and airport security; refocusing research on nuclear, chemical, and biological threats, and aggressively assessing intelligence about terrorists and their organizations.

The president also created a Terrorist Threat Integration Center to merge divisions from the CIA, the FBI, and other agencies into a single government unit to strengthen the collection and analysis of foreign and domestic terrorist threats and force the agencies to better communicate—just as O'Neill did, albeit on a smaller scale, when he named a CIA official to be his deputy at the FBI in 1995 and when he helped established the Alex station that dispatched an FBI agent to work at the CIA in 1996. CIA Director George Tenet was placed in charge of the center and given full control over the collection and evaluation of all information relating to terrorist threats—not the FBI—after giving his full assurance to Bush and Congress that his agency would become more aggressive in fighting terrorism. (After all, one of the single greatest embarrassments to the U.S. intelligence community was the fact that John Walker Lindh, a young Californian who joined Al Qaeda and personally met bin Laden, was not working for the CIA.)

FBI Director Robert Mueller also pledged that the bureau would make counterterrorism its top priority, and he directed resources toward fighting extremists bent upon destroying America, including the hiring of hundreds of analysts, linguists, and experts on information technology. Perhaps even more important, Mueller said he would change the rigid culture and "bureaucratic intransigence" that not only contributed to O'Neill's forced retirement, but to the mind-set that caused officials at headquarters to ignore warnings from field agents about possible terrorist activities. Those alarms that terrorists might be attending American flying schools and involved in an imminent suicide mission could conceivably have prevented the September 11 attacks. The director's promise provided recognition that many of the agents who were trained by O'Neill to think out of the box would now be embraced, because their unique insights might hold innovative solutions for fighting terrorism. Many of those agents have been left to wonder, and correctly so, whether the events that took place on September 11 would have been altered if the visionary O'Neill had been allowed to return to Yemen to pursue the "dots" that were leading to bin Laden, and ultimately to the plot to destroy the Twin Towers, the Pentagon, and the Capitol.

No less a counterterrorist luminary than Mary Jo White, the Manhattan U.S. attorney whose office had prosecuted every major international terrorism case in the 1990s, addressed the true measure of O'Neill's unsung accomplishments when she received the first award given in O'Neill's name by the Respect for Law Alliance on January 17, 2002. White had not been in agreement with everything O'Neill had done. She frowned upon his so-called night job of socializing, and would have preferred that he had been less brusque.

But in accepting the award, White focused on the true measure of O'Neill's life: that he contributed more to recognizing and fighting terrorism than any one man, and that the relations he had forged laid the groundwork for the successes that have been made in the struggle against the scourge of international terrorism. "In that struggle, we are inspired and motivated by John O'Neill as the symbol of how single-minded and brave we all must be. He was a relentless and unmovable warrior and patriot. And we cannot begin to say enough or to thank him enough for all he did and the sacrifices he made, including the ultimate sacrifice."

Despite O'Neill's acknowledged vision and professional successes, there remained at least one detractor whose opinion did not soften about O'Neill, even after his death: Barbara Bodine, the former U.S. ambassador to Yemen who had clashed with O'Neill in Yemen. In October 2000, when O'Neill led the investigation into the USS *Cole* bombing in Yemen, which killed seventeen U.S. sailors, Bodine hindered his effectiveness. The ambassador went so far as to accuse him of everything from political insensitivity to lying, and ultimately took the unprecedented step of barring him from returning to Yemen to continue the hunt for Al Qaeda operatives. In the weeks after September 11, Bodine did not alter her opinion about O'Neill. The career diplomat continued to deride O'Neill's efforts in particularly unkind terms, especially considering the manner of his death. Bodine told the *New Yorker* that O'Neill "did not discover" bin Laden and that "too much" had been made of whether O'Neill was in Yemen or not. "So the idea that John or his people or the F.B.I. were somehow barred from doing their job is insulting to the U.S. government, which was working on Al Qaeda before John ever showed up. This is all my embassy did for ten months. The fact that not every single thing John O'Neill asked for was appropriate or possible does not mean that we did not support the investigation." In *Esquire* magazine, she went even further, insisting O'Neill was "dishonest" and a liar, although perhaps only to women. Whatever aspect of O'Neill inspired Bodine's intense opposition, her behavior, both in Yemen and after O'Neill's death, is something she will have to live with.

Following the Iraqi war, Bodine was called upon to serve under General Thomas Franks as part of the civil administration rebuilding that country. Her selection appeared to vindicate her position against O'Neill. But she was quickly removed from her post after J. Paul Bremer, a terrorism expert and admirer of O'Neill, was sent to take over the chaotic effort to restore order. As for the other women in O'Neill's life, those he hurt the most, each claimed that she would forgive him if she could speak to him now. Perhaps the most important person in his life, his mother, lost her other Johnny, her husband, around Christmas, 2002. She continues to drive her cab in Atlantic City, and she is working on a book about her son's childhood.

Throughout his life, O'Neill believed in the best in all of us, and brought that belief alive day after day, and hour after hour, with a passion and intensity and joie de vivre that rubbed off on others. He spent six years at the tip of the spear in the fight against international terrorism, and he tried hard to convince the Clinton administration that bin Laden would mount a massive strike on U.S. soil. Right up to the end of his life, in the collapse of Twin Towers, he insisted: "We are due . . . for something big."

Knowing that Manhattan's most famous international landmark was in the crosshairs, how could O'Neill have walked away from the FBI and left the vanguard of the only fight that mattered to him? The answer in the end has to be that O'Neill was only one man, trying to change a whole culture of law enforcement, and was finally slowed down by his own very human limitations. One committed man can unleash great evil, as bin Laden proved on September 11, and the tragedy of that day, and O'Neill's death, was the devastating reminder that one man committed to fight the good fight is never enough. O'Neill knew this better than anyone, and was a master bridge builder. He knew better than anyone where the enemies of America would take their fight, and that the only answer to that threat was banding together, reaching out to our friends in other countries, uniting to oppose these enemies of humanity.

When John O'Neill arrived at FBI headquarters as the special agent in charge of the counterterrorism section in February 1995, he instantly found himself at the helm of the capture of Ramzi Yousef, the mastermind of the first attack on the World Trade Center and then the world's most wanted criminal. When he emerged from that three-day whirl of activity, O'Neill had found his calling in the global theater, where he would bring his considerable talents, his heart, and his passion, and fulfill that boyhood dream of becoming a valued agent with the FBI.

"I know of no more noble cause than to fight for that for which one has the greatest of passion," O'Neill wrote in a letter to a friend. "And so I say, rebellions left in the hands of good men will ultimately prevail.

"And the costs and suffering of the rebels will be small indeed."

NOTES

PROLOGUE

Information was drawn from interviews with Thomas Carney, Kevin Donovan, Carson Dunbar, Valerie James, Elaine Kaufman, Jay Manning, Michael Rolince, Mark Rossini, Gary Schweikert, Bruno Selimaj, Vincent Sullivan, Keith Weston, and Mary Jo White. I also used the July 2002 *Vanity Fair* article about Elaine Kaufman, and PBS's *Frontline* interview with Fran Townsend, October 3, 2002.

1. ON THE BOARDWALK

Recollections of Atlantic City, the early life of John O'Neill and insights into his college years and his initiation into the FBI were provided by the following people: Joseph Adams, John Blaha, Jack Caravelli, Fred Dalzell, Lee DeStefano, Anna DiBattista, Kevin Duffy, Warren Flagg, Frank Formica, John Heanon, Valerie James, Jay Manning, Dorothy O'Neill, Walter Roe, Murray Rosenberg, Marc Rossini, Lewis Schiliro, Mary Lynn Stevens, Kelley Thornton, Rex Tomb, and Kenneth Walton. Articles and other materials that enhanced the descriptions and history of Atlantic City were: "History of Atlantic City," Atlantic City Online; "Atlantic City," *Time*, December 6, 1982; "Casino Gambling," *Record*, August 17, 1986; untitled extract from *Business Perspectives*, June 22, 1999; Lawrence Wright's "The Counter-Terrorist," *New Yorker*, January 2002; the American University archives; and the George Washington University archives.

2. THINKING OUT OF THE BOX

Interviews with the following people provided insight in writing about O'Neill's experiences working in his first "office of origin" in Baltimore and his young married life: George Andrew, Herbert Better, Robert Bryant, Anna DiBattista, James Duffy, Neil Gallagher, Valerie James, Patricia Kelly, Kathy Kiser, Janet Murray, Kurt Schmoke, Gary Stevens, Mary Lynn Stevens, and Wes Wong. Additional information for this chapter was obtained from the following articles: Anne Fitzhenry, "Sentencing Postponed in Wedtech Case," *Washington Post*, January 29, 1988; "Mitchell Jury Selection," *Washington Post*, October 23, 1987; Larry Rosenthal, "Maryland Brothers Guilty on Several Counts in Wedtech Case," *Associated Press*, November 6, 1987.

3. "MY KIND OF TOWN"

The detailed recollections of the following people provided information about O'Neill's years living in Chicago: George Andrew, Grant Ashley, Anna DiBattista, Valerie James, Jay Manning, Kenneth Pierneck, Mary Lynn Stevens, and Jack Townsend. The following articles provided additional information: John O'Brien's "Keeping the Robbers in Check," *Chicago Tribune*, December 5, 1991; William Recktenwald and Patrick Reardon's "Crime-rate Drop Can't Hide Danger Despite 6% Decrease; Chicago is 5th in U.S," *Chicago Tribune*, May 5, 1994.

4. IN THE NAME OF GOD

Lengthy interviews with numerous individuals provided insightful information for this chapter on John O'Neill's involvement in the abortion-clinic violence investigation. They included FBI supervisors and special agents assigned to the case at the time and others: Robert Blitzer, Robert Bryant, Anna DiBattista, Kevin Giblin, Valerie James, John Lipka, Ray Mislock, Michael Rolince, and Debby Stafford. In addition, the following articles, books, and television reports were utilized as references: Mimi Hall's

"Abortion Fight Takes Deadly Turn," *USA Today*, March 11, 1993; Bill Kazor's "U.S. Marshals Outside Abortion Clinics After Shootings," Associated Press wire report, August 1, 1994; Tamar Lewin's "Abortion-Rights Groups See a Rise in Attacks on Clinics," *New York Times*, January 14, 1993; James Risen and Judith Thomas's *Wrath of Angels: The American Abortion War*, Basic Books, 1998; "Four Years After Last Bombing, Rudolph Still Missing," Associated Press wire report, January 27, 2002; newscast, *ABC World News Tonight*, March 10, 1993; PBS's *Frontline* interview with Fran Townsend, October 3, 2002.

5. **"YOU CAN'T MAKE THIS SHIT UP"**
Information was drawn from interviews with friends, supervisors, and agents directly involved in the capture and investigation of Ramzi Yousef, the 1993 bombing of the World Trade Center, and the plot to blow up New York landmarks, bridges, and tunnels. They included: Robert Blitzer, Robert Bryant, Anna DiBattista, William Galvin, Valerie James, John Lipka, Thomas Pickard, Lewis Schiliro, and Mary Jo White. In addition, the following materials were referenced: Peter Bergen's *Holy War, Inc.: Inside the Secret World of Osama bin Laden*, The Free Press, 2000; Jim Dwyer, David Kocieniewsky, Diedre Murphy, and Peg Tyre's *Two Seconds Under the World*, Crown Publishers, 1994; Simon Reeve's *The New Jackals: Ramzi Yousef, Osama bin Laden and the Future of Terrorism*, Northeastern University Press, 1999; Greg Myre's "Bombing Suspect Had Explosive in Bag When Arrested," Associated Press wire report, February 9, 1995; Richard Bernstein's "Behind Arrest of Bomb Fugitive, Informer's Tip, Then Fast Action," *New York Times*, February 10, 1995; David B. Ottaway's "Retracing the Steps of a Terror Suspect; Accused Bomb Builder Tied to Many Plots," *Washington Post*, June 5, 1995; Robert D. McFadden's "The Trade Center Verdict: The Mastermind," *New York Times*, November 13, 1997; John Miller, Michael Stone, and Chris Mitchell's *The Cell: Inside the 9/11 Plot and Why The FBI and*

CIA Failed to Stop It, Hyperion, 2002; The People of the State of New York against El Sayyid Nosair; defendant; Lawrence Wright's "The Counter-Terrorist,"*New Yorker,* January 2002; PBS's *Frontline* interview with Richard Clarke, October 3, 2002. Court cases: *United States of America* v. *Usama bin Laden et al.,* S798 Cr. 1023; *United States of America* v. *Omar Ahmad Ali Abdel Rahman et al.,* S593 Cr. 191 (MBM); *United States of America* v. *Ramzi Ahmed Ousef, Abdul Hakim Murad, Wali Khan Amin Shah,* S1293 Cr. 180 (KTD).

6. THE BIRTH OF AL QAEDA

This chapter draws on interviews with George Andrew, Robert Blitzer, Robert Bryant, Jack Caravelli, Frank Ciluffo, Thomas Corrigan, Anna DiBattista, James Duffy, Neil Gallagher, Kevin Giblin, Jerry Hauer, Valerie James, John Lipka, Raymond Mislock, Louis Napoli, Marc Rossini, Lewis Schiliro, Maurice Sonenberg, Mary Lynn Stevens, and Mary Jo White. Additional information was obtained from the following publications: Peter Bergen's *Holy War, Inc.: Inside the Secret World of Osama Bin Laden,* The Free Press, 2000; James Brooke's "World Briefing Asia: Japan: Death Sentence for Cult Leaders," *New York Times,* June 27, 2002; *Catastrophic Terrorism: Imminent Threat, Uncertain Response.* McCormick Tribune Foundation, June 2000; John Cushman's, "Death Toll About 300 In Oct. 3 U.S- Somali Battle," *New York Times,* October 14, 1993; Jim Dwyer, David Kocieniewsky, Diedre Murphy, and Peg Tyre's *Two Seconds Under the World,* Crown Publishers, 1994; "450 Combat Soldiers Return Home From Somalia," *Associated Press,* December 19, 1993; Michael Gordon with Thomas Friedman's, "Details of the U.S. Raid in Somalia: Success So Near, A Loss So Deep," *New York Times,* October 25, 1993; Michael Gordon with John Cushman Jr.'s, "Mission in Somalia: After Supporting Hunt for Aidid, U.S. Is Blaming U.N. for Losses," *New York Times,* October 18, 1993; Gwen Ifill's "President Defends American Presence in Somali,"

New York Times, September 18, 1993; Gwen Ifill's "The Somalia Mission:" Overview; U.S. Mixes Signals To Somali General on Its Next Steps," *New York Times,* October 8, 1993; Roland Jacquard's *In The Name of Osama Bin Laden: Global Terrorism and the Bin Laden Brotherhood,* Duke University Press, 2002; Michael Ledeen's *The War Against The Terror Masters,* St. Martin's Press, September 2000; Donatella Lorch's, "Talks on Somalia Suspended by U.N.," *New York Times,* March 18, 1993; Donatella Lorch's "Somalia's Leaders Reach Agreement," *New York Times,* March 29, 1993; Donatella Lorch's "Troops Storm Somali Chief's House but He's Gone; U.N. Attack in Mogadishu Follows Hours of Bombing by U.S.," *New York Times,* June 18, 1993; Donatella Lorch's "U.N. Denies It Is Seeking Somali Clan Leader's Arrest," *New York Times,* June 19, 1993; Donatella Lorch's "After Raid, Somalis Struggle With Anger and a Weariness," *New York Times,* October 17, 1993; Emily MacFarquhar's "The Rise of Taliban: A New Force of Muslim Fighters Is Determined to Rule Afghanistan, Pakistan," *U.S. News & World Report,* March 6, 1995; Nicholas D. Kristof's "Roundup in Japan: The Overview," *New York Times,* May 17, 1995; Chitra Ragavan et al., "New Life in an Old Probe," *U.S. News & World Report,* April 2, 2001; Simon Reeve's *The New Jackals: Ramzi Yousef, Osama bin Laden and the Future of Terrorism,* Northeastern University Press, 1999; The Al Qaeda Manual; The People of the State of New York El Sayyid Nosair, defendant. 14030/90; Terrorism in the United States: Special Retrospective Edition, Department of Justice, 1999; *United States of America* v. *Ramzi Ahmed Yousef, Abdul Hakim Murad, Wali Khan Amin Shah,* S1293 Cr. 180 (KTD); *United States of America* v. *Mohammed A. Salameh, et al.,* S593 Cr. 180 (KTD); *United States of America* v. *Eyad Ismoil,* S1293 Cr. 180 (KTD); Stuart Wavell's "Secret of the Saudis," *Sunday Times of London,* October 21, 2001; *United States of America* v. *Usama bin Laden et al.,* S798 Cr. 1023; PBS's *Frontline* interview with Richard Clarke, October 3, 2002.

7. THE OBSTRUCTIONISTS

The following people were among those who contributed to his chapter: George Andrew, Anne Beagen, Robert Blitzer, Robert Bryant, Jack Caravelli, Anna DiBattista, James Duffy, Kevin Giblin, Valerie James, Thomas Pickard, Lewis Schiliro and Mary Lynn Stevens. Interviews for this chapter were conducted with key FBI personnel, including several involved in the Khobar Towers investigation: Robert Bryant, John Lewis, John Lipka, Raymond Mislock, Debby Stafford, and Michael Rolince. Other information was obtained from Peter Bergen's *Holy War, Inc.;* Douglas Jehl's "Bombing Saudi Arabia: The Overview; Saudis, Aided by the FBI, Seek Blasts Clues," *New York Times*, June 27, 1996; Steven Erlanger's "Bombing in Saudi Arabia: The Witnesses: Survivors of Saudi Explosion Knew at Once It Was a Bomb," *New York Times*, June 26, 1996; David Johnston's "Charges Near in Bombing at Saudi Base, U.S. Aides Say," *New York Times*, June 13, 2001; "The Khobar Bombing," *U.S. News & World Report*, July 23, 2002; Ahmad Mardini's "Gulf: Saudis Warned of More Attacks," Inter Press Service, November 15, 1995; Chitra Ragavan et al., "New Life in an Old Probe"; Simon Reeve's *The New Jackals: Ramzi Yousef, Osama bin Laden and the Future of Terrorism;* Siobohan Roth's "Al Khobar Towers: A Case of Futility," *American Lawyer Media*, September 20, 2001; Philip Shenon's "Saudi Truck Bomb at a U.S. Complex Kills 11, Hurts 150," *New York Times*, June 26, 1996; Philip Shenon's "23 U.S. Troops Die in Truck Bombing at Big Saudi Base," *New York Times*, June 26, 1996; Philip Shenon's "Bombing in Saudi Arabia: The Security;" *New York Times*, June 27, 1996, and "FBI Finds Clues to the Truck Use in Saudi Bombing," *New York Times*, June 30, 1996; Patrick Tyler's "The Saudi Exit: No Sure Cure for Royals' Troubles," *New York Times*, April 30, 2003; "US Troops in Saudi Arabia Target of Holy War," Agence France Presse, May 12, 1997; Afshin Valinejad's "Iran Criticizes U.S. Indictment in 1996 Khobar Bombing," Associated Press wire report, June 22,

2001, and "Iran and Saudi Arabia Rebuke U.S.; Enemy and Ally Both Angered by Charges in Barracks Bombing," *Miami Herald*, June 23, 2001; Elsa Walsh's "Louis Freeh's Last Case," *New Yorker*, May 14, 2002; Stuart Wavell's "Secret of the Saudis"; Benjamin Weiser's "Man in the News: Reputation for Tenacity, James Brien Comey," *New York Times*, December 2, 2001. Court cases: *United States of America* v. *Usama bin Laden et al.*, S798 Cr. 1023. *United States of America* v. *Ramzi Ahmed Yousef, Abdul Hakim Murad, Wali Khan Amin Shah*, S1293 Cr. 180 (KTD);

8. SILENCING THE CRITICS

The following people were among those who assisted in recreating the events in this chapter: George Andrew, Joseph Billy, Thomas Corrigan, Kenneth Maxwell, Anna DiBattista, Sal Emilio, Kevin Giblin, Neil Herman, Valerie James, James Kallstrom, Thomas Pickard, Michael Rolince, Lewis Schiliro, and Mary Lynn Stevens. Materials from the following sources were also used: Dan Barry's "FBI Questions Salinger on Crash Claim," *New York Times*. November 10, 1996; Peter Bergen's *Holy War, Inc.: Inside the Secret World of Osama bin Laden*; CIA simulation video of TWA 800 disaster. Dennis Duggan's "Kallstrom's Maelstrom," *Newsday*, July 17, 1997; The Hotline's "TWA 800 Conspiracy? Salinger Sees a Catcher in the Lie," *American Political Network, Inc.*, November 8, 1996; N. R. Kleinfield's "The Crash of Flight 800; The Overview: TWA Jetliner Leaving New York for Paris Crashes in Atlantic," *New York Times*, July 18, 1996; Barry Meier's "The Fate of Flight 800: The Airline," *New York Times*. July 23, 1996; Blanca Monica Quintanila and Robert Kessler's "An Apology to Navy/TWA Missile Theory Loses an Advocate," *Newsday*, November 6, 1997; Simon Reeve's *The New Jackals: Ramzi Yousef, Osama bin Laden and the Future of Terrorism*; Reuters's "TWA 800 Shot by U.S. Missile, Salinger Claims," *Palm Beach Post*, November 8, 1996; James Rutenberg and Hester Jere's "A Chunk of Hope Found," *New York Daily News*, July 29,

1996; Roberto Suro's "Crime All But Ruled Out in TWA Crash; FBI Details Exhaustive Probe; Focus Now on Mechanical Failure," *Washington Post*, November 19, 1997; Don Van Natta and Matthew Purdy's "Salinger the Crash Theorist Raises More Eyebrows Than New Questions," *New York Times*, November 17, 1996. Court cases: *United States of America v Usama bin Laden et al.*, S798 Cr. 1023.

9. O'NEILL TAKES MANHATTAN

Interviews for this chapter were conducted with: Louis Anemone, Joseph Billy, John Blaha, Mark Chidichimo, Joseph Cantemessa, Thomas Corrigan, Anna DiBattista, Lorraine Di Taranto, Carson Dunbar, Thomas Durkin, Jerry Hauer, Neil Herman, Valerie James, James Kallstrom, Jay Manning, Kenneth Maxwell, Lewis Schiliro, Gary Stevens, and Mary Jo White. Articles consulted include: Frank Bruni's "Rampage at the Empire State Building: The Scene," *New York Times*, February 24, 1997; The Hotline's "TWA 800 Conspiracy? Salinger Sees a Catcher in the Lie," *American Political Network, Inc.*, November 8, 1996; N. R. Kleinfield's "Rampage at the Empire State Building: The Suspect," *New York Times*, February 25, 1997; Clifford Krause's "Rampage at the Empire State Building: The Weapon," *New York Times*, February 25, 1997; Robert D. McFadden's "Rampage at the Empire State Building: Overview," *New York Times*, February 24, 1997; Dan Morrison's "Chemical Chills/Sarin Scare Was False Alarm," *New York Newsday*, March 31, 1997; Matthew Purdy's "Rampage at the Empire State Building: Overview," *New York Times*, February 27, 1997; Blanca Monica Quintanila and Robert Kessler's "An Apology to Navy/TWA Missile Theory Loses an Advocate," *Newsday*, November 6, 1997; Reuters's "TWA 800 Shot by U.S. Missile, Salinger Claims," *Palm Beach Post*, November 8, 1996; Roberto Suro's "Crime All But Ruled Out in TWA Crash; FBI Details Exhaustive Probe; Focus Now on Mechanical Failure," *Washington*

Post, November 19, 1997. Murray Weiss's "1,100 Phone Lines Tapped Daily: Feds," *New York Post,* January 15, 1997.

10. THE MAN WHO KNEW

Interviews with key figures directly involved in the events discussed in this chapter included: Louis Anemone, Anne Beagen, Joseph Billy, Robert Blitzer, Jack Caravelli, Frank Ciluffo, Thomas Corrigan, Anna DiBattista, Kevin Donovan, Carson Dunbar, Joseph Dunne, Richard Friedman, Jerry Hauer, Valerie James, James Kallstrom, Louis Napoli, Kenneth Pierneck, Lewis Schiliro, and Mary Jo White. Additional materials for this chapter were obtained from the following sources: Sylvia Adcock's "TWA 800, The Final Report," *New York Newsday,* August 22, 2000, and "TWA 800, The Final Report, Tragedy's Lessons," *New York Newsday,* August 20, 2000; Devlin Barrett's "I Came to the U.S. to Kill Jews," *New York Post,* July 21, 1998, "Convicted Terror Thug Goes Berserk," *New York Post,* July 24, 1998, and "Terror Suspect Nailed for Fraud," *New York Post,* December 4, 1998; Peter Bergen's *Holy War, Inc.: Inside the Secret World of Osama bin Laden;* Daniel Benjamin and Steven Simon's *The Age of Sacred Terror,* Random House, 2002; Bill Hoffmann's 'Life for Subway Terrorist out to Burn the Jews," *New York Post,* March 2, 1999; John Miller, Michael Stone, and Chris Mitchell's *The Cell: Inside the 9/11 Plot and Why the FBI and CIA Failed to Stop It,* Hyperion, 2002; Simon Reeve's *The New Jackals: Ramzi Yousef, Osama bin Laden and the Future of Terrorism.* CIA simulation video of TWA 800 disaster; National Strategy Forum, speech by John P. O'Neill, chief of international terrorism, operations, FBI, delivered June 11, 1997, at the Chicago Athletic Association; *Patterns of Global Terrorism,* published by the U.S. Department of Justice, Office of the Coordinator for Counterterrorism, April 1996; The Al Qaeda Manual. Court cases: *United States of America* v. *Usama bin Laden et al.,* S798 Cr. 1023; *United States of America* v. *Omar Ahmad Ali Abdel*

Rahman et al., S593 Cr. 191 (MBM); *United States of America* v. *Ramzi Ahmed Ousef, Abdul Hakim Murad, Wali Khan Amin Shah,* S1293 Cr 180 (KTD).

II. "THEY CAN STRIKE ANYTIME"

The following people were among those who provided central information to this chapter: Joseph Billy, Jack Caravelli, Kevin Donovan, Sheila Horan, James Kallstrom, David Kelley, Patricia Kelly, Kenneth Maxwell, Raymond Mislock, Louis Napoli, Thomas Pickard, Kenneth Pierneck, Pat Pogan, Michael Rolince, Lewis Schiliro, Keith Weston, and Mary Jo White. Additional materials were obtained from the following sources: Peter Baker and John F. Harris's "Clinton Admits to Lewinsky Relationship, Challenges Starr to End Personal 'Prying,'" *Washington Post*, August 18, 1998; Dan Balz and John Harris's "Clinton More Forcefully Denies Having Had Affair or Urging Lies," *Washington Post*, January 27, 1998; Daniel Benjamin and Steven Simon's *The Age of Sacred Terror*, Random House, 2002; James Bennet and Don Van Natta Jr.'s "Lewinsky Said to Detail Clinton Affair," *New York Times*, August 7, 1998; James Bennet's "Testing of a President: The President; Appeals to Democrats with Pleas for Their Forgiveness," *New York Times*, September 10, 1998, "Testing of a President: The Overview," *New York Times*, August 8, 1998, and "U.S. Fury on Two Continents: U.S. Cruise Missiles Strike Sudan and Afghan Targets Tied to Terrorist Network," *New York Times*, August 21, 1998; David Broder's "Composed in the Center of the Storm," *Washington Post*, January 28, 1998; Pamela Constable's "Terrorist Leader 'Safe,' Afghan Hosts Declare," *Washington Post*, August 21, 1998; Alan Feuer's "Bombing Suspect Is Said to Admit He Felt 'Duty to Kill Americans'" *New York Times*, March 20, 2001; Barton Gellman and Dana Priest's "US Strikes Terrorist-Linked Sites in Afghanistan, Factory in Sudan," *Washington Post*, August 21, 1998; The Hotline's "TWA 800 Conspiracy? Salinger Sees a Catcher in the Lie,"

American Political Network, Inc., November 8, 1996; Roland Jacquard's *In the Name of Osama bin Laden: Global Terrorism and the bin Laden Brotherhood*, Duke University Press, 2002; Michael Ledeen's *The War Against the Terror Masters*, St. Martin's Press, September 2000; Vernon Loeg's "U.S. Wasn't Sure Plant Had Nerve Gas Role; Before Sudan Strike, CIA Urged More Tests," *Washington Post*, August 21, 1999; Robert D. McFadden's "Bombings in East Africa: The American Dead," *New York Times*, August 10, 1998; James McKinley Jr.'s "Bombings in East Africa: The Overview," *New York Times*, August 9, 1998; Donald McNeil Jr.'s "The Terror Verdict: The Reverberations," *New York Times*, May 31, 2001; Steven Lee Myers's "After the Attacks: The Overview; U.S. Offers More Details on Attack in the Sudan," *New York Times*, August 24, 1998; Deborah Orin and Vince Morris's "Missiles Hammer Terrorist Targets—U.S. Clobbers Sites in Sudan and Afghanistan," *New York Post*, August 21, 1998; Deborah Orin's "Furor over 'Nerve Gas'; Reporters in Sudan Saw Only Drugs," *New York Post*, August 25, 1998; Blanca Monica Quintanila and Robert Kessler's "An Apology to Navy/TWA Missile Theory Loses an Advocate," *Newsday*, November 6, 1997; Marilyn Rauber and Brian Bloomquist's "Prez Makes Sorry Statement: Blast from Party Bigs Forces Sexgate Apology," *New York Post*, September 5, 1998; Reuters' "TWA 800 Shot by U.S. Missile, Salinger Claims," *Palm Beach Post*, November 8, 1996; Simon Reeve's *The New Jackals: Ramzi Yousef, Osama bin Laden and the Future of Terrorism*; Benjamin Weiser's "Going on Trial: U.S. Accusation of a Global Plot: In Embassy Bombings Case, the Specter of a Mastermind," *New York Times*, February 4, 2001; Roberto Suro's "Crime All But Ruled Out in TWA Crash; FBI Details Exhaustive Probe; Focus Now on Mechanical Failure," *Washington Post*, November 19, 1997; Benjamin Weiser's "Man Charged in Bombing of U.S. Embassy in Africa," *New York Times*, October 9, 1999, and "U.S. Faces Tough Challenges to Statements in Terrorism Case," *New York Times*, January 25, 2001;

Court cases: PBS's *Frontline* interview with Fran Townsend, October 3, 2002; *United States of America* v. *Usama bin Laden et al.*, S798 Cr. 1023.

12. SO NICE THEY NAMED IT TWICE

Interviews with the following people provided pivotal insights: Louis Anemone, Anne Beagen, Joseph Connor, Thomas Connor, Thomas Corrigan, Anna DiBattista, Thomas Donlan, Joseph Dunne, Neil Gallagher, Jerry Hauer, Valerie James, Elaine Kaufman, Patricia Kelley, John Lewis, Thomas Pickard, Kenneth Pierneck, Patrick Pogan, Bruno Selimaj, Lewis Schiliro, Mary Lynn Stevens, and Keith Weston. Additional information was obtained from the following sources: Kenneth Bazinet's "No FALN Apology Who Accepted Clemency Talks, Seeks Understanding," *Daily News*, September 13, 1999; Peter Bergen's *Holy War, Inc.: Inside the Secret World of Osama bin Laden*; David Briscoe's "State Department Warns Americans on Bombing Anniversary," Associated Press wire report, August 5, 1999; James Gerstenzang's "In Helping Gore, Clinton Seeks to Cement Legacy," *Los Angeles Times*, August 8, 1999; David Johnston's "Federal Agencies Opposed Leniency for 16 Militants," *New York Times*, August 27, 1999; Neil MacFarquhar's "Clemency Opens Old Scars for Sons of Bombing Victim," *New York Times*, August 23, 1999; John Miller, Michael Stone, and Chris Mitchell's *The Cell: Inside the 9/11 Plot and Why the FBI and CIA Failed to Stop It*; Simon Reeve's *The New Jackals: Ramzi Yousef, Osama bin Laden and the Future of Terrorism*; Katherine Seelye's "Clinton to Commute Radicals' Sentences," *New York Times*, August 12, 1999; Paul Shepard's "On the Anniversary of U.S. Embassy Attacks, Albright Vows Bombers Will Pay," Associated Press wire report, August 7, 1999; Edward Walsh's "NTSB Report Faults Co-Pilot in EgyptAir Crash; Study Does Not Offer Conclusion on Why Man Flew Plane into Atlantic in 1999," *Washington Post*, March 22, 2002; PBS's *Frontline* interview with Richard Clarke, October 3, 2002; Thomas Connor, testimony before Congress, September 21, 1999.

13. THE VOICE OF GOD

The following people contributed information to this chapter: Giovanni Adamo, Joseph Dunne, Sal Emilio, Jerry Hauer, Alan Hoehl, Valerie James, James Kallstrom, Elaine Kaufman, David Kelley, Isabelle Kirshner, Kenneth Maxwell, John Miller, Raymond Powers, James Roth, Lewis Schilio, Keith Weston, and Mary Jo White. Additional information was obtained from the following sources: Paul L. Bremer's "Dealing Fairly With Terrorism," *Boston Globe*, June 22, 2000; Adam Buckman's "Got the World on a String; Millennium Coverage Is What TV Does Best," *New York Post*, December 27, 1999; Bob Drogin's "Anti-Terrorism Panel Finds U.S. Tactics Fall Short," *Los Angeles Times*, June 4, 2000; Erik Eckholm's "Pakistanis Arrest Al Qaeda Figure Seen as Planner of 9/11," *New York Times*, March 2, 2003; David Halbfinger's "A Peaceful Party: In the City's Bunker, Much Ado About Not Much as the Celebrations Proceed," *New York Times*, January 1, 2000; David Johnston's "Major Catch, Critical Time," *New York Times*, March 2, 2003; Eric Lichtbau's "U.S. Indicts 2 Men for Attack on American Ship in Yemen," *New York Times*, May 16, 2003; Vernon Loeb's "U.S. Is Urged to Preempt Terrorists; Panel Proposes Unfettering CIA, Tracking Students," *New York Times*, June 4, 2000; John Marzulli's "Secret Plan to Safeguard City NYPD Would Mobilize, Seal Site of an Attack," *New York Daily News*, December 30, 1999; "Man Jailed on Arrival with 200 Pounds of Mysterious Powder, Timers," Associated Press wire report, December 16, 1999; PBS's *Frontline* interview with Fran Townsend, October 3, 2002.

14. THE BRIEFCASE INCIDENT

Insights and recollections for this chapter were obtained from George Andrew, Anne Beagen, Neil Gallagher, Valerie James, Isabelle Kirshner, John Lewis, Barry Mawn, Thomas Pickard, Michael Rolince, Marc Rossini, Lewis Schiliro, Joseph Valiquette, and Mary Jo White. The following are some of the additional materials used in this chapter: Peter Bergen's *Holy War, Inc.: Inside the Secret World of Osama bin Laden;* Josh Meyer's "Broder Arrest Stirs Fear of Terrorist Cells in U.S.," *Los Angeles Times,* March 11, 2001; John Goldman's "Response to Terror," *Los Angeles Times,* January 17, 2002; Simon Reeve's *The New Jackals: Ramzi Yousef, Osama bin Laden and the Future of Terrorism;* "Tragedy Averted; Accused Millennium Bomber Had No Problem Getting Passport, Jury Told," *Edmonton Sun,* March 14, 2001; PBS's *Frontline* interview with Fran Townsend, October 3, 2002; James Risen's "Terrorism Panel Faults U.S. Effort on Iran and 1996 Bombing," *New York Times,* June 4, 2000; James Risen's "Tied to Many Plots, An Elusive Figure Who Came to U.S. Attention Late," *New York Times,* March 2, 2003.

15. THE TIP OF THE SPEAR

The following people provided recollections for this chapter: Stephen Corbett, Thomas Donlan, Kevin Donovan, Mike Dorsey, Gary Fitzgerald, Valerie James, David Kelley, Patricia Kelly, Barry Mawn, Robert McFadden, Patrick Pogan, Michael Rolince, Joseph Valiquette, Kenneth Walton, and Mary Jo White. The following are some of the source materials used for this chapter: Barbara K. Bodine, ambassador to Yemen, biography, U.S. State Department; John F. Burns and Steven Lee Myers's "The Warship Explosion: Blast Kills Sailors on U.S. Ship in Yemen," *New York Times,* October 13, 2000; John Burns's "Tolls Rises to 17 in Ship Blast, as U.S. Hunts Suspects," *New York Times,* October 14, 2000; Eric Eckholm's "Pakistanis Arrest Qaeda Figure Seen as Planner of 9/11," *New York Times,* March 2, 2003; Michael Gordon's "The Warship Explosion: Military Analysis," *New York Times,* October 14, 2000; David Johnston's "Major Catch, Critical Time," *New York Times,* March 2, 2003; Eric Lichtbau's "U.S. Indicts 2 Men for Attack on American Ship in Yemen," *New York Times,* May 16, 2003; John Miller, Michael Stone, and Chris Mitchell's *The Cell: Inside the 9/11 Plot and Why the FBI and CIA*

Failed to Stop It; Steven Lee Myers's "Whose Holy Land? U.S Officials Tell of Getting Warning Last Month, but Say It Was Too Vague," *New York Times,* October 14, 2000; "Yemeni President Calls USS *Cole* Attack 'Very Well-Planned,'" CNN.com, October 18, 2000; PBS's *Frontline* interviews with Fran Townsend and Richard Clarke, October 3, 2002; James Risen's "Tied to Many Plots, An Elusive Figure Who Came to U.S. Attention Late," *New York Times,* March 2, 2003; "Statement by the President on Middle East Situation and USS *Cole,*" the Rose Garden, U.S. Navy, October 12, 2000.

16. FACE-TO-FACE WITH THE ENEMY

The following is a partial list of people who contributed to this chapter: Stephen Corbett, Thomas Donlan, Kevin Donovan, Michael Dorsey, Joseph Dunne, Thomas Durkin, Gary Fitzgerald, Gregory Fried, Mary Galligan, Jerry Hauer, Valerie James, David Kelley, John Klochan, Jay Manning, Barry Mawn, Kenneth Maxwell, Robert McFadden, Pat Patterson, Michael Rolince, and Joseph Valiquette. Other information for this chapter was obtained from: Peter Bergen's *Holy War, Inc.: Inside the Secret World of Osama Bin Laden,* The Free Press, 2000; John Burns's "Yemeni and U.S. Teams Focus on Boat Used to Attack *Cole,*" *New York Times,* October 22, 2000, "Investigators Discouraging Speculation in *Cole* Attack," *New York Times,* October 23, 2000, and "No Special Alert for *Cole* Before Bombing, *New York Times,* October 25, 2000; Diana Elias's "Video Suggests Bin Laden Men Perpetrated *Cole* Bombing," *Washington Post,* June 20, 2001; Erik Eckholm's "Pakistanis Arrest Qaeda Figure Seen as Planner of 9/11," *New York Times,* March 2, 2003; Gillian Flynn's "Weddings," *Entertainment Weekly,* December 15, 2000; David Johnston's "Major Catch, Critical Time," *New York Times,* March 2, 2003; Eric Lichtbau's "U.S. Indicts 2 Men for Attack on American Ship in Yemen," *New York Times,* May 16, 2003; John Miller, Michael Stone, and Chris Mitchell's *The Cell: Inside the 9/11 Plot and Why*

The FBI and CIA Failed to Stop It, Hyperion, 2002; Steven Lee
Myers's "Failed Plan to Bomb a U.S. Ship Is Reported," *New York
Times,* November 10, 2000; Simon Reeve's *The New Jackals:
Ramzi Yousef, Osama Bin Laden and the Future of Terrorism,* North-
eastern University Press, 1999; James Risen's "Tied to Many
Plots, an Elusive Figure Who Came to U.S. Attention Late," *New
York Times,* March 2, 2003; Patrick Tyler's "Yemen, an Uneasy
Ally, Proves Adept at Playing Off Old Rivals," *New York Times,*
December 19, 2002; Benjamin Weiser's "Bin Laden Linked to
Embassy Blast by an Ex-Soldier," *New York Times,* October 21,
2000; "Remarks of the President," Cole Memorial Service,
United States Navy, October 18, 2000; "U.S. Envoy Escapes
Yemen Hijack," CNN.com, January 23, 2001; "Hijack of Yemen
Jet Foiled; Passengers Safe," AirDisaster.com, January 24, 2001;
"US Diplomat Safe After Yemen Hijack," BBC News, January 23,
2001; "Yemeni Plane Carrying U.S. Ambassador Hijacked," Asso-
ciated Press, January 24, 2001; "Hot Stuff Galore at Tommy
Wedding," *New York Post,* December 5, 2000; "Correction: Gos-
sip," *New York Daily News,* February 22, 2002.

17. FORCED OUT

The following people were among those who provided insight
and information for this chapter: Grant Ashley, Frank Ciluffo,
Anna DiBattista, Lorraine Di Taranto, Kevin Donovan, Neil Gal-
lagher, Mary Galligan, Jerry Hauer, Alan Hoehl, Valerie James,
James Kallstrom, Elaine Kaufman, Barry Mawn, Kenneth
Maxwell, Robert McFadden, Thomas Pickard, Marc Rossini,
Joseph Valiquette, Jeff Wharton, and Mary Jo White. The follow-
ing are some of the materials used for information in this chapter:
"Atta Stayed at Hotel Near Flight School in Madrid," Associated
Press wire report, March 3, 2002; Walter Berns's *Making Patriots,*
University of Chicago Press, 2001; Massimo Calabresi's "Missing
Link," *Time,* July 10, 2001; David Cloud and Neil King Jr.'s "U.S.
Faces Hurdles in Approach to USS *Cole* Probe," *Wall Street Jour-*

nal, July 6, 2001; Dale Eisman's "Case Marches Toward Justice," *Virginian-Pilot,* April 22, 2002; Douglas Frantz's "Search for Sept. 11 Suspect Focuses on Visit to Spain," *New York Times,* May 1, 2002; Douglas Frantz, Don Van Natta Jr., David Johnston, and Richard Bernstein's "Inside the Hijacking Plot," *New York Times,* September 10, 2002; James Graff's "Bust in Madrid," *Time,* December 3, 2001; "Hijackers Met in Spain, Report Says Meeting Took Place Weeks Before September 11," Associated Press wire report, July 1, 2002; David Johnston and James Risen's "FBI Is Investigating a Senior Counterterrorism Agent," *New York Times,* August 19, 2001; Ron Kampeas's "FBI's Global Role Causes Culture Clashes," Associated Press, August 12, 2001; John Miller, Michael Stone, and Chris Mitchell's *The Cell: Inside the 9/11 Plot and Why the FBI and CIA Failed to Stop It;* Walter Pincus and Vernon Loeb's "Bin Laden Called Top Terrorist Threat: 'Global Network' Active, Tenet Says," *Washington Post,* February 8, 2001; Sebastian Rotella's "Suspected Hijacker Tied to Madrid Cell," *Los Angeles Times,* November 23, 2001; "Sept. 11 Hijackers Plotted Attack in Spain," Agence France Presse, June 30, 2002; "Spain–Al Qaeda Probe Details Sept. 11 Plotters' Spanish Connection," *Financial Times* Information, June 30, 2002; "War Chant—Bin Laden Urges 'Blood, Blood and Destruction,'" *New York Post,* June 20, 2001; PBS's *Frontline* interviews with Fran Townsend and Richard Clarke, October 3, 2002; "A Letter to Lou Gunn," *Frontline,* PBS, October 3, 2002.

18. SEPTEMBER 11, 2001

The following people were among those who contributed information to this chapter: Giovanni Adamo, Diane Becker, Robert Bryant, Charles Campisi, John Cantwell, Jack Caravelli, Mark Chidichimo, Christopher Cincotta, Stephen Corbett, Anna DiBattista, Richard Dienst, Thomas Donlan, Joseph Dunne, Michael Fabozzi, Neil Gallagher, Kevin Giblin, Jerry Hauer, Valerie James, James Kallstrom, Elaine Kaufman, David Kelley,

Patricia Kelly, Kathy Kiser, Rodney Leibowitz, Jay Manning, Barry Mawn, Robert McFadden, Louis Napoli, Dorothy O'Neill, J. P. O'Neill Jr., Kenneth Pierneck, Raymond Powers, Gary Schweikert, Lawrence Silverstein, Gary Stevens, Mary Lynn Stevens, Robert Tucker, Robert Von Etten, Jeff Wharton, Eugene White, Mary Jo Whyte, and Wes Wong. The following sources were among those used for this chapter: Douglas Frantz and Desmond Butler's "Germans Lays Out Early Qaeda Ties to 9/11 Hijackers," *New York Times*, August 24, 2002; Douglas Frantz, Don Van Natta Jr., David Johnston, and Richard Bernstein's "Inside the Hijacking Plot," *New York Times*, September 10, 2002; Robert Kolker's "O'Neill Versus Osama," *New York* magazine, December 17, 2001; Graham Rayman's "Agent's Death Sparks Emotions in Case," *New York Newsday*, October 11, 2001; John Miller, Michael Stone and Chris Mitchell's *The Cell: Inside the 9/11 Plot and Why The FBI and CIA Failed to Stop It*, Hyperion, 2002. Simon Reeve's *The New Jackals: Ramzi Yousef, Osama Bin Laden and the Future of Terrorism*, Northeastern University Press, 1999; James Risen and David Johnston's "FBI Account Outlines Activities of Hijackers Before 9/11 Attack," *New York Times*, September 27, 2002; The Al Qaeda Manual; Peter Sampson's "True American Hero Laid to Rest; FBI Agent Died at WTC Helping People Escape," *Bergen Record*, September 30, 2001; Patrick E. Tyler's "Yemen, an Uneasy Ally, Proves Adept at Playing Off Old Rivals," *New York Times*, December 19, 2002; Lawrence Wright's "The Counter-Terrorist," *New Yorker*, January 14, 2002.

EPILOGUE

The following are some of the materials used in this chapter: Jean-Louis Brugiere's "Homage to our FBI 'Colleague'," *Le Figaro*, September 19, 2001; Martin DeAngelis's "A Local Boy, a Tragic End, a Hero's Funeral," *Press of Atlantic City*, September 28, 2001; Andy Geller's "Mob Destroys Saddam Statues: Looting in Streets of Baghdad," *New York Post*, April 10, 2003; Andy Geller and Brian Blomquist's "Osama Behind Lethal Blasts—Bushy, Saudis Vow Justice as bombing Toll Hits 30," *New York Post*, May 14, 2003; Frederick Halia's "Lest We Forget: Anti-Terrorist Expert John O'Neill," *Brooklyn Record*, September 28, 2001; David Johnston's "Threats and Responses: Intelligence Gathering, CIA Director Will Lead Center to Combine Agencies' Information on Terror Danger," *New York Times*, January 29, 2003; Niles Lathem and Andy Soltis's "Qaeda Car Bombers Kill Yanks in Riyadh," *New York Post*, May 13, 2002; Neil Lewis's "After Sept. 11, A Little-Known Court Has a Greater Role," *New York Times*, May 3, 2002; Eric Lichtblau's "FBI, Under Outside Pressure, Gets Internal Push," *New York Times*, December 2, 2002; Neil MacFarquhar's "Saudis Are Shaken as Jihad Erupts at Their Front Door," *New York Times*, May 16, 2003; Peter McAleer's "His Influence . . . Will Be Enormous," *Press of Atlantic City*, September 28, 2001; Robin Pogrebin's "John O'Neill Is Dead at 49; Trade Center Security Chief," *New York Times*, September 23, 2001; Dana Priest's "CIA Is Expanding Domestic Operations: More Offices, More Agents with FBI," *Washington Post*, October 23, 2002; David Rosenbaum's "Threat and Responses: The Advisors," *New York Times*, September 11, 2002; Eric Schmitt's "U.S. to Withdraw All Combat Units From Saudi Arabia," *New York Times*, April 30, 2003; Richard Stevenson's "Threats and Responses: The President: Signing Homeland Security Bill, Bush Appoints Ridge as Secretary," *New York Times*, November 26, 2002; "The Blame Game," Editorial Desk, *New York Times*, May 17, 2002; Patrick Tyler's "Yemen, an Uneasy Ally, Proves Adept at Playing Off Old Rivals," *New York Times*, December 19, 2002; Patrick Tyler's "The Saudi Exit: No Sure Cure for Royals' Troubles," *New York Times*, April 30, 2003; Patrick Tyler's "A Nation Challenged: The Attack," *New York Times*, August 8, 2001; "At Least 183 Dead in Bali Bombings," CNN.com, October 13, 2002; PBS's *Frontline* interview with Fran Townsend, October 3, 2002; speech given by Mary Jo White, Respect for Law Alliance, John O'Neill Pillar of Justice Award, January 17, 2002; story by Pat Milton in the Marine Corps Law Enforcement Foundation magazine, December 2001.

LIST OF
INTERVIEWEES

Joseph Adams, guidance counselor, Holy Spirit High School, Atlantic City, New Jersey

Giovanni Adamo, maître d', Elaine's

George Andrews, FBI head of counterintelligence, New York City, retired

Louis Anemone, NYPD chief of department, retired

Grant Ashley, FBI deputy director, criminal investigative division, FBI headquarters

Anne Beagen, FBI special agent, New York City

Diane Becker, co-manager, Elaine's

Tim Bereznay, FBI deputy assistant director for the counterintelligence division

Roy Bernard, owner, Kennedy's restaurant

Herbert Better, former assistant U.S. attorney, Baltimore, Maryland

Joseph Billy, FBI special agent in charge, counterterrorism New York City

John Blaha, supervisory special agent FBI National Academy training, retired

Robert Blitzer, FBI assistant deputy director, counterterrorism, retired

Robert Bryant, FBI deputy director, Washington, D.C., retired

Gregory Bujack, State Department worldwide diplomatic security chief, retired

Charles Campisi, NYPD chief of internal affairs

John Cantwell, NYPD detective

Jack Caravelli, National Security Council director; CIA expert Russian affairs and weapons of mass destruction; Department of Energy director of international nuclear material and protection and cooperation

Thomas Carney, bartender, Elaine's restaurant

Dr. Marvin Cetron, author and president of Forecasting International Ltd.

Frank Ciluffo, Homeland Security Administration, and formerly of the Center for Strategic and International Studies, retired

Christopher Cincotta, NYPD detective sergeant, retired

Joseph Connor, New York banker

Thomas Connor, New York banker

Joseph Cantemessa, FBI special agent in charge of operations, New York City, retired

Stephen Corbett, Department of Defense Counterintelligence Program Manager for Force Protection Detachments, Naval Criminal Investigative Service

Thomas Corrigan, FBI-NYPD joint terrorist task force, NYPD detective, retired

John Crimmins, special agent, Naval Criminal Investigative Service, retired

Fred Dalzell, orthopedic surgeon, Atlantic City

Anna DiBattista, director of national sales for corporate travel for the Windham Hotel and Resorts, New York City

Richard Dienst, attorney, New York City

Martin Dillon, author

Lorraine Di Taranto, FBI support staff, New York City

Robert Devine, New York businessman

Thomas Donlan, FBI assistant special agent in charge, domestic terrorism, New York City

Kevin Donovan, FBI Assistant Director in Charge, New York City

Michael Dorsey, deputy assistant director, Multiple Threat Alert Center, Naval Criminal Investigative Service

James Duffy, FBI supervisory agent, retired

Kevin Duffy, manager, Elaine's restaurant

Carson Dunbar, FBI special agent in charge, administration, New York City

Joseph Dunne, NYPD first deputy commissioner, retired

Thomas Durkin, former counsel to the archbishop of New York

Abdel Emam, owner, Atlantic City Cab Company

Sal Emilio, Alcohol, Tobacco and Firearms Bureau special agent; joint terrorism task force

Richard Esposito, newsman

Michael Fabozzi, detective, NYPD

Gary Fitzgerald, FBI-NYPD joint terrorist task force, detective, retired

Warren Flagg, FBI special agent, retired

Frank Formica, businessman, Atlantic City, New Jersey

Gregory Fried, surgeon, NYPD

Richard Friedman, president, National Strategy Forum

Neil Gallagher, FBI deputy director for national security, FBI headquarters

William Galvin, FBI assistant director in charge, New York City, retired

Jerome Hauer, assistant secretary, Office of Emergency Public Health Preparedness, Department of Human Services; director of the mayor's Office of Emergency Management, New York City, retired

John Heanon, sergeant, Atlantic City Police Department

Alan Hoehl, NYPD chief, retired

Sheila Horan, FBI supervisory agent, counterterrorism, Kenya, Africa

Valerie James, vice president of sales and marketing for Sunny Choi

James Kallstrom, FBI assistant director in charge, New York City, retired

Elaine Kaufman, restaurateur, Elaine's

David Kelley, assistant United States attorney, Southern District, New York City, chief of counterterrorism and organized crime

Patricia Kelly, State Department special agent in charge of diplomatic security services

Raymond Kelly, NYPD police commissioner; U.S. Customs commissioner, retired

Bernard Kerik, Deputy Minister U.S.–Iraq: Civilian Administration; former NYPD commissioner

Isabelle Kirshner, former Manhattan assistant district attorney

Kathy Kiser, FBI special agent, retired

John Klochan, FBI assistant special agent in charge, National Security Division, New York City

Ted Lebb, New York Cops Foundation

Rodney Leibowitz, dentist, NYPD

John Lewis, FBI deputy director for national security, FBI headquarters, retired

John Lipka, FBI special agent in charge, Denver, Colorado, and former counterterrorism supervisor

Jay Manning, FBI assistant special agent in charge of foreign counterintelligence, New York City

James Margolin, FBI special agent, New York City

Robert Martin, NYPD commander, special investigations division, retired

Kenneth Maxwell, FBI assistant special agent in charge, counterterrorism, New York City, retired

Barry Mawn, FBI assistant director in charge, New York City, retired

Robert McFadden, Division Chief, Counterterrorism Department, Naval Criminal Investigative Service

Philip Messing, reporter, *New York Post*

John Miller, Los Angeles PD homeland security; former ABC-TV correspondent

Raymond Mislock Jr., National Security Council director, retired; CIA director for worldwide security, retired; FBI special agent in charge of counterterrorism, Washington, D.C., retired

Lisa Monaco, attorney general's office, Department of Justice

Janet Murray, a friend of O'Neill from Baltimore

Louis Napoli, detective, FBI-NYPD joint terrorist task force

Pat Patterson, FBI assistant director of training, Virginia, Quantico

Thomas Pickard, FBI deputy director, retired

Kenneth Pierneck, senior director of intelligence, homeland security; FBI program manager for counterterrorism and counterintelligence

Patrick Pogan, detective, FBI-NYPD joint terrorist task force, retired

Raymond Power, director of security, Rockefeller Center; former NYPD chief of operations

Michael Rolince, FBI special agent in charge of counterterrorism, Washington field office

Murray Rosenberg, owner of the Yellow Cab Company, Atlantic City, New Jersey

Mark Rossini, FBI supervisory agent detailed to the CIA counterterrorism center Alexandria, Virginia

James Roth, FBI legal counsel, New York, retired

Lewis Schiliro, FBI assistant director in charge, New York City, retired

Kurt Schmoke, mayor of Baltimore, retired; assistant U.S. attorney, Baltimore, retired

Gary Schweikert, vice-president and managing director, Plaza Hotel

Bruno Selimaj, owner, Bruno restaurant

Anthony Senft, NYPD detective

Lawrence Silverstein, CEO, Silverstein Properties

Maurice Sonnenberg, president, Foreign Intelligence Advisory Board; vice-chairman, National Commission on Terrorism

Debby Stafford, FBI acting supervisory special agent of the terrorism task force, Kansas City, Missouri; Osama bin Laden unit chief, headquarters; supervisory special agent, Khobar Towers, Saudi Arabia

Mary Lynn Stevens, vice-president for external relations for a large military credit union

Vincent Sullivan, FBI counterterrorism behavior assessment, New York City

Rex Tomb, FBI unit chief, public affairs, headquarters

Richard Torykian, Lazard Frères director, cofounder Marine Corp–Law Enforcement Foundation

Robert Tucker, special assistant Queens district attorney, retired

Joseph Valiquette, FBI supervisory special agent, New York City

Robert Von Etten, Port Authority director of security, World Trade Center, retired

Kenneth P. Walton, deputy assistant director of the FBI criminal investigative division; deputy assistant director in charge of the FBI, New York City, retired

Keith Weston, detective chief superintendent, Scotland Yard, London, England

Jeffrey Wharton, president, Silverstein Properties, World Trade Center, retired

Mary Jo White, United States attorney, Southern District, New York City, retired

Eugene Whyte, lieutenant, NYPD office of deputy commissioner for operations

Philip Wilcox, State Department, coordinator for international counterterrorism, retired

Wesley Wong, FBI programs manager, New York City

TIMELINE

JUNE 1970: O'Neill joins the FBI as a clerk and tour guide.

JANUARY 23, 1971: O'Neill marries his high-school sweetheart, Christine Shutz, in Linwood, New Jersey.

JUNE 1974: O'Neill graduates with a bachelor's degree from the School of Justice at the American University in Washington, D.C.

JULY 1976: O'Neill is appointed a special agent of the FBI.

OCTOBER 1976: O'Neill is assigned to the FBI field office in Baltimore, where his investigative assignments include foreign counterintelligence, organized crime, and white collar crime.

JUNE 1978: O'Neill earns a master of science degree in forensic science from George Washington University in Washington, D.C.

JANUARY 1980: Saudi millionaire Osama bin Laden joins the mujahedeen fighters in Afghanistan against Russian invaders.

JULY 1984: O'Neill separates from his wife, but they never divorce.

1986: Bin Laden opens the first of his six training camps in Afghanistan.

APRIL 1, 1987: O'Neill is assigned to FBI headquarters, where he serves as a supervisory special agent in the white collar crime section.

1989: Bin Laden opens a service office in Peshawar, which he calls Al Qaeda, or "The Base," to engage in a global recruitment of Muslims for jihad, or holy war.

JANUARY 1991: O'Neill is appointed chief of the governmental fraud unit at headquarters.

JULY 1991: O'Neill is named assistant special agent in charge of the FBI Chicago office with overall responsibility for violent crime, white collar crime, and drug and organized criminal activities.

NOVEMBER 1991: Bin Laden flees his native Saudi Arabia and eventually settles into a lavish estate in the Sudan.

FEBRUARY 26, 1993: The World Trade Center is bombed. Six people are killed and more than one thousand injured.

OCTOBER 3, 1993: Eighteen U.S. servicemen are killed when bin Laden and Al Qaeda–supported rebels shoot down three Black Hawk helicopters in Somalia.

AUGUST 1994: O'Neill is designated inspector in charge of a nationwide, multiagency task force investigating murder, domestic terrorism, and violence at abortion clinics. He also continues to work as the ASAC of the Chicago office.

JANUARY 1, 1995: O'Neill is promoted to chief of the FBI's counterterrorism section at FBI headquarters with the overall responsibility for the planning and direction of all international and domestic counterterrorism investigations.

FEBRUARY 5, 1995: O'Neill spends three days orchestrating the capture in Pakistan of Ramzi Yousef, the mastermind of the 1993 World Trade Center bombing.

MARCH 8, 1995: Bin Laden issues a rambling communiqué denouncing the Saudi royal family for allowing the U.S. military to establish bases in their country.

MARCH 9, 1995: O'Neill becomes the first FBI official to warn his supervisors that Osama bin Laden is becoming the greatest threat to U.S. national security.

APRIL 19, 1995: The Alfred P. Murrah Building in Oklahoma City is struck by a massive bomb, killing 267 people and injuring more than 1,000 others. O'Neill heads the investigation.

APRIL 22, 1995: Special Whitewater Prosecutor Kenneth Starr questions President Clinton and First Lady Hillary Clinton privately about their failed Whitewater real estate deals in Arkansas.

JUNE 21, 1995: President Clinton signs nationwide Presidential Decision Directive 39, which gives the FBI lead responsibility for investigating terrorism in the U.S. and abroad.

NOVEMBER 15, 1995: A two-hundred-pound truck bomb rocks the Office of the Program Managers for the Saudi Arabian National Guard (OPM-Sang) that houses U.S. military personnel. Seven people are killed, including five Americans, and sixty others are injured.

JANUARY 1996: O'Neill creates "Alex station," which for the first time positions an FBI agent inside the CIA. He simultaneously names a top CIA official to serve as his deputy of counterterrorism at FBI headquarters.

JANUARY 22, 1996: First Lady Hillary Clinton becomes the first wife of a sitting president to be subpoenaed in a criminal investigation, and she testifies the following day.

APRIL 28, 1996: President Clinton testifies on videotape as a defense witness at the first Whitewater trial.

MAY 31, 1996: Saudi officials convict and immediately behead four suspects in the OPM-Sang bombing before O'Neill's agents can interrogate them.

JUNE 26, 1996: A truck bomb destroys the Khobar Towers residence in Saudi Arabia that houses U.S. Air Force personnel. Nineteen American servicemen are killed and four hundred others are wounded.

JULY 3, 1996: President Clinton testifies on tape at the second Whitewater trial.

JULY 17, 1996: TWA Flight 800 explodes and crashes shortly after takeoff from JFK International Airport in New York. All 230 crew members and passengers are killed.

AUGUST 23, 1996: Bin Laden issues a frightening call to arms to harm Americans and Jews.

JANUARY 1, 1997: O'Neill is named special agent in charge of the national security division at the FBI's flagship office in New York City, with responsibility over all aspects of FBI counterterrorism and counterintelligence operations.

FEBRUARY 23, 1997: A Palestinian national fatally shoots a Danish tourist and wounds seven others during a rampage on the 108th-floor observation deck of the Empire State Building in New York City.

MAY 12, 1997: Bin Laden tells CNN that he can no longer guarantee the safety of American civilians should they get in the way of future attacks, which he says will be heard "in the media."

JUNE 11, 1997: O'Neill delivers a prophetic public speech about the danger posed by bin Laden and other islamic fundamentalist radicals. O'Neill warns that the terrorists have the capacity to strike on American soil anytime they choose.

JULY 1997: Osama bin Laden is secretly indicted by a federal grand jury in Manhattan for terrorist activities, including involvement in the tragic 1993 "Black Hawk Down" incident.

JANUARY 7, 1998: Former White House intern Monica Lewinsky denies in a sworn court affidavit that she had an affair with President Clinton.

JANUARY 16, 1998: Prosecutor Starr receives permission to expand the investigation into whether President Clinton and his close friend Vernon Jordan encouraged White House intern Monica Lewinsky to lie under oath about her affair with the president.

JANUARY 26, 1998: President Clinton angrily declares he "did not have sex with that woman, Monica Lewinsky."

FEBRUARY 22, 1998: Osama bin Laden announces the formation of the World Islamic Front for Jihad against Jews and the Crusaders with Dr. Ayman al-Zawahiri of the virulent Egypt Jihad Group and the Egypt Islamic Group at his side.

APRIL 15, 1998: First Lady Hillary Clinton testifies for five hours before a grand jury probing her role in the Whitewater real estate scandal.

MAY 26, 1998: Bin Laden holds a press conference in Afghanistan warning "of good news to come."

MAY 28, 1998: ABC-TV airs an interview with bin Laden predicting "a black day for America."

JUNE 1998: New York Mayor Rudolph Giuliani builds a multimillion-dollar emergency command center "bunker" inside the World Trade Center despite doubts from O'Neill and NYPD.

JUNE 1998: O'Neill's personal car breaks down in New Jersey and he allows a girlfriend to use a bathroom in a secret FBI garage, a violation that causes him to be suspended for fifteen days.

JULY 17, 1998: Prosecutors issue an historic subpoena ordering President Clinton to testify before a grand jury.

AUGUST 6, 1998: Monica Lewinsky testifies before a federal grand jury about her relationship with President Clinton.

AUGUST 7, 1998: Two four-hundred-pound truck bombs destroy U.S. embassies in Kenya and Tanzania in Africa, killing 247 and injuring more than 5,000. O'Neill immediately declares that bin Laden is behind the attack.

AUGUST 17, 1998: President Clinton addresses the nation, and confesses that he had intimate relations with Lewinsky.

AUGUST 21, 1998: President Clinton launches ineffective Tomahawk missile strikes at a bin Laden camp in Afghanistan and a pharmaceutical plant in the Sudan in retaliation for the two African embassy bombings. The FBI was never advised of the upcoming strikes. O'Neill claims the president used outdated intelligence in selecting the targets.

SEPTEMBER 11, 1998: Prosecutor Starr issues a salacious 445-page report on Clinton and Lewinsky listing eleven grounds for impeachment.

SEPTEMBER 28, 1998: President Clinton vows not to resign.

NOVEMBER 1998: O'Neill orders the expansion of his Al Qaeda squad in New York.

NOVEMBER 24, 1998: O'Neill is passed over for promotion to deputy director of the national security division at FBI headquarters primarily because of the "car incident."

DECEMBER 19, 1998: President Clinton is impeached, but declares he will fight.

FEBRUARY 12, 1999: House of Representative acquits Clinton of the impeachment charges.

AUGUST 11, 1999: President Clinton grants clemency to sixteen imprisoned members of a Puerto Rican terrorist group linked to a dozen killings and more than 130 bombings in American cities. Critics say the decision was made to help First Lady Hillary Clinton's run for the U.S. Senate in New York.

OCTOBER 31, 1999: An EgyptAir flight crashes shortly after takeoff from JFK International Airport in New York, killing all 217 people on board. O'Neill's agents quickly suspect the erratic pilot was solely responsible.

DECEMBER 12, 1999: Ahmed Ressam is arrested at U.S–Canadian border bringing explosives into the U.S. as part of a plot to carry out bombings timed to the millennium 2000 festivities. O'Neill and his agents capture the remaining suspects in Brooklyn before New Year's Eve.

JANUARY 3, 2000: Al Qaeda terrorists attempt to bomb the USS *Sullivan* in Yemen, but their bomb-laden skiff sinks from the weight of hundreds of pounds of explosives.

JANUARY 20, 2000: Top Al Qaeda leaders meet in Malaysia, where they plan an attack on the USS *Cole*. Among those attending are Khalid Shaikh Mohammed and two September 11, 2001, hijackers.

MAY 2000: O'Neill is passed over for promotion to head the FBI New York office.

JULY 2000: O'Neill's briefcase containing a classified report on his terrorism programs is stolen from an FBI retirement seminar in Florida. Although the material is quickly recovered without incident, the breach prompts an internal probe.

OCTOBER 12, 2000: The USS *Cole* is attacked by two Al Qaeda suicide bombers in Yemen, killing seventeen sailors and wounding dozens more.

OCTOBER 15, 2000. O'Neill arrives in Yemen to lead the U.S. investigation of the USS *Cole* bombing, and is immediately confronted by Barbara Bodine, the U.S. ambassador to Yemen.

NOVEMBER 23, 2000: O'Neill returns to New York, where he continues to head the investigation of the USS *Cole* bombing and other national security matters.

JANUARY 2001: Ambassador Bodine refuses to allow O'Neill to return to Yemen, making him the first FBI official in history to be denied "country clearance" by a State Department official.

JULY 5, 2001: O'Neill arrives in Spain to speak before the Spanish national police about the role of international policing in the fight on terrorism, and he begins to contemplate retiring from the FBI, which did not fully support him against Bodine.

JULY 8, 2001: Mohammed Atta, a key mastermind of the attack the World Trade Center, also arrives in Spain to meet with other suspected hijackers to finalize the plan.

JUNE 16, 2001: FBI Director Freeh and O'Neill decide to pull their agents out of Yemen because of the threat level, but U.S. Ambassador Bodine orders the Marines to keep them hostage, locked inside her embassy compound.

JUNE 21, 2001: Bin Laden releases a hundred-minute videotape in which he kneels and fires automatic weapons, rejoices in the attack on the *Cole*, and asks Muslims to come to his camps because the "war" against the Americans is beginning.

AUGUST 16, 2001: O'Neill accepts a job as director of security at the World Trade Center.

AUGUST 19, 2001: Three days before his retirement, the *New York Times* publishes a story reporting that the FBI is investigating O'Neill's "briefcase incident."

AUGUST 22, 2001: O'Neill spends the last day of his thirty-one-year career at the FBI signing orders for the FBI to return to Yemen to continue the USS *Cole* investigation.

AUGUST 23, 2001: O'Neill starts his new job as director of security at the Twin Towers.

SEPTEMBER 11, 2001: O'Neill and more than 2,800 other people are killed when the World Trade Center is struck by hijacked commercial jets, and destroyed.

OCTOBER 7, 2001: President Bush orders U.S. military attack in Afghanistan of bin Laden camps and the Taliban.

SEPTEMBER 11, 2002: The U.S. mourned the tragic first anniversary of the Attack on America, as Ramzi Bin al-Shibh, a key 9/11 mastermind, was captured in Pakistan.

OCTOBER 12, 2002: On the anniversary of the bombing of the USS *Cole*, 183 people, most of them from Australia, were killed when bombs destroyed two crowded nightclubs in Bali.

NOVEMBER 2002: President Bush creates a department of homeland security, bringing together nearly 170,000 employees from twenty-two agencies in a new cabinet-level agency to better safeguard America's cities, airlines, and borders.

MARCH 19, 2003: U.S.-led coalition troops invade Iraq to oust Saddam Hussein's regime and find weapons of mass destruction.

APRIL 9, 2003: U.S.-led coalition troops take Baghdad, Iraq, where hundreds of jubilant Iraqis stomp on a toppled statue of Saddam Hussein and drag its severed head through the streets.

MAY 12, 2003: At least nineteen Al Qaeda terrorists—most of them Saudis—carry out a massive four-bomb attack at an apartment complex in the capital city of Riyadh, Saudi Arabia, killing thirty people, including eight Americans, and wounding nearly sixty others.

MAY 16, 2003: More than forty people are killed and scores injured when five bombs detonate simultaneously in Casablanca, Morocco.

PHOTOGRAPH
CREDITS

INDEX

Abbas, Abu, 394
Abdullah (Crown Prince of Saudi Arabia), 128, 135
abortion clinic investigations. *See* VAAPCON (Violence Against Abortion Providers Conspiracy) investigations
Abouhalima, Mahmoud, 94
Abu Sayyaf (Bearer of Swords) group, 82, 83
Adams, Joseph, 11, 15
Aden Harbor terrorist attempt, 272–73
Aden Hotel, 297–99
ADIC (assistant director in charge) position, 73, 276–77
Adid, Mohammed, 98–99
Afghanistan
    bin Laden camps in, 81, 109, 315, 334
    bin Laden move to, 122–23
    Taliban, 95, 122–23, 177, 197, 219, 393
    U.S. attacks on, 216–23, 393
    U.S. support of bin Laden in, 95
    war in, and terrorism, 181–82
African embassy bombings, 179, 203–27, 237–38, 392
    bin Laden, Al Qaeda, and, 5
    O'Neill's entertaining of African officials in New York City, 4
agents, O'Neill's relationships with
    in Baltimore, 21–22, 26–27
    in Chicago, 38–44, 64–66, 71–72
    concern about families of agents, 212–13
    concern for agents, 308
    in New York City, 157, 233–35
    in Washington, D.C., 92–93
Age of Sacred Terror, The, 222
Agnew, Spiro, 26
airplanes. *See* jetliners
Ajaj, Ahmad Mohammed, 82

Albright, Madeline, 216, 222
Alcohol, Tobacco, and Firearms (ATF) agency, 260
Alex CIA-based station, 119, 396
Al Faran, 111
Alfred P. Murrah Federal Building bombing, 103–5
al-Gamma'a Al-Islamiya, 195
Al Jazeera, 99, 287
Al Qaeda. *See also* bin Laden, Osama
    African embassy bombings and, 203–5
    building of, 98
    Egyptian embassy bombing by, 116
    investigation of, 91–109
    meeting in Madrid, 340–41
    meeting in Malaysia, 273–74
    millennium attack plans, 245–46, 262–63, 265–66, 270, 273
    O'Neill's warnings about, 5–6, 270–74, 321, 360, 390–91
    U.S. attacks on, 393–95
    USS *Cole* bombing and, 291, 315–16, 333–35
Al-Sayegh, Hani, 134–35
al Zawahiri, Ayman, 145, 195, 225, 272, 287, 317
ambition, O'Neill's, 73–74
American Airlines Flight 11, 364–65
American Airlines Flight 77, 365, 370
American Bandstand (television show), 30, 49
American University, O'Neill at, 15, 17, 19
Andrew, George, 26–27, 52, 92, 113–14, 141–42, 274–75
Anemone, Louis, 169–76, 191, 236
antiabortion violence investigations. *See* VAAPCON (Violence Against Abortion Providers Conspiracy) investigations

Anton's Loyal Opposition restaurant, 34
apartment, DiBattista's, 241–42
apartments, O'Neill's
   Chicago, 37, 49
   New York City, 154–55
Armed Forces of the Puerto Rican
   National Liberation (FALN), 70,
   238–41
Armed Islamic Group, 219, 249
Army of God, The (manual), 61, 62
Arnett, Peter, 177
Arté's, 154
Aryan Nations, 70
Asahara, Shoko, 96
Ashley, Grant, 38–43, 50, 52, 53, 279, 346
assistant director in charge (ADIC)
   position, 73, 276–77
ATF (Alcohol, Tobacco, and Firearms)
   agency, 260
Atlantic City
   O'Neill's early life in, 7–15
   O'Neill's funeral in, 384–88
Atta, Mohammed, 273, 340–41, 354,
   361–64
Aum Shinrikyo (Supreme Truth) Cult,
   96–97

Ballast, Jack, 140
Baltimore field office job, O'Neill's, 21–33
   cooperation with U.S. attorney, 23–26
   corruption investigations, 26–28, 32–33
   family life and separation from his wife,
   29–32
   gang investigations, 22–23
   pornography investigations, 23–26
   relationships with agents, 21–22, 26–27
   relationships with women, 30–32, 34
   transfer from, to Washington, D.C.,
   33–35
Barbados visit, 110–11
barbecue at Quantico, 124–26
Barrett, Jim, 63–64
Basilan, 83
Batouti, Gameel, 243–44
Baumgart, Stephen, 352
Beagan, Anne, 120
Beekman Hotel, 154
Beirut bombing, 76
Benjamin, Daniel, 222
Bergen, Peter, 177

Berger, Sandy, 94, 197, 219, 238, 251
Bernard, Roy, 385
Berns, Walter, 339–40
Bhutto (Pakistani Prime Minister), 81, 83,
   88
Billy, Joseph, 149, 155–57, 202, 207,
   211–12, 216, 218, 387
bin al-Shibh, Ramzi, 273, 341, 395
bin Laden, Osama. *See also* Al Qaeda
   African embassy bombings and, 206–7,
   213, 222–23, 227
   attempts to buy enriched uranium,
   117–18, 146
   and Black Hawk Down incident, 98–99,
   145–46, 190–91
   camps in Afghanistan, 81, 109
   family business, 298
   as financier of terrorism, 78–79, 83
   indictments of, 190–91, 194, 237–38
   Khobar Towers bombing and, 128–29,
   134
   holy war declaration by, 144–45, 177–79
   leaving Sudan for Afghanistan, 122–23
   O'Neill warnings about, 5–6, 164–65,
   186–87, 202–3
   Saudi Arabian royal family and, 97
   Saudi contract on life of, 177
   speeches by, 195–97, 287, 333–35
   in Sudan, 97–98
   U.S. attack on Afghanistan and, 219, 221
   USS *Cole* bombing and, 333–35
bin Sultan, Bandar, 125
Black Gangsta Disciple Nation, 44–47
Black Hawk Down incident, 5, 98–99,
   145–46, 190
Blaha, John, 17, 134, 167–68
Blitzer, Robert, 62, 69, 70–71, 79–80, 87,
   92, 104–6, 119, 186, 209
blowback, 95, 218
Bodine, Barbara, 270–72, 289, 292–93,
   297, 299–300, 303–12, 316, 317–22,
   324–33, 342–44, 347, 354, 397–98.
   See also USS *Cole* bombing; Yemen
Bojinka Plot, 84–86, 90, 139
bomb-smuggling case, 247–63
Boo-G, 47
Bosnia, 109
Boston Blackies bar, 43
Brannon, Bill, 51
Bratton, William, 158

Bremer, J. Paul, 275, 398
briefcase infraction, 279–83, 288, 336, 346–50, 385–86
Bright Line policy, 199–200, 236, 282
Britton, John, 63–64
Bronfman, Edgar, 274
Brooks, Michael, 131, 385
Bruno restaurant, 4, 154, 231, 356
Bryant, Robert "Bear," 57–59, 62, 64, 71, 80, 90, 100–101, 104–5, 114, 119, 121, 126, 130, 132, 383–85
Bulger, James "Whitey," 277
Bunn, John, 267, 274, 392
Burt, John, 60
Bush, George H. W., 135
Bush, George W., 185, 375, 377, 392–96

Campisi, Charles, 382
Cantemessa, Joe, 154
Cantwell, John, 383
Caravelli, Jack, 7–8, 11–13, 15–16, 30, 94, 116–19, 196–97, 220–21, 375, 387
Carey, Mariah, 322–23
car infraction, 197–202, 209, 235, 365
Carney, Thomas, 3
Caro, Dana, 26–27
Caruso, Tim, 300
Catholic religion, O'Neill and, 11, 51, 106, 108, 166–68, 194, 213
Cedars of Lebanon restaurant, 331
Center for Strategic and International Studies, 102, 342
Central Intelligence Agency. *See* CIA (Central Intelligence Agency)
Centro's restaurant, 48
Chicago field office job, O'Neill's, 35–75
abortion clinic violence investigations, 57–70, 74–75. *See also* VAAPCON (Violence Against Abortion Providers Conspiracy) investigations
cooperation with Chicago Police Department and gang investigation task force, 38, 43–47
kidnapping investigations, 39, 42–43
lifestyle during, 36–37, 47–48, 51–53
promotion to, 35
relationships with agents, 38–44, 64–66, 71–72
relationship with Anna DiBattista, 67–68

relationship with Mary Lynn Stevens, 50, 66
relationship with Valerie James, 48–51, 66–67, 72–74, 75
transfer from, to FBI headquarters job in counterterrorism, 70–71
Chicago Police Department, 38, 43–47
Chidichimo, Mark, 161, 374
Childs, John, 111
China Club, 362–63
Christmas, 149, 194, 259, 324
CIA (Central Intelligence Agency)
Jack Caravelli at, 12
Clinton Administration distrust of, 94
dispute with, 114
murders at, 95
relationships with, 116–21, 124–26, 351–52
TWA Flight 800 simulation, 143–44, 193
Cibo's restaurant, 326
Ciluffo, Frank, 102–3, 342
Cincotta, Christopher, 383
Cité restaurant, 4, 154, 331
Clark, Carol Higgins, 380
Clarke, Richard, 79, 80, 101–2, 113, 120, 233, 347
clemency grant to Puerto Rican terrorists, Clinton's, 238–41
clerk-agents, FBI, 20
Clinton, Bill
abortion clinic violence and, 57, 62
clemency grant to Puerto Rican terrorists, 238–41
international terrorism and, 94, 185–86, 196–97, 205, 391–92
Lewinski scandal, 196, 214–20, 223
National Commission on Terrorism, 275–76
pardon of John Deutsch, 282
Presidential Decision Directive 39, 103, 105, 156, 175
relations with Yemen, 271
response to African embassy bombings, 214–23, 251
response to Khobar Towers bombing, 126
response to millennium terrorist threats, 248, 250–51
response to USS *Cole* bombing, 313–14

Clinton, Hillary, 239–40
Cohen, David, 114
Cohen, William, 219–20
Cole. See USS *Cole* bombing
college years, O'Neill's, 15–20
Collingwood, John, 348
Connor, Joe, 239–40
Connor, Thomas, 240–41
contacts. *See* networking, O'Neill's
cooperation, O'Neill's
    with Chicago Police Department, 38,
        43–47
    with CIA, 116–21, 124–26, 351–52
    between intelligence agencies, 102–3,
        105, 141–42, 395–96
    international, 4–5, 105–6, 119–20,
        191–92, 270, 274–75
    with New York City law enforcement
        agencies, 155–57, 169–76, 236–37
    with U.S. attorney in Baltimore, 23–26
Corbett, Stephen, 326–27, 331–33, 376
Cordier, Robert, 368
Corrigan, Thomas, 93, 142–43, 160–64,
    189–90, 233–34, 242
corruption investigations, 26–28, 32–33
counterterrorism job at FBI headquarters,
    O'Neill's, 70–151
    bin Laden and Al Qaeda investigations,
        95, 97–103, 121–24, 144–46. *See also*
        Al Qaeda; bin Laden, Osama
    Bojinka Plot and Phillipines Airlines
        flight bombing, 83–84
    capture of Ramzi Yousef, 79–80, 86–90
    capture of Wali Khan Anim Shah,
        112–14
    Clinton administration problems,
        94–95
    cooperation between CIA and FBI,
        116–21
    Egyptian embassy bombing, 116
    immersion in, 91–92
    international cooperation, 4–5, 105–6,
        119–20
    Khobar Towers bombing and Saudi
        Arabian obstruction, 124–35
    kidnapping of Donald Hutchings,
        108–12
    Oklahoma City bombing investigation,
        103–5
    OPM-Sang bombing, 115–16

Pan Am Flight 103 bombing, 76–77
    perspectives on, 93–95
    plot to assassinate Pope John Paul II,
        85–86
    promotion to, 70–75
    relationships with agents, 92–93
    relationships with women, 106–8, 110
    Tokyo subway sarin gas attack, 96–97
    transfer from, to New York City field
        office, 146–51
    TWA Flight 800 investigation, 139–44
    unheeded warnings, 5–6
    World Trade Center bombing plot,
        77–83
cruise-missile attacks on Afghanistan and
    Sudan, 216–23
Cunningham, Gregg, 63

dagger as symbol, 287, 335
Dalzell, Fred, 11
dancing ability, O'Neill's, 30, 49
Dar es Salaam embassy bombing, 204–5,
    211, 216. *See also* African embassy
    bombings
DEA (Drug Enforcement Administration),
    45
Dean, Diana, 247–48, 263
debts, O'Neill's, 231, 279. *See also* finances,
    O'Neill's
Deily, Lester, 169
Department of Homeland Security, 395
Department of Justice
    O'Neill as tour guide at, 17–19
    tour of Chicago with O'Neill, 45–46
Deutsch, John, 282, 348
Dhahran bombing, 4, 123–35
Diallo, Amadou, 236
DiBattista, Anna
    beginning of O'Neill's relationship with,
        67–68
    Christmas gift to, 323
    move to New York City, 241–42
    O'Neill's death and, 378, 383
    at O'Neill's funeral, 385
    O'Neill's relationship with, 80, 107–8,
        245
    O'Neill's resistance to ending
        relationship with, 233, 344–45,
        356–57, 361
    O'Neill's retirement and, 338–39, 342

revelations about other women and, 380–81
talks of marriage with, 148–49, 231–33
travel with, 110–11, 192
during World Trade Center attack, 368–69
Dienst, Richard, 357–58
Digler, Alan, 79–80
dirty bomb, 117
Di Taranto, Lorraine, 155, 351
divorce, O'Neill and, 31, 51, 107, 168
Dolan, Thomas, 376
domestic terrorism, 95, 103–5, 119. *See* terrorism
Donlan, Thomas, 235, 243–44
Donovan, Kevin, 291, 294, 300, 303, 306–8, 311
Dorsey, Mike, 299–303, 317
Drug Enforcement Administration (DEA), 45
Duffy, James, 24, 30, 109, 111
Duffy, Kevin, 14
Dunbar, Carson, 157–58, 201–2
Dunne, Joseph, 236–37, 246, 255–57, 264–68, 326, 367, 372, 383–85
Durkin, Thomas, 166–67, 386

Eddy, R. P., 14
EgyptAir Flight 990 crash, 242–44
Egyptian embassy bombing, 116
Egyptian Islamic Jihad Group, 145, 182, 195, 219, 225, 317
Elaine's restaurant, 3, 154, 155, 269, 362, 389
Emergency Management Services, New York City, 169, 172–73
Emilio, Sal, 140, 260–61
Empire State Building incident, 164
energy, O'Neill's, 28, 51, 150, 185, 321
entertaining as networking, 3–6, 274–75. *See also* networking, O'Neill's
Etten, Robert Von, 357
exit strategy, 162

FAA (Federal Aviation Administration), 141–42, 243, 264
Fabozzi, Michael, 383
Fadl, Jamal al-, 145–46, 164–65
FALN (Armed Forces of the Puerto Rican National Liberation), 70, 238–41

family, O'Neill's. *See* parents of. *See also* O'Neill, Dorothy (mother); O'Neill, John (father); O'Neill, John P., Jr. (son)
fatwa (call to arms), 129, 363
FBI (Federal Bureau of Investigation)
Baltimore field office job (*see* Baltimore field office job, O'Neill's)
bringing Yemeni officials to headquarters, 326–27, 330–31
Chicago field office job. *See* Chicago field office job, O'Neill's
Clinton's relationship with, 218
history of, 91
investigations in foreign countries, 226–37
as lead terrorism authority, 105
and NYPD terrorist task force, 287–88
legal attaché program, 133
New York City field office job. *See* New York City field office job, O'Neill's
O'Neill's early interest in, 7, 18
O'Neill's first job as fingerprint clerk and tour guide, 15–20
O'Neill's headquarters jobs, 33–35. *See also* counterterrorism job at FBI headquarters, O'Neill's
O'Neill's infractions at, 6, 197–202, 270–83
O'Neill's relationships with agents. *See* agents, O'Neill's relationships with
O'Neill's retirement from, 6, 53, 279, 330, 336–40, 344–54, 389
O'Neill's training at, 19–20
travel arrangements, 207–8
FBI, The (television show), 7
Federal Aviation Administration (FAA), 141–42, 243, 264
Federal Bureau of Investigation. *See* FBI (Federal Bureau of Investigation)
Feehan, William, 369
finances, O'Neill's
debts, 231, 279
generosity and, 14, 18–19, 233–35
living beyond means, 52–53
property settlement with wife, 345
World Trade Center job and, 346
fingerprint clerk, O'Neill as FBI, 15–20
Fire Department, New York City, 169–72
First on First, 154

Fitzgerald, Gary, 292–93, 309–12, 318, 321, 329–30
Fitzgerald, Mark, 299
Fitzgerald, Pat, 268
Flagg, Warren, 18–20
Foreign Intelligence Surveillance Court, 249
foreign investigations, 226–27
Formica, Frank, 13–14
France, 296
Franks, Tommy, 327–28, 398
Freedom of Access to Clinic Entrances Act, 62–63
Freeh, Louis, 58, 68, 71, 105, 129–35, 147, 199–200, 212, 213–14, 216–19, 235, 277–78, 280, 292, 301, 318, 320, 328–30, 342–41, 384
Friars Club, 166
Fried, Gregory, 326
Frozen Zone, Times Square, 264
fundamentalism, religious, 59. *See also* Islamic fundamentalists; VAAPCON (Violence Against Abortion Providers Conspiracy) investigations
funeral, O'Neill's, 384–88

gadgets, 27–28
Gallagher, Neil, 34–35, 235, 280, 282, 348, 385, 387
Galligan, Mary, 332–33, 395
Galvin, Bill, 88–89
Ganci, Peter, 369
gang investigations
    Baltimore, 22–23
    Chicago, 43–47
Gani name, 248, 251, 252
generosity, O'Neill's, 14, 18–19, 233–35
George Washington University, O'Neill at, 19–20
Ghost Shadows gang, 22–23
Giblin, Kevin, 59, 91–92, 97, 105, 121, 150, 355
Giuliani, Rudolf, 164–66, 169–73, 191, 257–58, 364, 372
Golden Maher hotel, 319
Gold Sardine piano bar, 51
Goodwill Games, 174–76
Governors gang, 44–47
Gray, Macy, 234
Griffen, Michael, 60–61

Ground Zero, 377–78
Guerrero, Alfredo, 124–25
Gulf War of 1991, 77, 82, 129
Gunn, David, 59–61, 63
Gunn, Louis, 330, 350

Hazmi, Nawaf al-, 273, 341, 352, 365
Hanssen, Robert, 348
Haouari, Mokhtar, 253, 262
Harkat-ul Ansar, 111
Harry Carey's club, 49
Hasert, Dirk, 111
Hatton, Leonard, 379–80
Hauer, Jerry, 172–73, 202–3, 234, 336–37, 348, 356, 362–63, 374, 377, 383
Heanon, John, 10, 14–15, 384
Herman, Neil, 147, 159, 162
Hezbollah, 126
hijackings
    Ambassador Bodine's, 327–28
    World Trade Center attack and, 364–66
Hill, Paul, 63–64
Hirsch, Seymour, 383
Hoehl, Alan, 265, 337–38
Holmes, H. Allen, 162–63
Holy Spirit High School, 11
holy war. *See* jihad (holy war)
Hoover, Larry, 45
Horan, Sheila, 208, 210–11
Horton, Ralph, 87–88
hospitals, terrorism and, 245–46, 293–95
Hurley's restaurant, 167–68
Hutchings, Donald, 108–9, 111–12

Ikegami, Haruki, 84
infractions, O'Neill's FBI, 6, 197–202, 270–83
insecurities, O'Neill's, 233
international cooperation, 4–5, 105–6, 119–20, 191–92, 270, 274–75
international terrorism, 76–77, 93–95, 119, 240–41. *See also* terrorism
Iran, 76, 129, 180
Iraq, 76, 77, 82, 117–18, 180, 394, 398
Irish background, 7–8, 13, 48
ISI (Pakistani Inter-Services Intelligence Agency), 123, 219, 224
Islamic Army of Aden-Abyan, 343

Islamic fundamentalists. *See also* Al Faran; Al Qaeda; bin Laden, Osama; Yousef, Ramzi
 FALN (Armed Forces of the Puerto Rican National Liberation), 70, 238–41
 O'Neill's speech about, 179–85
 O'Neill's warnings about, 5
Islamic Movement for Change, 115
Israel, O'Neill's views on, 357–58

James, Jay, 74, 166, 194, 266–67, 323–24, 326, 338–40
James, Valerie
 beginning of O'Neill's relationship with, 48–51
 car infraction and, 198–202
 move to New York City to live with O'Neill, 166
 on O'Neill, 10, 32, 59, 149, 274
 O'Neill's death and, 371, 373–74, 377, 383
 O'Neill's funeral and, 385
 O'Neill's relationship with, 66–67, 72–75, 90, 107–8, 148, 186–87, 231–33, 245, 259, 288, 322, 359
 O'Neill's retirement and, 344
 revelations about other women and, 380–81, 390
 St. Patrick's Day in New York City, 167–68
 trips with, 194, 279–81, 323–26, 338–40
 during World Trade Center attack, 363–65, 368
Japan, gas attack in, 96–97
Jautakis, Harold, 125
Jennings, Peter, 59, 378
Jerusalem, 182
jetliners
 Bojinka Plot to bomb, 84–86
 hijacking of Ambassador Bodine's, 327–28
 plot to attack World Trade Center with, 341, 352–53
 World Trade Center attack and hijacked, 364–66
jihad (holy war)
 bin Laden's declarations, 144–45, 177–79, 195–96
 O'Neill on, 181–85

John Paul II, Pope, plot to assassinate, 85
Johnson, David, 346
Jordan, 265–66, 270, 328–29
Judge, Mychal, 369, 371

Kahane, Rabbi Meir, 94
Kallstrom, James, 139, 141–42, 147–48, 158–60, 166, 192–94, 221, 258, 349, 386
Kamal, Ali Abu, 164–65
Kammerdener, Charles, 188
Kansi, Mir-Aimal, 95
Karpiloff, Doug, 368, 374
Kashmir, 111
Kaufman, Elaine, 3, 362, 385
Keane's Steakhouse, 377
Kelley, David, 268, 308, 311, 367–68, 372, 385
Kelly, Patricia, 209–11, 225–26, 234, 305, 322, 385
Kelly, Raymond, 248
Kennedy's restaurant, 154
Kenya embassy bombing, 203–4, 209–11. *See also* African embassy bombings
Kerik, Bernard, 368, 372
Khalil, Lafi, 187–90
Khobar Towers bombing, 4, 123–35
kidnappings
 Chicago, 39–43
 terrorist, 108–12
Kirshner, Isabelle, 252
Kiser, Kathy, 21, 27, 29–30, 33, 209, 374, 385
Kiss My Ass (K. M. A.) Day, 340
Klinghoffer, Leon, 394
Klochan, John, 328–29
K. M. A. (Kiss My Ass) Day, 340
Koresh, David, 104
Kuwait, 77, 82, 129

Latin Kings gang, 45
Lebb, Teddy, 359
Lee, Wen Ho, 282, 348
Leery, Stephen, 173
legal attaché program, FBI, 133, 183–84
Leibowitz, Rodney, 358
Les Halles restaurant, 71
Lewinski scandal, Clinton administration and, 196, 214–20, 223
Lewis, John, 116, 132, 235, 275, 348

Libya, 76–77, 180
lifestyle, O'Neill's
  in Chicago, 36–37, 47–48, 51–53
  entertaining as networking, 3–6, 274–75.
    See also networking, O'Neill's
  in New York City, 153–54
Lindh, John Walker, 396
Lipka, John, 62, 64–66, 69, 71–72, 86,
    120–21, 124, 125, 130–31, 133, 139,
    150–51, 385
Lopez, Kathy, 290, 294–95
lying, O'Neill's, 32, 49–50, 390

McAllister, James, 33
McFadden, Bob, 315, 318–19, 331, 376,
    378
McTureous, Robert, 290
McVeigh, Timothy, 104, 392
Madrid, terrorist meeting in, 340–41
Mafia, 4
Maizar, Ghazi Ibrahim Abu, 187–90
Making Patriots, 339–40
Malaysia, terrorist meeting in, 273–74, 341
Mangan, Keith, 111
Manhattan. *See* New York City
Manning, Jay, 36–37, 324–28, 384–85
Marine Corps Law Enforcement Dinner,
    356–57
marriage. *See* O'Neill, Christine Shutz
    (wife)
Mawn, Barry, 277–79, 280, 282, 292,
    320–21, 327–29, 331, 348–49,
    367–68, 372–73, 385–86
Maxwell, Kenneth, 223, 249–50, 256–57,
    259, 262, 332, 343–44, 354, 358–60,
    367–68, 371–73, 384–85
Meskini, Abdelghani, 252–63, 270
Midhar, Khalid al-, 273, 341, 352, 365
military as lead terrorist organization, 275
millennium
  bombing plot, 247–57, 259–63, 270, 273
  preparations for, 245–46, 257–58,
    263–69
Miller, Bill, 87
Miller, John, 47, 197
Mislock, Raymond, 69–70, 126–28,
    130–32
Mohammed, Khalid Shaikh, 341, 395
Morales, William, 239
Morange, William, 252

Mosabbah, Abdel Rahman, 187–90
Mottola, Thomas, 234, 322–23, 337
Moussaouri, Zacarias, 352–53
mujahedeen (holy warriors), 78, 95, 109,
    129, 272
Mueller, Robert, 396
Muller, Robert, 368
Murad, Abdul Hakim, 85–86
Murphy, Bernie, 198
Murray, Janet, 30–31
Muslim community, New York City, 157
Muslim fundamentalists. *See* Islamic
    fundamentalists
Mutual of New York, 166

Nagana, Sam, 204
Nairobi embassy bombing, 203–4, 209–10.
    See also African embassy bombings
Naji, Homoud, 314, 331
Napoli, Louis, 189–90, 217, 223–26, 375
Nashiri, Abd al-Rahim al-, 315
National Commission on Terrorism, 275
National Security Council, 12, 196–97
National Strategy Forum speech, 179–85
NTSB (National Transportation Safety
    Board), 243–44
Naval Criminal Investigation Service
    (NCIS), 293–94, 376
networking, O'Neill's
  entertaining as, 3–6
  seeking expertise, 355, 357, 359–60
  using contacts to help friends, 274–75
New Jersey field office, 202, 235
news, terrorism and, 184
New Year's Eve millennium
  bombing plot, 247–57, 259–63, 270, 273
  preparations for, 245–46, 257–58,
    263–69
New York City field office job, O'Neill's,
    146–354
  African embassy bombings, 203–27
  Al Qaeda squad, 93
  Ambassador Barbara Bodine and
    terrorist threat in Yemen, 270–73
  bin Laden and Al Qaeda perspectives,
    93, 177–87, 190–91, 194–97, 202,
    273–74. *See also* bin Laden, Osama; Al
    Qaeda
  briefcase infraction, 279–83
  car infraction, 197–202

Clinton administration issues, 214–23, 238–41, 275–76
cooperation with law enforcement agencies, 155–57, 169–76, 236–37
EgyptAir Flight 990 crash, 242–44
Empire State Building incident, 164–66
Goodwill Games, 174–76
international cooperation, 191, 270, 274–75
lifestyle at, 3–5, 152–55, 231–46, 322–24
loss of promotion at, 235–36, 276–78
millenium bombing plot, 247–57, 259–63, 270, 273
millenium preparations in, 245–46, 257–58, 263–69
New York Times story, 346–50, 389
O'Neill's ambition and, 73
Palm Pilot incident, 276
promotion to, 146–51
relationships with agents, 157, 233–35
relationships with women, 192, 194, 231–33, 241–42, 245, 338–40, 342, 344–45
retirement from, 336–40, 346, 350–51
St. Patrick's Day, 166–69
sarin gas incident, 169–74
subway bombing conspiracy, 187–90
terrorist concerns, 139, 237–38
TWA Flight 800 investigation, 159–64, 192–94
USS *Cole* bombing, 287–335, 342–44, 354
World Trade Center job, 337–38, 345–46, 351–63
World Trade Center terrorism plot, 340–41, 352–53
New York Times article about O'Neill, 346–50, 389
Nichols, Terry, 104
night life, O'Neill's. *See* lifestyle, O'Neill's
Nosair, El Sayyiud, 94
NTSB (National Transportation Safety Board), 243–44
Nye, Danny, 231

O'Brien, John, 43
O'Connell, Jeff, 121
O'Connor, John Cardinal, 155, 166–68, 322–23, 386
Odeh, Mohammed Sadeek, 203, 212

Office of Professional Responsibility, 200, 281–83, 288, 345–46
Ofli, Mary, 204
oil, O'Neill on, 134
Oklahoma City bombing, 103–5, 392
Old Ebbitt Grill, 67, 71
Olympic Games in Atlanta, 139
Omar, Mullah Mohammed, 123, 177, 221
Omari, Abdulaziz al-, 361–64
O'Neill, Bob (uncle), 10
O'Neill, Carol (daughter), 31
O'Neill, Christine Shutz (wife)
dating, 14–15
family life with, and separation from, 29–32
marriage to, and birth of son, 16–17
at O'Neill's funeral, 385
post-separation relations with, 53, 72
property settlement with, 345
September 11 call from, 366
O'Neill, Dorothy (mother), 8–11, 68, 349, 384, 398
O'Neill, John (father), 8–11, 384, 398
O'Neill, John P.
author's relationship with, 158–59, 389–90
Baltimore field office job, 21–35. *See also* Baltimore field office job, O'Neill's
capacity to digest information, 22–23, 28–29, 92
Chicago field office job, 35–53. *See also* Chicago field office job, O'Neill's
college years and first job as fingerprint clerk and tour guide at FBI, 15–20
cooperation of. *See* cooperation, O'Neill's
counterterrorism job at FBI headquarters. *See* counterterrorism job at FBI headquarters, O'Neill's
death of, 371, 376, 382–84
early life in Atlantic City, 7–15
energy of, 28, 150, 185, 321
FBI headquarters job in Washington, D.C., 33–35
finances. *See* finances, O'Neill's
funeral of, 384–88
infractions at FBI, 6, 197–202, 270–83
legacy of, 389–99
lifestyle. *See* lifestyle, O'Neill's

O'Neill, John P. (*continued*)
  New York City field office job. *See* New
    York City field office job, O'Neill's
  Palm Pilot incident, 276
  parents of. *See* O'Neill, Dorothy
    (mother); O'Neill, John (father)
  personality of, 11, 12–13, 158, 201–2,
    233–35, 389–91
  relationships with agents. *See* agents,
    O'Neill's relationships with
  relationships with women. *See* women,
    O'Neill's relationships with
  reputation of, 157–58, 389–90
  retirement from FBI, 6, 53, 279, 330,
    336–40, 344–54, 389
  son. *See* O'Neill, John P., Jr. (son)
  speech about terrorism, 179–85
  style of entertaining and networking,
    3–6, 274–75. *See also* networking,
    O'Neill's
  suggestions for National Commission
    on Terrorism, 275–76
  terrorism warnings of, 5–6, 164–65,
    186–87, 202–3, 270–74, 321, 360,
    390–91
  wife. *See* O'Neill, Christine Shutz (wife)
  World Trade Center attack and. *See*
    World Trade Center attack on
    September 11
  World Trade Center job, 337–38,
    345–46, 353–63
O'Neill, John P., Jr. (son), 16, 29–30,
  204–5, 360–61, 366, 371, 373–77,
  383, 386–87
Ong, Betty, 364–65
Operation Archangel, 250, 264
OPM-Sang bombing, 114–16, 121–22, 123
Ostro, Hans Christian, 111
Owhali, Mohammed Rashed Daoud al-',
  97, 197, 203, 212

Pagan, Dylcia, 239
Pakistan
  African embassy bombings and, 212,
    223–24, 226–27
  relationships with bin Laden, 123, 177,
    219
  terrorists in, 83, 86–88
Palestinian Liberation Front, 394
Palestinians, O'Neill's views on, 357–58

Palm Pilot incident, 276
Pan Am Flight 103 bombing, 76
parents, O'Neill's. *See* O'Neill, Dorothy
  (mother); O'Neill, John (father)
Parker, Ishtiaque, 86–88
Pasta Tutti restaurant, 51–52
Pataki, George, 375
Patterson, Pat, 321, 360, 367
Pearl, Daniel, 108, 112
Pentagon, attack on, 370
personal life, 31, 50–51, 390
Peter Cooper Village apartment, 154
Pfeifer, Raymond, 369–71
Phil Donohue Show, The (television show),
  57, 63
Philipines Airlines, 84–85
Pickard, Thomas, 87–89, 114, 140–41,
  143, 147, 161, 208–9, 212, 235,
  277–78, 280, 346–48
Pierneck, Kenneth, 38–39, 41, 43–44, 45,
  46, 47–48, 50–52, 200, 208, 216, 218,
  236, 375–76
Plaza Hotel, 362
Pogan, Patrick, 169, 206–7, 234, 288
police departments
  Chicago, 43–47
  New York City, 169–76, 187–88, 236,
    250, 252, 263–65, 287–88, 378–79
pornography investigations, 23–26
Powel, Colin, 343
Powers, Raymond, 250, 355, 359–60
Presidential Decision Directive 39, 105,
  156, 175
Pressley, Frank, 203–4
Prince of Darkness nickname, 52, 342
Principals Committee, 251
public corruption investigations, 26–28,
  32–33
Puerto Rican terrorists, Clinton grant of
  clemency to, 238–41

Qaddafi, Muammar, 76–77
Qatar, 113–14
Quantico, Virginia
  barbecue at, 124–26
  O'Neill's training at, 19–20

Racketeering Influence and Corrupt
  Organizations Act (RICO), 24, 43, 47,
  62

Rahman, Blind Sheikh Abdul, 77, 81, 82, 94, 95, 145, 161, 188, 287
Rainbow Room, 154
Reagan, Ronald, 76–77
Reeve, Simon, 81, 88
religion
   O'Neill's Catholic, 11, 51, 106, 108, 166–68, 194, 213
   religious fanaticism, 59, 179–85. *See also* Islamic fundamentalists; VAAPCON (Violence Against Abortion Providers Conspiracy) investigations
Reno, Janet, 57, 62, 68, 69–70, 105, 156, 212, 238, 262, 268, 277–78, 280, 301
reputation, O'Neill's, 21–29, 157–58, 197–98, 389
Respect for Law Alliance, 397
Ressam, Ahmed, 248–50, 262, 270
retirement from FBI, O'Neill's, 6, 53, 279, 330, 336–40, 344–54, 389
Reuwer, Kenneth, 294
Reyes, Ed, 84
Rice, Condoleezza, 336
Richard, William, 197
RICO (Racketeering Influence and Corrupt Organizations Act), 24, 43, 47, 62
Ripley, John, 194
Risen, James, 346
Rockefeller Center, 355
Roe, Walter, 19
Rolince, Michael, 74–75, 150, 212–13, 333, 343, 351, 354
Rosenberg, Murray, 9, 10
Rossini, Mark, 134, 339–40
Roth, James, 260
Roubaix Gang, 251
Rowley, Coleen, 352–53
Russia, 117

Sadat, Anwar, 182, 195
Saddam Hussein, 82, 117–18, 129, 327
Safir, Howard, 258, 323
St. Patrick's Day, 167–69
Salameh, Mohammed, 94
Saleh, Ali Abdullah, 271, 295–96, 310, 316–17, 327, 393–94
Salinger, Pierre, 144, 160, 193
Saluté, 1545
Salvi, John C., III, 74–75

Sapha-i-Sahaba party, 83
Saracini, Victor, 364
sarin gas
   New York City incident and, 169–74
   Tokyo subway attack, 96–97
Satar, Mohammed Yahya Ali, 327
Saudi Arabia
   bin Laden and, 97, 99–100, 177
   Khobar Towers bombing in, 4, 123–35
   OPM-Sang bombing in, 114–16, 120–21, 123
   relationships with, 121–24, 127–35
Schelly, Jane, 112
Schiliro, Lewis, 89, 95, 139–40, 165, 200–202, 206–7, 213, 216–18, 235–36, 244, 258, 276, 359
Schmoke, Kurt, 23–26
Schwalier, Terry, 124
Schweikert, Gary, 362, 381–82
Seagram, 274
secrecy, O'Neill's, 390
Selimaj, Bruno, 5
September 11 World Trade Center attack. *See* World Trade Center attack on September 11
Sessions, William, 58
Shah, Wali Khan Anim, 90, 112–14
Shannon, Rachelle Ranae (Shelley), 61, 62–63
Shehhi, Marwan al-, 341, 365–66
Sheikh, Ahmed Omar Saeed, 108–9, 112
Shelton, Henry H., 222
Shutz, Christine. *See* O'Neill, Christine Shutz (wife)
Silverstein, Larry, 337–38, 345, 349, 374
Simon, Steven, 222
Slater, Elizabeth, 204
sleeper cells, Al Qaeda, 265
Sodi, Thalía, 322–23
Somalia, 5, 98–99, 145–46, 190
songs, O'Neill's, 231
Space Needle, 249, 257
Spain, 338–42
Spanish Police Foundation, 338, 341
special agent in charge (SAC) position, 73
special agent position, 20
Stafford, Debby, 62, 65, 69, 126–27, 130–31
State Department, 113, 118–19, 305

Stevens, Gary, 22, 27–29, 31, 33, 35, 58,
    174, 374, 388
Stevens, Mary Lynn
    beginning of O'Neill's relationship with,
        34
    on O'Neill, 148
    O'Neill's death and, 381, 387–88
    O'Neill's relationship with, 66, 106–8,
        232
    O'Neill's request for exclusivity, 50
    O'Neill's retirement and, 339, 344
    planned trip with O'Neill, 356, 362,
        387–88
    during World Trade Center attack,
        371–72, 377–78
"Stinky" nickname, 17, 167
Stuyvesant Town apartment, 153, 166
Sudan
    bin Laden in, 97–99, 122
    as sponsor of terrorism, 76, 180
    U.S. attack on, 216–23
Sullivan, Vincent, 4–5
Supportive Crisis Incident Response
    Group, 300
Supreme Leaders gang, 45
Swartzendruber, David, 86
Sweeney, Amy Lynn, 365
Syria, 180

Taha, Abu Yassir Ahmed, 195
Taliban, 95, 122–23, 177, 197, 219, 393.
    See also Afghanistan
Tanzania embassy bombing, 204–5, 211,
    216. *See also* African embassy
    bombings
task force
    Chicago gang investigation, 38,
        43–47
    FBI and NYPD terrorist, 287–88
taxi business, O'Neill family, 8–10, 52
technology, 27–28
Tenet, George, 121, 222, 238, 336
terrorism. *See also* counterterrorism job at
        FBI headquarters, O'Neill's
    counterterrorism division and separate
        divisions for domestic and
        international, 119
    domestic, 95, 103–5, 119
    Giuliani's brainstorming sessions on, 191

international, 76–77, 93–95, 119,
    240–41
O'Neill's speech about, 179–85
O'Neill's warnings about, 5–6, 164–65,
    186–87, 202–3, 270–74, 321, 360,
    390–91
United States response to, 93–95, 239–41
worldwide terrorist network, 78–79
Terrorist Threat Integration Center,
    395–96
Tigers of the Gulf, 115
Tiller, George, 61, 62
Times Square millennium celebration,
    257–58
Tokyo subway gas attack, 96–97
Tomb, Rex, 18, 19
toughness, O'Neill's, 26
tour guide, O'Neill as FBI, 17–19
Townsend, Fran, 68, 113–14, 209, 249,
    268–69, 277, 282, 306, 323–24, 336,
    351, 369, 380, 384–85
Townsend, Jack, 38, 44–45
travel arrangements, FBI, 207–8, 293–94
Tucker, Robert, 355, 361–63, 374
Turki, Abdul Hamid, 111
TWA Flight 800 investigation, 139–44,
    159–64, 192–94, 392

United Airlines Flight 93, 365
United Airlines Flight 175, 365–66
United States
    CIA. *See* CIA (Central Intelligence
        Agency)
    FBI. *See* FBI (Federal Bureau of
        Investigation)
    lack of cooperation between intelligence
        agencies, 102–3
    policy toward terrorism, 93–95
    presidents. *See* Bush, George H. W.;
        Bush, George W.; Clinton, Bill;
        Reagan, Ronald
uranium, bin Laden's attempts to buy
    enriched, 117–18, 146
USS *Cole* bombing, 5, 288–322, 324–35,
    342–44, 350–51, 354, 397–98
USS *Duluth*, 318
USS *Normandy*, 144, 160
USS *Sullivan*, 272–73, 319–20
USS *Tawara*, 318

VAAPCON (Violence Against Abortion
Providers Conspiracy) investigations,
57–70, 74–75
failed attempts to make a national
conspiracy case, 68–70
formation of FBI task force, 62–63
murders by John Salvi, 74–75
murder of David Gunn, 59–61
murder of John Britton and Jim Barrett,
63–64
O'Neill's preparation for, 92
O'Neill's selection for, 57–59
relationships with agents, 64–66
relationships with women, 66–68, 75
religious fanaticism and, 59
shooting of George Tiller, 61–62
Verni, Thomas, 164
Vice Lords gang, 45
Vietnam War, O'Neill and, 15–17
Voice of God speaker system, 265
Von Essen, Thomas, 171–72
VX nerve gas, 216

Waco incident, 104
Wag the Dog (movie), 219–20
Walton, Kenneth, 157, 171, 256, 287
wardrobe, O'Neill's, 47, 65–66, 161,
170–71
warnings, O'Neill's, 5–6, 164–65, 186–87,
202–3, 270–74, 321, 360, 390–91
Washington, D.C.
Chicago vs., 36
field office authority, 208
O'Neill's jobs at FBI headquarters in,
33–35. *See also* counterterrorism job at
FBI headquarters, O'Neill's; FBI
(Federal Bureau of Investigation)
Watson, Dale, 347
weapons of mass destruction, 117
Wedtech Company case, 33
Wells, Paul, 111
West Berlin disco bombing, 76–77
West Nile virus, 237
Weston, Keith, 213
Wharton, Jeff, 337, 356, 360–61, 368,
374
White, Mary Jo, 95, 155–57, 185–86,
190, 209, 227, 268, 308, 349, 384–85,
397

white collar crime division, O'Neill at,
26–27, 33–34, 58
Whyte, Eugene, 379
Williams, Kenneth, 353
Windows on the World restaurant, 154,
288
women, relationships with
Anna DiBattista. *See* DiBattista, Anna
Valerie James. *See* James, Valerie
married woman, 32
Janet Murray, 30–31
O'Neill's death and revelations about,
380–81, 390
Christine Shutz. *See* O'Neill, Christine
Shutz (wife)
Mary Lynn Stevens. *See* Stevens, Mary
Lynn
Wong, Wesley, 22–23, 370–71
Woodward, Michael, 365
work ethic, O'Neill's, 34–35
World Church of the Creator, 70
World Islamic Front for Jihad against Jews
and the Crusaders, 195
World Trade Center
bombing of, in 1993. *See* World Trade
Center 1993 bombing
O'Neill as head of security at, 6,
337–38, 345–46, 351–63
September 11 attack. *See* World Trade
Center attack on September 11
as target, 191, 321, 360
Windows on the World restaurant, 154,
288
Yousef's threat to destroy, 89–90, 95
World Trade Center 1993 bombing, 77–90
Bojinka Plot and Phillipines Airlines
flight bombing, 83–84
bombing plot, 77–83, 94
capture of Ramzi Yousef, 79–80, 86–90,
392
O'Neill's speech about, 180–81
Pan Am Flight 103 bombing, 76–77
plot to assassinate Pope John Paul II,
85–86
World Trade Center attack on September
11, 185, 363–88
airline hijackings, 364–66
O'Neill's activities during, 364–71
O'Neill's death, 371, 376, 382–84

O'Neill's funeral, 384–88
plot, 340–41, 352–53
reactions of O'Neill's friends and family,
    367–80
revelations about O'Neill after, 380–82

Xydis, Elaine, 65, 71

Yemen
    Ambassador Barbara Bodine, 270–72,
        289, 292–93, 297, 299–300, 303–12,
        316, 317–22, 324–33, 342–44, 347,
        354, 397–98. *See also* USS *Cole*
        bombing; Yemen

bringing Yemeni officials to FBI
    headquarters, 326–27, 330–31
failed terrorist attack on USS *Sullivan*,
    272–73, 319–20
President Saleh, 393–94
terrorism in, 98, 270–73
U.S. counterterrorism actions in, 394
USS *Cole* bombing, 5, 288–322, 324–35,
    342–44, 350–51, 354
Young, Dennison, 386
Yousef, Ramzi, 77–90, 94, 95, 139, 188,
    194–95, 399

Zubaida, Abu, 273, 395